Sunrise to Sunrise

One Man's Journey through History:
China, The Philippines and
World War II Internment

by Vincent H. Gowen

[handwritten signatures]

Trafford
PUBLISHING

Order this book online at www.trafford.com/06-2278
or email orders@trafford.com

Most Trafford titles are also available at major online book retailers.

Note for Librarians: A cataloguing record for this book is available from Library
and Archives Canada at www.collectionscanada.ca/amicus/index-e.html

Printed in Victoria, BC, Canada.

ISBN: 978-1-4251-0520-4

*We at Trafford believe that it is the responsibility of us all, as both individuals
and corporations, to make choices that are environmentally and socially sound.
You, in turn, are supporting this responsible conduct each time you purchase a
Trafford book, or make use of our publishing services. To find out how you are
helping, please visit www.trafford.com/responsiblepublishing.html*

*Our mission is to efficiently provide the world's finest, most comprehensive
book publishing service, enabling every author to experience success.
To find out how to publish your book, your way, and have it available
worldwide, visit us online at www.trafford.com/10510*

 www.trafford.com

North America & international
toll-free: 1 888 232 4444 (USA & Canada)
phone: 250 383 6864 ♦ fax: 250 383 6804 ♦ email: info@trafford.com

The United Kingdom & Europe
phone: +44 (0)1865 722 113 ♦ local rate: 0845 230 9601
facsimile: +44 (0)1865 722 868 ♦ email: info.uk@trafford.com

10 9 8 7 6 5 4 3 2

Dedication:

Over his long life Vincent Gowen taught generations of students of all ages including:

The boys at St. Paul's School, Anking (1915-1919)
Shen Ch'uan-ling and his wife, Nanchang (1921-1922)
Mary, Lucy and Peter Ts'ai, Nanchang (1921-1922)
The girls at St. Lioba's, Wuhu (1923-1927)
The boys and girls of St. James School, Besao (1927-1942)
The boys and girls of Camp Holmes High School, Baguio (1942-1944)
The boys at Lakeside School, Seattle (1946-1950)
The Monday Morning Group, Bainbridge Island
And many others whom he tutored individually

To all his students, these memoirs are dedicated.

also by Vincent Gowen:

Sun and Moon

Village on the Yangtze

Follow Me: On Becoming an Active Christian

Contents

Illustrations

Acknowledgements

The Text

Vincent Gowen penned these memoirs over 40 years ago. A published novelist and accomplished stylist he wrote prose that needed little editing. We wanted his manuscript to reflect events as accurately as possible, however. With hindsight we now know some facts and observations to be inaccurate, or need balance from other views. Also we thought additional context and explanation might be helpful to 21st century readers. We used footnotes to do this.

Many people helped. The late James J. Halsema, knowledgeable about pre-war Philippines and World War II Internment, gave us invaluable comment and suggestions and directed us to useful resources including those in his own extensive library. Donald E. Mansell read the entire manuscript with great care. Fresh from researching his authoritative account of our Camp Holmes/Bilibid Prison internment experience Don gave detailed useful comment and advice while acting as unpaid editor who spotted typos and other errors that had eluded previous readings of the manuscript. Fred Maerkle, steeped in Chinese culture and language, read carefully the China portion of the manuscript and provided helpful comment, despite pressures of a new assignment.

Melanie Rigby of "Editor for You" provided editorial suggestions. Francis Gray, Rob Sherwood, and William Bartsch reviewed earlier drafts and had useful comments. Betsy Herold Heimke shared original materials and illustrations. Others, though they hadn't read the full manuscript, provided insights, and shared stories including Michael Shaffer, Curtis Tong, Katherine Ream Sobeck, Frederick Crouter, and others who attended the Baguio/Bilibid 2007 reunion. Members of the 37th Division, also at the reunion, particularly Gene Pope, and Joe Konya and his son Mark Konya contributed stories and identified resources..

Maps, Photos and other Illustrations.

Beverly Hunter, head of Piedmont Research Institute, helped to create the first four maps which required extensive research to find the appropriate databases. Jim Halsema's library (now with the MacArthur Memorial Library in Norfolk, Virginia) included early post-World War II contour maps of the Philippines that formed the basis of Map 5. Map 6, based upon Robert Ross Smith, *"Triumph in the Philippines,"* Map IV, also draws on information in maps found in Connaughton et al, *"The Battle for Manila"* and a pre-war map of Manila from James W. Zobel of the MacArthur Memorial Foundation.

VHG was an avid photographer. Using a succession of cameras that he named after flies -- Firefly, Dragonfly, Mayfly and others – he systematically recorded the people and places where he lived and worked. Most photos used here are ones he took. For the Philippines before the war we had several albums of photos that survived the War that could be scanned or photographed digitally for a suitable image. From China we had almost nothing until recently we found a canister of some thousand or so black and white negatives. They had survived Yangtze River travel, treacherous roads into the mountains of Luzon, Japanese occupation when they were hidden at great risk by loyal Igorot friends, and a postwar sea voyage to the U.S. Though many had been lost and others degraded in quality, eighty years later we have been able to piece together a photographic account to parallel many parts of the narrative.

For the internment portion of the memoirs neither VHG nor anyone else had a camera - with one exception a young, mining engineer, Rupert Foley. For his smuggled camera he had one roll of film, kept throughout the war, and developed successfully some three years after. One has been used here courtesy of his son Robert. The wonderful drawing of Camp Holmes, 1943, by Fern Harrington (later Fern Harrington Miles) is from her book *"Captive Community."* courtesy of the Baptist Historical Society. Ralph Longway, Betsy Herold Heimke, and Ralph Kuttner kindly provided photos used in this section. The seven photos at the end of this section are official Army photos that have been widely used in publications about internment and the Battle of Manila. The American Red Cross probably took the photo entitled "Mail Line".

Geoffrey Gowen
June, 2007

Preface

THERE'S AN IMAGE I have of my father from the years when I was growing up. It's summer. He's in his study… a room neither my brother, Geoffrey, nor I entered uninvited. I can smell old books and pipe tobacco, worn leather and in the August air the occasional whiff of newly cut grass mixed with the scent of low tide. Daddy is seated at the desk next to the window and more likely than not he's writing in one of the many stiff backed notebooks that lined his bookshelves. At times he was working on a lesson plan for one of his summer students. Often he was composing a sermon or a lecture, But in his later years, after he retired, he was penning this volume…his memoirs.

My father enjoyed reliving his past. Many a breakfast conversation was centered around, "In my day," and because he had kept a diary from the age of 15 on he was able with accuracy to look back on Seattle at the turn of the century. He could recall the days in China when he was a young bachelor and later a married and newly ordained priest. He reminded us of the Philippines, before World War II when we lived among the rice terraces of northern Luzon then during the war when we were interned in Baguio.

Twenty-three years have passed since his death. The room that was his study no longer exists. The smell of old books and pipe tobacco evaporated years ago. But his memoir lives on and in it we still have my father's account of one man's days long gone and times since past.

Ann Gowen Combs
June, 2007

Introduction:
Apologies to Nobody

MEMOIRS, REMINISCENCES, AUTOBIOGRAPHY — whatever we choose to call them — all attach large importance to the letter "I". If the "I" belongs to somebody famous or scandalous a reader may be admitted into counsels that shaped history or to intrigue that shocked its contemporaries. A Winston Churchill or a Casanova is sure of his public. But when the "I" is neither famous nor scandalous, it is doubtful whether he has the right to stuff a book with his unremarkable doings, much less to flatter himself that anyone, except possibly his grandchildren, will want to read about them.

The "I", then, in these pages matters little. Its subject has never made headlines nor is he likely to make the history books. He has significance only as he is representative of countless thousands who have endured history rather than made it, thousands who have lived through times and in places that do matter greatly.

For me, these times and places compressed into one lifetime three distinct epochs: one so primitive as to be haunted by spells and magic; another violently medieval; and the third a 20th Century "civilization" in which men attained an efficiency in slaughtering one another such as neither Igorot head-axes nor the carelessly wielded guns of Chinese mercenaries could rival. Since it is the aspirations of nobodies that make up the society to which we belong, perhaps a nobody is entitled to write the story of his life if merely for a revaluation of the events that comprised it.

The America in which I grew up seems as remote as the grass villages of the Luzon Cordilleras or China's flagstone roads grooved by a millennium of wheelbarrow traffic between walled cities. I was born in British Columbia, but at the age of four I accompanied my parents to Seattle, arriving there only a few weeks before another arrival of larger interest – the docking of the steamship Portland with the first considerable cargo of gold from Alaska. Gold quickly inflated Seattle's importance. Its first settlers had set an extravagant goal when naming the beach on which they landed in 1853: "New York

1

Alki" ("Alki" in Chinese jargon means "by and by"). Now, thanks to the Gold Rush, "by and by" had arrived. Seattle became the starting and the landing point for ships of every kind. Adventurers, avidly seeking instant fortune, made the grueling march up Chilkoot Pass to the Klondike, or suffered the rough voyage across Bering Sea in anything that could float to be dumped ashore on Nome's gold-bearing sands. Other more seaworthy ships soon extended the newly opened trade routes to Japan and China, and to the Philippines where Dewey's bloodless victory at Manila achieved for our republic the heady prestige of an Empire.

My share in these months of change was fragmentary. Across the top of a first grade blackboard I still can see, lettered in coloured crayon, the slogan "Remember the Maine," and recall the echo of sea-battles off Cuba. My most cherished Christmas gift in 1898 was a cardboard replica of the flagship *U.S.S. Brooklyn*, which I towed by a string from room to room of our First Hill home. Manila-bound steamships – the *Tremont* or *Shawmut* – swung at anchor in Elliott Bay crowded by their still active rivals, the three-masted sailing ships which plied the traditional path around Cape Horn. The sight provided exultant stimulus to a small boy's fancy. Some years later, when I was old enough to explore Seattle's waterfront on my own, these square-rigged ships still were docked at the foot of the First Hill, their bowsprits overreached Railroad Avenue. For me their magic had not dimmed. Once I was permitted to accompany a Seaman's Institute chaplain aboard one of them – a German ship – and to have lunch with its captain. The seaworthy compactness of his quarters inspired in me an instant and burning ambition to "go to sea." The nearest I ever came to fulfilling it was to pause irresolute by the gangplank of a Blue Funnel liner while trying to muster courage to offer my services as a cabin boy.

But Seattle, at the beginning of the 20th Century, had other horizons to catch a young boy's imagination. While it was still something of a makeshift town, built largely of wood, there were business blocks constructed solidly of red brick in a respectable style which critics were beginning to deride as "General Grant." Whatever the town's crudities, they were tempered by the domestic appeal of quiet streets leading securely through the leafy shade of many trees. Broad green strips provided parking for carriages drawn by high-stepping teams.

Seattle, at this time, was impatient to become big. Frantic for more people, more factories, larger payrolls, it seemed to believe that by multiplying inhabitants it could enrich, not stifle, individual happiness. Soon – much too soon – trees were sacrificed to make way for gaunt forests of telephone poles, power lines. The broad green parking strips were sliced and sliced again to expedite ever more motorcars. The noise of grinding gears replaced the clop-clop of horses' hooves. All too swiftly the makeshift peaceful town was engulfed in the craze for bigness. "New York Alki" threatened to become "Jersey City New." Smoke from factory chimneys begrimed the once clean air of sea and forest, while swarming vacationers scattered their litter across beaches and spilled trash along forest trails. Although I was still in my teens, with the normal boisterousness of a growing boy, I still can recall an almost violent resentment against this zeal for bigness.

My resentment against bigness, however, did not extend into the area of personal ambitions. My own were big enough. I came from a home well furnished with books. My father, who later was to inaugurate and head for many years the Oriental Department of the University of Washington, had a scholar's library packed to the ceiling with interesting volumes. He once estimated that he read, on an average, 220 volumes a year and, what is more, remembered what he had read. But he did not force books on me. In this, as in many other matters, he was wise. Often an outsider can do more to electrify a boy's natural indolence than the most sympathetic parent. In my case it was a schoolmaster who lighted the spark.

At the age of eleven I was enrolled, with my younger brother[1], at De Koven Hall, a military school whose only military features were the blue uniforms we wore for dinner, the nondescript drills each day before classes, and the Civil War muskets which we warmed against our schoolroom stovepipe on frosty mornings. Bugle calls punctuated our school day as hour by hour they resounded across the solitude of Lake Steilacoom. When evening study hall crawled to its drowsy finish, we began closing books, putting away papers, tensely expectant of tattoo's resonant call. Barely were the long drawn-out strains concluded before we were dodging through dark trees to the school's main building, rumbling up three flights of stairs to our rooms, crowding two hours' suppressed chatter into the few minutes before taps. Only when the headmaster walked through the halls announcing, "Prayer time," and then "Prayer time's over – brush your teeth," was this chatter stilled.

Perhaps we prayed and brushed our teeth. I do not remember. What I do remember was lying awake after lights out listening, from miles across the prairie, to the plaintive whistle of Northern Pacific trains puff-puffing their way to Portland. A curious feeling of loneliness they instilled, the loneliness of an America spread through remote farms and solitary pioneer cabins. On winter nights the babble of coyotes sometimes broke into this quiet. Traveling in packs, they sounded like a troop of boys hell-bent on mischief.

This was exciting country to grow up in, and ours was a school to challenge both mental and bodily growth. Situated in the rolling prairies south of Tacoma and accessible only by horse-and-buggy or a five mile walk. De Koven Hall confronted miles of sparsely settled country. Often after

3

Christmas vacation, my brother and I trudged those miles dragging our suitcases and bending our heads to the wind and rain as we splashed through puddles too dark for us to see. At pleasanter times it was enticing country to roam. Its inhabitants were characters, like the genially profane proprietor of a "stand" to which we resorted for "pop" and cracker jack. Claiming to have belonged to the Jesse James gang, he held us in open-mouthed amazement over his own exploits as an outlaw. Nearby, at the State Insane Asylum (known now by a more prestigious name), odd inmates wandered at large through the hospital's spacious park, doing things as strange as the people of Gulliver's Travels. The Asylum barns had once been forts; the rifle slits cut in their log walls recalled Indian fighting days. Here Lieutenant U.S. Grant had been stationed. Within bicycling range to the south were the ruins of the Hudson's Bay Post at Sequalitchew Creek.

To growing boys these signs of the West's brief history stirred our curiosity, but they were less engrossing than the wild life still around us. Foxes, timber wolves, mink, muskrats, skunks, and an endless variety of birds crowded swamps and prairie. In pairs, we boys combed these areas for nests. If we found one, we posted its tree or bush with our trademark to warn of other claimants, and by school rule took one egg – and only one – for our collection.

But it must not be supposed that De Koven Hall depended upon situation and natural wildlife alone to prod a student's expectations. The enduring, and to many the strongest, stimulus came from our teachers. Not one of our faculty was a professional teacher and doubtless under present-day rules they could not have qualified for a certificate. This was our good fortune. The headmaster was a man who taught because teaching was in his blood; he could not have dreamed of doing anything but teach. To this he dedicated a wise understanding of boys and even wiser tolerance in handling them. Willingly he paid the teacher's price in life-long poverty for those rare moments of illumination which consecrate a teaching vocation – the perception of learning's proper impact upon the pupils entrusted to him for guidance.

If measured by its meager equipment, De Koven Hall was never more than makeshift. Its living quarters were spartan, a huge ramshackle building lighted by primitive acetylene burners and heated by a furnace that barely tempered the chill of the upper floors. But it was a monument to learning, with unique and effective features our modern-day schools might do well to copy. It had, for instance, no classes tied to yearly numerals. It had no graduations. Pupils went their own gait: when they had completed their courses they departed. This unorthodox arrangement was possible because the school required each boy to complete each day's work and satisfy each

4

day's punishment on that day. Nothing was carried over. The master in charge of detention saw to that, sometimes holding students almost to dinnertime.

We did without a gymnasium; we had no interscholastic sports. Except in rare instances no master supervised our play. Yet we played basketball (outdoors), we played baseball and tennis, we trained for track sports. We were always engaged in pick-up games of every sort, One O'Cat, Run Sheep Run, Prisoner's Base, Duck on the Rock. We did not expect to be coached or umpired. We were content with the most rudimentary equipment. For one of our favourite games, hockey, we cut our own sticks and never dreamed of waiting for ice, a rarity not to be counted on in winters usually wet and mild; we hacked at our home-made pucks across tough prairie grass.

All this I record because this school, so much nearer the pioneer's one-room schoolhouse than today's dazzling edifices, taught me both to play games and to read books. Zest for reading I owe to my first English master, a Johns Hopkins graduate, as well as an introduction to poetry, begun exactly where a boy's acquaintance with verse should begin, in Scott's *Lady of the Lake*. This master converted me almost too thoroughly. I became a pedant. I had to be assured that any work was an authentic classic before I would lend it my attention.

Fired by these exalted standards I debated for some time as to whether Jack London's *Sea Wolf* could qualify for tastes as pure as mine. Other books, unassailable classics, I read without hesitation, and too often without comprehension. Tennyson's *Idylls of the King* were a natural next step from the *Lady of the Lake*, though I could not grasp how lines without rime could be called poetry. More mystifying – and more boring – was Spenser's *Faerie Queene*, which I read from start to finish at the ripe age of thirteen. This I topped with the whole of Gibbon's *Decline and Fall of the Roman Empire* and Browning's *Ring and the Book*. None of these would I have completed except that I was reading after light's out. Propping a candle by my bed, shading it against any sudden emergence by the dormitory master down the hall, I plodded doggedly through their pages. For a young boy who understood less than half of what he read, Spenser and Gibbon and Browning should have been natural soporifics, yet somehow I kept awake long enough to blow out my candle.

Such feats do not gauge fairly my real awakening to the magnificence of poetry, to Keats and Shelley and my ever-loved Tennyson. Under their inspiration I resolved to be somebody. Spurred by my father's remark that he had read most of Shakespeare before he was twelve, I secured volumes of the Temple edition for my twelfth birthday and would hardly let them out of my sight, even sending for them on a summer vacation with the intent of converting a girl friend, older than I, to my new passion for Elizabethan drama. The intention was as premature as my incipient interest in the girl herself. It foundered on the word "whore" which occurred all too frequently in Shakespeare's scenes for me to risk offending her delicate ears.

Out of this reading came the firm conviction that if I was to become somebody, poetry must be my vehicle. I tackled all kinds, even inventing the Gowen stanza to vie with Spenser's, but put my mightiest efforts first into an epic whose Viking hero, Leifsonn, fled across northern Europe pursued by wolves, and next into a five-act tragedy in the blankest of blank verse. *Eldwardine* was its title and its heroine. If it did not match Shakespeare in quality it did rival his ingenuity in killing off its cast. Eldwardine, an Anglo-Saxon princess, succumbed to tuberculosis in Act Four, but to terminate Act Five her lover journeyed all the way to ruined Carthage. Only amid its desolate fragments could he give his own anguish an adequate setting. On Carthage's highest hill he stood, brandishing his sword as he raved against heaven – and fell dead, struck down by lightning.

These masterpieces perished, along with a vaulting ambition which would have made my growth top heavy had not the literary impetus of that first schoolmaster been balanced by his successor. Not long after his arrival, the new teacher offered a prize of five dollars to the boy who, in three months, could develop the most physically. This prize I set myself to win. Morning and evening I toiled at push-ups, at chinning the bar, at track. I took that prize by storm. When the master asked what he should get me with the five dollars, my answer was ready – a de luxe volume of Shelley. His was equally prompt. "No, I am getting you a tennis racquet," he said, "and I want your promise never to lend it to anyone."

Bewildered and disappointed, I was stuck with a tennis racquet which only I could use, and too thrifty to let it lie idle. It proved the first of many and transformed a scrawny bookworm into a solid-muscled boy, so intent on all outdoor sports that he could win a cup for track, and from memory recite the line-up of every big league baseball team for several years back. Tennis, baseball, soccer, badminton, I played them all yet, oddly enough, the change wrought by that first racquet did not dim my love of books. Two masters, with wisdom and understanding, had taught me both to read and to play.

At fourteen I was caught up in a flurry of diary keeping which swept through the school. For most, the craze was as fleeting as a spring day, but once started on my daily journal I never stopped. Until I lost the earlier volumes in the Second World War, I had testimony written at the time that ours was a happy school. We were indeed so engrossed by boys' activities, wholesome outdoor activities, that girls scarcely impinged on our thoughts. They were creatures from another sphere. Possibly I was protected by a veneer of literary innocence, by a "Sir Galahad complex," but I was not alone in regarding them in terms of knight errantry. Of prurient talk, of the sniggering habit of thought that provokes it, I recall almost nothing.

From De Koven Hall I progressed, at fifteen, to the University of Washington. Only by the grace of a tired examiner was I admitted. Having come from a non-accredited school, I was required to take entrance tests. Greek, Latin, English presented no difficulties. What I dreaded was Algebra. This obstacle I confronted in late afternoon when, to save time, the examiner sent me to the backboard. Algebraic formulas I could rattle off so long as they were confined to "a" and "b" and "x" and "y." but when they were applied to a man rowing upstream at so much an hour against a current carrying him downstream at something else an hour, I never knew where to apply the "a's" and "x's" to find out how long it took him. Time passed, while I floundered hopelessly. At last the examiner intervened.

"Suppose you change this plus to minus," he suggested, taking the chalk from me to demonstrate. "There, do you see: it comes out all right."

It took several more "helpful" suggestions to complete the exam, but he passed me. For him "x" must have meant what time he could be home for dinner.

Small though its enrollment, fewer than three thousand, the University of Washington had an English faculty equal to any in the country. One of its members, Vernon Louis Parrington, was the ablest teacher I have known. He could have walked the marble pavement at Plato's academy and by his discourse spurred his disciples to think. His three-volume masterpiece, *Main Currents in American Thought*, was an education in itself, and won for him a Pulitzer prize. By a lucky stroke my section in Freshman English was transferred to him from another instructor who had met with the class but once, barely time to call the roll and assign a textbook, Genung's ponderous *Rhetoric*.

This text Mr. Parrington (he prided himself on never having sought a Ph. D.) told us to sell back to the bookstore. He used no text, gave us no rules. All he had us do was write, write, write, while he read and commented on our work in class – a method so effective that to this day I cannot write a paragraph without recalling those comments. On this daily work we were graded; final examinations he dispensed with. As in our classes at De Koven Hall, day-to-day work outweighed in lasting usefulness any knowledge crammed feverishly at the semester's end. It was in his courses that I began to appreciate what great teaching can be, how magnificent and enduring its impact. There were moments of illumination so dazzling that no student willingly skipped class. His method was Socratic. Cleverly he veiled his own opinions while goading his pupils from a shrewd perception of their likes and dislikes into animated argument, often animated protest. Even the journalism

7

students he spurred into debating Predestination, and he brought all of us close to tears over the tragedy of Cotton Mather and Jonathan Edwards – big frogs in a puddle too small for them.

I had other professors to whom I was grateful, not least of them the patient, warmly literate teacher who for four years led me through Plato, Homer and Aristophanes, as well as the Greek lyric and tragic poets. My father's classes I dared not attempt. Even had I known that I was to spend thirty-three years in the Orient, I still would have been chary of enrolling. My father sought perfection, a quality which I was painfully aware he would not find in me.

Before undertaking his University work, my father had been rector of Trinity Church, the Episcopal Church's oldest Seattle parish. For both careers he was ideally fitted. As a scholar he was proficient in Sanskrit, Arabic, and Hebrew, and in the major European languages, even studying Russian to consult books on China not otherwise accessible. He had a shelf of books to his own credit, text-book histories of China and Japan, and other volumes ranging from history and biography to Biblical scholarship. Finest of these was his *History of Religion*, a work that, in its tolerant understanding of religious motives, managed to deal fairly with mankind's various types of religious expression. For years he was respected in the Far West as a foremost religious leader, gifted not only with breadth of mind but with the power to express that mind eloquently and to bring his thought down to the needs of countless people who sought his help in trouble.

So public a life naturally made inroads on the time he could devote to his family, yet I grew up in complete sympathy with his aims. He did not oppress me with those aims, nor was he sloppily permissive. He expected of his family his own detailed obedience to duty – three services on Sunday, a service every Friday, services daily in Lent. Except for Sunday School, from which, happily, I was soon emancipated, I did not rebel. At the age of seven I was singing in the choir. We practised three afternoons a week, and an hour with the adult choir on Thursday evenings. For this we were paid twenty-five cents a month, with five cents deductible for any service or practice we might miss. We might well have ended the month owing the church money, but absences were rare. Since there were no competing attractions, attendance was as natural as breathing. This choir training imbued me with a deep love for the Church's worship, for vestments and lights and the familiar wording of the ancient prayers. Today I cannot hear the morning and evening collects, written when Rome trembled from dread of the barbarians mustering behind the Alps, without echoes from every crisis of my own life.

None of this at the time, however, disposed me to follow my father's footsteps in the Anglican priesthood. Except for a vague notion of teaching college English, I had little idea what I wanted to be.

As a boy I spent some summers in the San Juans, a group of islands that border the extreme northwest boundary between the United States and Canada. Today they are thronged by tourists, their tide-propelled waters are noisy with outboard motors, but in those far-off years they were the quiet, little-visited edge of the continent. In spirit they were nearer the Spanish explorer who rivaled Cook and Vancouver in exploring their intricate waterways than to the less romantic exploitation of yacht clubs and trailer parks. Even their names bespoke Spain – Lopez, Rosario, Matia, Sucia. Their population was curiously mixed. On farms, adequate but never flourishing, lived pioneers who spoke with the bleak accents of hope annually postponed. Across from Canada had come other settlers, gentlemen farmers, younger sons of English and Scottish families, who had strayed far afield in search of a fortune that had eluded them. Orcas Island's prized apples, which had been the foundation of their hopes, now were scarcely worth the picking. Eastern Washington, with its apples assembly line picked and sorted, had stolen the markets.

At such a home, centre of a decaying orchard, I used to stay. It was a second home, so dearly did I love the family whose welcome never failed the most eager of anticipations. It had no modern conveniences. Every day a venerable horse was harnessed to fetch water on a wooden sled from a spring a hundred yards away. By hand the water-barrel was filled, and emptied a dipperful at a time. Yet the weather-beaten house breathed old-world traditions. On its walls hung oil portraits, one among them a great-grandfather who, as an English general, had directed red-coated infantry at Waterloo. On a table by the bay window was an ivory chess-set brought back from China by an uncle who had fought in the Opium War. The head of the family had studied at a German university, and the talk in the evening belonged to a period when men and women had time to talk. Every evening these talks were prolonged during twilight walks accompanied always by their two beautiful collies.

Shut off from ready communication with the more bustling life around it, served only by the rusty old steamships whose whistles echoed through the deep inlet thrice-weekly, East Sound was not only a place for retired men to drowse away their last years, but imaginative in its appeal to the young. I walked its dusty roads, climbed its one commanding mountain, Mount Constitution, to catch glimpses of sunlight reflected from the reefs of Victoria twenty miles away. I roamed the slopes of Turtle Neck seeking vainly the stones, places in the shape of an anchor, which some Spanish captain was reputed to have left as a marker. I explored the beaches and borrowed a tipsy, homemade skiff to brave tiderips alongside perpendicular cliffs, hazardous excursions to hunt out an abandoned gold mine or to drop

9

in on a whiskered hermit who had planted his log cabin and his orchard almost beyond access.

At every turn was the contrast between dozing, sun-filled valleys, whose only sound was tinkling cow-bells, and the forest, barely kept out of pasture by the split rails of snake fences, but my favourite haunt was a jutting promontory, Cockerel's Reef, where I would sit by the hour watching the tide glide past its rooks. I was not too late to see Indian canoes, dugouts with high prows carved into the crude semblance of a deer's head. Laden with salmon, the Gulf of Georgia's summer bounty, they would slip swiftly and silently by, eighteen or twenty men at their paddles.

The waters I gazed on were silent, too, seldom disturbed except by the raucous snorting of killer whales. But another sound sharpened my attention – the pulsating engines, Glasgow built, of the Canadian Pacific steamships, outward bound for the Orient or returning from sea. Often I heard them hidden within August fogs as they made the turn past Saturna light-house, but on a few thrilling occasions I saw one of the ships in the sunlight, the famous white Empresses, Empress of India, or China, or Japan, sister ships shaped long and sleek with a yacht's clipper bow. My thoughts went as passengers with them. Some day, I vowed I would travel and live and be somebody, get clean away from the humdrum of a frontier town to older, more fantastic ways of life.

Eventually I did get away, not by Empress from Vancouver – my Empress voyages were to come later – but in the Persia, an antique Pacific Mail steamship, from San Francisco[2]. Out the Golden Gate we steamed, past the Parallenes, far into warm seas where flying fish skimmed before our gently plunging bow.

The chapters that follow are the record of these ensuing years – years which were to end finally at that same Golden Gate. I returned as obscure as when I left, to a world incredibly different from what I had cherished in memory through the years as "home." But I did not come back empty. Although the war had reduced my luggage to a duffel bag, I brought with me experiences, recollections, friendships. For me, these had made an obscure life profoundly worthwhile. Few of us become great or famous, but most of us do follow a dream seeking to mature our own peculiar knowledge of what life has to offer. There is never any coming home to our youth. The world inevitably changes between our growing up and our preparing to die. But if ultimately we are to know content, we must so shape our course that in human terms we reach a worthy destination.

If to no one else but ourselves we must become somebody.

FAMILY

EARLY DAYS *(right)*
Lance, Joyce and Vincent circa 1900. (photo courtesy of Patricia Gowen Aitken)

THE SENIOR GOWENS *(below) Dr.and Mrs. Herbert Gowen, Port Blakely, June, 1939*

THREE GENERATIONS *(below)*
Top row, left to right: Joyce (Robbins), Vincent, Dr.Gowen, Mrs.Gowen, Rupert, Sylvia (Wells-Henderson) and Lance. Bottom row, left to right: Marvin (Robbins), Geoffrey, Ann, Ronald (Wells-Henderson) and Patricia ("Patsy"), Port Blakely, July, 1939

11

HOME   **"HOLLY RIDGE"**
(right) Oct. 1938.
Originally the home of
the manager of the
Port Blakely Mill
company on Bain-
bridge Island. Dr.
Gowen bought this as
a summer home in the
mid-1930s. It was the
site of many Gowen
family reunions. VHG
bought it in 1945 after
returning to the U.S.
and lived there until
his death in 1984.

THE SEATTLE HOME *(below)*
Feb. 1926. Located at 5005 22nd
Ave. NE in the University Dstrict.
VHG grew up in this home and
returned there on furloughs until it
was sold in the late 1930s when Dr.
Gowen retired.

Part I

China: 1913 to 1927

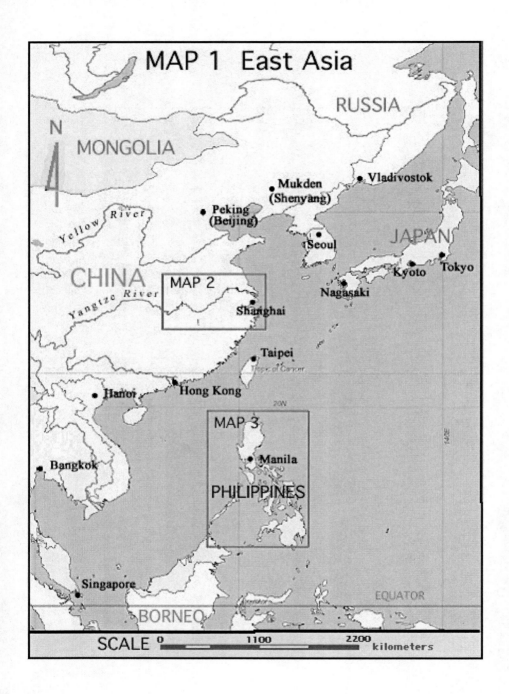

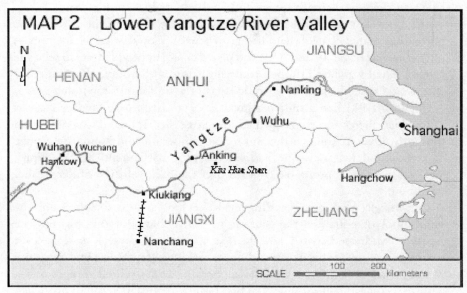

MAP 2   Lower Yangtze River Valley

NOTES:

1. Modern provincial names have been used above. Some have changed since VHG was in China as follows: Zhejiang from Chekiang; Jlangsu from Kiangsu; Hubei from Hupeh; Henan from Honan; and Jiangxi from Kiangsi.

2. The modern spelling of City names in China has changed from those used above as follows: Kiukiang to Jiujiang; Hangchow to Hangzhou; Anking to Anqing; Nanking to Nanjing; Hankow to Hankou.

3. The sacred mountain, Kiu Hua Is now known as Jiuhua Shan.

THE YEAR 1913 was the last of the 19ᵗʰ Century. It was the last year in which people of the West could believe in a civilization that by ballot, Bible, text-books, and bills of lading was to make men perfect, the final year granted the white man to believe that Nature or God had made him superior over all coloured peoples, black, yellow, brown, or red, and ordained him to rule over them to their advantage and, without apology, to his own.

As a boy of twenty, I arrived off Yokohama in the autumn of that *same* portentous year, *1913*. All that I had grown up to enjoy seemed secure forever; indeed, it was revolt against a life too placid that had prodded me to seek the Orient. I had watched Europe's recurring crises with a hope that some day they would explode, that they would smash the dullness of too much peace.

Japan in 1913 had acquired a great navy, a disciplined, modern-trained army. Her merchant ships girdled the seas; her trains ran swiftly and promptly. Over Yokohama that sunny November morning hung the smoke of a thousand factories. She had, moreover, a parliament, and elections, and was evincing a profitable concern over the backwardness of her weaker neighbours.

Of this Japan I got gleaming evidence long before sunrise from the lighthouses that marked the gateway to Tokyo Bay. But this was not the Japan I had dressed swiftly and hurried up to the dark deck to see. As we stole silently toward this new world, I was seeking everything a boy of twenty would seek, but looking to find it wrapped in the mysterious trappings of a culture strange and absorbing. The first beautiful portent was Fuji just when daybreak touched its snowy pinnacle and warmed slowly down the smooth outspreading slopes of its perfect cone.

Exploited though Fuji had been by gilt reproduction on a million cups and saucers, it surmounted this cheapness as it surmounted the smoking plain, too great to be marred, secure in its beauty and its magic. It was the truest introduction I could have had not to Japan alone but to the Orient; it presented a spiritual reality to which any newcomer from the West must keep his eyes alert or he will see only squalour, disease, filth. Now I appreciated what a Japanese friend back in Seattle had in mind when he heard that I, a brash youth of twenty, was going to China to teach.

"I wonder," he said, "that you have the boldness."

"The boldness" of Western intrusion thrust itself forward from every turn in this initial acquaintance with Japan - the boldness of Western might, Western commerce, Western science, the 19th Century trust in trade and empire, all apparent even before we dropped anchor.

Yokohama at that time had no docks. We moored amid a great fleet drawn from every maritime nation. Exactly at eight bells, sounded from scores of bridges, these ships in one magnificently concerted gesture flung out their many flags - British, French, German Austrian, Norwegian, Dutch, Danish, American, Japanese - while, a cable's length away, the British flagship, *H.M.S. Minotaur*, held divine service on the quarterdeck. This spectacle our captain, Scottish born but an American citizen from many years back, watched from the stern railing. With grave attention he head the *Minotaur*'s band play the hymns, The Church's One Foundation, and Glorious Things of Thee are Spoken; when they ended to the solemn strains of God Save the King, he did not even try to wipe away the tears that rolled down his cheeks.

Had he been entering Yokohama harbour, as I was, six years later, he would have seen more to weep over. The First World War had come and gone; the 19th Century had gone with it. Tokyo Bay still was crowded with ships but, except for the French flag aboard our ship, the only flags we saw were Japanese.

* * * * * *

A first day in a foreign land - for a young man at least - is bound to be indigestible. He will cram into it more than he can chew. Yet no later, wiser perception sees a lustre equal to those first enamel-bright impressions. Even such ordinary experiences as the swift, prompt transit by electric railway from Yokohama to Tokyo were exciting; their sameness was so different.

This was a day more exciting to live through than to describe. The wall and moats of the Imperial palace, for example, mean something new to every traveler, but they have had their sticky-sweet due in the prose of tourist bureau folders. Other memories of Tokyo recall broad avenues still unplagued by cars, yet scoured so frequently by winds sweeping up the dust like invisible brooms that we soon copied local practice: we turned our bodies before each gust and walked forward facing backward. Flagged down by policemen's swords, we turned also to avoid staring into the carriage which was carrying one of the Imperial princes to the palace.

This was not the only taboo. Japan had developed others which were to become, alas, more in keeping with modern custom than we anticipated. Chief among them, even in 1913, was a morbid watchfulness against spies, suspicion so acute that although our guide was the American military attaché (or perhaps because of it), he insisted that we not carry our cameras with us since he still was uncertain as to what could or could not be photographed in Tokyo.

The day left my companion Alan Lee, a young Englishman, and myself far from sated. We craved a deeper, more poetical initiation into the Orient's mysteries; what more natural than that we leave this to the enterprise of the rickshaw coolies whom we hired that evening in Yokohama. This notion the coolies themselves endorsed emphatically. When they suggested a tea-house, we were instantly agreeable, looking forward to a pavilion, its eaves uptilted, its crimson column set beside a lotus-strewn pool; there we would sit imbibing jasmine tea while the darkness, dimly lit by stone lanterns, vibrated gently to lute and flute and quaint-syllabled songs.

What we got was the second floor of a raffish building where no sooner were we seated than we were pounced upon by a flurry of mama-sans, all struggling to sit in our laps. Kimonos they did wear but so loosely that it was immediately apparent they wore nothing else. Over-plump and none too clean, they were too unseductive to make any strain on our virtue. We were as drastically untempted as we had been in San Francisco, a few weeks earlier, when exposed to the nauseous spectacles of the Barbary Coast, a Barbary Coast where one needed only a very minute sense of the fastidious to emerge pure as St. Anthony.

Our continence, however, was more than our ricksha coolies could understand.

"You wanchee high class girl?" they asked.

"No"

"You wanchee Eurasian girl"?

"No."

"You wanchee Russian girl?"

"No, we want to go back to our ship."

This lame end to a promising night reduced them to despair. For our own good they pleaded.

"What! You go home, people ask you Japanese girl how fashion, you say no have try - what thing?"

Despite this engaging lesson in pidgin English, our first exploration of Oriental mystery had bogged down before the most enticing mystery of all; so far as we were concerned the mystery of "Japanese girl how fashion" went unexplained. Today, thanks to the American G.I. it is a mystery no more. He "have try!"

The poetically transcribed mysteries of the Orient we were to see without advice of ricksha coolies, see for ourselves in Kyoto, one of the world's few perfect cities. Imaginations as young and susceptible as ours could not have framed better the rain-washed roofs of this one-time capital as we looked down on them from the massive wooden veranda of the Kiyomizu Temple. The late sun, breaking out from beneath rolled back clouds, reddened the wet glistening city. Behind the temple the eastern sky was clear; poised on the edge of a hill, dome-shaped, autumn-crimson with maple, the full moon waited its turn, long enough for the sun to disappear and for a flight of migrant geese, as rightly placed as the ink marks of a painting, to sweep across its white, flat circle. At this moment, as if to consecrate the day's end, a deep-tongued bell boomed across Kyoto's crowded valley.

The Japanese are co-workers with Nature; they even persuade it to conform to their artistic canon. Unless the European living there is willing to make a similar surrender, he remains an exile. His poignant apartness we felt in Nagasaki, a brooding city half smothered by the clouds hanging low on its circle of hills. Here were remnants of old imperialisms, Dutch and Russian, bleached high and dry above the receding wave of western conquest. At the English church the priest, for no reason that we could decipher, wept in mid-sermon. Into the hill-girt bay came to anchor a towering white liner, the *Empress of Russia*, promising home and swift escape from lands in which we would be forever strangers. Our hotel, its rose-garden still flowering forlornly in November, was a stopping-place where the lost souls of Joseph Conrad's novels might have yawned and drunk stupidly to ease their homesickness.

Everything about it was hushed, the slippered servants, the straggle of English weeklies, *Tatler, Bystander, Sketch, Punch*, heaped in an oppressive drawing-room, the dinner which we were to meet in many a bachelors' mess, fried fish, cold meat, boiled potatoes, stewed fruit on custard, a meal cooked without zest and served without flavour. This dinner left nothing more but to go to bed, to sleep as we could in rooms ponderous with gigantic furniture, chairs, dressing tables, chests-of-drawers, dragged half way round the world from London in the days when Victoria was queen. Nagasaki that night was the world's remotest corner, a stagnant backwater where nothing would ever again happen. It spoke only banishment, and made homesickness ache like a decaying tooth.

Out of Nagasaki, however, we escaped. Aboard a smart Russian Volunteer Fleet[3] ship, the *Poltava*, its hull throbbing as it picked up speed, its two buff funnels smoking dark clouds in its impetuous wake, carried its own assurance of the 19th Century. In an elegant saloon an ikon, signalized by a votive lamp, hung between portraits of their Imperial Majesties, the Czar Nicholas II and his sad-faced Empress.

For us this voyage, two nights and a day, meant the end of voyaging. We did not know whether to be glad or sorry. It might have meant mishap for my sleep walking friend: having sallied in pyjamas down the corridor, he was at a loss what stateroom to go back to; all had doors hooked open, all looked alike until, putting his hand on what he hoped would be his pillow, he put it on a woman's face. "Is that you, George?" she murmured. He did not stay for George's reply.

In my youth China was yellow, not red. Hundreds of miles off its coast the Yellow Sea reached out to remind us of this yellowness. Our ship was afloat on Chinese soil. The Yellow Sea is frighteningly yellow. The ocean is stained halfway to Japan by the vast outpouring of silt of the Hoang-ho[4] and the Yangtze, an outpouring matched only by the equally vast, unceasing flood of human life which spills on to a world less and less big enough to contain it.

The nearer we approached China across this mud-laden sea, the more its bigness daunted us. Yet the Shanghai at which we arrived finally after the tortuous channel of the Huangpu gave every evidence that China's bigness had been tamed. Singing in melancholy acceptance their chant of skimpy wages and endless toil, its coolies staggered beneath the unbroken chain of boxes, bales, crates which hauled from factory and warehouse to cram the holds of ships consigned to every great port in the six continents. A city reckoned by millions, Shanghai's smoking chimneys made foreigners rich. Along its Bund stood buildings so substantial that their empire of alien commerce promised to last forever. Few observers who noted the crass magnificence of this bustling city, the luxury of homes on Bubbling Well Road staffed by a hundred servants, the regal leisure of its clubs, the self-assured wealth of its shops, its banks, its great business "hongs," had the inner sight to remark that the houses which walled in brick and stone all this massive enterprise were built solidly on mud. It was an omen which the westerner, flourishing as he never could have flourished at home, chose to ignore; he overlooked the fragile crust on which all this was reared, unready believe that he lived daily and dangerously at the mercy of boycott, strike, riot, of sinister forces just learning to measure their strength.

None of these forebodings troubled me as we came ashore at the Customs jetty. Except for the hordes of coolies I might have doubted whether I was in China at all. Two or three hundred yards away was the American Post Office where I bought and affixed two-cent American stamps to send my letters home. This was but one anomaly in a city whose charter was treaties; under such mouth-filling terms as "extraterritoriality" they guaranteed every foreigner freedom from Chinese courts, Chinese laws, Chinese taxes, freedom indeed from all taxes. The only tax an American paid was the dollar he spent each year to register at his consulate. The treaties, all derived from the settlement of the mis-named Opium War[5], even guaranteed foreigners freedom from looting. Chinese soldiers had learned that, while they could plunder their own people with impunity, any attack on foreigners brought reprisals.

Shanghai was the impregnable bastion of this system, a European city erected on the mudflats where the Emperor's officials had hoped to confine its intrusive merchants in a swampy ghetto. Never did they imagine that this ghetto would dwarf in wealth and power the Chinese city which had schemed to keep uncontaminated by these aliens with big noses and faded

20

hair. Reluctant to be bothered with their uncouth affairs, the mandarins had told these squatters to administer their own community, in fact tossed them self-government like coppers thrown to a beggar. They could not have foreseen how this same self-government would prove so honest as to attract Chinese residents by the million, all eager to safeguard homes and property under the shelter of its utterly un-Chinese justice.

Shanghai shared other anomalies with all the treaty ports. To the newcomer the most puzzling was the currency, the figuring prices in dollars brought by the shipload from Mexico and worth only the silver they contained. Although the Chinese mints had begun to coin dollars, these too had no backing; in banks and hongs their value was tested by a shroff who bit them or rang them to assay their purity. As for subordinate coinage - a recent innovation - eleven or twelve ten-cent pieces made a dollar, or six twenty-cent pieces, whereas copper cents might well range up to three hundred. To complicate still further this book-keeper's nightmare, the standard of commercial exchange was not the dollar, wherever this "piece-of-eight" might have been minted, but the tael - and for this there was no coin. A tael was an ounce of pure silver; for centuries China had stumbled along under this cumbersome system which required merchants to carry with them ingots of unalloyed metal and, in every transaction too considerable for the square-holed coins, to slice off the desired amount of silver and weigh it on pocket scales.

These intricacies I was not likely to master in a day. I had come from Seattle where paper money was despised and the lowly penny used only by children to buy wine-balls and white peppermint lozenges, or pink wintergreen. Consequently, I was too proud to cumber my pockets with copper cents, and unloaded a heavy superfluity of these coins on my ricksha coolie, all in excess of his fare which I would not deign to pay in anything smaller than dimes. The result was a riot. This was the Orient's first lesson: to overpay is more hazardous than to underpay. Spotting me for a newcomer, and quickly joined by a mob of his fellows who came cawing like crows to his support, my ricksha man beat his breast and wailed and screamed; an old-fashioned actor performing King Lear could not have bettered his anguish. In a country where six dollars Mex. kept a family housed and fed for a month, pennies were not small change.

But Shanghai, as everybody told me, was not China. Nor was it home - but the dullest of boring substitutes. For the casual stranger, excluded from the social life that went on behind high walls, walls formidably topped with broken glass, the sole entertainment was at one of the settlement's two cinés. I could not have pictured amusement more lugubrious. Some time after eight-thirty a Portuguese pianist would emerge from under the stage, survey the smattering of patrons and, if there were enough of them, begin hammering out an overture. Late starting, late ending, these shows were protracted past midnight by an interminable intermission during which the handful present were expected to drown their loneliness at the bar. So much livelier was this refreshment than what the screen offered that some patrons stayed there through the second half. Such was Shanghai's nightlife in 1913 - unless one sought female society on Kiangse Road.

Six weeks later, on a Christmas visit to Shanghai, I looked up a friend aboard the *U.S.S. Helena*, a gunboat whose skyscraper stack had been built purposely high - so the British Navy declared - to prevent the American gobs from spitting down the smokestack and swamping the fires.

On the China Station, the American Navy lived vividly. Josephus Daniels, Woodrow Wilson's pious Secretary of the Navy, had not issued as yet his much resented order against alcoholic beverages aboard ship. My visit gave excuse for a bibulous afternoon and in my honour was broached a huge bowl of punch which was being mellowed for Christmas. It contained, I would swear, every known liquor, and it propelled us ashore in a mood so blithe that even Shanghai looked cheerful.

We soon were a party of twenty, all but myself officers either from the Helena or the cruiser Rainbow. First suffering some part of the picture at the Victoria, we adjourned to the old Carlton, a restaurant dismally suited to be a jury room, and thence by an understandable momentum to the establishments on Kiangse Road. Three in succession we visited, drinking champagne in the scented company of Shanghai's most lurid décolletage. At each house we lost some of our party. When, at three in the morning, my friend and I emerged from the third, we emerged alone - and he, I am convinced, only because he had assumed guardianship over my youthful morals.

The girls in Kiangse Road, most of them American and none, to my critical eye, enticing, were well acquainted with our Asiatic squadron. They followed the fleet on its yearly rounds, to Shanghai, Chefoo[6], Hong Kong, Manila, so that at each stop they could offer our stranded husbands the solace of home. In the great upset which was to follow World War I, the U.S. Navy also upset this cozy arrangement; it began bringing Navy wives to the Orient. Whether this was an improvement on Kiangse Road was hotly disputed. Navy wives were, reputedly, swept up from hotel lobby floors every Sunday morning. My Christmas visit to Shanghai, however, culminated in a celebration as blamelessly domestic as the God-bless-us-one-and-all pages of Charles Dickens.

I had made one return sortie to the Helena, even bringing Alan, on the wardroom's urgent request, to sample the famous punch. Ours became an exploit unique, I hope, in Navy annals - the capture of a gunboat by a sampan. Unchallenged we came alongside, unchallenged we climbed on deck and, for several minutes, beat on a door before we could make our shouts heard over the din inside. This was the mess-deck. The wardroom, to which a sailor finally led us, was submerged in calm. Prone around the punch bowl sprawled its victims, too lackadaisical to do more than invite us to help ourselves. But, to our dismay, even the punch was exhausted. Its potent ingredients had been so wantonly diluted that we could have drunk to Christmas just as blithely from the Huangpo flowing muddily by.

Bickerton's Private Family Hotel saved the day. Whether it was the hotel or the families it catered to that were private we never figured out, nor why a family hotel should admit bachelors like ourselves. But for the Christmas dinner Dickens himself could have imagined nothing better. At one huge table sat all its guests. Mrs. Bickerton, a woman of generous proportions, presided at one end, her husband, as thin as she was stout, at the other.

The dinner was no paltry affair of soup, salad, entrée, and dessert. Calories had not yet been invented, and there were servants to wash the dishes. Without a qualm we disposed of each course as it was borne in, soup and fish and a salad, roast beef with Yorkshire pudding, roast sucking-pig, roast goose, roast turkey, a second salad, then minced pie, plum pudding and of course, hard sauce, after which we tapered off on savoury, nuts, and fruit, and scorched our fingers in the blue flames as we delved raisins from a bowl of snapdragon. If we did not quite match the three-bottle men of earlier centuries, we did not scant a varied abundance of wines, sherry, sauterne, claret, port, and liqueurs, working off the drowsing effects of the repast by drawing-room games - not a kiss in the lot - which kept us upright until two in the morning.

Christmas 1913 - next year the world was at war, and Christmases like this belong now to a world as obsolete as the antiquarian rites which Washington Irving described with nostalgic gusto at Bracebridge Hall. What have we gained? - roads clogged with motorcars, skies noisy with jets, radio, television, vitamins, refrigerators and frozen foods, guided missiles, man-made satellites, nuclear bombs - and fear.

* * * * * *

The China of 1913 had not yet learned to live in the 19th Century, much less the 20th. Barely two years before, it had undergone one of those transformations, soon to become fashionable, whereby a magniloquent name was attached to a doubtful change. It was now the Republic of China, or, more literally, the Central Flowery People's Country, and as up to date as parliaments and parliamentarians (dressed in top hats and frock coats) could make it. The silk hats outlasted the parliaments by several years. As late as

23

1918 my cook rented for me, at fifty cents, a top hat in prime condition whose owner, a provincial assemblyman, was preserving it against a summons that never came - the call to resume his legislative duties. I wore it to celebrate a peace which proved to be no peace!

For thousands of years China had thrived as a great civilized power surrounded by neighbours too weak and (from the Chinese viewpoint) too inferior to challenge her ascendancy. It was an imperialism with no rivals, no curbs - except those imposed by its own recurring cycles of corruption and decay - to China's domination over adjacent countries like Tibet or Burma or Mongolia. Even when overrun by outer barbarians, by Mongols or Manchus, her culture, her social system, assimilated these conquerors till they ended by becoming Chinese. Her name, Chung Kuo[7], Central Country, was no extravagant boast; it spoke a fact. To this fact China owed her long existence as a country. Some strong claimant would set up a dynasty, Han, T'ang, Sung, Ming, Ch'ing, and, so long as his vigour was inherited by his descendants, China too stayed strong. When luxury eventually rotted away the dynasty, a period of internal conflict ensued; it might last even a century or two but, because no nearby country was powerful enough to do more than nibble at its over-extended boundaries, China always fought her way back to the renewed might of another great dynasty. Civil war had eliminated the weaklings.

Such leisurely adjustments were not feasible in 1911, when the Manchu[8] dynasty collapsed of its own top-heavy inertia. No longer was the earth centred in the round slab on the Altar of Heaven's concentric marble terraces. As T'ien Tzu, son of heaven, in the bitter early morning darkness of the Winter Solstice, the Emperor still did obeisance to Heaven; glittering in dragon embroidered robes he still prostrated himself to music played on instruments of jade, but the ritual was solemn pretense. China had been pushed to the fringe of the civilized world. Big-nosed men, repulsive-looking with blue eyes and straw-coloured hair, had brought soldiers and gunboats as well as merchants from their uncouth lands; not only had they forced China to do business with these barbarians but were dividing her into parts like the segments of a wheel which they called "zones of influence." Still harder to swallow, one of China's erstwhile vassals had copied their bullying tactics. The Japanese, the "Eastern Ocean Dwarfs," were using their nearness not to pay tribute but to make sure that China produced no new strong man. If Japan could prevent it, no new dynasty would rise from the ruins of the old.

All this was being played out in the autumn of 1913, although I rode into China, passing from the 19th Century to the Middle Ages in the less than two

24

hundred miles that separated Shanghai from Nanking, with little realization that I was heading into the most critical years of China's long history. It was a dismal ride. The train was slow and cold. From my compartment could be seen tiny snatches of farm obstructed and hampered by graves, by the round mounds heaped up in such inconvenient places as to block the ploughman at every furrow. Except for the graves, the country was a wearisome panorama of yellowing willows, houses put together crudely from dirty-grey tile, men and women garbed alike in jacket and trousers, in the dull uniformity of faded blue cotton.

Nanking quickened my interest. The train had passed from plains to treeless mountains when abruptly above moat and foothill loomed its stupendous wall. Reared on stones huge enough to be the handwork of giants, topped by massive battlements, it looked impregnable till one noted its shell-scarred towers. They told another story, recalling the past summer's warfare, which had demonstrated how vulnerable were its fortifications now that explosive shells had ousted arrows and iron cannon balls.

This wall, twenty-six miles long, enclosed far more open country than city. Some of these empty spaces had once been inhabited, like the flat wastes of the Tatar city, razed to its foundations in an earlier uprising. In Europe even small towns, insignificant in importance compared with Nanking, would have shone in the splendour of ancient buildings. Nanking had only one, its drum tower, a lump of crimson-washed brickwork, pierced by three arches, capped by a superstructure, long fallen out of repair but with upturned eaves that gave Ku Lou its single graceful touch. Through its arches poured the city's traffic. Its drum, however, was silent; it no longer beat out the hours. Of Nanking's eminence as capital of the first Ming Emperor, the Buddhist shepherd who as Hung Wu claimed the dragon throne in 1368 I found barely a trace. After I had acquired some recognition of Chinese characters, I discovered his name stamped on some cream-glazed bricks in the city wall. That was all. Hung Wu survived not in the living city but in the lonely solitude of his tomb at the foot of Purple Mountain[9].

For Nanking present miseries had blotted out both past and future. The city had just undergone a siege that ended in evicting Sun Yat-sen, the revolutionary leader whom fate had pushed into worldwide acclaim as China's first President. Although his name was to remain the rallying-point for an assortment of fanatics until - and after - his death in the middle '20's his term in office had been brief. Chang Hsun, first of the War Lords, had driven out both Sun Yat-Sen and his silk-hatted cronies; in their place, he brought back the queue - or pigtail, as in ruder days we called it - badge of fealty to the Manchu emperors.

The queue gave the Chinese populace some perplexed moments. One day, it had been death to appear with a queue, the next, death to appear without one. Taking their stand at the city gates, where revolutionaries had clipped the queues of all comers, Chang Hsun's blue-coated ruffians seized anybody who dared appear short-haired - a turn of events so probable that prudent Chinese had insured themselves by saving their severed queues ready for revived use.

Chung Hsun and the longhaired bullies who made up his private army took no stock in republics. Chang had promoted himself to general from the lowly post of groom to the late Empress Dowager. While it does seem, despite much privately expressed skepticism, that he could write his own name, his signature (to judge from a document I once saw) was an illiterate scrawl. In a country where good handwriting, the art of inscribing the ancient characters with distinction, could advance an official to the highest places in government, Chang Hsun was a boor, but a boor to be whispered about, not criticized openly.

He and his troops had burst upon Nanking like a horde of bandits, plundering, raping, killing. Not a house, except the sacrosanct homes of the foreign devils, had they spared. This was the Nanking at which I arrived after the chilly tedium of the train ride from Shanghai, a city prostrated by the horror it had suffered. On many of its doors still was chalked the character "ch'a" or "searched," put there in a vain hope that the successive bands of marauding soldiers would pass them by. Cowed and destitute, its inhabitants cringed before the dread of renewed brutality. Down the Hua P'ai Lou, its principal thoroughfare, I myself saw Chang Hsun ride in his closed carriage. Preceded by shouting cavalrymen who lashed anybody in his path, he tore along a street so narrow that the carriage could scarcely squeeze by. When his horses knocked down an old woman and left her sprawling on the ground, he did not halt.

The only people for whom China was healthy in those days were the foreigners. Killing foreigners was an activity which Chinese of every persuasion gladly would have assisted, but the game was not worth the price. Behind the tiny gunboats that paraded American, British, French, Japanese flags up and down the Yangtze lurked powers the Chinese were unready to provoke; they remembered the Boxer Rebellion and its bitter aftermath. European or American, the foreigners were spectators at a theatre, watching tragedy, but never truly part of it. An Englishman, eating tiffin aboard his houseboat by the river bank, could send his houseboy to demand that a Chinese cruiser stop shelling the forts until after his siesta - and expect to be listened to.

This curious immunity amid havoc characterized the American household to which we came. Nanking's foreign community consisted of three groups,

26

consular, commercial, missionary. Having been sent to China to teach in a mission school, we belonged to the last. But our present status was that of lodgers in a faculty home at the University of Nanking, at whose recently inaugurated Language School we had enrolled to study Chinese.

Alan Lee and I should have been termed missionaries by accident. Our only excuse for being in Nanking was that we were tired of Seattle. Alan, for some mystical reason, had conceived a hankering to go to Burma. I needed no persuasion to adopt Burma as my goal too; I would have embraced, indeed, any goal sufficiently remote from the sights I was used to, from a humdrum existence oppressed always by the duty set before me of seeking a Rhodes Scholarship.

Neither of us ever reached Burma. The nearest we could come was a teacher's job in China, where the Episcopal Church needed men for its mission schools. Flimsy though our credentials would have appeared, appraised by later pedagogical standards, we were accepted, accepted with no indication of what we were to teach. Before we sailed, however, I regretted my rashness. I had fallen in love (not for the first nor the last time!), and wrote the Bishop in New York who was handling our appointment that I could not possibly stay a full five years in China; two years was the most I could contemplate.

Bishop Lloyd did not argue. He replied very simply that, after I had seen what was being done in the overseas Mission, I would change my mind. He foresaw more than I. The two years stretched to thirty-three, and the two amateur teachers, appointed so casually, ended as missionary priests, dedicated to a cause which, on that first contact at Nanking, we neither understood nor believed in.

Christian missions 1913 were as 19th Century as the countries that had dispatched them. Their piety ran the entire gamut from the China Inland Mission, whose husbands - one disgruntled daughter said - lived on faith, their wives on hope, and their children on charity, to the Episcopalians, a spiritual aristocracy reputed (falsely) to enjoy a wine and tobacco allowance. The mission ranks included many able people, many good people, and many bigots.

Some thinking persons were moving to recognition that the Christian religion was the property of no one race or nation but an ideal as yet imperfectly practised in which all peoples, Oriental, African, European, must take their place as equals, contributing their specific racial talents to a world-wide unity of purpose. This alone, they felt, could guarantee an enduring peace. To most missionaries of that time, however, the activating motive was condescension: we are right and you are wrong. They had come not to ask the Chinese to become partners in work vitally important to Chinese and westerner alike; they had come to convert poor, benighted heathen.

My own preconceptions of life in China had been romantically vague - a bamboo hut built on stilts over a canal, and curry twice a day. I was lodged instead in a substantial brick house set apart, like most mission homes, from close contact with the Chinese. Walls enclosed the compounds, favouring an aloofness supposedly necessary to the missionary's health. Except that they were served by blue-coated servants watching in silence while their masters ate, the meals might have been those in any American home. The table talk, indeed, was more pious.

This piety was far harder to adjust to than the exotic existence I had anticipated. Being young and brash, I made little allowance for the hospitality that had been willing to take me in as a boarder. The naked display of religiousness shocked me, the bland certainty of the group at table that they were "saved," the twice-daily prayers voiced in terms of insinuating familiarity with God, and backed up by a use of the Bible both uncritical and superstitious - for these I was totally unprepared. I could only take refuge in the words of a speaker at the Nanking Association when he declared - the brightest of my memories from that first evening in Nanking - that "we are all cast in the same mould, but some are mouldier than others."

Nanking offered some truly mouldy specimens, fanatics spurred by a crusading conviction that any human being unbaptized was damned. My diary was unkindest in describing the Methodist missionaries who, by supplying room and board, had enabled Alan and me to study at Nanking. I wrote of them as the most dismal of our hardships. In retrospect, I wonder how they put up with me. I was fatuously blind to their part of the hardship. We were latecomers to the Nanking Language School, then beginning its second year of a classroom instruction which many earlier missionaries, compelled to puzzle through the rudiments of Chinese without such guidance, sniffed at as a questionable novelty.

Episcopalian students were a novelty even more questionable. It took fervent persuasion from our resident priests, who lived too far from the University of Nanking to lodge us themselves, before any mission would accommodate us. Only our Methodist hosts braved this risk. With sliding doors they shut off a front parlour for our occupancy. The arrangement had physical defects and spiritual: the bathroom was upstairs, far down a corridor to the utmost limits of the house; the living-room and the family's domestic activities were a keyhole's breadth away, a nearness that tended to aggravate doctrinal differences yawning between us like a deep gulf.

These doctrinal differences another lodger, a Wesleyan Methodist, Australian by birth, English by training, took on his shoulders to mend. He became the most uncomfortable friend it was ever my privilege to acquire. I stress the word "privilege" because what he insisted on doing put me

28

perpetually in his debt. Night after night he walked me up and down the quiet back streets of Nanking while he tore to pieces my most cherished beliefs and demonstrated, by sharp, probing logic, how frail was their structure. Often, in an agony of resentment, I groaned to be left alone, but he was relentless, baring every weakness, just as he deflated my conceit at the dinner table after I had made some swaggering quip, by inquiring behind the bland scrutiny of his glasses, "And have you any more funny stories?"

It is not easy to be a grateful to a friend so uncompromising, a friend who never made any easy accommodation to my likes. I am glad that I did have the good sense to be grateful, and to merit a letter which he wrote afterwards commenting on the rare fact that, candid though he had been, open-eyed to each other's faults, refusing a more slipshod friendliness, never once had we exchanged an embittered word.

Nearly forty years have passed since last I heard of Burgoyne Chapman, yet that friendship has not loosened. As he himself wrote, honed to a fine edge by Cambridge University debates, may have pruned from my convictions, he replaced by a theology that kept step as I matured.

The piety of our Methodist household did not wear so well. Not only was it their habit, after breakfast, to get down on their knees and - as a small girl once put it – "smell the chairs." But every Wednesday night they held prayer meeting. After absorbing this second-hand through the sliding doors, I volunteered to play the piano for these exercises.

My reasons were not entirely devout. I was kindling to romantic interest in one member of the household, the University president's secretary. Since dating was not in vogue in prim Nanking, this was one of the few ways I might win merit in her eyes.

As it happened, she had been gravitating toward the Episcopal Church. Long before we appeared, she had been studying the Book of Common Prayer. When her turn to lead prayer meeting coincided with Ash Wednesday, she was amenable to my suggestion that between us we use some portions of the Penitential Office appointed for that day.

Ash Wednesday, however, meant nothing to these Methodists. Neither did Penitence. How could it? They were saved. On hearing us both talk sin and repentance, even in the Prayer Book's sedate English, their instant conclusion was that we had been up to something, and were confessing our mutual trespass. Throughout the round-robin intercessions that emanated from the chair bottoms, our misdoing was on their minds: several persons prayed for her, two or three even tackled the hopeless task of praying for me!

Two years later, I got my revenge by marrying the girl for whom they had offered their assiduous prayers, but for the moment I was done with prayer

29

meetings. Having been given a box of cigars, a present from the British-American Tobacco Company's manager, I puffed them through the keyhole to such good effect that after the meeting we heard a maiden lady exclaim from the hall, as another of the faithful was trying to light her lantern, "I am sure that the gentlemen in the next room could give you some matches!"

These good people were more tolerant of me than I deserved. They put up not with me alone but with my dog, a tawny pugnacious little beast, half way between Pekinese and a Chow, a pet offered me by a stranger on the sad plea that he could not afford to feed him. This gift I compounded by paying its master twenty cents. Twice the dog ran away; twice his master brought him back, confounding those wise to the Orient, who were sure that I had been duped. They had not seen the sadness in the man's eyes.

Convinced at last, Hsi-tzu accepted his new home and new master. I had called him Hsi-tzu, or Happy One, thinking this was his name. What his master said was more likely (in the Nanking pronunciation) Ssu-tzu, or Lion, the species he belonged to. Both names were suitable. Nothing daunted him, nothing dampened his gaiety.

Where I went, he went, paying his respects to the kitchen while I had tea in the parlour. The ricksha men knew him and deferred to him and, on the one occasion when I forgot him, brought him home seated in lordly arrogance in his own ricksha.

Church he loved, thumping an accompaniment to the organ I was playing. To curb this distracting habit, I tried tying him outside the church door, but when the minutes ticked by with no worshippers appearing I went to investigate. Hsi-tzu was holding the congregation at bay. Not satisfied with holding off a congregation, Hsi-tzu welcomed the Bishop on his annual visitation with a nip in the ankle. The result, alas, was an inexorable edict: no dogs in the Mission. Sadly I transferred Hsi-tzu to Presbyterian friends; in their precincts, at least, he was safe from bishops.

* * * * * *

Presbyterian, Methodist, Episcopalian - these were but a fraction of the Christian sects competing for Chinese acceptance. It was the heyday of a movement destined soon to recede, like so much else that the 19th Century trusted would lead by orderly steps to a perfected world. "Ecumenical" then was no more than a faint whisper. Some missionaries had begun to question the absurdity of contaminating new converts with our doctrinal disagreements, the folly of fostering Chinese, Japanese, Hindu, African in our rigidly divisive patterns, yet nobody had thought out anything better. Our Chinese Book of Common Prayer was an exact copy of the American,

30

even to translating what in my choir-boy days used to divert me through a long sermon, the formula for finding the Golden letter.

Many of the missionary community were grappling other problems which threatened the essential bases of their faith. They were facing up to biblical criticism, to the theory of evolution, to the question of whether God had dictated His truths like cryptic oracles rattled off on a ouija board, or led man as a child is led, step by step out of infancy, and through normal liability to error, toward enlightenment, toward progressive awareness of the Divine character and what God expects of man.

These perplexities did not trouble us in the Episcopal Church. After all, Charles Darwin was an Anglican vestryman. We were not involved in a literal acceptance of Genesis. To many thoughtful persons in other missions, brought up to believe in a six-day Creation, and in Adam and Eve as the first human beings, the doubt cast on these chapters posed painful uncertainty.

I was taken, one evening, as guest to hear such issues discussed. In careful secrecy the group met at the home of Dr. Leighton Stuart, who became, a whole generation later, the United States Ambassador to Chiang Kai-shek's China. Before being admitted, I pledged myself to say nothing outside about the group, its members, its topics of study. Had some mission boards in America learned that their appointees were engaging in these heretical studies, they would have recalled the guilty parties post-haste. The Bible was their fetish. A squat, fat tome, bound in leather, fastened with brass clasps, it occupied a central lectern in their churches. No cross, no altar, no candle was permitted to dispute its eminence. It was enthroned for worship as stolidly as the gilded Bodhisattva in a Chinese temple.

The participants in these discussions were men and women gifted with good sense as well as judgement. Others sniffed the new learning like an intoxicating vapour. I remember, at a Union service in Wuhu, a Methodist minister who announced from the pulpit that the greatest men in history were Jesus of Nazareth, H.G. Wells, and Dr. Harry Fosdick. Out walked the fundamentalist half of his congregation, leaving few except Episcopalians to hear him finish, and they more from curiosity as to how he would support this uncouth selection.

His was an extreme case, standing out from a Protestantism whose creed had been narrowed to Thou Shalt Not - Thus Shalt Not Smoke, Thou Shalt Not Drink, Thou Shalt Not Play Cards (not, that is, cards printed with Kings and Queens and Jacks), Thou Shalt Not Look Happy on Sunday (mislabeled, the Sabbath). Many otherwise sensible people had reduced the process of what they called Salvation to scattering Bible tracts among the heathen. In earlier days, before China was open to missionary intrusion, some Christian champions even tossed packets of tracts overboard from passing ships in hope that they would wash ashore and give the fisherman who picked them up his chance to be saved.

By such accident he was expected to decide his eternal future, to choose heaven or hell. Quite solemnly some missionaries averred that when every human being had been given this chance - how a population predominantly illiterate could read these tracts was not explained - the Christ would return to divide sheep from goats.

This, of course, was overlaying China's already sufficient superstition with an imported one even less rational. In practice, however, religion to many of its missionary believers meant little more than the Puritan's code of abstention. It exhorted them to keep in mind always that this world is a vale of tears, their faith a crawling obeisance to a God Who never smiles. As the hymn put it:

"Weary of earth, and laden with my sin,

I look to heaven, and hope to enter in."

In choirboy days I had loved agonizing through the doleful tune to which these words groaned, and this in the supposedly worldly Anglican Church. If even we could insulate what we mouthed from what we really desired, small wonder that other denominations, inculcated with Puritan teaching, tainted by the morbid New England conscience, should accommodate themselves to the appearance, instead of the substance, of the virtues they extolled.

One Sunday in June, near the end of my year's study at Nanking Language School, I was talking to the college treasurer, the only Episcopalian connected with that worthy school. Having overstayed a visit to Shanghai, he had returned by the night train in bare time to pay salaries to faculty members, many of them itching to get away on their vacations. One woman, I knew, had instant need of her pay, for she was departing by train early the next morning. "Tell her I will be in my office after the union service," he asked me to relay. "She can pick up her cheque then." This message I transmitted. The woman was darting toward the office when a forgotten scruple halted her. "Oh!" she objected, "I couldn't think of going there now - getting my money on Sunday - but then added, "Suppose you get it for me, please." After all, I was an Anglican; one trespass more would make scant difference in my final reckoning.

About this time a deputation from the Nanking missionary community did come to the priest in charge of our work, Father Gill, a Virginian who could make bluntness so ingratiating that even those whose piety he rebuffed felt flattered.

"Mr. Gill," they began solemnly, "we have come to ask if you would give up smoking."

"Why?" he demanded, with a shrewd twinkle in his eyes.

"Well, you see, we teach our Christians that it is a sin to smoke."

"That's all right," he assured them exhaling blue clouds as he replied, "you can teach them any damn lie you please, but when you persuade me that it is a sin to smoke, then I will give it up."

Of Father Gill this rebuttal was quoted with admiration, as was a similar retort to a Methodist lady, whose piety, though seemingly as inflexible as the skull-tight set of her hair, had not stifled her sense of humour. She had approached him just after he did abandon his incessant addiction to cigarettes, not however in deference to moral argument but to his physician.

"Oh, Mr. Gill," she began," I am so glad that you have stopped smoking. You know, I have prayed and prayed –"

"Just a moment, Madame," he broke in. "The day I stopped smoking, I bought a bottle of whisky."

Such gay impertinence the Methodists would not have tolerated from me; I lacked the Virginian's grace. But my acquaintance with the Methodists was destined to be close, not simply because I married a Methodist, but because, long after Nanking, I was assigned to cities, Nanchang and Wuhu, where their work overshadowed all others.

More than once I was present at Methodist Thanksgiving dinners and once listened to a twenty-minute blessing while the gravy surrounding the turkey cooled to grease. At this first dinner God was addressed by an eccentric old man from Chicago, proprietor of a famous hotel. He had made his fortune more intelligently than he disbursed it, assigning a very large sum to indoctrinate the Chinese with his ideas of the Bible. What these ideas were he indicated, on that Thanksgiving Day, by predicting from explicit verses in Isaiah how Jamaica, Australia, and the other dismembered fragments of the British Empire would seek refuge under the Monroe Doctrine.

These citations I was too startled to set down, and no subsequent perusal of Isaiah has given me any clue. They would not have enhanced Isaiah's credit for accuracy. The British Empire, certainly, is dismembered, a breakup few would have expected in 1913, but the Monroe Doctrine, as sacred then as Motherhood and the Stars and Stripes, excites only puzzlement from the modern schoolboy. It has sunk into limbo with the "White Man's Burden" and Prohibition.

Into that same limbo has gone, in large measure, the Methodism I describe. It was too unctuous to seem sincere. Patiently its votaries used to give God pointers, addressing Him about His duties as one would remind an absent-minded old man. "Thou knowest," introduced many a prayer which told the Deity in discursive detail things He should have known, but evidently had forgotten. He had aged. Instead of the Divine Father he had settled back to being "Grandpa God."

The allowances which some Methodists made for God, they were less ready to make for one another. In one Chinese city where I lived two hospitals had to be built to accommodate the two physicians; they could not work together. Both were women, one a Chinese whom we nicknamed "Kaiser Bill" because she ruled her institution with the domineering forthrightness of an autocrat. Far from copying the Chinese habit of saying what her listeners hope to hear, she blurted her opinions, let the chips fall where they might. We loved her for it. At a discussion club which convoked the foreign community every three weeks to whet mind and tongue on varied secular topics, she was the sole Chinese member, and never backward on that account. No cramped nationalism nor cramped piety inhibited her thinking. Truly a citizen of the world, she was a gutsy character, ever ready to level the heaviest artillery against whatever provoked her ridicule. Love her though we did, it was with private thanksgiving that our particular fields did not require our working with her.

Later, I moved to another station where again the Methodists had doctor trouble, two male physicians this time, both Americans. Instead of building separate hospitals, their solution was to allow one doctor full time to plans and construction while the other treated the sick. This hospital even boasted a motor ambulance, gift of some generous American who had neglected to enquire whether there were any roads on which it could be operated. To keep its batteries charged, the ambulance was paraded up and down the Bund's bare half mile of highway, but patients still came by stretcher or by wheelbarrow.

From the compound adjacent to the hospital the wife of the minister-in-charge disappeared, one dark night. She was never found. At the base of the bluff which supported her house like an acropolis the Yangtze eddied in turbid flow, eager to drag any victim down beyond rescue from its silt-stained depths. Back of the house were swamps and rice-paddies, a cozy overlay as grasping as quicksand.

No sooner had he heard of this tragedy than the head of our Mission hurried up to volunteer for the search a gang of coolies who were leveling a site for our middle school. The bereaved husband shrugged off this offer. "Thank you very much," was his equable reply, "but after breakfast will do."

There the mystery rested. The missing wife, it was true, had been under treatment for some nervous disorder; there seemed little doubt that she had thrown herself into the River. Entirely logical was the husband's attitude: before breakfast or after breakfast would have made little difference in a search doomed from its outset to failure. But his calm unconcern was not echoed by the foreign community. To quiet conjecture he was transferred to California. In that state, more inured to clerical idiosyncrasies, he was awarded a new congregation.

Caricature comes too easy. Despite its fanatics, its bigots, its spiritual busybodies, its freaks, the missionary community deserved better than the ridicule which outsiders accorded it. Within its ranks were men and women of marked brilliance, profound scholarship, intelligent dedication to a purpose worthy of respect, people too whose brimming compassion moved them to regard their own lives of small account in ministering to the sick and abused. As a body - and with innumerable exceptions - their dominant fault was the fault of the lands, the denominations which had sent them, a racial arrogance that underrated Chinese culture and overrated their own. Their philosophy at times seemed to reach no further than desire to make the Chinese like themselves, blurred blotting-paper facsimiles, just as they planted Gothic churches where every detail of worship, down to the same morbidly self-centred hymns, copied the respectable Sunday habits of church-going America. America and Europe (Protestant Europe, that is) were successful, so the teaching ran, because they were Christian.

Four years of a world war were soon to knock the props from under both these claims, leaving their converts to question the value of a Christianity whose paramount success was the scientific ability, and willingness, to kill off their fellow-Christians wholesale.

* * * * * *

The War which erupted in 1914 was fought out in almost another world from China. I touch on it but slightly because it never actually intruded on our life. We greeted it, at first, with an excitement tainted by eagerness; here was drama on a titanic scale. Avidly we subscribed to news agencies, to illustrated weeklies, never dreaming that such subscriptions need extend beyond a few weeks until France and Russia, in climactic land battles, and Britain, in battle at sea, should settle once for all the Kaiser's impudent challenge. We could not imagine a whole generation of Europe's most hopeful young men massacred in muddy trenches. Even when casualty lists mounted we recognized but faintly that the grimmest casualty was to be the civilization which had bred us. Another more worldwide war was to complete the job, but in the years from 1914 to 1918 the West discredited itself irrevocably among the so-called backward peoples who had looked to it as the exemplar whereon to pattern their own growth to a fuller humanity.

For me and my friend, Alan Lee, the War promised merely the chance to escape a routine that was becoming as humdrum as life at home. We had heard that the British government would pay the way home of any who

35

volunteered to fight. Without troubling to confirm the report we decided to register at the British Consulate. Our motive was less than heroic. What we counted on was the free trip to Europe, the opportunity to see India, Egypt, the Mediterranean. By the time we reached England, we had no doubt, the War would be ended.

In Alan's case this registration was a natural step, since he was a British subject. My case was more complicated. Although I was Canadian-born and son of English-born parents, my father was a naturalized American; I would have been entitled to the same citizenship except that I had left the United States and taken up residence in China before my twenty-first birthday. The belief that by doing so I had forfeited my American citizenship gave a final push to my enrollment as a Briton.

I learned soon enough that the British government was paying nobody's passage home to fight. Volunteers enlisted at their own expense. This dampening news ended my participation in world War I: when the British government, four years later, did get around to granting free passage not to fight but to direct the Chinese labour battalions which were being recruited for work behind the lines, I was in hospital recovering from a nearly fatal case of pneumonia. Hostilities did not wait on my convenience.

If World War I ended for me before it even began, the results of my patriotic frenzy lasted longer, years longer. I was a British subject, paying annually the only tax to which I was liable, my small registration fee at the Consulate. When in 1915 I paid off the Methodists by marrying Mary Angeline Gillmore, the girl with whom I had dared clicking tongues and pursed lips in our ill-advised attempt to combine Ash Wednesday with their prayer meeting, I changed her too, though Illinois-born, into a subject of King George. Even before we were married in church, we underwent the ordeal of a Consular wedding, an ordeal so formidable, behind a barricade of leather-bound registers as ancient-looking as the Magna Carta, that we felt like prisoners haled before the bar to be sentenced.

Each year I had stronger regrets for my lost citizenship. Much as I valued my British ties, my British friends, and clung to my British accent, the fact remained that my home was in America, as was my wife's, and all our known relatives. To return as aliens to the land where we had grown up was a humiliation that cut sharper with every furlough.

Beside this humiliation there was inconvenience to embitter this experience of being admitted as strangers to our own country. In 1925, for example, in preparing for a second trip home (our first had been in 1919-1920, while I studied theology in New York), I wrote to the American Consul-General in Nanking asking if it would be at all possible for a clerk to come the ten

36

minutes drive to the Yangtze, as we passed through en route to Shanghai, and stamp our passports with a visa.

In normal times, I admitted, such a request would have been presumptuous, even though I expected to pay the trifling expense, but times were not normal. Riots in Shanghai, and their forcible repression by the International Settlements police, had set all the Yangtze ports seething. Not knowing what might happen in Wuhu, I was loath to risk the two days' absence necessary for a trip to Nanking.

The Consul-General's reply was a state paper. It sounded like a Bishop's charge to a Confirmation class. "As you are doubtless aware"" he wrote, "the entrance of aliens into the United States of America is not a business to be entered on in a light and perfunctory manner."

Humbly I wrote my apology, promising, of course, to appear in person. By setting the date for this visit ten days later, however, I allowed time for an answer to my further query: would my Canadian-born status have any bearing on his procedure?

No answer came. On the date set I embarked on the forty-mile voyage to Nanking. By this time the popular ferment was boiling over. On the Nanking streets I passed troops of Boy Scouts doing their daily good deed by pasting on every pole lurid exhortations to "kill the foreigner," appeals which I hoped they would not put into practice on me as I rode past in the much too public accessibility of a ricksha.

These echoes of violence did not intrude on the Consulate. In his quiet sanctuary, far from the madding crowd, the Consul-General received me with graciously worded apologies of his own. He seemed much less perturbed over the agitation swirling around his compound walls than by the inconvenience I had been put to in coming to Nanking. "I am terribly sorry you came down," he announced. Born in Canada, you don't need a visa; you can go in any time you choose." He was so polite about it, the perfect model of a Virginia gentleman, that I should have felt churlish to remind him of the ten days during which he might have told me this by letter. I did propose, however, that, having come, perhaps I would be wise to get the visa. This suggestion he brushed aside." No, that isn't necessary. You would just be wasting your money."

I departed in a glow. The trip had been worthwhile just for the pleasure of basking in his concern for my welfare. If all government functionaries could be so considerate, I mused, what a happy world this would be.

But there was a second act, which began, half way across the Pacific, when the purser of the *Empress of Australia* sent back my immigration form uncompleted because I had no visa. The consul's assurance he shrugged off. "Consuls," he scoffed, "never know what they're talking about." By his direction I consulted the Immigration officials who boarded the ship on our arrival at Victoria. To my delight, they vindicated the Consul – "Born in Canada? Go in any time you please."

My wife and I continued to Vancouver, stayed overnight with friends, came down the next evening so agreeably stimulated by Canadian hospitality that we had no doubt of walking straight aboard a Princess liner just preparing to cast off for Seattle. When consuls were backed up by the Immigration Bureau, what had we to fear? It was a rash conclusion. We were stopped at the gangplank.

"Here," you can't go aboard exclaimed the inspector. "This passport has no visa."

When I told him my story, he despatched me to an office a few steps away to confront another official. The prospect looked hopeless. The office had room for but one inspector, and three or four persons were waiting their turn ahead of us. Within the ten minutes before sailing time we despaired of getting our tangle straightened. How it happened I cannot imagine, but he did get to us. He even understood at first gasp my breathless explanation and was instant n his decision: "You don't need a visa, but you must pay the poll-tax."

Frantically I forked out the eight dollars. The officer waved it aside.

"Not here!" he protested. "You can't pay it here" - and, in response to my blank look – "You pay at the ticket office - at the other end of the pier."

The Canadian Pacific pier in Vancouver ranked among the world's longest; it seemed longer! Although convinced I was too late, I set off at double quick, reserved just breath enough to tell the ticket agent what I wanted, snatched up my receipt and at the quadruple quick dashed the interminable distance back, expecting I would arrive only to see the *Princess Kathleen* backing away from her dock.

A second miracle happened: the ship was still alongside. The Immigration people, I found out, do have a heart. They had held the ship, in fact had taken their stance on the gangplank to help us transact the last formalities.

Six months later, just before our permit expired, I had speaking engagements in Vancouver, just in time to collect again my eight dollars. When I applied for a new permit, however, the Immigration officer asked,

"Why did you pay the Poll tax?"

"Because they made me."

"You needn't have done so," he said, and after giving me a new permit, a permit apparently unlimited in its duration, added some candid advice:

"Put that British passport in the bottom of you suit-case, and don't ever get it out."

Three weeks later, when I crossed to Victoria for another talk, I brought simply a note from the British Consul in Seattle. This the inspector at Victoria merely initialed - and I was passed. The routine was growing, progressively, so much simpler that I began to hope I might eventually be paid for entering the United States.

To a thoughtful official I was indebted for the suggestion which changed me back from visitor to citizen. This came in 1939, at the end of my final six months as an alien. I had gone to the Seattle office to renew my permit.

"Where were you born?" the officer asked.

"In New Westminster, British Columbia," - and then, with a sigh, "about ten miles too far north." The man gave me a quizzical look.

"Did it ever occur to you," he asked, that you may never have lost your American citizenship?"

He explained further his office's desire to establish that, so long as a naturalized citizen was receiving his salary from an American organization, residence abroad did not forfeit this citizenship. If I were willing, they would like to confirm in my case their claim that such employment was the equivalent of American residence.

I was more than willing. Ten years earlier, I had married again, and long been oppressed by the anomaly that, while my wife and daughter carried American passports, my son and I were accounted British. Since I had taken no other oath of allegiance, the Seattle office was able to push the case. Within six weeks, while I was in New York I was notified that my papers were there awaiting my signature. Down to the New York office I hurried to receive the coveted document, my Certificate of Derivative Citizenship. Its number, A13368, remains filed in my memory.

* * * * * *

My immediate problem was what every missionary spoke of with awe as "the Language." No missionary could begin converting until he could make some show of speaking and reading Chinese. This did not help us in the schools; indeed, the first headmaster under whom I served tried to curtail my Chinese study. Since modern textbooks were not yet available in Chinese nor a Chinese vocabulary invented to make their subjects intelligible, we taught in English. Luckily, in my case, the Bishop overruled the headmaster; before assuming the role of teacher I was assigned a year's study at the Nanking Language School.

Language schools were an innovation. Though regarded skeptically by earlier students, who had had to blunder their way singly into knowledge of Chinese, they offered a method so sensible that one could only wonder why it had not been devised years before. What could be simpler than to gather each year's newcomers in systematized classes and supervise their first gropings into this formidable language?

Even with this aid my first lessons were frustrating. Having come six weeks late, I had missed preliminary explanations; without more ado I was closeted face to face with a Chinese teacher in a small, chilly cubicle. I knew no Chinese, he knew no English. Toying with the sparse wisps of hair on his chin, he beamed at me indulgently from beneath heavy eyelids, then suddenly grunted, "Fu." For a puzzled moment I thought he had said, "Fool," a description which at the time seemed to fit me exactly. Only by impatient signs and nods did he make me understand that I was to repeat "fu" after him. "Fu, fu, fu, fu," I kept mimicking first in the same low grunt, next with a rising inflection, a level inflection, a higher, descending inflection, and a final staccato "fu" so sharp that it made me jump.

From "fu" we progressed to "ho," and other sounds until I had become adept in the five tones customarily used in Nanking. Slowly I was learning that it made a difference whether my voice went up or down or stayed level, a difference that could be embarrassing, since these various ways of pronouncing "fu" gave it importantly various meaning.

Chinese would have been difficult enough had there been but one "fu" for each tone, but there were dozens. Each, of course, was based on a character, a written ideograph. In essence, it was a language spoken and written in words of one syllable, although actually these characters were combined to construct more complicated terms, as "ho" (fire) and "ch'e" (cart) to make "ho ch'e" (locomotive) or "ch'i" (gas) and "ch'e" to make automobile. But since, in all their thousands of years the Chinese had neglected to invent an adequate variety of sounds, each sound did duty for many words, words distinguishable only by the context in which they appeared.

This poverty of expression is indicated by the Chinese name for "people" – "pei hsing," or "hundred surnames." Pei hsing was no distortion of fact; there were probably fewer than a hundred surnames in general use, and in some Moslem districts only two or three. How the Chinese ever managed to publish a telephone directory is a puzzle I never investigated; if in the West we had had to thumb our way through hundreds of pages of Johnsons and Smiths we might have written notes instead - which is just what people did, Chinese and foreigner alike, in the China that I knew. Even in emergency a coolie carrying a "chit-book" from house to house was quicker, surer, than looking up a party or making his name intelligible to the operator.

This paucity of surnames also hampered romance. No Chinese boy could marry a girl with the same surname as his own. It narrowed the field. Providentially the Chinese had guarded against this dire chance by giving the prospective bride and groom no opportunity to fall in love. The groom's parents, with well-paid professional assistance from the horologers, picked his wife for him, a system which, however it may revolt our young people, has nonetheless produced the world's most prolific birthrate[10].

But Chinese surnames, in my language school days, were not an immediate worry. There was the soon regretted blessing of learning a language that had no grammar. After trying to master a tongue reduced to nothing but idioms, a tongue whose nouns could be adverbs or verbs or adjectives as the speaker chose, I sighed for the solid stability of "amo, amas, amat," for conjugations and declensions and persons and gender. Chinese seems as amorphous, as changeable, as an April cloud.

If I wanted rigidity, however, I soon got it in attempting to read or write Chinese characters. So intricate had these elaborations of picture writing become that they required anywhere from one to more than twenty separate strokes. Each stroke had to be written in its own particular way, its own particular order. With no alphabet, words could not be arranged as in our dictionaries. Yet Chinese scholars had not let this balk them. Dictionaries they contrived by dividing every character into two parts, a radical, which indicated - vaguely - its meaning, and a phonetic, which suggested its sound. Of these radicals there were 214 - all to be learned in order and by number. To look up an unfamiliar character, one first noted its radical, then turned to a list of all the characters based on that radical. Next, he counted the strokes in the phonetic and thumbed down the list till he reached the phonetics with that number of strokes. If lucky, he would then find the character he sought, and could turn to the number under which it was listed in the dictionary. Seldom did his quest turn out so simply. Most characters contained several common radicals, but only one counted, in this character, as its proper radical; the rest helped make up the phonetic. So confused could the student become in this guessing game that often he forgot what character he was seeking, and even if he found it he was little the wiser.

The Chinese written language, in 1913, was as distinct from the spoken language as Latin from English. Ten years later a movement similar to that which in Europe produced Dante and Chaucer was making its impact on the Chinese mind: the vernacular was being written in place of the ancient classical style but, when I arrived in China, a true scholar would have scorned to write in a style which any but the literati could understand. If he spoke on a formal occasion, he did not expect, nor even wish, to be intelligible. I once heard a provincial Commissioner of Education address a high school; that he was a man of the highest scholarly attainments his audience was unanimous in agreeing, for no one understood a word of what he had said.

41

My first instruction in writing Chinese characters was not in the classical tradition, with brush and with ink-stick dipped in water and dissolved like water-colours on an ink-stone. I had to practise with chalk on a slate blackboard. Each time I made a false stroke, my teacher scratched it out with a long finger-nail. The shivers he sent down my spine spurred me to learn rapidly.

Long finger-nails were a Chinese teacher's distinguishing mark. Like his overlong cuffs they proclaimed his caste, indicating that he did no menial work with his hands. Whether he compensated by the work he did with his brain was open to question. Teachers in China waxed proud from a prestige sharply contrasted to the lowly status we in America grant our pedagogues. Learning had long been the key to official rank. From ancient times the Chinese had operated a civil service. Based on a system of local, provincial, vice-regal, imperial examinations, it permitted the humblest boy to rise to the confidence of the Emperor, to become a Minister of State even though his qualifications, knowledge of the Confucian classics, ability to write a neat essay and to express it in praiseworthy characters, did not fit him - as history proved - to shine as an administrator.

Shortly before the Revolution this system had been abolished, but Nanking, a viceroy's seat, still held on to its vestiges in the now deserted examination halls. Radiating like the spokes of a prison were rows of tiny cells, unfurnished, open to the air, where the candidates had been sequestered for several days while they toiled over their papers. No communication with the outside was allowed; if an examinee died, his body was hoisted over the wall. To carry out still further the prison likeness, at the axis of the spokes stood a watch tower whence guards could look down each row and make sure no hard-pressed student sought aid from his neighbours. Abandoned, weed-grown, their tiles already tumbling down, these halls still whispered the hopes and disappointments they had sheltered so bleakly. I was barely in time to see this lingering reminder of Imperial days; a year or so later, the halls were replaced by a market.

But the tradition of the scholar outlived them. One of his privileges was never to be wrong, nor to admit ignorance even when ignorance was excusable. "I don't know," was not in his vocabulary. In the case of proper nouns or technical terms imported from outside China, this omniscience could lead to ludicrous confusion. Since Western names could not be reproduced alphabetically, the usual custom was to transliterate them into sounds resembling them - a resemblance usually remote: "Ya-mei-li-chia," for instance, as the equivalent of "America" The scope of Chinese sounds was too restricted to make such transliteration even half-way successful.

The problem was further complicated because these transliterations had to be set down in characters - and every character had its own meaning. Historical, geographical, scientific, religious terms all suffered this anomaly. Centuries earlier, Buddhism had confronted this difficulty: now Christianity, its Bible reeking with odd-sounding names, met the same puzzle, often with comic results as when Immanuel was transliterated into characters which meant, "Use a horse for interior profit!"

My teacher, baffled by a phrase from the Creed – "Pen-tiu-pi-la-to" - mystified me throughout an entire lesson by his involved and wholly unintelligible explanation of these five characters. His interpretation was a masterpiece. Never having seen this combination of characters before, he was extracting profound wisdom, wisdom bolstered by allusions to Mencius and all the sages, from an attempt to put in Chinese the name, Pontius Pilate.

The Chinese teacher also conferred on his pupils his own infallibility. A good teacher was rated by the excellence of his grades. To fail a student would have reflected on his skill; 96 or 97, therefore, were practically flunking grades. If the teacher, by a happy and not infrequent chance, had his own son in his class, or a nephew or even a cousin, automatically he marked them 100. Only an unnatural father would have done otherwise. In one school with which I was connected, classical teachers made sure that their classes would pass creditably by giving out their questions six weeks in advance. Not till the night before exams did the headmaster hear of this - and counter it with a new set of questions. Next day the students struck, claiming that the headmaster's action was unfair.

Even language students like myself, to whom grades mattered nothing, had to guard against their teachers' desire to please. I remember stuttering out a statement in laborious Mandarin, and then asking my teacher,

"Is that right?

"Yes." He replied, "it is very good, very good – ting hao"

"But would you say it this way?" Consternation flashed across his face.

"I!" he exclaimed, his hands raised as if to push out of sight the offending sentence, "I! Oh, no, I would never say it that way!

My acquaintance with the Chinese teacher - the old style teacher, perhaps I should make clear - was an odd introduction to the Chinese student. All the Chinese I had learned I was expected to forget, at least in the schoolroom, so that my pupils might learn English. Western learning had supplanted Confucius and Mencius as the key to success - but commercial success now was the goal. The treaty ports drained the back country of its more ambitious students and, in cities like Shanghai, any student with a good working knowledge of English could take his pick of the best jobs.

43

This working knowledge was best obtained at a Mission school. Although the Government schools offered similar courses, their teachers were inferior, their discipline so poor that the students tended to spend more time on strikes or in holidays protesting Japanese aggression than in the classroom. Despite superior instruction, Mission schools did have serious drawbacks: for one thing, their fees were high, but a grievance more objectionable in Chinese eyes was their requirement that all pupils attend chapel twice daily and study Christian doctrine. These drawbacks, nevertheless, did not check enrolment: the higher fees the rich boys paid, the scholarship boys had theirs paid for them; the religious provisions rich and poor accepted, but with a minimum of zeal. To learn English thoroughly they put up with the tedious sins of Hebrew kings and with yawning tours to Corinth and Ephesus.

Religion had never been the badge of a Chinese scholar. Confucius himself had been skeptical about the existence of Divine beings, singular or plural. There might be such spirits, he conceded, but the less men had to do with them, the better. What he had bequeathed was a system of ethics, ethics shaped to the smooth and high-principled operations of a bureaucracy. Actual religion the Chinese scholar turned over to his women folk, tolerating with bland condescension their Buddhist piety, or their dabbling in the uncouth mixture of superstition and vaguely apprehended mysticism which went under the name of Taoism. Only in old age, with death looming formidably on his life's horizon, would a Confucian scholar look to Buddhism, seeking secrets which Confucian teaching had been too matter-of-fact to admit. So with Christianity - to the student class, if it was acceptable, it was acceptable as a super-Confucianism, a system of ethics more up-to-date than the work of the sages and, it was hoped, better fitted to help China rival the Christian nations in guns and navies.

It was to be expected, then, that to the majority of Mission school students compulsory worship and compulsory religious study were a grievance. By such subtle impudence as snapping their fingers when the wafers were broken at Communions they demonstrated their resentment. Chinese students had begun to thrive on grievances. Whether their grievances were logical they did not bother to ask. After all, no one compelled them to enter a Mission school; they enrolled only because in the long run it would help them make more money. Similarly, their grievances against treaty ports ignored history. When Western nations, under the shelter of the so-called Opium War[11], crowded China's shores demanding the right to trade - a concession the United States forced on Japan through Commodore Perry - the Chinese authorities would not contaminate their own cities by admitting foreign devils. As in Shanghai, they sequestered the intruders on waste lands which the despised foreigner eventually made more desirable than the cities from which he had been barred.

A Swedish friend of mine once was walking on the outskirts of Wuhu, Yangtze port above Nanking, when he encountered some students. During casual talk they complained that the foreigners had stolen the best places. On every hilltop, they pointed out, were impressive foreign houses, flourishing foreign gardens.

"How old are you?" he asked. The oldest was twenty.

"Well," he remarked, "I have been in China forty years. I know more than you about those hills. When we first came, the Chinese would not sell us flat land; it was valuable for growing rice. They sold us, instead, barren, rocky hills. We built the houses, we planted the gardens" - he swung his arm in a circle – "look at those dozens of hills still empty, still barren. Why don't you do what we did?"

The boys were silent.

However illogical, this undercurrent of discontent seethed in every school. Eventually it rushed the students into welcoming Communism and made them raucous agents of disorder. The Chinese students' role in promoting riot has been copied by students in many countries; in China it came naturally because the students never had been looked on as mere schoolboys; theirs was a superior caste, humbly deferred to by a populace largely unschooled. No wonder they lorded it over the masses. Their blue cotton gowns reaching to the ankles, the long sleeves that half-hid their hands exempted them from manual labour, an exemption taken so seriously that a deputation once came to me to complain of an American teacher who had asked some primary graders, eight and nine year olds, to toss tennis balls. Although they were barely out of kindergarten, this sacred immunity from working with their hand already protected them.

As a result, Chinese schoolboys could not play baseball, nor even softball. Softballs, then half as big as sofa pillows, stung their tender hands so painfully that after one brief try I gave up the experiment. The skill they lacked with their hands, however, they made up with their feet. At their favourite game of soccer they were agile, swift, accurate - and often rabid. Playing informally among themselves, they took their games with easy good humour but, the moment they confronted another school, they played with hate in their hearts. At all costs they must not lose. To lose was nothing so simple as losing a game; it was to lose face - a fate worse than death!

In Chinese opinion, the happiest outcome was a tie game. Nobody was disgraced. If a Chinese team must be beaten, it preferred to be beaten by a lopsided score. It then could argue that it had been playing out of its class, like a Little League team playing the Yankees. This philosophy enabled it to

45

lose gaily to expert teams from the British gunboats, contests so amiable that they were a veritable love-feast, whereas contests with their own countrymen were murderous, and the outcome most dreaded, what we would value best, defeat by a close score.

One spring, our school and its foremost rival were engaged in semi-annual competition, a track meet to be followed by soccer. Every omen was bad. So nearly were the track teams matched that they came to the final event tied. The relay would decide the issue. The tension was electric, the air sultry with passion like the impending madness of a typhoon. Inwardly, everyone responsible for the track-meet was cudgeling his wits for some excuse to postpone the decisive relay, but no one was brave enough to be a coward. The show must go on.

Somehow, we squeaked through that crisis. The home team won, not that this mattered much, since the spectators were from rival, hostile schools; if anybody won, a riot had seemed inevitable. But the spark did not catch; the crowd dispersed knowing as we did that they would be back for a graver crisis in the morning. This was the soccer game.

By this stage, the Chinese teachers had thought up excuses for canceling the contest. True Confucian gentlemen, they had ready a choice of politely acceptable lies which would have saved the situation. The two schools' headmasters, one American, one English, would not listen. Their pupils were going to learn proper sportsmanship, damn them, or die in the attempt. Win or lose, they argued, any team should be proud of a close game. Never would they have a situation more perfectly devised to demonstrate the courage of fair play. A game is only a game.

The Chinese went away shaking their heads. They knew what would happen - and it did. The game began on a field whose sidelines were packed end to end by students from the other local schools. Each goal which the home team scored they jeered; each goal kicked by the visitors they applauded, until the unhappy moment when they drew level with the home team, 4 - 4, and provoked an exultant uproar that neither the referee could quell nor the home team endure. They refused to continue. Off the field, through a mob that had overrun the lines, they jostled their way, snarling, cursing, weeping.

Even now we congratulated ourselves that riot had been averted. The crowds dispersed, the visitors went to their dormitory to pack, the commotion was subsiding when with frightening abruptness the quiet was shattered by shouts of "Kill, kill, kill". In the upper hall the visiting team was fighting a rearguard action to escape the suddenly revived fury of their hosts. Boy Scouts were flailing them with staves; others had seized their black and scarlet flags and were tearing them to rags with their teeth. Like swimmers battling a whirlpool we were swept into the midst of it, struggling to curb the maddened frenzy of our own pupils. One teacher even rushed to a nearby police station to beg help.

"Who is fighting?" asked the officer. "Students?" He shook his head. He had no stomach for getting mixed up in a fight between students.

Meanwhile, the visiting team and their American coach had barricaded themselves behind the doors of their dormitory. To defend themselves, they tore rods loose from the iron beds. Though the home-students had gone to lunch - even Chinese wars stopped for meals - they had posted sentries to sound the warning if their guests tried to escape, a warning shouted with shrill promptness when the beleaguered team attempted a stealthy sortie.

Only the arrival of the town's foremost orator prevented murder. Mounting a table, taking off his long coat to act out his eloquence more graphically, he harangued the assembled students for upwards of an hour. Sweat poured down his face, his voice sagged to a hoarse whisper until, utterly exhausted, he could say nothing more. But the English headmaster saw - and had courage to seize - the crucial moment.

"I am going upstairs," he told his sullen audience, "and I shall escort our guests out of the building, out of the compound. I expect everyone of you to remain here."

They remained. The visitors departed, mollified by the promise of a sixteen course feast at Wuhu's best restaurant - and an era of teaching western sportsmanship came to an abrupt end.

Games against the local Sports Club, a team composed of the port's foreign residents, were less amicable. In one of these the American goal-keeper, a peppery Southerner, grew so irate over what he considered inexcusably rough play that he kicked a Chinese player while the latter lay sprawled on the ground.

The kick was little more than gesture, a tap so mild that the boy in question did not even know he had been kicked. But the spectators knew. Their uproar soon infected the team, whose temper began to seethe to a slow-boiling fury. Not only had the school been insulted but China too had been insulted, their four million "womb-brothers[12]" had been insulted by this act of brutal imperialist aggression! How the game managed to be played out in an atmosphere so volatile was a miracle unexplained. No sooner had it been concluded, however, than the offending goalkeeper walked over to the boy whom he had affronted.

"I am very sorry," he said.

In Western eyes this was handsome reparation; in Chinese eyes, he made himself contemptible. To his initial fault he had added the folly of admitting his mistake. Instead of recognizing that only a strong man would have the grace to apologize, the students despised him. Unfortunately, this man had to pass the school each morning on the way to his office; for months afterward, each time he walked past, he was taunted by voices calling out from the school's upper windows, "I am ver-ree sor-ree! I am ver-ree sor-ree!"

* * * * * * *

As a teacher I had learned, long before this instructive episode, never to pose as less than infallible. The art of a teacher, I had been told by my Bishop, was to teach a subject I didn't know. Unable to read a note, much less sing, the Bishop proved his point by training a boys' choir. I proved it by teaching Botany. When I discovered, one day, in dissecting a cosmos blossom, that I had explained it wrong, having failed to notice that the cosmos belonged to a special family, the compositae, I merely substituted a pink blossom for a white one and described it correctly. My prestige was unblemished, my class none the worse. They knew even less about cosmos than I - and cared less.

Those were the days before Dewey. Our methods were wrong, our textbooks monstrous. Who could have dreamed of leading Chinese students through the pages of so old-fashioned an author as Washington Irving, or letting them confuse an American Christmas with the antiquarian pedantry of Bracebridge Hall? Who was foolish enough to inflict on them the eight-hundred pages of Nesfield's Grammar, a volume originally designed to torture Indian students but just as effective in baffling the Chinese by its innumerable hair-splitting rules, its multi-syllabled names for every conceivable - and even inconceivable - quirk of the human tongue?"

Yet the Chinese students not only survived the defects of their education; they seemed to benefit by them. They emerged speaking creditable English. They were capable, the best of them, of getting up without advance notice to commemorate Shakespeare's birthday by a reasonable and well-phrased account of his lifework. If their studies did not fit them for the 20th Century, they did help them to see that the West, like China herself, had lived through other centuries than the 20th, and that the best way of meeting our present and shaping our future is by remembering and honouring our past.

None of this really suggests the life of a Chinese school as I knew it. For the most part it was orderly. From a distance it could be identified by an insinuating drone, the noise of students studying their lessons aloud, which was not unlike the murmur of a bee-hive or, more recognizably, the whir of machines in an old-fashioned factory. Quite aptly we thought of the school as the "wisdom works" and under its hypnotic rhythms learned to appreciate the Chinese habit of studying aloud. Whereas any break in the silence of Western study-halls will divert and distract every pupil, the Chinese pupil, swaying as he declaims from his text-book, is unperturbed by any disturbance short of an atomic explosion.

A Chinese school in those days supposedly was unharried by the social life that disturbs our American high schools. There were no dances, no contacts with girls beyond the Sunday morning chapel services when the boys had the exciting privilege of staring at the sleekly oiled pigtails of the St. Agnes girls who occupied the front pews. But the boys knew much more about these girls than they were presumed to know. They even established communication through the hymn books and prayer books left in the pews. How widely these circulated we were not aware until I chanced to open one and discovered reading matter of a very different sort from the prayers. It consisted of notes addressed by name to the more popular girls and written not in Chinese but in English. These notes were unblushingly anatomical and precise but expressed in terms culled from the dictionary in a combination as weirdly medical as it was naively obscene. What the boy never would have dared say nor the girl dared read in their native idiom they had no compunction about accepting in a foreign scientific jargon which for them disguised its lewdness. It reminded me of my own schoolboy meanderings through the dictionary and how innocuous the pursuit would become after such entries as "Whore - see Prostitute."

Chinese novels treated sexual activities with a frankness which did not skip details but, where we used to put asterisks, they described the culmination of erotic play in such poetic figure as "yun-yu" (clouds and rain). In the English worded notes scrawled through the Prayer books the frankness was there, but not the poetry.

Once a year, during the Christmas holidays, the schoolboys had a chance they never neglected to address the girls openly. This was in their Christmas plays. No matter how carefully these plays were censored, the result was always the same. Every actor felt gaily free to ad lib in whatever ribald terms came to his tongue. With the St. Agnes girls braving often freezing weather - for the stage was erected and the benches deployed outdoors - the boys soon warmed them into forgetting the bitter December night; using unflattering nicknames and indelicate physiological allusions, they managed to insult every girl present. This situation never varied. The girls knew they would be insulted, they came annually to be insulted - after which they would sever what tenuous ties bound the two schools, only to resume them next Christmas in time for a new and angrier breach. In a country where boy did not meet girl, these annual quarrels were a substitute for dating.

The only missionary I knew who dared curb the exuberance of the Christmas play was the Sister Superior of a convent school. Her girls had asked, and been refused, permission to add to their Nativity Play a dramatization of the Prodigal Son. The refusal did not deter them. After hurrying through the Nativity Play word for word as it was written, one of the cast announced a special attraction: they would now perform the highly moral and instructive story of the Prodigal Son.

The Sister Superior knew exactly what they had in mind, a candidly graphic portrayal of the scapegrace youth wasting his substance over harlots - it wasn't often that convent-trained schoolgirls could play harlot! She knew too how unconvincing would be his repentance, a minor item of the plot to which they would devote a few grudging words. Like Hollywood, they enjoyed making vice more plausible than virtue. Where would Samson have been without Delilah or David minus Bathsheba? But the Sister did not falter. Going to the stage, she announced, "Now we will not perform the highly moral and instructive story of the Prodigal Son." With these blunt words she sent the audience home.

This abrupt closure her girls accepted. A boys' school would have gone on strike. The girls, however, since they were not performing for boys - that would have been a breach of convention quite unthinkable - but entertaining only their relatives, submitted to this loss of face with no greater protest than a few tears.

* * * * * * *

The exigencies of the first World War pushed me, at the age of twenty-four, into the exalted post of headmaster. This job I held for two years, and managed without a single rebellion We did end slightly ahead of schedule, but this was due to a nation-wide strike, during which every school in China shut down to condemn what the students rated the supineness of Peking[13] officials in yielding to Japan.

My immunity to strikes was helped by the fact that my predecessor had suffered a strike just before handing over the school to my care. Like so much in China, this strike originated in problems of "face." One senior, rightly certain that he would fail his final examinations, had decided to escape embarrassment by breaking up the school and thus preventing a public graduation. To his cause he rallied four other malcontents. By resolute action these five boys panicked the entire school body into refusing classes.

The strike itself was comparatively mild. The students did not imitate a nearby school which had locked up its faculty in a storage compartment and then tossed the school dishes on top of them. We could be grateful too that no windows were broken, no books torn to shreds and scattered to the winds, and that the ringleader had not thought up the plan used elsewhere, a few years later, of halting exams by burning down the school.

50

The irony of this present strike was painfully evident when some ninety of the school's ninety-five pupils came, one by one, to the office to protest that they did not wish to strike - but "they make me." Who were "they?" - the five rebels, five browbeating ninety, the tail wagging the dog. Anyone wishing to comprehend recent Chinese history should note this example. What here in miniature was to recur, time and time again, on the national scale. A country schooled in compromise, schooled to stay with the herd and - as our expression goes – "not to stick its neck out," is cravenly at the mercy of a small aggressive group. Accustomed to paying tribute to bandits, tribute to war-lords, China was quick prey for the Communists.

This strike enabled the faculty to proscribe all potential trouble-makers but, as headmaster, I soon imported a few of my own. This time it was "face" in a new guise. Our wholesale expulsions had depleted our enrolment, and also our finances. Twice a year the boys brought their "hsueh fei," fifty silver dollars, which our shroff rang or bit, coin by coin, to make sure that they were an honest weight in silver. When two boys from up-country chanced to pay their fees in Spanish dollars of the French Revolution years (1789-1793) I was as excited as a pirate unearthing a chest full of doubloons. But to the shroff (whom we nicknamed "Adonis" in reverse tribute to a face which could not have squeezed in one additional pock-mark!) these were not dollars; impassively he assayed them at ninety cents apiece. A century's handling had rubbed off too much silver.

Our receipts in dollars were vitally involved in the school's maintenance, since the New York office, if it was to make deficits, preferred two or three years' advance notice. To make ends meet, therefore, I had to risk admitting from an upriver school some doubtful applicants, boys who had been suspended for a semester but whose ban had been lifted.

"Face" forbade their returning to their own school; "face" soon made them troublesome in ours. The problem was provincial loyalties, then the most potent type of Chinese patriotism. The Chinese were provincials first, nationals second, an attitude analogous to that assumed by citizens of our own southern states who were Virginians or Carolinians before they were Americans. In the case of these newcomers, pride over their Hupeh ancestry made them unwilling to take orders from the school's prefects, all of them natives of Anhui and qualified for their office by two years' probation. Their recalcitrance, moreover, was abetted by one of the faculty, a fellow provincial known to the school as the "Hupeh Consul." If the school was not to be broken up, our only course was to forestall trouble. Trusting no one except the principal Chinese teacher and my American colleague, I summoned the four dissidents while the rest of the school were in study hall, set coolies to packing their pigskin boxes, and told these four Hupeh boys that for their sake as well as ours I was refunding their money and requiring that they leave. All this we conducted in a room illuminated, for dramatic effect, with but one green-shaded student lamp. They pleaded, they argued, they even begged permission to say good-bye to their fellow students in study hall - a plea we were not gullible enough to grant. Too well we knew the incendiary effects of student oratory! So long did they argue that the time came for concluding study hall, but I had held up ringing the bell; the only clock, luckily was in the corridor, well out of sight. Fifteen minutes late, but with nobody else aware of what was happening we inched the four trouble-makers to the gate where, with relieved sighs, we clanged and locked it behind them.

Next day ours was a different school. Never have I seen the students happier. Thankful that the crisis had not pushed them into an unwelcome strike, the boys laughed and sang. That they could have resisted the call to strike did not occur to them. As for me, until the term's end I tutored two of the boys whom I had dismissed, and sent them on to another school where their record was excellent.

This was our gravest episode, a warning of how oddly emergencies can flare up in China. It left no scars. Ours became a school to be proud of; when the boys, dressed in white uniforms for some gala occasion, marched through the city to the martial incitement of their drum and fife corps, our hearts swelled over the admiration they provoked from the populace lining the pinched streets to watch them go by. In my mind's eye I used to go over the roll of these eager youngsters from the top form to the lowest, picturing them one by one; literally, I could not recall a single student for whom I did not cherish warm affection.

I had worked with them, played with them, shepherded them on picnics and on Christmas Eve when they did the waits, singing Christmas carols from compound to compound and coming, incidentally, into almost pitched battle with rival waits from the Choir School over which group announced "Peace on earth, good will to men!" I had assigned most of them their English names - a current fad to which they were attached - and amused myself by suggesting Reuben (which closely follows the Chinese pronunciation of "Japan" - and waiting to see how many excuses except the real one they would give for politely declining this name. This passion for magniloquent names once had given me an eminence unrivalled in history. As headmaster, I was supposed to spank any lower schoolboy who had incurred five demerits. On this particular afternoon I whipped both Wellington and Napoleon!

After five years in its classrooms and two years as its headmaster I was homeward bound. In farewell the students planned a tea-party. My American colleague reluctantly altered the wording of the first invitation which they had composed in English to circularize the foreign community: it began,

"Owing to the joy of the students of St. Paul's at the departure of Mr. Gowen on furlough, etc. etc." This final sample of my shortcoming as a teacher of English I would have cherished - or did they mean it!

The tea-party was monumental. The boys prefaced it by sending a committee, all wearing their best silk gowns of sober greens and blues, to escort me from my home across Anking. To my embarrassment, they paraded me through the town's most crowded streets and, to make these crowds even larger, heralded our coming by cannon crackers and daylight fireworks.

Under the school's wide spreading acacias they had set out tables for their guests, foreign and Chinese, and benches for the school and, in solitary majesty a table for me. The ceremonies, like the refreshments, followed a pattern which the Chinese had perfected through centuries. There were ceremonial tributes, speeches of unblushing flattery, and the presentation of a "pien," a silk banner. This I valued above all else. The Chinese, as I knew, had many gradations of politeness, politeness in some cases for form's sake alone, or politeness doled out with partial and limited enthusiasm. But a "pien" they never gave unless they meant from their hearts every pleasant word.

The culmination of these rites, however, shattered tradition. It introduced a feature which, in the three thousand years since Confucius, had never graced - or disgraced! - such an occasion. Although one of my limited talents had been the convincing imitation of animal noises, I still was taken aback when, very formally, the master of ceremonies requested that I bark like a dog.

I did. For better measure I whinnied and moo-ed and bleated, and even haw-hawed like a north China ass. I crowed like a cock, put on a cat fight, and started all the neighbourhood wonks yapping by the extended range of my canine noises.

On this note the ceremonies ended, ended with impressive dignity as the boys formed a procession to parade once more through the city. The "pien" they carried before me, illuminating it with huge paper lanterns so that the public might read my virtues. They set off rockets, set off long strings of firecrackers and, when they arrived at the steps of my home, they sang in English, "Good-bye, my lover, good-bye."

Even now, as I remember that June evening across nearly half a century, my inclination is not to laugh, but to weep.

* * * * * * *

"In China but never of it," would describe accurately enough the thousands of foreigners, European and American, who spent their active lives in a country eternally alien to their tastes and ambitions. Only a fraction of these

53

foreign residents wished to know China; only a fraction of the Chinese had any desire to know the foreigner. In his desire to nurture mutual sympathy between the two the missionary had an advantage: he had to learn Chinese to pursue his vocation. But even he lived apart in a walled compound subject not to Chinese control, to Chinese laws and courts and taxation, but to the consular jurisdiction of his own country. This system, known by the cumbersome title of extraterritoriality, outlasted my time, but it was merely symptomatic of a subtler extraterritoriality, and extraterritoriality of social habit which impelled all but the most fanatically dedicated missionary to shut himself up within tiny Western enclaves where he could live as he might have lived in America or England, eating Western food, entertaining Western friends, dispensing with all reminders of China except, of course, that most efficient of labour saving devices, the Chinese servant.

Some of these restrictions were abetted by Chinese custom. Chinese men, for instance, entertained quite apart from their women folk. An American doctor, in playing host to a Chinese general, overlooked this to his own discomfiture; he invited his women nurses to be present. When the general and his staff began offering these American women the endearments usually lavished on sing-song girls, international friendship chilled.

In the years following the 1911 Revolution, the segregation of the sexes still held, although two movements had begun inroads on the conservatism which confined women within the high blank walls of their homes. No longer were women's feet bound, deformed into pegs that restricted their walk to a painful hobble. No longer were girls denied the privilege of attending school. In interscholastic contests girls even competed publicly in drills and games, exposing their faces, their trim blue-clad figures to the common gaze in exhibitions that would have been branded, but a few years earlier, as indecent. But the larger number of upper class women still remained house-bound. Seldom did they emerge except on the days after New Year's, when they could be seen, festively attired in skirts of scarlet satin but perched, crudely and uncomfortably, on the narrow side ledges of the wheelbarrow in which they were being trundled over cobblestones to visit friends and relatives.

Unlike the women's, the men's social life was enjoyed away from home. They met their friends at feasts in the restaurants. For these feasts - unless missionaries were present! - a sufficient supply of sing-song girls might be ordered by the host. Each girl sat on a stool slightly back of the man to whom she was assigned. Her part in the evening's gaiety, however, was much less lurid than rumour would have us imagine. She might drink a little wine, but she was occupied mostly in singing falsetto to her own squeaky accompaniment on the "hu-chin," a crude violin. Often she went on to another feast after the shark's fins had been served, the ceremonial moment when the host acknowledged by formal toasts the presence of his guests. At this stage, Chinese etiquette permitted the guests themselves to proceed to other entertainment, a provision which has enabled me to attend three feasts in one evening.

For a people obsessed with "face" the Chinese evinced a peculiar disregard for what we call the "trimmings." Just as their homes were plainly and even bleakly furnished, their restaurants were ramshackle structures to which mangy dogs off the streets found easy admittance, brushing against the feasters as they scrounged for the bones which the latter spit out on the bare wooden floor.

The level of table talk was low, mostly routine banter exploding to raucous guffaws in the drinking games which were the feast's main entertainment. Of these games the most usual was "slippery fist." No game could be simpler, a duel wherein two contestants, each extending a fist, threw out simultaneously any number of fingers and called what he hoped would be the total disclosed by the two hands. If one man, for instance, had thrown out three fingers and called seven while his opponent at the same instant had shown four fingers, the loser had to drink a cup of wine. Each man in turn went the rounds of the table, taking on his fellow guests for two out of three victories. At a table of twelve this could result, for those less nimble, in considerable drinking, although the cups were so tiny and the Shaohsing wine, poured warm from teapots, was so mild that I have drunk more than fifty cups with no dizzying effects. Kaoliang, an approximation of vodka, was more potent, and when some Chinese journalists inveigled me into a bout with "beh-lan-di chiu," a particularly explosive brandy, I manufactured an urgent appointment which I kept in short order.

Slippery fist, I had soon learned, is not just a game of chance. Every man has his weakness - his "mao ping" as the Chinese call it - the tendency to display some particular number of fingers oftener than others, two, for instance, or three, or even none. A quick-eyed participant soon notes and registers his opponent's "mao ping." The game is played at such a headstrong pace, to the accompaniment of a rhythmic tab, that there is little time to think. Chinese custom however did sanction "putting on a hat" (tai mao tzu), the addition of a further tag so seldom used that it could throw the nimblest feaster off his stride. This tactical device helped me hold my own.

The attraction of a Chinese feast belongs where it should - in the food. My first feast, nevertheless, gave me so painful a belly-ache that I had decided these exotic repasts were not for me. One more try, however, I was urged to make, a fortunate second attempt, for I noticed that whereas I had been crunching up and swallowing the dried water-melon seeds that garnish the meal like nuts at a Western dinner, the others merely cracked the seeds with their teeth to get at the soft kernel. When they heard how thoroughly I had been eating the brittle shells they were more shocked than amused. Ground glass could not have been more indigestible.

These feasts often ran to twenty-four courses of fish, meat, chicken, and game in concoctions too complicated to describe. Each course was placed in a bowl on the table. From the bowl the guests helped themselves, reaching for tidbits with their chopsticks. An attentive host also plied his guests individually with choice morsels, a practice more hospitable than hygienic, although he might, if sensitive to Western notions, run his chopsticks through his mouth to clean them before doing the honours. In a few cases I have even seen hosts employ a separate pair of chopsticks, but properly to enjoy a Chinese feast it is best to forget hygiene.

The ceremonial peak of the feast was attained with the shark's fins, a dish so substantially reinforced with chicken that to me it was chicken soup. For such courses a porcelain spoon was also provided. Since Chinese food is cut up in the kitchen, knives are never needed; few customs lowered the foreigner to a more barbarous level in Chinese eyes than his use of knives at the table.

Before dessert the spoons were rinsed in a bowl of hot water, sure preface to "pa-pao fan," a glorified rice pudding made of eight precious ingredients, of which the tastiest was lotus seeds. This dessert was no indication that the feast was nearing its end; on the contrary, it merely gave the feasters their second wind for many more of what we would designate as entrée courses. Among these was pressed duck, pulled apart by the guests' joint use of their chopsticks from the crisply browned skin down to the last tender morsel of meat on the bones. But the severest test of a foreigner's skill with chopsticks were pigeons' eggs, soft-boiled without the shells. To exert just the right pressure without breaking them demanded a violinist's touch. When I passed this test I ought to have been awarded a diploma.

Rice, the mainstay of ordinary Chinese meals, had almost no part in a feast. It was served only at the end when pheasant, chicken, pork, fish, all sliced paper-thin, were dropped with vegetables into a copper chafing dish where water, already boiling, was kept hot by flames from a saucerful of burning wine. These flames soared in luminous tongues, blue, crimson, yellow, as they surged against the copper pan.

Feasts for me became a happy addiction, so long as I did not ask what I was eating. I recall vividly the host who honoured a visitor from America not only with sixteen appetizing courses but with running commentary, much too explicit, about what each dish consisted of. No sooner had the guest escaped than he disgorged his meal. The Chinese can make an old shoe tasty; they can do the same with any part of any animal - and they waste nothing.

Never would it occur to them to be squeamish about the anatomical details of what they are relishing.

To me the most remarkable demonstration of a Chinese cook's skill was a Buddhist meal. Some monasteries had their own restaurants; not content with serving neither fish, flesh, nor fowl, they restricted each meal to but one ingredient. Generally, this would be bean curd, sauced in so many varied ways that it could not be monotonous. I attended one Buddhist feast in the house of an old official whose wife, the "lao t'ai-t'ai," kept her religion with scrupulous abstinence. From the savoury appearance of the dishes, brought in steaming profusion to the table, this abstinence looked no more ascetic than eating broiled lobster for Lent. Bean curd they were, but prepared in the shape of fish or chicken or meat; not only did thy look like fish or chicken but tasted like them, yet vegetables and vegetable oils alone had been compounded to create these convincing flavours.

Despite the perfection of their own cooking, the Chinese in the post-Revolutionary years had developed a fad for Western meals, the reverse of our craze for the Cantonese distortions which we label "chop suey" and "chow mien." Western restaurants sprang up where the fashionable diner-out could gorge himself on sardines and tinned salmon. It was my ill luck to have a student whose father owned such a restaurant, and shortly before my departure from Anking this pupil honoured me with a meal.

To eat my way through corned beef and pork-and-beans on a July afternoon, with temperature and humidity both in the high nineties, would have been bad enough, but my host mixed with it an act of Chinese munificence which was disastrous. He followed the custom often practiced by Chinese hosts of ordering, as a generous gesture, several additional courses. At a feast this does not matter; a guest need only nibble at each dish as it appears. Since he has nothing in front of him but a small pewter saucer, he can help himself once or twice with his chopsticks and stop. In this case, I was the only guest and faced with the appalling prospect of eating my way through four extra courses of Vienna sausages and meat-balls cooked with spaghetti. As deftly as I could I tried to slip to the dogs some of the greasy surplus heaped on my plate; there was still enough to send me home bloated, and feeling the first uneasy symptoms of dysentery. In lieu of a stomach pump I dashed to the medicine chest which, fortunately, in those benighted days, was amply supplied with castor oil.

The Chinese ordinary food - or "pien fan" - I came to like so well that for nearly a year I and another American, a young bachelor like myself, had our meals sent up from the school kitchen. Ours was "teacher's chow," twice as expensive as the food dished out to the students. In American money, this extravagance cost us two dollars a month. I saved enough to buy an engagement ring; he financed a vacation in Japan.

These meals provided all the rice we could eat and four assorted bowls of meat, fish, eggs vegetables. Never outside China have I been able to match their palatable variety, certainly not at the so-called Chinese restaurants where American taste and a limited, one might say straitjacketed, knowledge of what to order has restricted the catering to bastard dishes like chop suey and chow mien.

Even chop suey and chow mien are appetizing if eaten on rice, as the Chinese eat "pien fan." The bowl must be heaped with these viands and then held to the mouth so that rice, vegetables, meat, shrimp can be shoveled in with the chopsticks. For proper enjoyment this mixture should be inhaled, and inhaled noisily. To eat noisily is good manners; it shows appreciation of the food just as a rumbling belch afterwards compliments one's host. Americans who reject rice and lap up chop suey or chow mien with forks have never tasted Chinese food. There is an art to blending the several ingredients with the rice so as not to swamp it with too much liquid or salt it disagreeably by pouring in too much soy sauce; this art can be practised only with its proper tools, with chopsticks. It is an art worth learning.

"Pien fan," like everything else, the Chinese celebrated with a proverb:
"I wan hao,
Lian wan kou
San wan chu."
In translation:
"One bowl good,
Two bowls enough,
Three bowls, a pig."
When confronted by the steaming hot dishes, the heap of flaky rice, I did not stop at two bowls!"

* * * * * * *

Two adjectives the Chinese prized which we do our utmost to reject: old, and fat. Seniority, of course, comes with the years, if one is lucky enough to live that long - a chancier achievement in China than in the West. The likelihood of becoming fat was even more uncertain. Chinese preoccupation with food is illustrated by the common greeting which they exchanged, "Chih kuo liao fan mo?" "Have you eaten?" instead of "How do you do?"

It was never an empty formality in a country where food cannot be taken for granted. "Give us this day our daily bread," was an Oriental petition, a petition which China, always haunted by flood, drought, and famine, could

58

echo from the heart. Even in the Yangtze regions, the most favoured part of the Eighteen Provinces[14], starvation lurked. For millions the success or failure of each year's harvest spelt life or death. The weather bred an excitement which we, who measure its importance in terms of picnics and galoshes, cannot appreciate - unless we live in a dust bowl.

Never a year comes in which some part of China is not a dust bowl. I can remember the riverside city of Anking taking steps to implore rain. Because the sun shines from the south, the south gates were closed, a measure that compelled the water coolies to hoist their wooden buckets of Yangtze silt up and over the city wall. Prayer flags by the thousand were strung across the streets, triangular bits of paper inscribed with the one desperately repeated character, "yu," or rain. When these flags accomplished nothing, the officials imposed a series of public fasts – "meatless days," we would call them - and eventually snatched the gods from the cool aloofness of their temples and set them out in the courtyards to suffer, unsheltered, the noon sun's blistering heat. Not till these futile expedients had been abandoned did the rains come.

In north China nature was harsher. This I saw at first hand the summer of 1921 when I undertook supervision of a famine relief centre at Yungching, fifty miles south of Peking. Never have I seen a less prepossessing town. But the country around it, though a daily mirage disguised its dryness, was even more dismal. Before the drought, floods had smothered the best fields with ten feet of gravel; after this, for three years, no rain at all had fallen.

To this desert I fell heir, inhabiting a drab little house in a drab village. All the houses were the same, grey tile, dilapidated and dusty. Centuries of traffic had worn down the streets till one had to scramble three and four feet up a sharp slope to the doorways. Human sounds were muted by despair. The liveliest noise was the braying of jackasses.

Once every four or five days we had a distribution. Spindly-legged scarecrows staggered in from ten or eleven miles away to present the tissue paper tickets, given out at the last distribution, which indicated how much wheat they were to receive at this. These men who came were the ablest bodied members of their families, the only persons strong enough to carry their little sacks of grain the endless hot walk home. They were a sight to weep over, so thin that I would not have been startled to see daylight shining through the stark framework of their ribs.

What their allotment should be had been decided by my predecessor. Personally he had inspected every village in his area and pried into house after house. His reception was always the same: as he bent low to enter the dark, smelly interior, the inhabitants, clumsily courteous, never failed to drop the curtain on his neck, dismaying him with the nightmare possibilities of lice - and typhus.

At one door he was halted.

"There is a mother inside with a newborn baby," a villager explained, whereat there came from within the unmistakable lowing of a cow.

"The new baby has a pleasant voice," observed my predecessor, and marked this family off his list. To own a cow was affluence.

My duties were less exacting. Chiefly I kept and disbursed the funds used to buy grain. Since this money had to be imported from Peking by train and mule-cart, my predecessor had persuaded the buyers to accept, in lieu of silver dollars, the paper currency issued by various foreign banks in Shanghai. These bank-notes, he assured them, were as good as silver - which could not be said of Chinese currency. But no sooner had he got his first shipment of paper from Peking than a French bank, the Banque Industrielle, failed. Immediately the buyers panicked. It did not count with them that our currency was all the issue of such rock-stable institutions as the Hong Kong Shanghai Bank, and the National City Bank of New York. They wanted Mexican dollars.

My first job then was to total the currency on hand and package it for shipment back to Peking. Not daring to trust any Chinese in this delicate task, I sat up half the night counting and recounting dollar bills, of which there were twenty thousand. These bills were possessed of seven devils. They did every possible trick to thwart me. They stuck together, they dropped on the floor. On one count they would be 97 to a packet, on the next, 99. Both counts were wrong. Dollars were gyrating before my eyes in a demonic dance.

The rest of the night I lay awake waiting for bandits. Since Yungching had no bank, not even a store, where I could deposit this money, I kept it under my camp-cot. In the Yangtze region this would have been a sure invitation to robbers, but the northerners were, as the Chinese of other areas described them, "lao shih" – which in the dictionary meant "honest," but in common speech, "stupid."

How "lao shih" they were was demonstrated by the simple method we used to transport what in Chinese eyes was a fortune. We employed a coolie, at six Mexican dollars a month, to carry this money a half day's mule-cart journey to the railway, and several hours by train to the International Red Cross office in Peking. Furnished with a railway pass good all the way to Mukden[15], he could have decamped to Manchuria before we knew he was missing. Even if his imagination could not compass a defection so profitable and so safe, the greater miracle was that no one else thought of robbing him. His errands were well known, yet he went and came – as he had been doing for months – without interference, returning the currency, fetching back twenty thousand silver dollars in boxes whose weight and labels advertised their contents. Whatever Bret Harte had to say about the "heathen Chinee,"[16] this could not have happened in Christian America!

But it must be admitted that Christian America had sent the money in the first place. I was confronted by an ironic fact: we were buying our grain in the famine district. The populace was starving simply because the wealthy Chinese (which included the officials) had pushed the price of wheat beyond the reach of ordinary people. If they starved, their fate did not ruffle the rich families. They would let beggars die at their gates and feel that they had been generous in buying a cheap coffin into which they had to fit the corpse by breaking its stiffened, contorted limbs. This was as far as their social conscience stretched. It was American social conscience, quick to the need of an alien people half way around the world, that kept alive sufferers for whom their own "womb-brothers" felt no concern.

Some Chinese even attempted to thwart this relief work. The local magistrate, sole ruler of an area larger than most American counties, had offered the Red Cross a simple scheme.

"Don't bother with staff and organization," he had urged. "Send the money to me. I will take care of the starving."

Because the Red Cross was not gullible enough to accept his kind offer he put every obstacle in their way and, after their work was concluded, and the foreign supervision withdrawn, tried to imprison on trumped up charges the Chinese members of the Yungching staff. China is not an easy country to show benevolence to, nor does such benevolence win thanks.

These, happily, were problems outside my sphere. I was present at every distribution, endeavouring to look intelligent though well aware, as were the Chinese staff, that my presence or absence made no difference to the efficacious operation of their system. They at least appreciated American munificence. They were volunteers, working for subsistence only – as were we all – and no hint of corruption ever tainted their performance – hard exacting toil done both with cheerfulness and compassion.

In only one situation did I regret the politeness they showed me. This was on our trips to other distribution centres. Our conveyance was by mule-cart, the world's most picturesque and most frustrating expedient for travelling two miles an hour. Picturesque I call it because a mule-cart is a handsome vehicle; its shafts, its wooden body, the sturdy wooden spokes of its two wheels are varnished and polished till they shine, and over the cart, as over a covered wagon, is a tent of blue cloth.

Into this tent the guest of honour is ushered, there to suffocate in unventilated heat, and to fend off flies, while his inferiors sit outside on the shafts, dangling their legs, able to breathe, to adjust themselves to the lurches which, inside the tent, toss the luckless rider from side to side. North China then had no roads, just ruts intermittently paved with deeply grooved stones; the mule cart had no springs. Riding inside was like being aboard a gale-tossed ship that struck rocks at every pitch. I would much rather have walked, but walking was not proper, any more than riding on the shafts, to so exalted a personage.

The net result of each distribution was a sackful of the tissue paper tickets which the recipients of grain had presented before receiving their allotment. These I stuffed into a box and despatched to Peking where the auditors supposedly checked the out go against the wheat we had purchased. Each time I got in reply an indignant letter from the English accountant requesting that I kindly sort them out first and arrange them neatly in order to facilitate his book-keeping. This I did not even try to do. The tickets had been written in "grass character," a cursive style as individual as our handwriting and more indecipherable than a doctor's prescription; they were presented torn, crumpled, stained - as one would have expected from the sweaty hands in which they had been clutched, a precious passport to life itself. Had I been aided by a corps of philologists trained in guessing at Cretan inscriptions, I still could not have got them sorted in a way to satisfy the auditors. My flippant suggestion that they burn the lot and trust to our honesty put them into cold shudders. To ask an auditor to trust any man's honesty, even if the man has volunteered to stifle, at no pay, in a sun-baked village in northern Chihli[17], was as unethical as requesting a surgeon to perform an abortion. By nature auditors must trust nobody. So we enjoyed our irascible correspondence to the end.

I was glad of this chance to be disagreeable; I had to be irascible to somebody. I was beginning to bray like Yunching's jackasses. The only foreigner in this desolate town, I inhabited quarters once occupied by an English priest, a man of indubitable piety, if the makeup of his library was a true index. Each day dragged by like a year. My loneliness and boredom were aggravated, moreover, by dysentery, picked up on the Peking train. Yungching's only physician spoke no English. Plucking up courage to visit him, I came face to face with a shaggy dog as huge as a black bear and so antagonistic to foreign devils that his master tugged with all his strength to hold him back while I described my symptoms. Since a Chinese medical vocabulary was not my forte, this took some doing. When I had concluded, the doctor pondered for a moment then asked, "What would you advise?"

I did not return, preferring the bloody flux to being consumed by his dog. But I did learn at least that sulphas magnesium on the shelf in my quarters was Epsom salts. For the remainder of my sojourn in Yungching I lived well salted.

Whether we were upsetting Nature's balance by keeping alive people who, even in the best of times, had so little to live for I did not ask. Each day I became more preoccupied with keeping myself alive. Had I been given only a lifetime in Yungching to look forward to, I doubt if I would have prolonged the effort. Fiercely hot in summer, bitterly cold in winter, life on these plains drove its bond-slaves to scratch unrewarding fields with a wooden plow for a sparse yield of grain, and to scour the soil for autumn's dead grass to keep even lukewarm the brisk stoves on which families lived and slept with their ailing children, their bedbugs, their lice.

Elsewhere in China any social encounter was prefaced by an invitation to "he ch'a" – to drink tea. Here the invitation was to "he shui" – to drink water, not spring water nor even river water but subsurface water tainted with alkali. For centuries the occupants of these plains had accepted this bitter drink as their lot, a fate they would be presumptuous to question.

The Red Cross did question it. By an ingenious contraption, a large wooden wheel which a man revolved with his feet like a caged squirrel, they sank bamboo pipes below the alkali deposit and started an artesian flow of sweet water. This one permanent improvement in Yungching's existence I hope outlasted our work. The immediate improvement which terminated our work we owed to Nature. This was rain.

It came unbelievably when we had given up expecting it. Yungching had a proverb:

"Shou pu shou
Ch'ih yueh er shih t'ou,"

roughly translated,

"Whether there is to be harvest or not will be known by the 21st of the 7th moon."

This deadline we had almost reached when the clouds began rearing great pillars high toward the zenith, not the haze clouds we were resigned to, nor the daily mirage, the lakes that bore fleets of ghostly junks sailing down the horizon, but huge, black thunder clouds. So overwhelmingly dark grew the sky that we held our breaths, waiting on the vast spectacle, hoping any minute for the downpour it promised. Lightning flashed, thunder rumbled, a sharp breeze lifted the dust in whirls – and, as quickly, the clouds thinned, the sun, shining fiercer than ever, steamed us with its humid blast. Back into the sobbing hopelessness of despair sank the village.

Next day promised the same tantalizing story. Thunderheads again towered to impossible heights. The whole sky darkened, the earth took on twilight grey. Although we were past believing rain could fall, that it would ever fall, our hearts still strained to the foolish expectation that this time it must come. We could see the storm veiling the far plain, obliterating the willow trees as it rushed nearer and nearer until suddenly, incredibly, it was here, rain in a great deluge bringing life, laughter, release from despair. Mad with excitement, people rushed into courtyard and street; they let the water soak them to the skin, let it scour the grime, let it sluice away the misery of three fearful years.

This was no brief shower. The drought was broken. There would be harvests and food. Nothing remained for me but to gather up the hundred or so Mexican dollars still unspent, my votive offering to the auditor, and start lumbering in a mule cart through roads no longer dust but mud, mud that splashed up to our axles. At Langfang, the railway station, I did not even wait for the Peking express but clambered aboard a freight train, taking shelter in the caboose. "Shelter" is a mis-statement. None of us, the cheery train crew and I, could dodge the leaks, the continuous shower-bath from a roof more sieve than shelter, but I rode to Peking completely comfortable from the sheer joy of being wet.

* * * * * * *

To say that Peking is unique is to use the word exactly. There is no other city like it. Unfortunately, it is as unique in China as to the rest of the world. It is almost the only worthy reminder of China's long and intricate past. Because China built flimsily, no country of her antiquity has left so few monuments of its past. Except for the Great Wall, little that is truly ancient survives. Even Peking is not ancient by European standards. A drum tower and a bell tower remain from the time of Kublai Khan; among the city's tallest structures, they like the gates were erected not to exceed 99 Chinese feet in height lest they impede passage of the good spirits, whose domain commences at a hundred feet. But Peking as we know it was laid out on Mongol foundations by the Ming Emperor, Yung Lo who moved his capital here from Nanking about 1426.

Yung Lo died in 1436. His is the first of the thirteen northern tombs that commemorate the Emperors of his dynasty. Most of them, perhaps all, have been broken into and plundered since I saw them in 1922. They occupied a complex of mountain valleys far to the north of Peking, valleys so lonely that no village, barely a cultivated field, flourished in their neighbourhood.

I had come straddling the kapok stuffed sack with which my donkey was saddled. The approach to the tombs, I know, began with a monumental arch divided by tall marble columns into seven parts. I know also that the arch was about seven miles from the railway at Nankow, a reasonable distance

64

affording me time, I hoped, to inspect at least one tomb and return to Nankow in time for the late afternoon train. But when I reached the arch and asked the donkey-driver where the tomb was, he pointed with his chin to a spot of gleaming yellow so remote that I dismounted from my donkey, knowing that if I were to arrive at the first of these imperial temples, I must set a faster pace than my beast would consent to.

For nearly two hours I plodded, following the broken pavement, much of it marble, along which had jolted the funeral carts of the dead Ming Emperors. In Chinese thinking, Majesty must have space. Dead or alive, the sons of Heaven could not be approached hastily. Great intervals apart were triumphal pillars, columns supporting heaven, and a stone tortoise labouring under a massive stela. Next I passed between pairs of elephants, camels, horses, immense figures, and between warriors and statesmen, a silent company stationed here five centuries ago to watch greatness go to its grave. Sun, rain, snow, sandstorms driving down from the Gobi Desert, had beat upon them, but they still kept watch.

By my arrival at the tomb I was so hot and thirsty, and the time left me to linger was so brief, that I had to choose between antiquity and beer. My vote was beer. I sought out the little pavilion where it was sold. Once refreshed, however, I gambled on time to visit Yung Lo's temple, a yellow-roofed building I had seen from afar, green-roofed, too, where shrubs had lodged and were breaking down the luminous tiles. This temple was upheld by pillars of laurel, eighty feet tall, hauled from Burma, and still as sound as when they were erected sixty-odd years before Columbus discovered America. In its vast interior, as large as the nave of Westminster Abbey, stood but one object, the gold-lacquered spirit tablet of the Emperor who created modern Peking. His ghost dominated the empty, silent hall.

Beyond the temple was the tomb, an artificial mound which could have been mistaken, in its overgrowth of pines, for a natural hill, except that one climbed through a tunnel, pausing to note the round stone which had shut the mausoleum and sealed in, if tradition be correct, not only the Emperor's body and his treasure but the host of men-servants and maid-servants despatched to serve his needs in the halls of the dead.

Out of the tunnel I emerged on the hill top where the final tablet, a monolith, had been reared to celebrate Yung Lo's glory under his posthumous name, Ch'eng Tsu. Time was passing; much as I longed to linger, to sit on the grass and soak in the sombre traditions of this vast, ghost-peopled valley, I could not delay. Frantically we urged the donkey back to Nankow by a more direct route, and managed the impossible: out of breath but with ten minutes to spare, I rushed to the railway station – only to hear that the train would be four hours late! Kipling was right: it is foolish to hustle the East.

Disappointing, as were the four hours I had to waste in Nankow's dingy hotel when I could have occupied them so valuably in the haunted valleys where the Ming Emperors slept away centuries, I doubt whether a longer visit could have impressed my imagination with memories more vivid. There if anywhere time is not a matter of minutes or hours but of sensation. One's mind bestrides history.

The same keenness of sensation was awakened by the spectacle of the Great Wall. China is not a nation; it is a world. Its isolation it maintained and cherished because it was the centre of civilization. No other people possessed anything worth borrowing, Mongols, Tatars, Europeans, Japanese, they all were barbarians who might make a show of brute strength but who lacked the true elements of the superior man.

In keeping with this attitude the Chinese have not called their country China, a name of uncertain origin. China is Chung Kuo, the Central Country, an arrogance matched only by the Romans when they named their sea the Mediterranean. Around China, so its people thought, the world revolved. Their destiny was not merely national; it was cosmic.

Glimpses of this attitude I caught as I marvelled at the immutable vigil kept by the stone figures through whose ranks passed the staggeringly heavy coffins of the Ming Emperors. It was revealed by the imaginative boldness that was satisfied to place in a lofty, pillared temple, ancient China's largest building, one sufficient object of veneration, a gold-lacquered spirit tablet, nothing more. In Peking itself a score of palaces and temples witnessed to this simple statement of a greatness unchallenged for all time. The noblest is the Altar of Heaven.

Many great buildings serve this altar, outstanding among them the Temple of Heaven, its round conical roof glowing a deep, fathomless blue, and the Hall of Enlightenment, a rectangular structure topped by seeming acres of sea-green roof. In this hall the Emperor fasted and prepared for the solemn rites of the Winter solstice when, in freezing darkness long before dawn, he ascended the Altar.

Chinese Emperors heightened their awful dignity by utilizing hours when man normally would be asleep. In these same dark hours their custom was to hold audience. Courtiers and ministers of state, summoned to the Imperial presence did obeisance long before cockcrow, kneeling, kowtowing, holding before their eyes an ivory board in order not to stare at the Son of Heaven, not to profane by vulgar sight the vision of His timeless Majesty. Only by report could they picture him, clad in the stiff gold-embroidered dragon robes, as he sat on the dragon throne. Over his head hung the silver ball of justice, suspended from a ceiling as lofty and as brilliantly painted as the panelled ceiling of a gothic church..

All this China's 1911 revolution destroyed. Frock coats and silk hats ousted mandarin robes. Politicians, springing up like weeds, flourished rankly till they were mown down by military despots, warlords whose private armies bargained for battles and subsisted not by fighting but by loot.

These changes had made the Altar of Heaven, when I saw it, an empty portent, a tourist's attraction. Yet even in the broad light of day it bespoke the assurance of the unseen, the numinous, that had created it. It is a series of concentric marble terraces rising to the topmost platform. Up these terraces the Emperor ascended in rites set to unearthly music, rites accompanied by jade bells and pheasant-feathered lutes. On the platform, before the prestigious circle of marble, set flush with the marble pavement, he paused. The exact centre of the altar, the exact centre of the earth, this stone was the centre of civilization, of culture, a centre which the Chinese shuddered to see desecrated by outer barbarians.

No matter what humiliation they had suffered from foreign devils and eastern dwarfs, the Chinese down to the humblest never wavered in believing that theirs was truly the Central Country. Foreigners, they admitted, might be clever in a boorish, mechanical way, but their achievements ranked low in the Chinese scale of values. As far back as 1921, when airplanes had not overrun even Western skies in today's noisy numbers, I have watched the reaction of Chihli peasants to their first sight of a 'plane. Far from being astounded, they gave it barely a glance. "Just another fool foreign invention," they seemed to say as they turned back to their fields.

What the Chinese of those days vociferously craved was the means of making "our China" strong, making it in fact as well as tradition the Central Country. From hope of such fulfilment they welcomed Chiang Kai-shek and, when he failed them, they turned to the Communists. But in doing so they lost their own spiritual centeredness. After centuries of proud, serene aloofness, they not only surrendered to the barbarians, they mimicked them.

* * * * * * * *

Except in Peking and its environs China has few monuments to her past. In the Yangtze valley, where I lived, the T'ai P'ing rebellion[18] had obliterated the population as well as its monuments. Driven by a compulsion of Christian heresies, racial hatreds, inflated and insane ambitions, it scourged China like an eruption of locusts. For fourteen years it raged, the bloodiest war in history. Before its collapse in 1864 it had run up a death-toll reckoned at twenty million. Most of the Yangtze cities had to be repeopled by immigrants from upriver. They swarmed into areas emptied by massacre, soon replacing the dead but powerless to replace their customs, their continuity with the past.

It was my fortune to be assigned, for two years, to the one city that held out against the T'ai P'ings, the great city of Nanchang, capital of Kiangsi. Eighty miles south of the Yangtze, Nanchang was reached by a train which took most of a day to travel those eighty miles. A year earlier, I had nearly broken my kneecap while running to catch the 7:58, a commuters' train to New York, so that I need not wait for the 8:01. Yet so swiftly does one adjust one's self to the pace of another world, another century, that when bound from Kiukiang[19] to Nanchang I used to arrive at eight, walk down the track a mile to board the single first class car before it was shunted into the station, and then wait for the train's departure, advertised for eleven o' clock, though we considered it on time if it got away before noon. This procedure, so necessary if I were to get a decent seat, soon seemed to me as natural as my commuter's pell-mell haste at East Orange.

On my first trip, however, I had not learned this trick – and I got no seat. The two first class compartments were so overstuffed with portly officials that I did not even make a feint of squeezing myself in; I sat, instead, on the car's open steps.

By accident I had hit on the most effective measure I could have chosen; I was causing the railway to lose face. The spectacle of a foreign devil sitting on the car's platform steps was too flagrant an advertisement of the line's shortcomings. The conductor and his retinue soon were on the spot begging me to go inside.

"But there is no room," I objected.

"Oh yes, there is plenty of room."

He was correct. Most of the dignitaries I had seen jammed into the first class compartments were friends come to bid their colleagues good-bye. But the officials who remained appeared anything but happy at having a foreigner intruded into their midst. Their objections the conductor countered by holding up my ticket. I actually had <u>bought</u> a ticket, phenomenon so startling that it silenced further argument; my fellow passengers – every sleek occupant of the compartment – were travelling on passes.

Two thirds of the way, which we had covered at a stolid twenty miles an hour, we reached a bridge, a construction bridge. Built to last two years, it had lasted ten. So long as it continued to stand, the Chinese saw no reason to replace it. It offered manifest handicaps. Since it was too frail to hold up the line's powerful locomotive, the train was hitched on to a switch engine, reputedly a relic of the New York "El," which huffed and puffed across the bridge and crawled the remaining miles to Nanchang.

On later trips I took no chances with this bridge but followed other passengers to the open platforms. If the trestle collapsed, we should not be trapped inside the car. We all poised, ready to jump, as the bridge creaked and swayed, but not for several more years did its luck run out. When it did fall, some two hundred persons perished with it, a tragic accident, the Chinese conceded – but think of the years it had been used without falling! At least they did not term its eventual collapse an "act of God."

At the end of this tedious journey the train still stopped short of Nanchang, which was separated from the station by the mile's width of the Kan River. This stream, across which passengers and freight had to be transported by sampan or barge, could be turbulent in a strong wind, and dangerous when spring freshets had swollen its muddy waters.

Nanchang was not a spectacular city to approach. Its walls were low, its houses a ramshackle clutter roofed with grey tile. But it was a proud city, a rich city; its streets took their names and their character from the different handicrafts that kept them bustling. I liked best the streets where furniture and chests were being made of camphor-wood. Their fragrance overpowered the smell of open drains, what a friend of mine, a singer, once set to song as "the Chinese national air!" Unlike most Chinese cities, however, where the "fen" buckets, the buckets of night-soil are carried to the fields uncovered, with perhaps a palm leaf to keep their nauseous contents from slopping on to the stones, Nanchang required that these buckets not only be covered by a lid but sealed around the edges with wet clay. Yet there were still smells enough to make the Chinese national air a palpable fact. Indeed, after long residence in China, I half convinced myself that fresh air was tasteless, like meat without salt.

Through the city, however, extended a string of lakes, the Tung Hu, or East Lakes, supposed rivals of the His Hu, the famed West lakes of Hangchow. If they could not match the latter in splendid temples and ornate pavilions, they did have their own beauty, especially in the pearl-grey of early dawn when the willow trees, blurred like puffs of smoke, overhung their blurred reflections. At the lake's edge we could hire boats, complete with chairs and tables, and drink hot tea while the boatmen poled us through China of the willow pattern; we even attempted dinner parties, putting the guests in one boat, the kitchen in another alongside so that the servants could pass across the hot dishes which they had prepared, and prepared appetizingly on the most rudimentary equipment, no ovens, no thermostats, just small earthenware charcoal stoves. These were meals compounded of poetry, begun under the glow of paper lanterns and concluded in the white light of the moon, lifting its radiant circle above the eastern mountains.

Nanchang's escape from the T'ai P'ings was so clouded in mystery – for its walls, neither high nor impregnable, invited attack by water or by land – that one was tempted to credit the legend of the Governor's wife, dressed as a peasant, who went into the besieging camp to sell straw sandals. The T'ai P'ing warriors laughed at her, for the sandals she held up for sale were three times the size any of them could wear.

"Ai ya, you stupid woman!" they exclaimed. "Who would buy sandals that big?"

"Big!" retorted the woman. "They fit the men of Nanchang perfectly" – whereat the T'ai P'ings, unwilling to combat giants, lifted their siege and withdrew.

But they had come close to capturing this City of Southern Affluence. In one wall still could be seen the broaches they had made by exploding coffins filled with gunpowder.

Despite these rumours from the past, Nanchang was as casual about its history as London. The one record it cherished was of never having been looted, a record soon to be broken. To a Westerner, especially one like myself from a region that could look back barely half a century, Nanchang's neglect of its few antique remnants was deplorable. Except that I had a teacher who shared my antiquarian passion, I might never have discovered one of the most beautiful of the city's forgotten treasures, a huge iron incense burner, dated from the Han dynasty, two thousand years back. Left open to the skies with no trace of the temple which must have sheltered it, it had sunk to being a prop for the bed-boards the women of its slumlike neighbourhood were purging of lice and bed-bugs.

Perhaps the Chinese were wise in paying greater deference to a living memorial, a camphor tree planted in the T'ang dynasty and still thriving after a thousand years. In the autumn, when it bloomed, Chinese by the hundred walked the five miles to the Taoist temple in whose courtyard it stood. Since the Taoists are a non-exclusive religion, ready to adopt any deity, it was not surprising that they saw, in the five stems growing up through a hollow Trunk, the hand of Buddha. In this temple modern inventions were utilized to serve ancient customs. On its shelves was a host of spirit tablets, tablets of the temple's many benefactors, but instead of the usual gilt characters the dead men were honoured by porcelain plaques on which had been copied from photographs stiff portraits of the deceased.

I paid my visits to this temple outside the pilgrim season. At this time the monks led so quiet a life among their galleries of the dead that I could relish the abbot's disclaimer to my apology for disturbing this tranquil routine. They were pleased, he told me, to have guests for, without such visits, they heard nothing but the singing of the birds.

70

If Nanchang had no monuments, its life was monument enough, that stream of custom and habit, of hope, love, gaiety, despair, which had poured, generation after generation, through the centuries. Even the countless reminders of death testified to this immemorial continuance of life. A pastime I indulged in was to wander across the adjacent hills and remark the gravestones placed before the round mounds of the dead. All were lettered in similar style and dated with the dynasty and the year of the reigning Emperor. Most, of course, belonged to the last dynasty, the Ch'ing or Manchu era, but I came frequently on Ming dynasty graves, and even on stones from the short-lived Yuan, or Mongol, dynasty. Week after week I kept searching, hoping some day to come upon one from the Sung dynasty or the T'ang. If there were such, sun and rain had effaced the record.

These mounds, heaped so as not to disturb the earth spirits, with exactly the amount of soil dug out for the coffin were everywhere, in the fields, around the villages, wherever the geomancers had located them. They were an ever-present reminder that the land had been much lived in, while their sameness was not so much a protest against death as an acceptance. Chinese funerals paraded the streets of Nanchang with a panoply of hired mourners, all dressed in unbleached muslin and all pumping out tears in a fantastic imposture of grief; but once out of the city, where there were no crowds to stare, mourners and bands were paid off, the coffin's rented trappings dismantled, and the dead man conveyed to his grave quietly and simply.

The Chinese people's vitality came from the soil to which it was natural that they should return. Their names might be washed out by the storms of centuries but their spirit, the subtle pervasive influence of their continuous human activity, remained in a landscape they were content to live in, not to tamper with, not to exploit. They had come to an accommodation with Nature such as made them, in a rare sense, deeply responsive to natural scenery. They even granted their scenery the privilege of solitude.

This may have been due to the unchanging pattern of their culture. No one could claim for the Chinese that innate respect for beauty both in nature and in man's handiwork which characterizes the Japanese and the older generations in Europe. There still persisted, however, in the crafts the delight in design common to all civilized peoples before the factory and the assembly line stifled pride of workmanship. Generally, these crafts flourished in particular localities: one went to Ningpo for the best carpenters, to southern Anhui and Canton for artists in porcelain, and again to Anhui for the families that retained the secret of how to make embossed ink-sticks and pocket sun-dials. At Anking I commissioned some Ningpo carpenters to copy for me two beds that I had seen illustrated in the International Studio. These beds were pictured with angels on each post, a detail I had omitted, from doubt as to what Chinese carpenters would do with mediaeval angels! On second thought, I decided to substitute Chinese lions, beasts which the carpenters carved, of course, by hand in the traditional style one comes across in many a Chinese temple. Since the lions had not been included in our original estimates, I asked the "lao pan," the boss, how much extra I owed him. "Nothing," he replied, "we enjoyed making them."

Throughout Chinese art runs the rhythm of the Four Seasons. They are signified in numberless sets of watercoloured scrolls, in the wrought iron panels of lanterns, in the decoration of porcelain jars, lacquer screens. The season modulations are the pervading theme of Chinese poetry. The Chinese lived through winter, spring, summer, autumn; he felt the wholesome discipline of their discomforts, the damp, often bitter cold of winter, the stifling, humid summers, and so enjoyed more keenly the explosive outburst of spring blossoms, autumn's sunlit haze when days that began with frost warmed to eighty at noon.

The discomforts as well as the glory of the Chinese seasons I learned to relish. Foreigners in China made more equable provision against the weather than the Chinese, but our heating was still rudimentary – two or three rooms warmed by coal-grates, the rest as icy as the inside of a refrigerator. In my first year of teaching I lived in rooms entirely unheated; twice the pitcher in my bathroom froze solid. To feel warm enough to read or write I would stir my blood by running a lap around the track. Since I taught all day in unheated classrooms, with temperature during a cold spell hovering at the freezing mark, I grew inured to this austerity, though never quite used to seeing women attend dinner parties in formal evening dress and then don cloaks at the dinner table to cover their bare shoulders.

The Yangtze region was midway between the continental winters of north China and the semi-tropics of the South. By Chinese reckoning it was not cold enough to require more warmth than could be supplied by an extra layer of cotton-padded garments. What fuel there was went to cooking – charcoal for the well-to-do, dried grass for the poor. Women would scurry to catch the sticks from a magpie's nest that was being knocked down from a telephone pole. In the outposts foreigner and Chinese alike bought his hot water from a hot water shop. All our bath water was fetched by coolies in wooden buckets, a function of such importance that my coolie interrupted a dinner party to tell me my bath was ready!

In summer the Yangtze region was super-tropical. During one hot spell the thermometre for six weeks did not record lower than eighty-five even at night; in the day time it rose to a hundred, and the humidity close behind it. Although our only relief came from the torrential downpour of a typhoon, I loved the summers. The great heat, the perpetual stridency of the cicadas exhilarated me. Shorts and shirt were all the costume one could tolerate; a sash replaced a belt because belt leather stained, and into the sash was looped a Turkish towel, which one used continually to mop away the sweat. Yet we endured these summers without benefit of ice. Since most foreign houses had underground cisterns to collect rain water, we cooled food and drink by hanging it in a wire cage inside the cistern. To drinking water thus chilled a few spoonfuls of lime juice were an addition more refreshing than ice. Tea we drank – as it should be drunk – hot. Houses we kept cool and free from flies by closing the shutters and leaving only the slats open. Mosquitoes were discouraged by our burning punk under tables and chairs and, if we sat outside at night, by putting our legs inside pillow cases. Mattresses of course were too hot for sleep; bamboo mats over a thin pad were more comfortable. By such expedients we adapted ourselves quite tolerably to heat and humidity; we engaged daily in brisk sets of tennis and managed an existence which we were cheerfully willing to accept as normal. Flat statements are treacherous but I am convinced that endurance of alternating heat and cold keep the human body better tuned, more resilient, more adaptable than the man-made uniformity of climate which the United States now regards as necessary.

Chinese life, however, and Chinese reactions cannot be gauged by the life of foreigners in China. The latter were independent of hardships from which millions of China's population could never hope to be freed, poverty, insanitary crowding, bruising toil. Comparisons, to be valid, must be made with Chinese of the more affluent classes, with merchants, officials, teachers. Among these even the rich did not overvalue comfort as we do. Their homes were built to a design that never varied except for adding more sections, surrounding more identical courtyards, to accommodate more kinsfolk, more concubines and servants.

Every house faced south, every house contained the same furniture, made sometimes of richer materials, more ornately carved and inlaid, but hard, straight-backed, unyielding. Each great family lived its own complete existence behind high walls; its stone-paved courtyards flourished with trees and flowers and singing birds while at the back was a miniature landscape set in a pond, an island around which one could walk a protracted circuit and admire tiny bridges, pagodas, pavilions. Here the Four Seasons passed in review, neither blurred nor ignored. Nature was welcomed into the heart of the family.

This accord with Life that underlay life can best be explained as a product of Chinese philosophy, the pantheism which Lao Tzu clothes in paradoxical phrasing, though long before his time it must have been the essence of Chinese character. Its principle is acquiescence, not resistance. Nature, by these standards, was not a spectacle nor a show-piece, not a lure to wring dollars from tourists, not a backdrop for the frantic activity of the skier or the pest at the throttle of an outboard motor boat; it was a harmonious configuration of mountain and plain and river to be sought out reverently for the peace it conferred.

This accord I felt most genuinely in autumn, felt it indeed from my first days in Nanking, when I looked up to Purple Mountain – "Golden Purple Mountain." The Chinese call it – glowing in sunlight that overlaid its treeless slopes like a patina. November voyages up the Yangtze brought kindred impressions, again bright sunshine and the vignettes it revealed as the steamship slid along the brittle river-banks – peasants at rest against stacks of harvested reeds and puffing blue smoke from their water pipes while a water buffalo nuzzled them like an overgrown dog.

On the hills outside Nanchang this serene mood seemed to lay an inviolable spell. For miles I used to wander, coming often to groves of camphor trees, as shapely as oaks but with leaves that never lost their green gloss. In their shade a little steam would trickle beneath bridges heaped up from slabs of rough-hewn granite. Cattle basked in the meadows, a scene exceptional to Nanchang whose inhabitants, unlike Chinese elsewhere, used milk, bought it indeed from dairymen who drove their cows from door to door and milked them into bamboo containers at each gate. Wild life abounded; geese by the hundreds foraged in the marshes; pheasant rocketed from covert under the crimson turned foliage of the heavenly bamboo tree. The candleberry too was bright in autumn colours, and the t'ung tree whose fruit, quince-like in appearance, gave out a sticky sap now applied to paints and varnishes but used by Chinese children to mend their fans.

My walks always took me a few hundred yards farther to a point where the valley began narrowing to a mountain gorge, the traditional site for a temple. Here I could be sure of tea and enjoy a chat with the monks, whom I usually found sunning themselves like their two or three well-fed cats in the late season's warmth. They belonged to this unhurried landscape - mountain, water, trees; the secret of its peace was in their wrinkled smiles, their gentle speech.

* * * * * * *

While still in Nanchang I was invited by a high official to tutor three of his children, two sisters, fifteen and thirteen, and a boy of twelve. At the same time, his neighbour, third ranking officer of the province, asked that I teach his grandson and his grandson's bride. To accommodate both groups a single classroom was set aside and furnished with desks, chairs, and blackboard. So began two memorable years in a profession which the Chinese esteemed above all others, the post of tutor. Each time I entered or departed the huge gates of the "kung kuan," the blue-uniformed soldiers on guard brought their rifles to the salute.

These two families, though closely allied, had widely different backgrounds, a vastly different routine. Shen lao-ye, "grandfather Shen", was an official of the old school. He had been stationed at the Chinese Legation in London, where he had witnessed the final splendours of Queen Victoria's reign. Out of this residence abroad he had brought home a smattering of English, English long since gone to seed. He and his wife, Shen t'ai-t'ai, were models of integrity, Shen lao-ye worthily personifying the Confucian ideal of the "chuntzu," the superior man, the t'ai-t'ai setting forth Buddhist piety at its best. Even to look at them, one saw in the kindly, disciplined restraint of their faces the inner harmonies of a life well lived. It followed naturally that the lao-ye should be a superlative Chinese scholar, so greatly honoured for his calligraphy that the public considered it only proper for an official of his high rank to devote a fortnight to inscribing a pair of scrolls congratulating the military governor's mother on her sixtieth birthday.

I hope the military governor gave this tribute its right value. He was of the new order. Although his mother was not even present in Nanchang, he sent out invitations to her birthday celebration some six weeks in advance, a forehandedness which reaped him two or three hundred thousand dollars in gifts. By contrast, on Shen lao-ye's sixty sixth birthday, his grandson rooted me out of school to share the felicitations. When I enquired why the invitation had not been issued early enough for me to prepare a suitable gift I learned this custom of inviting guests on the day itself was the old courteous way of indicating that gifts were not expected.

Shen lao-ye's grandson was following his grandfather's footsteps in his practice of calligraphy, but acquiring this ancient art by methods oddly up-to-date. He had a book filled with photostatic copies of illustrious Chinese documents; over these he placed tissue paper in order to trace these masterpieces line for line until he had developed his own free hand. A young man in his early twenties or even his late 'teens, he had been interrupted in his schooling by the onset of tuberculosis, a disease against which he was slowly losing ground. The inactivity this necessitated was more than usually bitter, for he had shown such promise as a runner that he had represented China in the far Eastern Olympics at Manila. Quiet, considerate, quick to smile, an aristocrat to his finger-tips, he was not the academic equal of his eager young bride – she had to be held back lest she embarrass her husband – but he was a youth who attracted both affection and respect until I regarded him not as a pupil but a friend, and cherished our many gay times in his grandfather's "kung kuan." My status as tutor gave me access to all the family doings, the feast, the amateur theatricals, the evenings spent at chess or mah-jong. The most festive of these celebrations centered in the birth of a son, the assurance of a new generation to manage the old filial rituals of a family that had come close to dying out.

The father of the two young sisters and younger brother who made up the other part of my class was as remarkable as Shen lao-ye. Although he had never been out of China, he spoke flawless English, flawless in grammar, flawless in choice of words and – still more noteworthy – flawless in intonation. Such an achievement spoke much for the Hong Kong schools which had trained him. Mr. Tsai's father had been, if I remember correctly, the first *compradore* for the great British firm, Jardine, Matheson and Company, handling with skill that great responsibility which made him the colleague of the British manager – or t'ai pan – and himself director of the company's huge Chinese staff and interpreter of business policies first conceived and formulated in English. The son, however, was in the employ of the Chinese Government; he was serving with the Salt Gabelle.

Many years before, the Chinese Maritime Customs had set the pattern on which the Salt Gabelle was shaped, a pattern highly profitable to China and providing, indeed, her only dependable revenue. In return for loans made under the auspices of several Western powers, among them the United States, the Customs had been turned over to foreign administration as a lien on this debt. So honest had been this administration that, after collecting the interest and such part of the principal as was due, it had collected a large annual surplus for the Peking government. It had extended its sphere to the provision of a Postal Service, prompter, more efficient and more trustworthy than its American counterpart. In my nearly fourteen years of China I cannot remember losing any mail, a feat more than ever amazing when one recalls that my mail was not even addressed in the language of the country, yet the ratio of foreigners to Chinese in the Postal Service was not more than one to two hundred. Tribute though this must be to the type of foreigner appointed to this work, it is equally a tribute to what the Chinese can do under leadership which they respect.

The Salt Gabelle was the late-comer in these debt-serving administrations. Its organization differed in having two heads, a Chinese and a foreigner jointly managing each district. How such a system operated elsewhere I do not know, but in Nanchang Mr. Ts'ai did the work while his English colleague had only to contribute his signature where required at the end of each month. So light were his duties that, after the shooting season had ended, he went to pieces from sheer boredom. No reflection was this on Mr. Ts'ai, with whom he served in perfect amity, but proof that two heads are not necessarily better than one.

76

Mr. Ts'ai and his wife exhibited a rare and perfect blending of two cultures, English and Chinese. They succeeded in being both progressive and conservative. If an education as happy in its results could have moulded a few thousand more of China's prominent officials, there would have been no room for the Communist revolution. The complete integrity of Mr. Ts'ai's outward career was just as evident in his home. Many a happy hour I enjoyed with the Ts'ais and their children (not to forget their white, curly-haired poodle) and I had the fortune to be admitted on the informal terms which made me welcome at ordinary meals – or "pien fan" – and to impromptu amusements not as a guest but as a member of the family. With them, as with the Shens, the traditional relationship of teacher and pupil was honoured, next to that of parent and child, as civilization's strongest bond.

The Ts'ais' pleasantest relaxation was the unusual one of cooking. To escape too zealous assistance from their many servants was not easy. Hidden away in a small room of their "kung kuan," they tried to conceal an oil cookstove on which they practised their experiments – experiment is a name worthy of the dishes they prepared. When I enquired before Christmas what gifts they might relish, I discovered that what they wanted most was pyrex oven-ware. They were the only Chinese I knew who could set before Western guests a Western meal, complete even to salad, which could satisfy the most critical taste. Their Chinese meals were equally remarkable; instead of the sixteen or twenty four courses normal to a Chinese feast, they served only eight but each course not only delicious in itself but chosen to take its proper place with the others.

This exceptional privilege of entry into the life of two aristocratic Chinese families made me much envied by other members of the missionary community. One of them, with reproach on his tongue, asked me how soon I was going to utilize this opportunity to "convert" Mr. Ts'ai. He was shocked by my opinion that Mr. Ts'ai did not need converting. In one of many profound talks, Mr. Ts'ai had told me that his sister was Christian and his children had his ready permission to become Christian but that for himself he would be disloyal to his ancestors if he abandoned the traditional sacrifices.

I considered this my one perfect class, the kind of class teachers dream of but never expect to see realized. Not once did I need to reprimand the two girls and the boy whom I met eagerly each day. Their work was always done on time, always carried out to the letter, carefully, efficiently, thoughtfully. In their improvised classroom they were models of alert interest, Mary, fifteen years old, gentle and sweet-tempered, Lucy, thirteen, winning friends by her quick, mischievous smile, Peter, twelve, bright-eyed with intelligence and a hopeful ambition that drew on deep springs of laughter and deeper springs of grave intentness, an unprompted determination to excel.

My association with these charming youngsters went beyond the schoolroom. Twice a week they came to my house, where it was their parents' wish that they absorb the niceties of Western etiquette. Young Shen Ch'uan-ling often came too. Out of these occasions quickened an affection such as any teacher who loves teaching will prize for its ability to transcend his career by a mutual trust and understanding that no longer needed take into account differences of age or status. There were games we played together, informal talks outside the classroom, walks on the city wall. To well-bred Chinese girls, spending their leisure at home, this last was adventure. Dog and all, they bubbled with excitement when we emerged from the little back gate and scrambled up the dilapidated stone wall, stopping to stare at the city's grey roofs or to peer through battlements at the teeming streets outside. But when they grew so bold as to urge me into bringing them home through these teeming streets, I was too startled to refuse.

We were almost a parade. The crowds that always thronged the narrow, stone-flagged street gaped at the spectacle of two well-born "ku-niang" being convoyed openly by a foreign devil. For me the walk was an ordeal, so embarrassed was I by such publicity, by the shock we were dealing Chinese convention. But the girls were not in the least embarrassed. The shops, the hurly-burly of a busy thoroughfare, the water-coolies splashing along, the rikshas jostling pedestrians and casually indifferent to the strident warning of their bells, the pedlars singing out in jingles the tastiness of skewered crab-apples, this hubbub combined for the children in the gayest of explorations, a blithe sortie into a world they knew chiefly by hearsay. They were regretful when we arrived at the kung kuan's entrance, sorry when the amazed gate-keeper swung open his huge, ponderous doors to admit us.

A teacher's vocation labours under the sad necessity of annual good-byes. He commits his youngsters to the world knowing that, despite their promise of seeing him often, if he has done his work well they will look forward, not backward. But separation from these pupils whom I had been tutoring came prematurely. I was transferred from Nanchang. Tears mixed with our farewells at the railway station.

Shen Ch'uan-ling I never saw again. I remember him handsome as ever that last morning, clad in the velvet jacketed elegance of a young aristocrat to whom life offered everything except health. Ours had been a wistfully happy understanding which he signalized by cutting for me out of soapstone the seals for stamping my Chinese signature. These personal seals are always gifts; one does not buy them. Making them is the work of a scholar, and the office of a friend. When he became more proficient, Shen Ch'uan-ling promised, he would cut me seals of jade. This promise he was not able to keep. Death intervened.

The Ts'ai children I did see once more, a summer or two later: their mother brought them to visit me at Kuling, the mountain resort where I was staying. We had tea and played games with a tennis ball converted into a shuttlecock.

"Look at them," exclaimed their mother, watching Mary and Lucy as they dashed into the game's excitement, "They are just like boys! I cannot do anything with them!"

But her eyes glowed with pride.

* * * * * * * *

From Nanchang to Wuhu was a journey into a different world. Wuhu was a treaty port; ocean freighters came three hundred miles up the Yangtze to moor alongside its crumbling banks and load the rice which it exported in larger quantities than any other port in China. Aside from a considerable foreign community, it had few noticeable distinctions. Most of the buildings to be seen prominently from the river housed foreigners. The commissioner of Customs lived palatially on his hill; the oil companies each had a hill, as did the missions. The Spanish Jesuits had a huge cathedral. The bishop of the Anglican diocese to which I was attached had been consecrated Bishop of Wuhu, but soon changed his see and his title to Anking to obviate – so rumour had it – the laughter which the mere mention of Wuhu provoked each time he was introduced to an American audience. Whatever his reasons, the change had its drawbacks.

Anking was proclaimed for miles up and down the Yangtze by its towering pagoda, the river's most impressive. Legend had made this city, capital of Anhui province, a ship, the pagoda its mast. In the pagoda temple were anchors to preserve the city from being swept downstream by the Yangtze's impetuous currents. West of Anking's grimy walls glittered the rocks of Ta Lung Shan, the Great Dragon Mountain. Admittedly, the bishop had chosen for his cathedral a more appealing site than Wuhu, but inaccessible to all who wished to consult him. To arrive at Anking, visitors steeled themselves to be prodded out of their comfortable staterooms at three in the morning and dumped into the murky confusion of an overloaded barge. To depart they waited at the riverside for a downriver steamship which might arrive at any time between nine and midnight. Many a weary night I have squandered watching impatiently for the red and white masthead lights of the Jardine steamer to appear around the bend above Anking, or for the triangularly placed white lights of Butterfield and Swire. Since Anking was a closed port, these British ships could not tie up to a hulk but turned into the current while an outsized sampan made fast with grappling hooks.

The sampan men were not eager to be carried far; by frantic shouting they hustled their passengers up the gangway, the steamer too was impatient to get going; its crew were rushing their passengers off with the same impetuous tumult. The two streams, arriving and departing, met in voluble frenzy on the gangway's slippery steps, blocking each other with baskets, pigskin boxes, crates of poultry, in a scrimmage so easily matched that it was a wonder anyone ever got on or off and no wonder that occasionally a luckless passenger was jostled into the dark river.

Embarking or debarking at Anking was a football game without umpires. Eventually one side broke through its opposition and began moving until, by a nightly miracle, the sampan had disgorged one set of passengers and crammed within its bulwarks another. Never quite sure how I had got aboard, I would stagger up two more companionways, emerging from pandemonium to the somnolent peace of First Class European – the top deck. It was like ascending from the Inferno to Paradise. In winter I would find a coal fire still burning on the hearth in the saloon, a saloon usually empty, for Yangtze passengers went to bed early. Ordering a hot rum toddy I would sink back into a leather chair and let rum and glowing coals warm my frozen limbs. Around the corners of the deck-house shrilled the wind while the steamer throbbed across shoals on her dark passage downstream.

Yangtze travel was the advertiser's dream of tranquil luxury – comfortable cabins, attentive servants, complete respite from the clock in the leisurely processes of waking and dressing. Tea and toast in bed gave way, when one felt up to them, to a hot bath, and breakfast, and a day spent in a deckchair watching the River's mild beauty, watching reedy banks slip by, willow-girdled villages, distant mountains, whose furrowed slopes the sun picked out in gentle undulations of light and shadow. To remind us that we were in China a pagoda would come into view, a white spire piercing the blue sky. So relaxing were these voyages that I dreaded getting back to the world, and prayed for the occasional night of fog when the ship had to anchor, and Shanghai was postponed till late in the second day.

Even the older ships gave this gift of complete release from shore-side cares. Some indeed, were so old that their passengers slipped back half a century to side-wheelers. Such were the vessels of a pioneer Chinese firm, the China Merchant Steam Navigation Company; ungainly craft they appeared, their paddle –wheels straining out the Yangtze in muddy-crested foam beneath huge round paddle-boxes, while atop the deck-house the walking-beam kept up its perpetual see-saw. Oldest of these was the *Kiangfoo*, reputedly knocked down and transported in cases from the Mississippi. Like all her company's ships she was painted the yellow she had worn in Imperial days. Old though she was, and sluggish against the downstream current, *Kiangfoo* was better liked by Chinese passengers than any of her modern successors, partly because they respected her venerable estate, but also because she had never suffered a serious accident. She was a "joss" ship. Her cabins belonged in a sailing ship, in the clippers that were traversing the oceans when she was launched; they were not copied from hotel rooms, as was soon to be the fashion. These ancient craft were a floating tradition, and so were the officers who manned them, English, Norwegian, Dutch, most of them grown up in sail. The Chinese were even slower than the Japanese of the same era in learning how to handle their own ships; they made do with foreign deck-officers. Their engineers too were traditional, Scotsmen straight out of Glasgow, shrewd, companionable men who kept their machinery throbbing so smoothly as to allow these engineers unlimited leisure on deck where, in talk to the passengers they ranged the Seven Seas. It was one of these Scotsmen, filling his pipe from leaf tobacco he himself had cured in rum, who voiced for me the most compact of all philosophies: Never trust a man who says "Ya" for "Yes."

On my removal to Wuhu, however, I saw the River from another angle. I travelled by junk. This was as much a practical measure as romantic, for it saved crating furniture or going to elaborate lengths to pack books and dishes and porcelains. All I did was hire a small junk at Anking, where my stuff had been stored, and have everything stowed in the hold. On top of this cargo the laodah, the junkmaster, and his crew laid floor boards. These boards were my bed, allowing me just enough headroom under the curved, matting shelter amidships so that I could sit up and read. On good days I pulled out one of my wicker chairs and sat in solitary state on the deck forward. The crew were quartered aft, and with them my cook, who served me Chinese meals, buying provisions each evening from the villages where we tied up – and wielding, as his wand of office, the ivory chopsticks which I had brought for my exclusive use!

What the river steamers travelled in a night took us a week. We could move only in fair weather, for my furniture, although it occupied much room, made very light ballast. When the winds were strong we bounced around so strenuously that I feared lest my dishes be smashed.

But our start had been propitious, favoured by bright sunlight and a wind in the right quarter to drive us forward. Since junks of this river type do not tack, a following wind was necessary to our progress. We were one of a fleet, our brown sails, like the others' pierced horizontally by bamboo poles that did the work of roofing points. Neither swift nor easily maneuverable, we plodded along fast enough to overtake huge timber rafts, overbuilt with

81

villages where families lived for weeks and months and helped their down stream drift by plying long sweeps, or "yu-lo," to the rhythm of a drum. By evening we had shoved our squared bow against the muddy bank of our first stopping place, the village of San Kiang K'ou.

Next morning broke with rain and wind, too stormy for any junk to loose its moorings. On the second morning we did cast loose, but only to make one turn into the rough water and hurry back to shelter. I had long since exhausted the attractions of San Kiang K'ou, a straggle of houses along the river bank. As my private yacht lacked sanitary conveniences, I had to go ashore from time to time, not having the aplomb of the crewmen, who squatted over the side in full sight of the populace and let nature take its course. They, of course, attracted no attention, but a foreign devil thus employed would have drawn spectators by the hundred, all gaping intently and commenting loudly over processes we prefer to keep private. On shore my search for privacy had luck but little better. No matter how far I slipped past the village nor how carefully I picked some nook screened by hedges, I soon had my public!

After two days and three nights of San Kiang K'ou, we finally broke away, lured by the promise of sunshine. The promise was deceptive. By noon the wind was kicking up such a sea that I insisted on our seeking shelter. We were off an island which looked entirely suitable. The boatmen thought otherwise. We were in pirate territory, they argued, and sure to be attacked if we lay over for the night. Our only recourse was to get round this island and steer for Wei Chia Pao, a village a mile or so across the River. The laodah put two men ashore, one pulling a line attached to our mast-head, the other, a rope fastened to the bow. Straining against the wind and helped by the laodah's manipulation of the yu-lo, we warped around the point and sped upstream to the security of Wei Chia Pao.

My one inspection of this village, an excursion attended by a motley entourage of children and dogs, deceived me for the moment into thinking that we were back at San Kiang K'ou. Yangtze villages have a family likeness, a family composed entirely of poor relations.

By this time I was growing inured to the casual quality of River travel. The outside world of newspapers and mail had disappeared across a horizon almost shut out by the high banks of a stream that had receded to its mid-winter low. Shrunk though it was, the Yangtze was still a giant, never less than a mile wide; hour by hour it pushed seaward often against storms that lashed its brown waters into a turbulence which only the large junks, the sea-going lorchas, dared face.

Some years before, I had gone for a night and a day up the Grand Canal.[20] Compared to sailing the Yangtze it was like railway travel contrasted to an ocean crossing. On the Canal we travelled indeed in trains, trains of houseboats towed by a steam launch. Each houseboat was divided into small compartments set below the deck line and each pierced by two tiny windows and a door. All night, all day, we were aware of fellow passengers barely removed from us by the thin boards dividing their compartments from ours. Children wailed, old men snored, groaned, kept tapping out their brass pipes; we were beset by high-pitched talk, by laughter, by mothers crooning their babies to sleep, and at all hours by the shrill voices of tea-boys as they squeezed along the narrow decks and stopped from door to door to scream their wares. Scenery there was none. The canal banks shut us in. Only when the launch ran aground, which happened every few hours, and we were free to scramble up to the top of the dyke did we realize that we were travelling twenty or thirty feet above the surrounding country. When we arrived, after dark, at our destination we had to descend a slope to the lamplighted gate of the city. For two thousand years, instead of dredging its accumulating silt, the Chinese had gone on building up the dykes of this narrow waterway until it overhung field and town - a perpetual menace.

Travel on the Yangtze was more spacious, and lonelier. On fair days we had company enough: the junks moved in a stately procession or spread across the river's broader reaches like a flock of huge-winged birds, but there were times when we seemed as remote from other human contact as if we had been set afloat in far stretches of the Pacific. It was a different river from what the steamship's passengers, comfortably settled in deck chairs, looked down upon as they sipped their Bovril. Its shipmen lived to themselves, and I found myself doing the same, measuring the days not by thought of what was happening in America or Europe or even in the port I was headed for but by the villages it would be our lot to tie up in each night, and by the sociable small talk of the tea-houses, the dark, dingy hovels, smothered by smoke from lamps fed with vegetable oil, which to the junkmen offered all the heady excitement of return from sea.

But still through foul weather we came at last to a metropolis, Tatun, and on the final day to clear sunshine, and a fresh breeze that sped us, amid a fleet of sails, toward our destination. The wind did not last; our sails drooped idle, their pattern of bamboo poles reflected from the Yangtze's glassy surface. But Wuhu was in sight. Hours would go by before we reached it, for we had to navigate the curves of an immense "S" in the river's tortuous course. The current dragged us around these interminable bends. Seated forward in my wicker chair, absorbing all the warmth of the February sun, I was sorry to contemplate my journey's end, sorry when it came time to step ashore and to pick up again the needless complications of an existence which telegraphed its troubles from continent to continent.

* * * * * * * *

Wuhu initiated me into the life of a treaty port. It contained a considerable community of Europeans and Americans whose reason for being there was trade, China's hypothetical four hundred million customers. As in other ports they lived outside the Chinese city but, quite differently from other ports, their homes were scattered over a wide area, not squeezed into each other's back yard. This was a happy contrast to settlements like Kiukiang, where there were rumoured to be twenty-one families and twenty cliques, the only person exempt being the doctor's; everybody had to stay on good terms with him! In Wuhu the foreign residents lived so far apart that when they met at the Club, as they met almost daily, they were glad to see one another.

This friendliness had some restrictions. When I first arrived, the wife of the Commissioner of Customs, the colony's social arbiter, gave me a list of the people on whom I could call without compromising my status. She was maintaining the old world distinction between "indoor" and "outdoor." The office staff of an oil company, for example, could join at the card table or the billiard table with the staff who handled machinery at the installation, they could associate at the Club, but they could not be invited to dinner together.

Certain other rivalries sometimes came to the front. In the absence of a consul – except the Japanese, who didn't count! – the question was always moot as to who was the community's proper leader. Any attempt by the Commissioner of Customs to assert such dominance was resented and often rebuffed by other residents who claimed that, although he might be – as usually he was – British by nationality, in function he was a Chinese official, and not entitled to speak for the foreign community. This rivalry produced one episode, exceptional in Wuhu but typical of other ports.

One December, word came that a British monitor, *H.M.S. Mantis*, would be in port for Christmas, news which prompted the senior British resident to summon all British subjects to meet and plan entertainment for the ship's company. Unfortunately, he set the meeting at the Customs Mess, the bachelor quarters of the Customs staff's junior members. To this, of course, the occupants had agreed but no sooner had his invitation gone the rounds of the port than he received a curt reminder from the Commissioner that he and he alone could call meetings on Customs property. Once again the chit coolies trudged from house to house carrying a notice that the meeting at the Customs Mess to plan entertainment for *H.M.S. Mantis* had been cancelled – only to be followed, an hour later, by a new notice, this time from the Commissioner of Customs, inviting British subjects on the same date and at the same time to meet at the same place, the Customs Mess, to plan entertainment for the sailors of *H.M.S. Mantis*.

Childish exhibitions of this sort were not peculiar to the China ports; they simply were more conspicuous. Under the conditions of outport life, it is amazing how well these tiny foreign enclaves conducted themselves, amazing that in a port like Wuhu there was so little quarelling and – still more remarkable – so little scandal. Westerners in these settlements lived always under double strain, the strain of preserving amicable relations in their own group, so confined that every face, every voice, became too familiar, and the infinitely tenser strain of their relationship to the Chinese. Marked off by alien features, alien complexion, alien habits and speech, they lived not just in a glare of publicity but of notoriety. Everything they did was known, gossiped about, misinterpreted. Often it had its amusing side as with the newly married Asiatic Petroleum company manager who had put a wedding gift, a framed copy of the once sensational nude, September Morn, over his mantel, only to overhear his compradore explain to some Chinese touring the house, "That is a picture of his wife."

Because, in the large, their contact with Chinese was closer, the missionaries felt this constraint less. Racial distinctions vanished. But the ordeal of being stared at never lessened. Few things did I enjoy more than strolling through Chinese streets, yet I generally wore dark glasses; these ostrich-like tactics somehow made me feel invisible.

Missionaries, from the nature of their work were more sensitive to Chinese opinion, and some were morbidly sensitive, stultifying themselves at every turn with,

"What will the Chinese think?"

To this the best reply was given by a breezy colleague who assured one queasy questioner,

"They think everything you do is crazy – so why worry!"

Much that was unfair has been written, sometimes by missionaries, about the secular residents of the China ports. They have been abused as mere money-grabbers, bleeding the Chinese for what they could extract, obtuse to Chinese culture, swaggering rough-shod over a cowed people; they have been denounced as carpet-baggers, adventurous, unscrupulous upstarts who in their own countries would have been ill-paid clerks yet presumed to impose themselves as lords on the East they were exploiting.

Little of this was true. After the first World War some riff-raff did drift out to the China coast; they began compromising Western credit by fly-by-night schemes, but the foreign community as a whole had won Chinese trust by its honesty and integrity. The Chinese knew better than Westerners themselves where to draw the line.

85

I boarded a Yangtze steamer with the wife of a friend, both of us bound for Shanghai. She had been bragging about the convenience of her chequing account in a new bank which permitted cheques for less than ten dollars. Aboard ship we each wrote a cheque for our passage to Shanghai. Presently the boy returned, saying, "Compradore no savee this cheque, Way Foong more better." "I see the convenience," I remarked smugly, as I replaced my friend's rejected cheque with one drawn on my account. The compradore was prescient. Not long afterward the new bank failed, involving in its heavy losses many American depositors.

The Wuhu residents included few, if any, adventurers. The harshest criticism that could be made of them was that they knew too little of China. Missionaries too were liable to this criticism: while in Nanchang, I was visited by an English archdeacon who had come from the coast by roads seldom travelled by foreigners. He appeared just after I had acquired a long sought treasure, the Nanchang Fu Chih, or Annals of Nanchang, a work in twenty-nine volumes beautifully printed a century before from hand-cut wooden type. Eagerly I produced it for his inspection. "Yes," he remarked, casually turning a few pages, "but these books are always so full of legends and myths which you don't want!"

There was, similarly, the reply of a missionary from Japan to a professor under whom I had studied and who had asked him questions about Japanese Buddhism. "Oh," he retorted, "we have no time to bother with Buddhism. We are superseding it."

Just as too many missionaries studied Chinese only to put across their own argument – they had come to tell, not to ask – so too many Westerners in commerce limited their Chinese to what they could utilize in making sales. But there were many exceptions, even in the trading community, men pursuing their own lines of interest in Chinese art or Chinese religion.

It was the interest of two Englishmen, one from the Asiatic Petroleum Company, the other from the Customs, which led me in their company to visit Kiu Hua Shan[21], the Mountain of the Nine Flowers, one of Buddhist China's four sacred mountains. Travelling in an A.P.C. motor launch we steered inland from the Yangtze at Tutung and soon were winding along a stream clear as green crystal into a sequestered valley where life drowsed serenely indifferent to the fret of the world we had come from.

The hillsides flourished with groves of camphor and pine, and between them were meadows where cattle grazed and bamboo swept up the slopes in plumed waves. In the evening, after shallow water had forced us to anchor, we sat on deck utterly relaxed by a sense of peace which it was impossible to believe that bandits could ever disturb. From farm roofs and brick kilns blue smoke and grey twirled idly toward a windless sky. Kiu Hua Shan, towering to an outline as sharply serrated as a giant's jawful of teeth, had all the components of a Chinese painting, abrupt cliffs entwined by a scarf of mist, mysteriously disappearing valleys, the day's last sunlight picking out furrowed glens and loitering on the peaks.

At night fireflies by tens of thousand danced around, a luminous spectacle we could not admire undistracted because mosquitoes, outnumbering even fireflies, pounced so savagely that, unable to sleep under their assault, we shortened a long night as best we could by much beer, and talk keyed to splendid nonsense.

Next morning, our chair bearers met us. A harder way of earning a living I cannot imagine; the chairs themselves were heavy, their wooden frames roofed and enclosed with rattan, yet we had but two men to a chair, two men stiffening to the pressure of the poles across their shoulders as they bore us mile after mile through the foothills. Each man's hire for three days of such toil amounted to about a dollar in American money. During these three days they were to walk no less than fifty miles and to climb and descend two thousand feet not by easily graded zig-zags but up and down rough stone steps. Whereas Chinese without compunction employed their fellow men as beasts of burden, few foreigners could feel easy over such staggering service. We ended our three days by tripling the agreed sum and, no doubt, starting China's age-old economy on the road to inflation.

After a day's travel through spectacularly beautiful country, ravines often framed by the lofty half-circle of a bridge, we began the final climb, a climb so steep that at times we were sitting on their necks. Since this was not the pilgrim season we saw none of the devotees who could be met with at other times. Hundreds of miles they used to come, stumbling along the rutted wheelbarrow tracks that passed for roads, plodding through the towns' frantic activity, carrying on their backs a shrine into which smoking incense sticks had been inserted, pausing every few paces, no matter how they impeded traffic, to prostrate themselves in the road.

Much more cheaply we entered the gates of heaven, the arches spanning the path. Each gate was numbered, the First Gate of Heaven, the Second Gate of Heaven, and so on in mounting series to the dizzying heights of T'ien T'ai. From temples beside each gate we could hear monks droning their sacred syllables, O-mi-t'o-fu, the Chinese alliteration of Amitabha, or Buddha, and glimpse their prayer wheels spinning. The whole mountain was occupied in worship or meditation. Clinging to shelves of rock on the bare face of every precipice were hermitages which an alpine club would have had trouble reaching. Almost at day's end we wound into a broad upland valley. Here was Kiu Hua Shan's chief settlement, a concourse of white-walled monasteries, all – except a 16th Century library – rebuilt after their destruction by the

T'ai P'ings. None of them pretentious, they half hid themselves in the serene company of great trees.

Most beautiful of all was the monastery where we lodged, the Shang T'san T'ang, or Hall of Meditation. Its pilgrim quarters, empty at the time, were immaculately clean. A miracle in itself, no bedbugs disturbed our sleep. From a wrought iron balcony grazed by trees that rose forty feet to the first branch, we could look down upon a mountain stream tumbling through a narrow, boulder-strewn gorge. Its music, pleasantly tinkling, mingled with the faint echoes of Buddhist chants, the sharper tones of bell and drum, heard at all hours from long before dawn, when the monks began reciting their daily office.

Monasteries, Buddhist or Christian, have much in common. Each consecrates the day's changing phases by appropriate worship. Only half awake we could hear from our hostel chamber the Buddhist equivalent of Mattins; some of the later offices we attended, watching from a gallery that overlooked the temple. Although not conversant with the liturgical idiom nor with the rubrics that dictated the right use of bell and drum, two of us came profoundly under the influence of those offices, sung as they were in the benign presence of a gigantic, kindly-faced figure of Buddha; the third member of our party thought them no better than shallow routine. But the lofty sanctuary, three stories high, impressed us all. Its most unusual feature was a sky-light that revealed not only the great Buddha and his accompanying divinities but every detail of the fine carving expended on the altar and even on the sturdy roof beams. It revealed also what we were to note in Kiu Hua Shan's other temples, the dedicatory tablet to "the reigning Emperor." Eleven years after the Revolution these shrines still did not recognize the Chinese Republic.

Like Buddhism's other sacred mountains, Kiu Hua Shan honoured a Boddhisatva, one of the special manifestations of Buddhahood. The particular divinity signalized here was Chin Ti-Tsang, in this earthly incarnation a Korean prince who, twelve hundred years earlier, had established himself here to become in effect the patron deity of the lower Yangtze. His tomb, reached by precipitous steps and capped by tower and pagoda, looked down upon the far-spread plains of the Great River, a site aptly supporting Ti Tsang's guardianship of the millions who inhabit that rich alluvial region; for the sake of these millions he had foresworn his well-earned right to Nirvana and engaged himself to toil amid the world's misery until the last human soul had been redeemed.

Some earnest of his spirit we gained from an evening talk with the Abbot, a man of gentle speech and interested in connecting his belief with ours. There were other attitudes less praiseworthy: a young neophyte came to me, as I was setting up my camp-cot, and suggested himself as a bed-companion. When I declined, he became quite surly. Like any centre of professional religion, Kiu Hua Shan presented the high and low extremes of faith, and often queerly mixed. Some aspects of its sanctity revolted us.

In the last category were the mummies set cross-legged on several of the altars. This phenomenon was not confined to Kiu Hua Shan; several temples in and around Wuhu displayed these dessicated saints. The recipe for attaining this type of sanctity (as published in the China Journal) requires the candidate to subsist for months on flax-seed and minute quantities of water until he has lapsed into a comatose state where only the vapour of his breath on a mirror can indicate that he is not dead. This state may last for weeks. When all sign of breathing has ceased, his body is doubled up in a huge earthenware jar and packed around with charcoal. After three years the jar is broken: if the body has decomposed, he obviously was not a saint. If it is intact, it then is gilded, robed, and placed in a temple where it so closely resembles the other, man-made figures that, in all that I have seen, only the stubble of a beard piercing the gilt betrays the fact that this once was a live man.

These mummies I resented. They lacked, when one recognized what they were, the serene dignity of the man-made figures, what with unfair implication we term "idols." In Nanchang I once visited a factory where these figures were being made, fold on fold of grass linen wrapped around a central core of carved wood, then lacquered and gilded and painted. I even photographed them, gods still incomplete because the little cavity left open at the back awaited the sacred characters, the talisman, which at their consecration would be sealed in to give them souls. These are not gods in our meaning of the word but symbols, aspects of the divine exhibited in visible, humanly intelligible shape.

But a dried corpse, the withered shell of not only an outlived but deliberately stifled life, for me at least did not share their dignity nor offer any worthy reason for veneration. It was as meaningless as the Christian hermits, our civilization's earliest flagpole-sitters, posing on pillars. Like the Puritanism which has defaced Christianity from our early centuries it presented sainthood not as embracing responsibilities but escaping them.

Perhaps they had more meaning than I perceived, perhaps they were a grim reminder that Buddhist philosophy, though generally softened in China to accommodate human cravings, is essentially nihilist. To be happy is to become nothing. Many must be dissolved into the unseeing, unthinking, unfeeling power that underlies and breathes through all existence. Absorbed in Nature he must shake off the pangs of personality.

In this respect the monasteries of Kiu Hua Shan lived in peace with their mountain valley. They were one with its trees, its massive rocky cliffs, its low, rain-spilling clouds. There were no cathedral spires, no challenging towers; the only loftiness was exhibited by T'ien T'ai, whose monastery surmounted a precipice a thousand feet above our heads. Everywhere were notices, it is true, imploring pilgrims to pay for gold leaf to repair the T'ai P'ing devastation of sixty years before by gilding gods and temples. We watched one craftsman at work on a carved figure – he kept still to be photographed in a twelve second time exposure! But what splendour such builders produced was quite incidental to the lovely accord of plain white walls and grey tile roofs, growing out of their quiet mountain valley, never seeking to dominate it.

Two days in a place as sacred as Kiu Hua Shan are too few to appreciate it adequately or even fairly. It sheltered charlatanry as well as pious devotion, the commercialism that preys on pilgrims as well as holiness. But we came away awed by a sense of nobility. Gladly we would have stayed longer and let this soak into our souls. Even though each of us reacted to its influence in different ways, and one of us quite critically, we gave the place our respect.

I, for one, remembered the retort made to a friend of mine who, on an earlier visit to Kiu Hua Shan, had been facetious about the fat-bellied god of wealth, often referred to as the laughing Buddha.

"What is he laughing at?" he demanded.

The monk to whom he put this question did not, for a moment, hesitate over his reply

"He is looking at you," he said.

* * * * * * * *

Kiu Hua Shan, it goes without saying, was a far cry from Wuhu. In Wuhu we seldom saw a consul; we paid him a dollar a year to register us, the only tax of any kind that we paid except the 5% tariff on goods imported from abroad, and went about our affairs with nobody, native or foreign, to give us orders. Because, unlike most treaty ports, we had no concession, no area set apart for our occupancy, we had no municipal council, no regulatory body of any kind. We still were subject, naturally, to the laws of our respective countries but, unless we started murdering people, or indulging a taste for embezzlement, we were a happy no-man's land where neither the Chinese authorities nor our own presumed to trouble us. This in itself would suffice to bathe my memories of China with a golden glow - no taxes, no regulations, but a freedom such as our present bureaucrat-ridden world is too tightly shackled even to imagine.

The Wuhu community did not abuse this freedom. Laws could not have made them more law-abiding, and this despite the fact that their backgrounds were dissimilar, French, Belgian, Dutch, Scandinavian, Italian, Czech, Portuguese, as well as British and American. Their bond was the English language, in which all were fluent. Many of them were brilliant men, a fact always evident at the dinner parties, which were the port's commonest social entertainment. These dinners were an end in themselves, not a prelude to the theatre nor, except on special occasions, even to cards or dancing. Guests were invited for eight, expected to arrive not before eight-thirty and, after sherry or gin-and-bitters, to sit down after nine. The seating was formal, the dress formal, and the meal itself a carefully planned series of courses each matched to the right wine. Dinners of this kind, of course, depend on an abundance of servants, on the hostess's serene assurance that nothing is left for her to do but give the number one boy a glance when she wishes plates removed or glasses filled.

One thing was not left to the servants – the table talk. Whether the cosmopolitan nature of the guests was responsible or the proper stimulus of the wines I cannot say, but rarely have I known any social gathering to match the scintillating quality of the conversation. Up and down the table it sparkled with a wit and verve that compelled everybody's interest and precluded that bane of good dinner talk, the breakup into two or three topics discussed simultaneously in a competition of a raised voices. It was an art practised so skillfully and gracefully by men and women alike that they chimed in like the players in chamber music.

Before the port wine the ladies withdrew, the host moved to his wife's chair, and started the decanter on its solemn round, each man passing it from his right hand to his left and taking care that it neither moved backward nor touched the table. Joining the ladies could be a delayed business, but not always for the naturally assumed reasons: ribaldry often took second place. One host, a passionate adherent of Voltaire, held us at table for an hour with lengthy quotations in French which he flattered us by assuming that we understood as fluently as he spoke them. Straining to look intelligent and laugh in tune with his soft-voiced chuckles we waited restively till his wife sent a servant to prod her abstracted spouse.

On another occasion I lingered, long after the port, with a friend, a zealous Roman Catholic convert who, years later was to end his days in West China as a Franciscan friar, but not till after a career so recklessly wild that his employers, spurred by the British government, shipped him home. On this particular night, long before he assumed the brown habit of St. Frances we were drawn into argument about the efficacy of Prayer. Fortified in his case by a bottle of Benedictine, and in mine by a bottle of Curacao, we talked ourselves into a stalemate. By midnight, when we were reminded of our duty to the drawing-room, we had been forced to abandon our discussion: neither of us could pronounce "efficacy."

It might be guessed that the Wuhu community was not exactly abstemious. This was true not only of Wuhu but of any treaty port. China hands were redoubtable drinkers. The captain of a British cruiser, transferred suddenly from the East India squadron to meet the Communist menace in 1927, told me that the Nanking residents in six weeks had drunk up stocks of liquor calculated to last their wardroom two years on the India station. Yet this drinking leaned to gaiety rather than ugliness. Never have I forgotten the withering remark of a Scotsman to whom I remarked in jest, "If this keeps on, I shall be under the table."

"Gentlemen," he chided, "are never under the table."

This standard characterized pretty fairly the port's social life. Any man whom liquor made either maudlin or combative suffered not just the disapproval of his fellows; he risked the punitive censure of his company. One old company made its Wuhu manager postpone his marriage for a year until he had proved able to abstain from alcohol for an entire year.

Alcohol flowed freest on national holidays, particularly the British and American. British subjects celebrated both Empire Day and King's birthday, Americans held open house on the 4th of July. These observances began with champagne and cocktails at noon, and to them were invited both the Chinese officials and the Japanese consular staff. Toasts of course were proposed, it being my function, whether the day were British or American, to translate these toasts for the Chinese guests. These versions I had my Chinese teacher prepare in advance, since they called for properly formal remarks in high-flown literary style. That my remarks never bore the slightest resemblance to the toast offered in English did not matter. The senior British resident, for example, was the most nervous of speakers. His toast never varied: "Gentlemen, I wish to propose the health of His Most Gracious Majesty, King George," yet to make sure that he should not forget this brief sentence he brought it typewritten; even while he read it, his hand shook and his tongue stammered over each word.

I then launched forth on my teacher's masterpiece, welcoming their "jade toes graciously advancing," and paraded an ornate series of mixed metaphors. This speech I had memorized, for the elegant rhetoric could not be tampered with any more than Milton could have been mixed with James Whitcomb Riley. It lasted perhaps five minutes. Although interpreters are always more long-winded than the speakers they struggle to explain, five minutes to translate one sentence would have been excessive in any country but China.

To the beaming officials it was exactly what the august occasion required. They now could turn their attention to the drinks.

A major sport of these national holidays was to get the Chinese officials drunk. Into this sport the officials themselves entered with a will. They were never concerned about preserving a dignified appearance; intoxication in public, as anybody visiting a Chinese restaurant could note, was no more blameworthy than it would have been to an 18th Century English squire. When the men of the foreign community came up to them one by one to click glasses, they did not hesitate to drain theirs. By the hour's end they were affably maudlin. This state their bodyguard expected; for these soldiers to support their staggering masters to their rickshas, or even to carry them, was routine.

The same methods were attempted with the Japanese consul and his staff, but in their case without success. Smilingly the consul would take the glass proffered him, but after a sip or two he would hide it behind a flower vase or in some other place conveniently inconspicuous until the club-house was gaily studded with the Japanese consul's cocktails. Only once did any member of his staff ever display undue gaiety. The next week, he was shipped back to Tokyo.

After the hosts, whether British or American, had slept off their noonday toasts, they returned to the Club for tea and to stage games for the children. One Fourth of July the Americans signalized by serving mint juleps, and imbibed so freely of their own mixture that none of them woke up for tea. After a half hour's wait the British took charge, passing around tea-cups, managing the children's games and at last – in the words of one Briton – avenging Cornwallis's surrender.

The usual end of festivities was a concert. To make this a success the port preferred, if available, the services of a gunboat. The British sailors, in particular, were adept at such entertainment, too adept, in fact, if they had been given too much beer. Their sketches were clever, one of the most amusing a caricature of an Anglican clergyman under the name of the Reverend Cuthbert Cheene. The sailor who put on this caricature did so with an ultra-refined Oxford accent (if there is such a thing!), - yet in actual life he spoke only cockney. The pride of a ship's concert, however was its songs. Each song had a great many verses, starting out innocently but growing more ribald the further they progressed. To make sure that his men stopped in time, the captain sat in the front row, barely an arm's length from his performers.

British sailors were not served spirits, but beer could do strange things to their discretion. Close to the start of one concert they embarked on a very promising song about the adventures of a tom-cat. Its refrain was, "It can't last very, very long." The refrain was prophetic. By the third verse the captain was restless, by the fifth he was squirming. Just as the sixth was getting under way he shot up from his seat. The song stopped. At his signal the men began "God Save the King" – and the concert was over.

Measured historically, China outport life itself did not last very, very long. Whether it was more artificial than life at home is doubtful, but beneath its surface lurked always a sense of exile, of ominous undercurrents. Its fervent engagement in sports, in tennis, soccer, golf, its absorption in social pleasures, hid but thinly the fact that it was a life pursued in sufferance. Pressing at its gates were the teeming masses of China. Never far out of mind was the thought of how quickly they could be spurred to become mobs and incited by hot-tongued agitators to smash down these gates. When this agitation was turned ever more fiercely against Japan I remember the words of a French Jesuit whom I used to visit:

"Our turn will be next."

World War I marked the turning-point. Even before this war Japan had initiated the steps of aggression which were to solidify China as a nation, but the absorption of the Western powers in their own cat-and-dog fight set Japan free to push this aggression to absolute domination of her great, sprawling neighbour. In the 1890's she had defeated China only to have Europe snatch from her hands the fruits of victory. This time she was confident that no outside power could prevent what seemed China's certain vassalage. But she forgot to take into account the Chinese themselves.

In the 1890's China had not learned to think as a nation. South China took no part in the war with Japan; it was the North's war. Twenty years later the Revolution, futile though its apparent results, had fomented a nationalism which was to react like a nest of hornets to each attack. Japan had to back down from her first demands, the infamous 21 Demands pressed on Peking in 1915, but she smoothed her first blunt approach too late. Every measure she tried only embroiled her further with this new and unexpected China. She was confronted by a resistance she could neither crush nor conciliate, a habit of resistance which did not stop with opposing Japan. As the French priest had predicted, our turn was next.

Few would have guessed this in 1918 when the European war terminated in armistice. In response to Woodrow Wilson's invitation China had declared war on Germany, she had responded to the clarion call to make the world safe for democracy. To Wilson's appeal, however, she only gave lip service; her real motive was to participate in the peace conference and to checkmate what she foresaw would be Japanese claims on her own territory, especially on the German interests in Shantung which Japan had displaced to substitute her own.

94

In the first world war China did almost nothing, but when it came to celebrating the Armistice she outdid her allies. By huge mass assemblies of rejoicing, by innumerable holidays, by fireworks and flowers and feasts she seemed bent on convincing the world that her part in the war had been the most glorious of all. A visitor would have thought China had won the war single-handed. Anking, where I was then living, came behind no other city in the jubilance of victory. The school year nearly disintegrated under the pressure of endless rehearsals, all coming to a climax in procession after procession – schools, guilds, soldiers – marching endlessly through streets literally walled and roofed with chrysanthemums.

In the final procession I took a spectacular part. The French Jesuit priest had arranged that the Postal Commissioner (an Englishman) and I have lunch with him and that we go in sedan chairs to the Civil Governor's *yamen*[22], where Père Noury was to be a speaker and China's Allies honoured in a great assembly and feast. For a state appearance of this kind I needed a silk hat to match the frock coat, outgrown by several inches, which the Commissioner, a friend of long standing, had given me. To supply this need did not look simple, but I remembered the one rule that always worked in China: when confronted by the impossible, entrust your problem to the cook. When I sent "Ta su-fu" out on the street to find me a silk hat, he showed no surprise. In half an hour he was back with a top hat that fitted me perfectly; he had rented it for fifty cents from a member of the long extinct Provincial Assembly. In my hastily acquired dignity I could have passed for an ambassador.

The huge gathering in the courtyard of the Governor's *yamen* was perhaps the only one of its kind; it was certainly the last, the single occasion of which the heroes were Western barbarians, China's Allies in a war she had won without firing a shot. Our popularity made us acutely uncomfortable. To see this great open space packed with the students from the many government schools, all in uniform and waving our assorted flags, to see them according the place of honour to their often reviled rivals, the mission schools, these were distinctions to which we had trouble adjusting ourselves. But we did not have to adjust ourselves long. In a few months we were back in our usual role of villain.

China soon learned that to be on the winning side was not sufficient. She lost the peace. At the bargaining table Japan had the louder voice. Although her participation in the war had amounted to little more than seizing for her own use Germany's Far Eastern colonies, no nation from an exhausted and war-weary West dared challenge this occupancy, certainly not by force nor on behalf of a China whose soldiers understood no military activity except civil war.

The outcry which greeted the Treaty of Versailles was to swell, with ominous momentum, through the 1920's. The unwonted "Love your neighbour" theme of the Armistice celebrations was quickly displaced by "Hate days," an exercise at which the students were much more adept. Japan still was the main target, but anti-Western hatred gathered steam with each passing year. Slowly China was learning how critically the slaughter of 1914-1918 had enfeebled her one-time conquerors. The time was vanishing when a tiny gunboat, mustering perhaps thirty men, had only to drop anchor alongside a city of half a million to guarantee the security of its hundred foreign residents. A train en route from Nanking to Peking was seized by bandits, and its passengers, many of them American or European, forced to trudge barefoot into the mountains whence, for six weeks, the Peking legations, despite the armed might they represented, strove ineffectually to get them released. Our old immunity was crumbling. People noted parallels to Boxer days, but this was not an uprising bred of fanatic superstition: the West now being challenged had been digging its own grave.

None of us who lived through those years understood where it all tended but the immediate signs of change were uncomfortable enough. No longer would I have dared sail down the Yangtze; I would have been taken and held for ransom. Two years later, the Shanghai police fired on a Chinese mob. The country seethed. In Nanking, which I had to visit at the time, boy scouts, complete with staves and water canteens, were placarding the telephone poles with exhortations to kill the foreigner. The only person unperturbed by this turmoil was an Anglican priest, an Englishman, whom I stopped to see. Seated in his sparsely furnished lodging, eating Chinese crullers which his servant bought on the street, he was reading, without a Greek lexicon, a tragedy of Sophocles.

Most of us could not emulate his serenity. We watched the creeping threat of communism, hatched in the south, but beginning to reach out hungrily toward the rich provinces of the Yangtze. In 1925, Sun Yat-sen died. He was of the type that succeeds better as agitator than administrator; many regarded him as the froth on the wave that unseated the Manchu dynasty. Pushed out of office in Peking, he had eventually taken control of his native Kwangtung and its great port, Canton. Although, in this hotbed of revolutionary ardour, his rule was notable chiefly for his welcome to Russian agents and their doctrine, he continued to shine in Chinese eyes as China's supreme patriot. On his death a determined effort was made to deify him, to make him a second Lenin. His body was embalmed and placed in a glass coffin, for which a mausoleum was erected in Nanking. At the time of his death his name was potent. Even the least politically minded of the foreigners who made up treaty ports like Wuhu could not shut their eyes to its menace.

After Sun Yat-sen's death probably every school in China held memorial exercises. I attended one such meeting in the boys' school to which I was attached in Wuhu. A Chinese teacher had been delegated to give the funeral oration. While we were waiting for the boys to assemble he chatted with the rest of the faculty in our staff room; his moments of final preparation were certainly not Lincoln's at Gettysburg. He was laughing, smoking cigarettes, telling flippant jokes. Not for a moment, we would have said, did sorrow for Sun Yat-sen cloud his mind.

Yet the instant he entered the assembly hall he became a changed man. When he began his speech he faltered, wiped his eyes, choked on his words as if overpowered by a grief too tremendous to express. Slowly he gained headway against this emotional tide, his voice rising, his gestures beating out every strident phrase, until his audience sobbed and groaned in a response so furious that I half expected them to tear us limb from limb, the two or three foreigners on the platform, and to burst out of the hall hell-bent on a sortie of arson and murder. But at the right moment he hushed them. He knew exactly what he was doing. His entire speech was acting, clever acting, nothing more. Sun Yat-sen meant nothing to him. What he saw was the opportunity to align himself with the winning side in a civil war soon to split China. Profiting by this chance he gave up teaching; teaching had no future. He turned to Communism, made his home an agency for flagrant propaganda, a meeting-place for conspirators, not because he cared one way or the other about the abuses it was supposed to correct but only because it opened a sure way to wealth and power. Against such a menace logic was dumb.

Sun Yat-sen was dead, but his heir, Chiang Kai-shek, was very much alive. Aided, almost encircled, by Russian military advisors, Russian diplomatic advisors, he converted the threat of Communist invasion into fact. The first Yangtze treaty port to be overrun was Kiukiang. Wuhu, two hundred miles nearer the sea, knew that it was living on borrowed time. A feeling of "After us the deluge" possessed the foreign community. It gave bent, entertainingly enough, to a cycle of elaborate costume parties.

First of these was at the Commissioner of Customs mansion, which had been transformed into a cherry orchard. For weeks the Commissioner's gardeners had been making artificial blossoms. The high-ceilinged rooms glowed with spring's delicate colours as his guests, some of them wearing kimonos specially ordered from Shanghai, assembled in the great hall.

Other dinners followed, the most notable one at which the Deputy Commissioner, a Frenchman, was host. Preparing for a party advertised as East of Suez, with any costume in order from a burnoose to a g-string, he spent two months transforming his main rooms into a Turkish seraglio. All this he did himself, using cardboard to put in a false ceiling, false walls, false columns. The painting also was his handiwork, designed as a brilliant background for the Bakst[23] costumes which he had copied from a book of prints for his own dress and his wife's. So overwhelming was the scene on which the doors were opened that his guests were too stunned to be gay. Dinner began as solemnly as the Mass.

Sir Edward Grey, the British Foreign Secretary, when at the outbreak of war in 1914 he made his often quoted remark that the lamps were going out all over Europe, and that we should not see them lit again in our time, showed a prescience even vaster than he knew. It included not one World War but two; it included a Western ascendancy which, whatever its faults, maintained justice and schooled its subjects in ways of peace and freedom more adequately than the rabid nationalism of countries prematurely born, or the Communist imperialism of a Russia that has outbid the Czars in the tyranny it seeks to clamp on men's minds and bodies. Civilization's lights were to be extinguished by nothing so obvious as the savage blackness of war but in the glare of a bomb exploded over Hiroshima. In that awful brightness man's security was to be extinguished forever.

Compared with what was to happen the extinction of China's treaty ports was but a tiny footnote to history. Yet they had seemed so substantial. After living in cities like Anking and Nanchang, where we dwelt always under the threat of mutinous troops or agitated mobs, I thought of Wuhu as a bulwark of safety[24]. Little did I guess how shaky that safety was to prove. We must review first, however, the endless tangle of civil war in which, neutral though they tried to be, the treaty ports were involved. They were to vanish like the votive lights we use to watch from the banks of the Yangtze.

On the fifteenth of the eighth moon, tiny boats, each illuminated by a paper lantern and bearing a food offering, were set adrift on the River's powerfully moving current. The moon, of course, was at its full – Chinese months always began with the new moon – and the night was aglow with heat into which the first autumn coolness had not yet insinuated its foreboding of winter. Yet bright though the moon shone, it could not dim the twinkling radiance of these little boats, whole fleets of them, green, yellow, red, swiftly moving down stream. The food they carried was an offering to the spirits of men who had been drowned, spirits which, neglected, might prey on the living and drag new victims beneath the water. When the candles inside the lanterns guttered out, the Chinese believed that their gifts of food had been accepted.

The sight never failed to stimulate my imagination, the spectacle of coloured lights by the score gleaming on the River's surface, and then their disappearance one by one until but two or three remained. With a concentration almost frantic I would watch those final survivors: the blue light would vanish, then the yellow, but a single green light would continue headlong down stream, defying extinction – and then, when we half hoped it might outlive its doom, it was gone. There was a sudden emptiness of moonlight flooding the Yangtze's glossy turbulence.

The treaty port lights too went out quickly when their season was over. They were like so much else on what the White man had prided himself, so much out of which he expected to evolve a world where freedom and justice (in Tennyson's words) "would slowly broaden down from precedent to precedent." But man was ahead of himself. His achievements were as frail as the paper lanterns, coloured yellow and red and green and blue; for a moment they shone bright, only to be snatched all too soon into darkness by the evil spirits of hatred and jealousy, of suspicion, fear, and cruelty.

The lights are out; in the dark ages through which we grope it is doubtful if we shall ever see them lit again.

* * * * * * * *

When I first went to the Orient, the Republic of China was little more than a year old. The new order had been hailed in America with extravagant expectations, in Britain more guardedly. So narrowly had China escaped being divided between several European powers that the pessimist could not be faulted for seeing no future promise but weakness, a weakness not likely to be corrected by imposing on China's chosenly aloof world an unfamiliar political system.

Fifty years and several revolutions later, China has swollen to a huge menace, threatening the free world by a military strength, and an intention of using this strength aggressively, such as we dare not measure. Those who knew China best would have been the last to predict what China did with that strength in North Korea. The German Emperor's prediction of a Yellow Peril – which men used to ridicule – has turned out an uncomfortable reality. Like everyone who lived in China through the chaotic years of the first Republic I am still asking the question, How did it happen?

The fall of the Manchu dynasty in 1911 should have been no surprise. It had lasted not much short of three centuries, the normal span of the more durable dynasties. Concubines, eunuchs, court favourites had sapped its strength as they had corrupted its predecessors, the Mings, the Sungs, the T'angs. In the past, after each dynastic collapse, China had awaited some leader strong enough to found a new Imperial family. Often she waited a hundred years or more while competing factions fought to ascend the dragon throne. Occasionally, as with the Manchus, the new leader came to power at once by destroying the weakened remnants of the preceding regime. But however the change was managed, it was managed with but little outside interference. In her remote corner of the world China towered supreme; she had no neighbors able to challenge her right to work out her own destiny. Mongols and Manchus, it is true, did conquer her, but only to let Chinese civilization conquer them.

In 1911 the situation was unique. No strong man had toppled the Manchus; they had destroyed themselves. Li Yuan-hung, the general whose army had dealt the terminal blow, had been pushed into greatness. An amiable nonentity, he could not have been more surprised by the easiness of his success. The uniqueness of the setting in which this success was won lay in the fact that China now was part of a larger world. Not only were there several powerful nations concerned about her future, and with armed might poised to shape that future to their own ends, but there were new ideas, less tangible yet potent as a tidal sweeping upon her from abroad.

These novelties had their most conspicuous proponent in the perennial agitator, Sun Yat-sen, who seized upon the Revolution as his chance. He dragged in his train a republic, a parliament, a swarm of provincial assemblies solemnly decked out in frock coats and top hats. Under his prompting, the Chinese were incited to discard all the beautiful symbols of Imperial rule.

This feverish eagerness to reject the past showered unexpected emolument on those, like myself, lucky enough to arrive in China just after the institution of the Republic. Official coats, magnificently embroidered, were a drug on the market. I bought several, one of the 18th Century from the middle years of Ch'ien Lung, its background of plum-coloured satin solidly overlaid with gold threads all couched with peacock's feathers. The price was the usual one – about eight dollars. Such was the glut of these official coats, every one splendid with dragons, that a friend of mine bought for his brother in America a dozen of them so that the brother and a select group of classmates could drape themselves in this exotic finery for a college reunion!

I had gone to China advised by a knowledgeable acquaintance to search out porcelains in apple green celadon; little did I anticipate the treasures offered me, treasures so attractive even to my untrained eye that the curio-dealers drained every dollar I could spare, and more that I could not spare. So brief was this period, during which the Chinese in their fine republican frenzy took little account of how valuable were the things they were unloading, that in six months many of the bargains had gone. A dealer, for example, who had sold me a string of amber beads, a hundred in all culled from the strings worn by mandarins, soon offered me five times and eventually ten times the Mexican $15.00 which I had paid for them. Word had got around that in

Europe and America these rejected insignia of the Court dress were worth infinitely more than the song they were selling for.

Only one Imperial relique did I have trouble securing, the triangular, yellow dragon flag. When I mentioned this to my dealer, he gave a start of alarm and glanced around to make sure that no servants were within earshot, then promised he would try to get one. Some days later, in the privacy of my bedroom, he produced a dragon flag[25], extracting it with utmost caution from the inner recesses of his clothing. The dragon flag had been superseded by a five-striped flag representing the nation's five races, Chinese, Mongol, Manchu, Moslem, and Tibetan[26] – which, a generation afterwards, was to be ousted by Chiang Kai-shek's trite Kuomintang flag. In 1913, to possess the Imperial flag could have cost the owner his head, yet undoubtedly thousands of Chinese preserved it as they kept stored away their severed queues which, though badge of servitude to the Manchu rulers, they were more than ready to wear again if another revolution should restore their vogue.

The queues never came back to favour, but the dragon flag might have waved again under Yuan Shih-k'ai, the astute official who took over the Presidency from Sun Yat-sen. "What would China do without Yuan Shih-k'ai?" I used to hear during my first years in China. Not too long afterwards we were to receive the unhappy answer, but in the meantime Yuan had come within an ace of seating himself on the dragon throne as first emperor of a new dynasty, the strong man whom China needed.

Unfortunately, there was a blemish in his past which liberal Chinese could not forgive. In 1898, when the Emperor Kuan Hsu, long suppressed by his aunt, had conspired with his advisor, K'ang Yu-wei, to convert China into a constitutional monarchy, Yuan Shih-k'ai blabbed his secret to the formidable old Dowager, Tzu Hsi. If Kuan Hsu's attempted reforms had succeeded, the 1911 revolution might never have happened, but Tzu Hsi's eyes were only for the past, not the future. Seizing again the long usurped reins of government, she kept her weakling nephew prisoner in his palace until ten years later when, feeling her own death imminent, she seems to have had him poisoned, too vindictive to let him survive her harsh domination.

By this treachery – as it was regarded, though Yuan claimed with probable sincerity that his act was in China's best interest – Yuan established himself in such prominence that the nation looked to his leadership after the Manchus had fallen. An able and firm administrator, he deserved this eminence. As president he checked the Revolution's incipient anarchy.

Next, he had himself elected emperor, not of course by popular vote – popular elections are an experiment which China has never tried – but by select groups meeting in the several provinces. To start the ball rolling, the "safe" provinces voted first. Like Julius Caesar, Yuan Shih-k'ai put up the polite pretence of refusing the crown – and like Caesar he never got it.

In the spring of 1916 I saw the proclamations posted announcing the date when he would assume the Imperial dignity under the name of Hung Hsien. As customary at the start of a new dynasty, they were printed in vermilion. But before he could ascend the dragon throne, a revolt intervened. It began in Yunnan, remotest of the Eighteen Provinces, where Yuan would be hard put to squelch it. Although it gave every semblance of a spontaneous uprising, the force impelling it was not secret. Japan had no mind to see China ruled by a strong man. She had rushed to profit from the European War by presenting her 21 Demands which, if accepted, would have degraded China to a vassal state. Aware that Britain, France, Italy, Germany, and Russia were too deeply engaged to interfere, she had begun the long, cannily calculated march toward the East Asia Co-Prosperity Sphere and World War II. To achieve this, she needed a China weak and divided.

So swiftly did the revolt spread that Yuan himself was taken by surprise. He made a fatal mistake: he hesitated – hesitation which had but one result, the cancellation of his ascent to the throne. To revert to the title of President proved futile; he had suffered what to the Chinese is a fate worse than death – a monumental loss of face. His death, a few weeks later, consummated the tragedy. Whether he died from disease or poison or (the view accepted by most Chinese) from a broken heart matters little. The strong man had fallen, leaving China prey to the little men, the War Lords.

China, until the communists seized power, has seldom known a strongly centralized government. The Emperors ruled more by the mystical prestige proper to Sons of Heaven than by might of arms. Even when Yuan Shih-k'ai was strongest, he had no truly national army to support him. The armies belonged to the provinces where each military governor kept his own troops, responsible only to him. In general, they were poorly trained, poorly disciplined, uncertainly paid. Their military talent was exercised chiefly in practicing the goose-step and blowing bugles incessantly from early morning till late at night. Slovenly clad in padded, dirty-grey uniforms, they were scarcely separable from the bandits out of whose ranks many of them had been recruited. While Yuan Shih-k'ai was President, their master, the War Lords, paid him allegiance; after his death they were on their own, serving Peking only when this suited them. Each was sovereign in his own province. Theoretically, the *Tuchün* – as he came to be called, in succession to such picturesque titles as Tutuh! – consigned political administration to the Civil Governor, an arrangement like Rome's two consuls; as in Rome, the man with the army became boss.

*Tuchün*s were of many kinds. In Anhui we had one so suspicious, so fearful for his own safety, that on the few occasions when he had to venture out of his yamen, he first had all the shops boarded up along his route to the Yangtze, all doors and windows shut, all cracks plastered with paper, and he then deployed his troops facing the houses and with their back to him. This man, Nye Tzu-chung, had such a terror of assassination that he would board a gunboat to journey two miles down river to the parade grounds, where he would come ashore again to watch his troops drill. Eventually, his power crazed him. Knowing the arbitrary rages into which the tiniest provocation would drive him, his family would not let his grown son come into his presence lest, in an eruption of anger, he should order the youth shot – a sentence which they knew that his enemies would rush to execute before he had cooled enough to change his mind.

With men like this wielding absolute power, the situation that followed Yuan Shih-k'ai's death was simple to predict. It sank into civil war between ever changing forces. Coalitions formed, battled, dissolved. Last year's enemies were next year's allies. In classical Chinese fashion no war was fought to an ultimate issue; a loop-hole was left for the defeated general's escape, the victor knowing full well that his turn would come when he would expect from his enemy in victory the same favours, the same chance to escape which he himself had accorded him in defeat.

When a *tuchün*'s power began slipping, the signs were easy to read: he stopped paying his troops. The average tenure was about three years, during which the military governor would milk his province of all the wealth he could exact, even to enforcing payment of taxes as much as thirty years in advance. Such payment his successor would ignore; people would begin paying their taxes over again until many communities, a half century ago, actually had paid their way into the 21st Century.

The clearest signal that the *Tuchün* was about to decamp was given by the wheelbarrowmen. When we saw wheelbarrows stored in the gatehouse, we knew that they had bribed the gateman to keep them in what was still the inviolate sanctuary of a foreign compound. Bitter experience had taught them that, on the governor's disappearance, his soldiers would collect their back pay in loot, and then impress the wheelbarrowmen into transporting their plunder, a service for which their only remuneration would be blows and cursing.

It always happened this way, until robbery and rape were normal hazards against which the citizenry took what few precautions they could muster. But the foreigner was still immune. Western retaliation had been so inevitable that mutinous troops avoided trouble by looting only their own people, a safer diversion. Furthermore, foreign goods were difficult to dispose of, foreign silver too heavily alloyed to be marketable. But fear of foreign gunboats was the major reason why we could live unharmed while the city around us was being torn apart. It did not matter that the gunboats could have done little or nothing to protect their nationals; the flag, usually the White Ensign, was sufficient.

One January, when disorders threatened Nanchang, the British admiral sent us *H. M. S. Woodlark*, little bigger than an armed launch. Her complement was two officers and twenty-six men; her fighting equipment, two pompoms. One of these, the forward gun – so a navy legend insisted – had been crammed so often with slugs to shoot wildfowl that it was useless for warlike purposes. When the admiral came on inspection he would be shown the after gun, which had been kept in perfect condition, and then conducted below for drinks while the good gun was being shifted forward, over his head, and mounted on the foc's'le to be approved a second time. What truth there was to this story I won't vouch for - it was told of every gunboat in the Yangtze Patrol – but the little *Woodlark*, whether she had one good gun or two, obviously was not equipped to take on a city of seven-hundred thousand people. Despatched to the rescue because no larger ship could have navigated the shoals to Nanchang, she was reassurance to the tiny foreign community and, oddly enough, a comfort to many Chinese.

My first experience of Chinese soldiers on the loose was at Anking. Without warning on a hot night in early September we were awakened by rifle fire, an outbreak so near that when the houseboy came running upstairs shouting, "Ch'iang ta!" "Robbers!" I feared for one ghastly moment that bandits had burst into the compound. By the time I had dressed, not daring to light a lamp and fumbling stupidly for my clothes, it was evident that the shooting, while all around us, was not inside our walls. Bright though the moon was, we could see nothing of what was happening, but we heard enough to panic the imagination, the point-blank report of guns, men shouting, the clatter of agitated voices in a hundred Chinese homes. After an hour of these alarms, during which I made sure that the gateman had the front gate staunchly bolted, the shots grew fewer, the noises drifted away until long before dawn all was quiet. Only with daylight did we learn what had happened. A small detachment of troops had first killed their colonel and then plundered the silver shops and pawn shops, all of them our close neighbours.

Before day-break the mutineers went into hiding, too few to confront the city openly. What the people now feared was a large body of soldiers, five thousand in all, camped outside the city walls. These threatened to break into the city at nightfall and complete more thoroughly what the garrison had begun. The whole day Anking was in a state of siege, the gates closed, river water hoisted in buckets over the city walls. When I came home after dark from across the city, I took wry amusement in noting that the many interior gates, barred barricades designed to shut off each important street in a crisis, had been pulled tight – but left unpadlocked. The policemen, who normally would have challenged me at every barrier, had vanished. They had no stomach for opposing mutinous troops on a rampage.

What weighed most on our courage was the silence that descended on the city at nightfall. Ordinarily in this stifling heat, which the full moon seemed to radiate with a searing brightness that dazzled the eyes, a Chinese town laughed and gossiped and cried and yawned and groaned and grunted and snored in a public hubbub which did not subside until long past midnight. Into the streets families would haul their bamboo cots to get what gasps of humid air they could snatch, or at least to swelter with their neighbours in sharp-pitched chatter. Anking in summer was a huge outdoors dormitory.

This night, however, everyone was within doors cowering behind barricaded gates. Not a sound rose from any of the houses adjoining our compound. Anking had become a city of the dead. So tense was this fearful silence that when I sat outside on the lawn talking to a friend we conversed in whispers – and even our whispers seemed to resound from wall to wall. Like the frightened populace smothering in the steam-bath heat of their dark, airless houses, we were waiting. The whole town was waiting. From far out in the country we could hear a dog barking, but nothing else; any moment we expected the stillness to be shattered by rifle shots, blood-curdling yells. Finally, about two o'clock, too exhausted to listen further, I went to bed and, happily, to sleep.

I was awakened by the sun shining bright on my bed. Nothing had happened. The threatening troops, we learned, had been bought off by the Chamber of Commerce.

Other situations came with which Chambers of Commerce could not cope. In January 1927, after half the lower Yangtze had been overrun by Chiang Kai-shek's Communist forces, the governor of Anhui, still allied to Chiang's opponents, requested from the Wuhu Chamber of Commerce Mex. $300,000 to pay his soldiers. To this demand the merchants were ready to submit; a $300,000 ransom was cheaper than being looted. But when the governor told them to pay the sum into his account with a Shanghai bank, the Chamber demurred, knowing full well that any money deposited in the *Tuchün*'s Shanghai account would never reach his troops.

The merchants' refusal to pay this blackmail soon brought reprisals. Again there were shots at night, but this time the looting was orderly; the soldiers who did the plundering were directed by their officers. Disdaining hit-or-miss plundering, they confined their attack to the banks, the silver shops, the Post Office. Officers signaled each attack by blowing whistles and, when satisfied, recalled their troops with whistles, aligning them in formation before marching to their next objective. To make sure that no assets had been overlooked, different detachments followed on another in raiding the same victims. A Chinese friend in the Postal Service told me that the Post Office was looted five times; much of the night he spent at guns' point, expecting to be shot. The profits from the night's orgy amounted to several million dollars, an increase great enough to prove to the Chamber of Commerce that a *tuchün's* request is not wisely dismissed.

Yet two months later this same *tuchün* turned over to Chiang Kai-shek. In a public proclamation he accepted the Kuomintang's principles of democracy, freedom, and justice, and posed, unblushing, as a saviour of his country. He was not the only one. Once it became clear that Chiang's was the winning side, warlords by the dozen tumbled into his camp – which explains why Chiang Kai'shek's government, a generation later, collapsed from its own corruption. Under new slogans and a new flag, these robber barons continued their extortions, and Chiang had no choice but to accept them, to rule through them, and to let them besmirch his name in the eyes of the people.

Chinese wars, after all, always had been fought in this way. Victories were not by combat but by negotiation, and the loser rewarded by the winner. After the second World War, when the Communists gathered strength and Chiang Kai-shek's star was on the wane, these grafting officials sought a similar accommodation from the newest victors. To their discomfiture, the Communists were less sensitive to the niceties of Chinese military tradition: they negotiated, they made peace with their new allies, they accepted them but then – in gross disregard of Chinese etiquette – they shot them.

* * * * * * * *

Since Mao Tse-tung's victory in 1948 and its ominous sequel in Korea, people in the West have forgotten – if they ever knew - that China's first communist revolution came to a head twenty-one years earlier, in 1927, and under the leadership of Chiang Kai-shek. Although the Western nations took strong measures to halt the overturn, measures such as for the time appeared to have checked the Russian-inspired and Russian-abetted threat, this for treaty ports was the beginning of the end.

Led by Great Britain, the West joined forces to meet this crisis. Britain alone transferred some thirty ships to the China Station and dispatched 27,000 soldiers to garrison Shanghai against the grim likelihood of a general massacre. To this force the Americans, Dutch, Spanish, Portuguese added their detachments while the French guarded their own concession – and the

Japanese held aloof, hoping that Chinese resentment of these forces would lessen their own unpopularity. The mainstay of the army so hastily transported was a battalion of Coldstream Guards – the first Guards regiment ever sent east of Suez. Instead of resenting them, the Chinese seemed entertained by their notable visitors, whose name they translated in the newspapers as "Ping Shui Chun" or "Ice Water Troops!"

This singular lack of resentment was shown by two Chinese soldiers who approached friends of mine in the street and asked what they must do to join the British Army.

"But why do you want to join the British Army?" asked my friends.

"Oh, we like their uniforms; they have so many brass buttons – and the soldiers look so well fed."

"But if you joined the British you might have to fight your own people."

"Ah, that doesn't matter – pu yao ching – we don't mind!"

The guardsmen on sentry duty outside General Duncan's Bubbling Well Road headquarters were a spectacle that engrossed Chinese crowds by the hour. In untiring admiration they gawked as the sentries marched way from each other until two hundred yards apart when, at precisely the same instant, they turned and in perfect step marched toward each other to their meeting-point outside the General's door.

Soldiers under such discipline were, to the Chinese mind, more effective than a battle although, by Anglo-Saxon standards, their discipline was not called on to match the heroism displayed by British sailors, three months earlier, at Hankow. Never once employing force, this small detachment held the British Concession against the daylong provocation of a mob that showered them with brickbats and mocked them with defiant taunts. Coolies would rush up to their line, baring their breasts, daring the sailors to fire, and getting in retaliation nothing worse than cockney jests from armed men whose only defence was their sense of humour. The lives of many Americans and Europeans scattered throughout central China depended on the restraint these men showed.

At Wuhu too the Navy bulked large. We benefited by the assignment of destroyers from the Mediterranean, first *Verity*, late in 1926, then in turn *Wild Swan, Wyvern, Wolsey*. So suddenly had these ships been shifted to China that they had gone direct from target practice in Greek waters, leaving the wives of the squadron stranded at Malta where they had just set up housekeeping for what should have been a two years' tour. However discomforted they might have been by this dislocation of their social life, the officers of those ships were a tonic to ours.

For the men, the stay was more irksome. Since a crisis so tense limited their excursions ashore, the captain of *Verity* asked me to lecture to his crew about

107

China and the Chinese customs about which they were doomed to learn only by hearsay. So well did this talk go that the men themselves requested me to request the captain to request me to give a second lecture – which request he granted gladly! The British sailor was more diffident toward authority than the American; he would have been shocked speechless had he heard the captain of an American destroyer hailed at a ball game by, "Here comes Benjie." His diffidence I learned more embarrassingly when I invited a petty officer to tea.

Sharp to the minute the man arrived; his departure was less prompt. He stayed, in fact, until too late to return by his six o'clock liberty boat. Conversation lagged. Everything we talked about dragged almost immediately to a dead end. Since he made no move to go, I had no option but to invite him for potluck. It was a meal of mumbled monotones spaced out at inordinate length by tedious, frantic silences. At last, the meal was done with; we returned to the drawing room – but still he showed no sign of departing. In the end I was forced to ask him whether he did not have to return to his ship; the hour was almost nine o'clock, and the last boat, I knew, left at nine. With an alacrity that startled me, after the evening's snail's pace, he jumped to his feet, said good-night, hustled out the door like a schoolboy dismissed from detention.

Next morning I mentioned his stay to the captain.

"But he was waiting to be dismissed," the skipper explained. "You should have told him to go. Poor devil! He must have been on pins and needles all evening wondering how he could escape."

The China Station in happier days had been one of the royal Navy's most desirable assignments. Aboard *Hawkins*, the flagship, I met a lieutenant-commander who had spent an earlier tour, years before, on the Yangtze. In those idyllic times the ships had not yet been fitted with wireless, a blessed lack which permitted his gunboat, when the Yangtze was flooded, to stray far afield. As the river subsided, she was left high and dry until late the following spring. Completely and delightedly out of touch with Admiral and Admiralty, the ship's company enjoyed a winter's shooting in one of the world's most prolific game regions – pheasant, duck, geese, snipe, bustards, marsh deer, all were theirs for the asking. They might even have a go at tigers and leopards.

Those days, alas, were gone; the ships dispatched so hastily to preserve us from massacre had to put up with duller times. The arrival of American destroyers to share their vigil eased their boredom. Each navy suffered its own disability, the American because it could not serve drinks aboard ship, the British because it could not afford to buy drinks ashore.

In Shanghai, where his higher pay gave the American sailor a competitive advantage in the purchase of such commodities as female favour and strong liquor, it made him the centre of much combat with the men of other navies, and not least with the "limeys' as he called his more politely but less accurately named British cousins. In Wuhu, where neither women nor liquor could be bought, the two navies were really cousinly. Back and forth between destroyers the men went, the Stars and Stripes host one day, the White Ensign next, and few things stranger have I heard than the American gob calling out "Cheerio" to the British tar as they boarded their respective liberty boats at the pontoon.

It was the symptom of a collaboration between the two navies which was to bind them ever closer as the crisis in China worsened. For once, the Americans had the freer hand – topsy-turvy contrast with earlier years when boldness had been British policy. In 1908, for instance (as a British officer told me the story), British and American gunboats were anchored at Nanking when news reached them of a riot at Anking. At once, the British ship prepared to rescue its nationals, and its skipper, noticing that the American ship was getting up steam, asked the captain if he was going to the aid of the Americans at Anking.

"Nothing doing!" exclaimed the latter, "We are going to sea for target practice. This is an election year."

In 1927 things were different. Unfettered by tight orders, the American ships cruised up and down the Yangtze with guns swung out and crews itching for action. The British had no such licence. The Foreign Office was seeking to salvage its relations with Chiang Kai-shek's movement, and wanted no brash naval officer imperiling its diplomacy; consequently, the Admiralty had been pressed to warn all commanding officers that rabble-provoking incidents must be avoided; they were ordered to employ no force except – as a last resort – to save human life. Destroyer and gunboat captains were turning grey over the dilemma they confronted: whether they acted too quickly, or too slowly, they would be blamed.

To make this dilemma more harrowing, most of these skippers were lieutenant-commanders, two-and-a-half stripers, a rank of which the Royal Navy – thanks to the Washington Treaty[27] – had more than plenty. Unless they could gain their third stripe before they were forty-five, they would be retired on half pay. With the Admiralty seeking every excuse to weed them out, one mis-step meant a career cut short. Yet there was the tantalizing thought that the China crisis might afford chances of promotion if they did the right thing at the right moment – chances they would not have encountered in the duller peacetime routine.

One lieutenant-commander won his third stripe by utilizing just such an opportunity. Without firing a shot his destroyer and a little gunboat captured a whole Chinese army – five thousand men – and three generals who had commandeered a British river steamer. They intercepted the stolen ship, nudged it ashore at Kiukiang, cleared it of troops, and even made the generals tote their own baggage across the pontoon. Ironically enough, the Kiukiang populace, far from being pleased over this invasion by their own soldiers, stoned them as they came ashore. This exploit, so neatly carried out, was the envy of every two-and-a-half striper on the River.

In Wuhu, where several Chinese expressed to me their hope that Britain would send a strong force upriver to allay disorder, our secret knowledge of how little the Royal Navy dared attempt dimmed what comfort the ships might have brought us.

My connection with the Navy had grown steadily closer. Since the destroyers, detached one by one to Wuhu had no chaplains, I had consented to read the Church of England service each Sunday morning. My first ship was *H.M.S.Wyvern*. Unable to come before eleven, I was requested, if possible, to finish by eleven-thirty; at that time the week's allowance of rum was dispensed from an oaken cask decorated by bold brass letters that proclaimed, God Save the King. Even the Book of Common Prayer could not trespass on a rite so sacred. When I managed to end precisely at seven bells, and without stinting hymns or sermon, the captain promptly wrote to the Admiral's secretary recommending me for a temporary appointment!

This appointment I did not take up, but I continued to conduct the services, as requested, even graduating to a small cruiser, *H. M. S. Caradoc*, which had been sent to reenforce the *Wyvern's* successor, *Wolsey*. In *Wolsey* I was also allotted the captain's sea-cabin in case living ashore became too dangerous. Although I never occupied it, for the simple reason that when I needed it Wolsey had been sent on half hour's notice to Nanking, I was able to enjoy dinners in the wardroom, and the intriguing punctilio of a British naval mess. Every evening we had the toast to the King but because the Mess could not afford port wine each night, we drank the toast dry: the Mess president would rap the table with his little hammer, saying, "Gentlemen, the King," whereat all would lift empty glasses and repeat, "The King. God bless him."

If there happened to be wine for the toast, this came from some unfortunate who had broken Mess rules and been assessed a fine. These rules were stringent. Anyone coming late to dinner must first have his apology accepted before he could sit down; anyone reading at table was punished, even if his offense was no more than perusing the name and address on an envelope. But the rule which paid off most regularly was the one that forbade mention at table of any woman. By great good luck we had aboard another civilian refugee, an Irishman from the Customs Service, who could not open his mouth without advertising his predominant interest. His past had been an unbroken series of titillating conquests - conquests which kept us in liquor.

Wine and song we still could indulge in; the women were gone. They had been evacuated to Shanghai. To achieve this took a real emergency. Like many of the outport men, I belonged to the Wuhu Defence Corps, formidable name for a far from formidable body. We had guns, but to make sure that we did not use them *Wolsey*'s captain had commandeered our entire arsenal and put it under padlock – which was just as well since none of us had ever seen these guns, much less tried them. What damage we might have done to a Chinese mob was far less predictable than the damage to ourselves.

The glorious function of the Wuhu Defence Corps degenerated into waking people, people who did not intend to be awakened. Each of us was assigned families on whose doors he was expected to pound, with instructions that all women assemble at the Butterfield & Swire hulk before daylight.

Daylight had come before I could get the families on my beat even to acknowledge this summons. Some time between three and four a handful of gravel tossed on my verandah would startle me out of bed – the signal that the situation was critical. Hastily, between yawns, I would grope for my clothes, stumble down stairs, set out on my rounds. Most of my clients were missionaries; only after turning a deaf ear to my knocking would they consent at last to give me grudging heed. Their excuse was always the same: they could not desert their flock. From some the plea was valid; the Sisters, for instance, had a girls' school which they could not disband to the winds. From the majority such a statement was silly. It was not their absence but their presence that endangered their flock, who would be risking their own safety if they had to protect or try vainly to secrete anybody as conspicuous in China as a foreigner.

When the emergency finally burst about our heads, however, it had been heralded by warnings so ominous that most of the women were ready to go. The crisis had been precipitated by the Governor's turn-over to the south, to Chiang Kai-shek and the Communists. This had let loose agitators of every brand – "every firebrand," would describe them better. To make matters worse a Jardine ship, *Kutwo*, had sunk a Chinese military launch, traveling on a dark night without lights. A hundred and twenty soldiers, it was rumoured, had been drowned.

Although no reasonable man could have blamed *Kutwo*, agitation disdains reason. The culprit ship was detained at Wuhu under armed guard. By improvising a Spanish windlass, the Chinese even raised the sunken

111

launch and planned to parade the hundred and twenty bodies through the city. This parade never came off. Instead of the hundred and twenty corpses the promoters had hoped for, the number actually exhumed was too few to make the stink, both literal and figurative, on which they were counting. Furthermore, as the Chinese governor was demanding from Jardine's three thousand dollars apiece for men dead whom he would not have valued at three hundred dollars alive, he was not eager to disclose how few they were.

Hysterically distended, these events set the stage for a monster demonstration, scheduled to hail the revolution and, in the person of a Russian speaker, greet the Communist promise to deliver China from its Western persecutors. What this demonstration would bring in its train was a question to which our little foreign community could think up only grim answers.

Ceaseless inciting of hatred already had provoked violence. Schools had struck; pupils were busy haranguing their elders. They operated under a newly potent Students' Union whose leaders had broken down every barrier between the sexes, enlisting girls – and, as one cynic noted, always the prettiest girls – for their committees. Yet when they called together delegates from the mission schools to recite a long list of wrongs suffered at the hands of their foreign oppressors, it was a girls' school alone which was brave enough to disclaim any abuses. To the demand as to how their foreign preceptors treated them, they replied, "Like father and mother." Instead of complaints, they spoke of good food, a pleasant garden, and iron beds to sleep on.

"But you are forced to study the Bible and go to church," their inquisitor maintained.

"No," said the school's spokesman, "nobody forces us. We do this because we like to."

For this unexampled display of courage the girls were hooted at and cursed all the way home.

Aggressive disorder, however, broke out in another quarter, an attack on the Customs. Far from being spontaneous, this was fomented by a Chinese who saw his chance to seize the whole system of Native (or internal) Customs stations. On a visit to the Customs House that noon I had noticed the loungers collecting; as I walked away, some stones were thrown after me, an attack I ignored although it was an uneasy experience trying not to quicken my pace or look behind me while expecting any moment to be felled with a brickbat.

By late afternoon the loungers were a mob, spurred on by paid demonstrators. Miles upriver we could see a customs station going up in flames while immediately below us the mob were attacking the main office, their voices shrill with blood-curdling war-whoops as they began looting.

112

Since the promoter of this outbreak was interested only in wrecking the offices, the looting did not spread to the homes of the Customs staff on a hill a mile distant. Violence was still tentative. The worst sufferer was the Customs Club where frenzied Chinese hacked the billiard table with axes, tore the felt hammers from the piano with their teeth, and rushed on to rip apart the volumes of the library, a library collected in years past by a scholarly Commissioner and unique in its valuable and irreplaceable books on China. The old, beautifully printed pages were scattered to the winds to be gathered by peasant women for wrapping cabbages.

After guessing at this vandalism from what we could see of scurrying rioters and, worse yet, what we could hear, we waited only till nightfall to bring in the women from their outlying homes. The *Wolsey*'s captain had advised us that the British Navy was despatching a cruiser. When dawn came, there she was, anchored off the Bund, *H.M.S. Emerald*, six hundred feet long, an imposing and welcome sight. Her commander, Captain England, had wasted no time cutting loose the Jardine steamer, *Kutwo*, from the Chinese soldiers who had been holding her for ransom. Safely moored in mid-stream, she became a refuge to which he transferred the women. His boldness had dampened all resistance.

"When there is a bone of contention," he told me, "my policy is to remove the bone."

For some of us, however, the protection we could count on, even from a six hundred foot cruiser, was a question mark. We had duties on shore which we could not desert, while between us and the safety of the river bank the crowd was assembling, pouring toward the meeting place like columns of ants. On the level foreshore, in a piece of land ordinarily used for soccer games, a platform had been erected. Here, we knew, the orators of the day would whip their twenty thousand listeners into white-hot passion – of which we, watching from the hilltop, would be the first target.

We were a very small group. Among us were the Sisters for whom I was responsible. As their chaplain, it had been left to my judgement to tell them whether to go or stay. Actually there was no room for argument. They had a girls' school on their hands; until arrangements could be made with the parents, their pupils could not be turned loose. Except under the perfervid auspices of the Students' Union, whose interference we did not admit, respectable Chinese girls did not go out on the streets unchaperoned. Whatever our personal risk, we could not betray the trust imposed by families who expected that our first concern would be to safeguard their daughters. So we stayed.

With us was one other woman who had insisted on remaining with her husband. Neither she nor her husband was sylphlike; this is understatement

– their dimensions were rotund. Since our only escape route lay across two miles of rice paddy to the oil company installations where – if we were lucky – a destroyer would pick us up, the more agile of us faced the ludicrous prospect of fighting a rear-guard action while this couple waddled toward safety. But even this escape route was not left to us: at the most critical moment a company of northern soldiers, defeated in some action down river, came straggling single-file along the dykes we had counted on using.

Not until this disconcerting juncture did the wife see the light.

"Then I am not helping my husband at all," she exclaimed.

"Exactly," I told her. "You are making it almost certain that he won't escape."

"Oh," she mused. "I didn't think of that."

"We tried to tell you," I reminded her ungraciously; hers had been a door on which I had pounded vainly before dawn.

"Well, I'm ready to go now," she announced.

"And just how are you going now?" I asked.

The demonstration on the Bund was reaching its oratorical peak. To have attempted pushing through the tightly packed crowd would have been suicide. If the mob moved to attack us, we could expect no help from *Emerald*. Powerfully threatening though her guns looked, unlimbered and pointing shoreward, we knew their menace was a bluff. Before the ship could even know we were in danger, we should have been overwhelmed. Haunted by these thoughts every minute of the sun-bright morning, we sat rooted to our hill-top porch, wondering what the next hours had in store, what would happen when the meeting broke up.

From the speakers' platform came the high-pitched notes of Oriental oratory. What was being said we could not distinguish; its meaning we could guess at all too well. What we did not guess was the effect produced by the single Russian speaker.

His harangue, scheduled to blow high the flames of revolution, turned out farce. Chinese en masse are a volatile people, their reactions unpredictable. In this case the sound of Russian spoken, its gruff, guttural stresses, prodded the crowd's funny bone. Men began to laugh. Laughter changed to mockery. The tension of the assembly, already stretched to the snapping point, suddenly relaxed. The crowd recognized not a prophet inciting them to heroic violence but an awkward foreign devil speaking uncouthly.

None of this, of course, did we know at the time. We could make out what seemed to be laughter sweeping across the huge gathering, but, so far as we could tell, it was the crowd's response to some jeering hateful sarcasm. For hours we had kept vigil, exhausted by the meeting's tedious length yet dreading its breakup. When, after unbearable suspense, the end came, we watched through eyes strained by dread of what would come next, trying to hide from each other the expectation that we should be torn limb from limb by a mob whooping for the kill.

The crowd, closely packed, appeared to hesitate, moving backwards, forwards, like a huge, stupid monster sluggishly testing its strength. This monster the students were doing their utmost to lash into action. Their rabid summons we could hear all too distinctly,

"Kill the foreigners!"

"Burn the foreign houses!"

A fringe of the crowd broke off in our direction.

But there were saner forces at work. The Merchant Volunteers, an organization of local vigilantes, had determined to keep order. To secure this they were armed with long staves which they wielded with astonishing vigour. If a student came riding by seeking to inflame the crowd into violence, they knocked him off his bicycle, sent him sprawling across the hard ground. Breathlessly we followed every turn of this contest, whose outcome could be lethal, though it seemed to be waged by toy figures against the unreal backdrop of the British cruiser, her steel sides, painted light grey, glistening in the warm March sun, her white ensign barely fluttering above the Yangtze's muddy current.

The vigilantes won. Their shouted orders, enforced by their clubs, took effect. Headed by drums the procession had re-formed and slowly but ever more surely moved back toward the city. By mid-afternoon the field was clear, with but a scattering of litter to mark the crowd that had trampled flat its withered grass. Taking my chow dog to the Butterfield hulk, I passed him across the barricade which the *Emerald*'s landing party had erected, and watched him handed from sailor to sailor, licking their faces with his black tongue as he went.

Less nimbly I was boosted over the picket-fence bulwark to follow him aboard a steam pinnace and by a transition almost magical in its swift change from mortal peril to stalwart safety, up the companionway to *Emerald*'s quarterdeck.

A major of the Royal Marines greeted me. He put exactly the right question,

"What will you have, Padre?"

"A whisky soda," I answered. I did not need to remind him to make it stiff.

* * * * * * * *

The *Emerald* did not stay with us long. A smaller cruiser replaced her, *H.M.S. Caradoc.* But she remained long enough to dispatch the women of the port – or all who would go – under escort to Shanghai. It was an eerie, night departure, with lights out so as not to draw fire from the forts downriver, and white-faced wives peering anxiously through the gloom at the husbands they were leaving. *Emerald* even played host to other women who arrived from back country mission stations too late to sail in the *Kutwo.*

Large though she was, she had scant space for such hospitality. When two elderly spinsters arrived the best she could offer them was a junior lieutenant's cabin, a cabin liberally placarded with pictures from La Vie Parisienne. These alluring sketches of girls at every stage of undress were a startling foil to the two little missionary ladies, whose shiny serge skirts had been padded out by bustles and petticoats and, one need scarcely surmise, by woolen union suits, but however shocking their introduction to the French demimonde, to chemises slipping off pointed breasts and stockings gartered up to the swelling contours of naked, enticing thighs, the missionaries kept their composure.

Next morning one of the pair approached the Engineer Commander, mistakenly believing that it was his cabin she had occupied.

"I want to thank you for the use of your room," she said, "I shall pray for you," and, with a twinkle in her eye, added, "I think you will need it."

The Engineer commander was the one to lose his composure. A bearded, completely respectable man, he had no pictures on his walls except photographs of his wife and children.

One by one we persuaded the few remaining women to depart although, in the case of a woman doctor, "cajoled" rather than "persuaded" was the word. Room had been provided for her in a Butterfield & Swire steamer which the company's agent detained over night, but so violently anti-British was she, more rabid than the Chinese themselves, that she came to his office demanding that she be served Chinese "chow;" British food she refused to eat.

Exasperated by her complaints, the agent, a peppery Scotsman, told her to go to hell.

"Well, you're on your way," she retorted sweetly.

Hell, it turned out, was to be the lot of the Nanking community, forty miles down river. Our first sign of trouble came when the American Admiral Hough's flagship, *U.S.S. Isabel*, went tearing downstream at full speed, swamping sampans and rocking the moored hulks with her wash. I had gone to the Bund, unsuspecting any crisis, only to find that my other home, *Wolsey*, also, had departed pell-mell for Nanking.

At the club, in the terse dispatches sent to *Caradoc*, we snatched dismaying glimpses of what our sister port was encountering. On Admiral Hough's orders, we learned, the signal had been given for American and British ships to open fire. Before we could adjust our minds to the stupendous possibilities of this action, another dispatch came, saying,

"Cancel preceding order," and, hard on its heels, a further one,

"Have opened fire (at 3:40 p.m., I think it was) as a last measure to save human life."

Some human lives – we learned later – American, Japanese, Italian – already had been lost in what had swelled into an attempted massacre of all the foreigners in Nanking.

Slowly the details sifted through. The Chinese Sixth Army, the same Communist force, which had passed through Wuhu, had gone berserk. We ourselves had known unpleasant moments during their stay, for their officers, strutting along the Bund, each had been escorted by a pair of trigger-happy guards, mere boys brandishing cocked pistols. The luck which spared us all except the threat of violence had failed the Nanking community, but when it became evident that these grey-uniformed ruffians were bent on rape and plunder – outbreaks to which Nanking history has been peculiarly liable – a concerted attempt was made by the foreigners to transport their women and children to a place out of the direct path of the marauding troops. The refuge, prearranged, was the Standard Oil compound.

Nanking had a curious topography. Its wall, twenty-six miles in circumference, enfolded not only the densely settled city and the adjacent foreign compounds; it included also a ribbon of settlements alongside the road to the riverside suburb of Hsiakuan, but there were large hilly spaces of open country. On one of the hills, within the wall but also within sight of the Yangtze, the Standard Oil Company had located its staff, a site sufficiently remote to escape a mob's immediate attention yet visible to the warships at anchor.

Here, for a time, the refugees looked for security, but their hiding place soon was known. Unleashed by blood-lust, by the hatred of foreigners always latent in China, the soldiers began to converge on their victims. At this juncture, and not a minute too soon, a naval signalman who had been left ashore for just such an emergency, climbed to a rooftop to wigwag desperate warning of their peril. Soon his destroyer and her destroyer colleagues, British and American, laid down a barrage of gunfire around the beleaguered compound. Since the shells were bursting in open countryside, they were not hurting the Nanking populace but only men bent on mischief, the marauding soldiers.

The impact, however, was felt throughout Nanking. At the first noise of gunfire looting stopped, even in areas where no guns could have searched out the culprits. An amusing story was told of a foreign traveler, lodged at the

Bridge House Hotel in Hsiakuan, who was being relieved of his watch just as the cannonade commenced. So startled was the Chinese soldier engaged in robbing him that he handed his victim not only the watch he had just taken but another as well.

Our knowledge of these incidents drifted in later. For the moment, our concern in Wuhu was as to how our local populace would react to the news of foreign gunfire. Anxiously we braced ourselves against the upsurge of mob violence which, it had always been predicted, would follow such strong action. Every foreign community in China, we had been told, would be assailed by crowds roused to a frenzy over what would be reported as a fiendish massacre of their "womb brothers."

Nothing like this happened. Instead of inflaming the mob, this decisive bombardment quieted them. Our only uneasy moment came when Chiang Kai-shek, in his triumphant journey downstream toward Shanghai, stopped briefly at Wuhu – though my memory as to just when this visit occurred is so uncertain that it may well have come before, and not after, the Nanking trouble. However ecstatically he may have been hailed by his countrymen, Chiang Kai-shek to us was no hero but a menace, a menace enhanced by the Russian backing which he was so soon to disown.

His arrival at Wuhu was spectacular. Sighted long beforehand threading the snakelike bends of the Yangtze which make the approach to Wuhu exceptionally tortuous, the China Merchants steamship conveying the general had attracted a huge crowd. When the ship finally drew near, just before sunset, the crowd's concern – and ours – was where he would land. If he tied up alongside the foreign hulks, as had happened with one or two Chinese troopships, the British shipping agents and their families living aboard these hulks would have been overrun by the mob, certainly looted, perhaps murdered. Nor would murder have stopped there. Once again on our hill-top we had balcony seats to witness the unfolding of our own future.

This uncertainty the steamship's captain shared. Slowly his vessel slid along the Bund; the crowd followed. Off each foreign hulk its helmsman seemed to hesitate, wavering between ominous choices. By the time the big yellow-hulled steamship had finally pulled around into the current, preparing for a landing yet evidently still without orders, we had given up hope of anything but the worst. The crowd, vacillating from point to point, were as puzzled as we. But at last a decision had been made: slowly the ship picked up speed enough to bring her alongside the Customs pontoon, an official Chinese landing place. The danger was past. Chiang Kai-shek came ashore to be greeted hysterically by his multitude of worshippers.

Chiang did not linger; his crisis did. Although no outburst ensued on the Nanking bombardment, Communist activity was making the lot of the foreigner untenable. Northern soldiers, captured in the fighting, were quartered in our school chapel where propaganda officers mounted the altar to harangue them on Marxist doctrine. At the boys' school the pupils finally marched out, first snowing the landscape with the strewn fragments of their prayer-books and hymnals. For several days Communist instigators, who sprang up in their midst, had attempted to hold the student body together as a focal point of inflammatory agitation. Parents who came to get their sons were refused admittance. Some boys did escape, leaving their clothes and other personal possessions to be torn to shreds. Only when we cut off supplies to their kitchen did the school disband; their erstwhile leaders vanished, taking with them the funds to which they had compelled every student to contribute.

The same breakdown of public morale was flagrant in the town. Respectable members of the community, members of the gentry, were led through the streets bearing placards confessing their crimes; they were spit upon, beaten, stoned. In Kiukiang, upriver, where the foreign settlement impinged on the Chinese city, any foreigner who had to walk through the streets had also to get used to coming back dripping with spittle, filthy from head to feet, and to submitting to this vileness without a sign of resentment. In Wuhu it was our good fortune not to be living at such close quarters with the mob, but we were threatened with a boycott that would force all servants to depart and keep us from obtaining food. On consular instructions all men were now advised to remove to Shanghai unless their continued presence was needed to maintain, if only in fragments, the business agencies for which they were answerable. This small group, it was decided, should live in the hulks by the river and get provisions from the steamers passing through.

I had no excuse to remain. As for greater safety we were consolidating the port's dwindling population, I spent my last nights at the Asiatic Petroleum Company's Mess, whose members, recognizing sadly that in a matter of days their new imposing home, erected for all time of sturdy concrete on one of Wuhu's loftiest hills, would be overrun by Chinese soldiers, were engaged in a methodical project not to bequeath them the Mess's copious stock of liquor.

To complete this delectable duty with the persistence it required we kept late, not to say bibulous, hours – which made all the more unwelcome my summons to the telephone at seven in the morning. It was the British Vice-Consul, lent to us during the emergency by the Nanking Consulate, the only person of official position whom our multi-national community could look to. For a Consul to be calling at seven in the morning was more direful than the Acts of God against which insurance companies won't insure us; for him to be calling by Chinese telephone was catastrophic. Chinese telephone service was a confusion I never had acquired the wit to master, but the Consul, unfortunately, had underlings trained to unravel its dark mysteries.

His request was simple, but momentous: would I inform the priests at the Roman Catholic Cathedral that they were under orders to evacuate Wuhu and proceed to Shanghai. Since they did not speak English and nobody in the port spoke their native Spanish, he was calling on me, as the only Chinese-speaking foreigner left in port, to transmit this message. I could use Latin too, he generously suggested – an undeserved compliment. At that hour of the morning I could not have parsed "Amo, amas amat!"

The British were always getting unwelcome jobs shoved upon them. The care of Roman Catholic missionaries was specifically a French responsibility, one which they had assumed years before – probably because a Roman Catholic missionary murdered was the best of excuses for enlarging the French Empire. At this juncture, however, the French did not choose to be involved. Ironically enough, they had had a gunboat anchored off the Bund only a few days earlier, but when a mob was sighted tramping toward the Cathedral – and past it, though they did not stay to assure themselves of this – the gunboat had pulled up anchor and retired precipitately to Shanghai. Now that evacuation appeared necessary, the Spanish Consul-General in Shanghai turned to the British to supply the protection at which the French had defected.

The consul's request, of course, I accepted, though with trepidation. To get to the Spanish Cathedral required walking to the centre of the Chinese city, which no foreigner had entered since the Nanking bombardment. As I strolled across the fields to the city, my mind aggravated the dismal possibilities like a tongue tormenting sore tooth. Remembering the seething anger roused to murderous anti-foreign outbreaks after the British police in Shanghai, only two years before, had been pushed into firing on a riotous mob, I could not imagine that popular indignation now would be less rabid.

Fortunately, the hour was early, the streets surprisingly empty. The few passers-by glanced at me but showed no decided reaction to the foreign devil walking through their midst. They did not seem even to have heard of Nanking. Except that some one did toss a handful of gravel in my direction, there was no hostile gesture.

To the Spanish fathers Nanking was news. Cloistered within their high walls, they had been completely out of touch with the outside world. My message they received graciously, but their reply I could have foretold: they must consult their bishop.

"Bishops!" exclaimed the peppery British captain aboard Caradoc when I brought him this reply. "We might get something done if we could get rid of those God damn bishops!"

His outburst was pardonable. The Anglican bishop in Anking had stymied the evacuation of his missionaries. The Methodist women in Wuhu could not depart without their bishop's orders, a pretext that rang hollow to any who knew how little this functionary dared curb their comings and goings. Some years before, in apologizing to the Anglican bishop, Bishop Huntington, for an arbitrary and unfriendly course pursed by one of his women workers, he had explained that these women were a law to themselves.

"You have my sympathy," exclaimed Bishop Huntington.

"I need it, Bishop, I need it," was his fervent answer.

If ever a man needed sympathy now, it was the Caradoc's captain, whose responsibility these women suddenly had become. Not content with dealing out to his care French interest and Spanish, fate now had handed him the safekeeping of Americans. *U.S.S. Preble*, a flotilla leader despatched from Nanking for this job, had arrived with half her crew suddenly stricken with food poisoning. She had stayed just long enough for her captain to give us details of the attempted massacre in Nanking.

"Do you know," he said, still white with anger over all he had seen and heard, "that four American women were raped by Chinese soldiers?"

"Oh, for god's sake, don't tell that to the women here!" exclaimed the English captain. "They'll never go."

But they did go. The next day, we all went, all except the handful of men who were to stand siege on the hulk. We boarded a ship already jammed with refugees from upriver, many of them friends or acquaintances.

It is a sad experience saying good-bye to a dearly loved home, shutting the front door on familiar rooms and wondering, as I did, how soon it would be before these doors were forced open, before vandals would burst in to steal and smash and trample underfoot one's treasures. A few special things I tried to take with me, but a home cannot be crammed into a suitcase; the task of choosing what to take became so excruciating that I lost heart. For years I had bought things because they attracted me, porcelains, lacquer screens and cabinets, rugs, chests carved of camphor wood, lanterns of wrought iron, eggshell china. Each piece had its memories; I could recall where I had discovered it, how long I had bargained for it, the daily joy which its glowing colours had given me. So completely had they been wrapt up into the life of the household that to desert them, to leave them to the hideous, spiteful wantonness of ruthless spoilers was like betraying a trust, betraying gentle, affectionate friends. I blinked back tears; I was shutting that door on a large chapter of my own life.

On their hilltops stood all the port's houses reproaching us as the steamer hustled us away. Their gardens, bright with spring, still flourished from the care that never again would they receive; their windows looked out blankly

121

on the past. We all knew what our departure meant; the ebb tide had set in, the slow withdrawal of the white man's influence in China, in the Orient, the end to Empire, to imperial claims that despite all their shoddy littleness of practice, their shortsighted mistakes, their repellent arrogance, had been built on dreams commanding enough to spur fine loyalties and magnificent endeavour.

* * * * * * * *

Of the voyage to Shanghai I remember only that, some time during the night, we were shot at. Although our quarters had been protected by steel plates and sand bags, the sharp, close range reports sent me rolling out of my cot to the greater safety of the deck, a precaution at which one missionary scoffed.

"I went through the siege of Wuchang[28]," he boasted, next morning, "and I tell you, you never get used to it."

After living so long anxiously subject to the whim of Chinese mobs and Chinese soldiery, I for one found Shanghai too amply protected. Life there seemed dull. Warships of several nations crowded the Huangpu and national festivals were so frequent that they had to keep bunting ever ready to dress ship so as not to hurt Dutch or Spanish or French or Portuguese sensibilities. More alert were they than the British cruiser, anchored upriver, whose signal officer was puzzled, one May morning, to note that the neighbouring American and Japanese destroyers had laid out strings of flags to hoist at eight bells. Hastily consulting the calendar he was shocked to discover that it was his own British festival, Empire Day, which they were prepared to celebrate. Much embarrassed over an oversight which it was too late to remedy, he sent them word that flags at the masthead would be sufficient – leaving the overly foresighted Americans and Japanese to unstring all their pennants and return them to the locker!

Shanghai was more punctilious. It was stiffly martial, and the United States Marines stiffest of all. In patrolling their sector of the International Settlement they still wore uniforms that made no concession to comfort. While their British confreres met the Yangtze spring's mounting heat in the easy undress of shorts and singlet, they wore tunics buttoned tight to the throat. The Dutch, Spanish, Portuguese, and in their own special spheres the French and Japanese all made themselves comfortable, but not the U.S. Marines. Guadalcanal and the informality of jungle greens were an unbelievable fifteen years in the future.

Life as a refugee, however secure, was from the start boring. Remarkable though it was to see how pleasantly a hit-or-miss collection of dispossessed

122

families can set up impromptu housekeeping, the sense of emergency soon palled. In the college dormitory which bulged to bursting with noisy inmates our only excitement was watching Chiang Kai-shek, now turned anti-Communist, disposing of his recent allies. Every day his soldiers led condemned foes out to execution on a hill visible from our windows. They did not employ firing squads; Chinese marksmanship at that period was too undependable. Their victims they made sure of by compelling them to kneel, after which an officer walked behind the line and, pressing his pistol to the back of each culprit's head, toppled him with but one shot. Except to the poor wretches thus blasted into a gloomy hereafter, these executions lacked every feature of drama; they were a drily efficient and routine process of extinction in which corpses passed down the assembly line instead of cars.

My escape from the Shanghai doldrums came unexpectedly: an acquaintance, highly placed in the Indo-China Steam Navigation Company, the shipping subsidiary of the hugely important firm, Jardine, Matheson & company, offered me a job as a purser aboard one of Jardine's Hankow steamers. I wasted no time accepting an opportunity for which all my refugee companions envied me, the chance to get upriver and once again to be in the thick of events.

Pursers were a new venture for Jardine's; their appointment, to handle not the European but the Chinese passenger traffic, had come about by accident. For decades, Jardine's – rightly named the Princely Hong – had ignored the profits obtainable from this traffic. Profit in four figures or even five was chicken-feed to a company used to counting its gains in nothing smaller than millions. But now even Jardine's had been driven to plugging some of the leaks in its income. Few of these leaks were more considerable than the money which might have been collected from Chinese passengers. How much this amounted to nobody apparently had checked until accident pushed it under their noses.

The system long in vogue had been to farm out to a Chinese combine the right to sell tickets. For the round trip to Hankow[29], three days upriver, two days down, the combine had been paying Mex. $1300. When Jardine's, suddenly parsimonious, insisted on raising this to Mex. $2000. the combine struck, But Jardine's was not to be bluffed. Almost at sailing time they dispatched a man from the office to sell what tickets he could to the Chinese embarking on the next Hankow-bound steamer. The results were a revelation: for the upriver voyage alone he sold Mex.$9000 worth of tickets – clear gain, since the company was not obligated to provide its Chinese passengers either beds or food. For berth and board these passengers whatever their class, first, second, or steerage, had to make arrangements with the compradore. What the compradore's earnings must have been can be gauged from the fact that out of his monthly salary of about Mex $125 he was able to hire some ninety servants – or teaboys, as they were called. At no further cost to themselves, Jardine's sold these Chinese passengers only the right to be aboard ship.

This certainly was not chicken-feed. Venerable though it was, Jardine's did not falter longer in adjusting its timeworn policy; it went promptly to work enlisting Chinese-speaking pursers to manage this traffic in each of its eight or ten ships. In the larger ships the purser was given an assistant. My ship, the *Tuckwo*, rated such help, a generous arrangement though for the moment hardly necessary, since except from Kiukiang we were to take only through passengers en route between Shanghai and Hankow. The other way-ports, Chinkiang, Nanking, and Wuhu, were to be served by intermediate steamers. As a result of this pleasant system I had, during most of these voyages, not only nothing to do but an assistant to help me. My only duty was on the top deck, in the European quarters, where established oracularly in the smoking room, I announced each morning the moment when the sun was over the yard-arm, and the bar open. For this decision I did not depend on the sextant!

River travel had been always my delight; to be paid for this indulgence was an unexpected luxury. With no uniform as yet – although a ship's officer had suggested that we wear on our shoulders the clutching paw! – I felt more passenger than purser. After a gossipy evening with the Company's agent, who helped us sell tickets and otherwise learn our not very exciting duties, duties it was up to us as pioneers to invent, my assistant and I picked out a pair of cabins in the European class and retired. The cabins we selected were abaft the protection of steel plates and sand bags, but they were newer and larger. For such convenience we were more than willing to run the gauntlet of snipers' bullets.

Departures upriver from Shanghai were scheduled for midnight, but ships seldom got away before breakfast since there was a crossing some miles up the Yangtze so perilously beset by quicksands that no pilot would attempt it except in daylight. By midnight, however, passengers were aboard, the singsong chant of the coolies toting bales and boxes up the gang-planks had ceased; in profound silence, surrounded though we were by the arc-lit bustle of one of the world's great ports, we awaited the skipper's orders to cast off.

This produced the single moment of excitement. A strong east wind had begun blowing from Yangtzepoo, across river. The *Tuckwo* was a large ship, 350 feet long, but shallow draft, and with bulky top hamper. Before she could gather way, the wind banged her back against the pontoon, an event usual enough except that it alarmed one of our white passengers: to my astonishment a woman stuck head and shoulders out of a cabin window, a woman who had no business being aboard. The British authorities had been imperative in ordering that no white woman be given passage upriver. While I was trying to puzzle out how this passenger had slipped past us, I was confronted by a steward. There was a woman dressed as a man in cabin 6 he reported; now she wanted a bath. Should he prepare it in the men's bathroom, or the women's?

I soon was more concerned about the comfort of the women in steerage. They were accommodated by a long narrow latrine on the starboard side aft. The door to this latrine, I found on a first inspection, had been nailed shut, shut indeed so effectively that I had to call a ship's carpenter to force it open. Inside the compartment had been piled high with boxes and baskets – my introduction to "pidgin" cargo, the unauthorized and, of course, unmanifested goods for which payment had been made to members of the crew. Like many illegal things in China, "pidgin" cargo had such venerable sanctions that no ship's officer would dispute the right of each sailor to stow away a bit of freight on his own. Below decks every inch of unused space was crammed with articles to which everyone, even customs officers, turned a blind eye. Anybody misguided enough to do otherwise would have ended in the Yangtze some dark night, with a knife between his shoulders blades.

But to take over the women's latrine was overstepping "kuei-chu," or tolerated custom. Six days was longer than any woman could be expected to resist nature's call! I had instant support, therefore, in ordering the boxes and baskets removed. This was not the end of the business. Scarcely had the "pidgin" cargo been whisked away to hiding places less objectionable than we made a discovery still more shocking. Crushed down in the zinc trough of the latrine itself, a trough still giving malodorous witness to its ordinary uses, we uncovered a dozen Chinese stowaways. To save perhaps ten dollars in American money, they had paid a cook to hide them where for nearly a week they would be squeezed, barely able to shift an arm or a leg and overpowered by heat and stench such as made a clean, or even a full, breath impossible. No time did I lose in hauling down the offending cook and making him pay, for each of these miserable wretches, his full fare to Hankow.

This job done, I was free to return to the top deck, where the mystery of the girl in men's clothes was very slow unraveling. All we knew was that she was Russian, and therefore suspect. We had aboard some Soviet agents fleeing Shanghai and their turncoat ally, Chiang Kai-shek, for sanctuary under the Communist regime established in Hankow. One of our passengers, a Swede who understood Russian, used to seat himself near these men on deck and retail to us, later, the plans they discussed, plans suggested by the hills and channels through which the *Tuckwo* was passing. Here they would mine the river, there they would plant guns – vaunting how easily they could make the Yangtze impregnable. Just why the British authorities should permit agitators of this stamp to travel in a British ship we put down to stupidity until it was explained finally that Britain wanted them out of Shanghai, where their opportunities for mischief were graver than upriver.

To this delegation we attached the masquerading girl, setting her down as a spy until one of the ship's engineers, loth to waste the only female society on board, made her acquaintance and elicited her story. Far from being a communist, she was a White Russian, and her determination to flout the Admiralty's embargo was not political but sentimental. She had been the sweetheart of a Belgian in Kobe, an employee of the Belgian Bank. When his bank transferred the man to Hankow, his girl came in pursuit, fearful of losing him. Our first sympathies inclined to the man. As a boy, this young woman was no beauty; her face was sallow, her hair straight and stiff. On our next visit to Hankow, however, we revised our impression, even crediting the engineer's discernment. This time she visited the ship in her proper garb; the ugly duckling had become a swan, graceful, vivacious, pretty.

Our trouble with women did not end with the Russian girl. A German woman was the next to force herself aboard as a passenger. Middle-aged, sturdily – not to say, massively – built, she did not resort to any intriguing ruse but shook us off at the gang plank and locked herself all night in a cabin. She had been sold, she claimed, a round tip ticket and was entitled to return to Hankow where the shop she owned required her presence. In language that withered us with all the sins of the British Empire she added our private sins to a catalogue that overlooked nothing. Not till daylight, under threat of summoning police to break down the door, did we oust her. As she moved tempestuously down the gang plank our agent warned the room-boy who was carrying her baggage,

"For God's sake don't ask for cumshaw!"

Our chief trouble, however, was not with Russian women or German or even with the professional ladies of anomalous nationality whom we brought down river from Hankow. These last, it is true, did come near turning the sedate *Tuckwo* into an impromptu cabaret, making themselves so popular with our junior officers that the Captain came aft to remind his men they were employed to be engineers not entertainers. We were getting more than enough entertainment from Chinese guns.

The Yangtze then was the dividing line between the armies of North and South. Impartially their soldiers shot at us from either bank, expending more ammunition on us than on each other. Because of this hazard we traveled in convoy, escorted by a destroyer, and anchoring at night. The destroyer assigned to us, however, had been delayed near Hong Kong by fog. In its absence our escort was the *Kiawo*, one of the small powerful steamers built to steam the rapids that hampered access to Chungking and West China. These ships could accomplish in three days a journey which houseboats, towed by coolies straining against the pull of the ropes as they trod a precipitous path beside the River, used to manage in six weeks. As an escort, *Kiawo* was merely a gesture. Her only guns were pompoms; her protection, as with the rest of us, was sandbags and a smattering of steel plates.

Her fighting capacity the Chinese on the north bank, the anti-Communist forces, soon set themselves to test with a three-inch gun. Who we might be, friend or foe, did not matter; we were too tempting a target to ignore, for we had just anchored for the night.

Busy down below, I did not hear the opening of the cannonade, but the shooting had been disagreeably accurate. By the time I came on deck the *Kiawo* was circling the convoy. A gaping hole in her wardroom showed what the first shells had done; fortunately the wardroom had been empty. They had struck a bare two minutes after *Kiawo's* officers had been called to action stations. The gun which had done this damage was now bearing on a Butterfield coaster anchored just ahead of us. One shell had punctured her steel side; another, as I watched, exploded under her stern counter. When the next splashed half way between this ship and ours, our Chinese crew needed no further spur to break all records in pulling up anchor. Not till we had put five miles of the broad Yangtze between us and our assailants did we breathe easily.

The next evening, the South took its turn at bombarding us. This time it was the forts high on the hills that guard the approach to Chinkiang[30]. Nothing daunted, the little *Kiawo* again went into action. She did not hurt them, of course, but neither did they hurt us. What she did reach with her pompoms, however, was a machine-gun nest near the river's edge. Guns and men went flying in all directions, a tribute to her marksmanship and a spectacle to exult in – a tiny steamship daring to defy forts any one of whose volleys, puffing in white clouds out of the barren mountainside, could have sunk her.

Hoping for a night's sleep we anchored near a marshy island where snipers, if there were any, could attack only from sampans. Every light extinguished, we lay blotted out by darkness, our shadows merged into the shadows of the tall reeds – concealment so excellent that it nearly brought disaster.

Some time after midnight I was jolted out of bed by frantic shouts and then by the *Tuckwo's* rocking violently. Hurrying outside, I was almost too late to see the disappearing shadow which had stirred up this commotion. A Northern cruiser, afraid of being attacked at her anchorage in Chinkiang, had made a run for it. Unlighted herself, she had plowed at full speed through our darkened convoy and, by a miracle, missed colliding in turn with each of our six ships.

The rest of our voyage could not rival the excitement of these first two days, although snipers' bullets, occasionally hitting the *Tuckwo*'s steel engine house, kept us from forgetting that we were everybody's enemy.

At Nanking we lined up in an avenue of ships, meeting here a downriver convoy which stretched upriver beyond the protecting men-of-war. Over our heads South and North engaged in a daily duel between Hsiakuan, Nanking's riverside suburb, and Pukow, crossriver terminus of the railway to Peking. Every noon, while the officers of *H.M.S. Emerald* brought their cocktails to the quarter deck to watch, the Hsiakuan fort aimed a few blasts at a prominent water tower near the Pukow station. For a month they shot at it; they never hit it.

Nightfall blotted out these hostilities. Nanking, Hsiakuan, Pukow all were suffocated under the darkness of fear. Not a sound could be heard, no sign that around us was a population of a million persons. The stars, slowly wheeling, a dog barking somewhere beyond the jet shadow of the hills, these only made the night lonelier. Blackness hid a city of the dead. Yet in midriver convoys and men-of-war blazed with bright merrymaking. Phonographs blared; motorboats chugged from ship to ship, taking passengers to visit friends and to celebrate their casual reunions in plentiful whisky soda. It was a weird turn to this civil war that here, in the heart of China, the only people who dared to laugh and sing were aliens, dwelling with the Yangtze for their moat. A cruiser or two made the difference.

Whenever we pulled alongside a way-port hulk, the Royal Navy sent a guard aboard; before we departed, they combed the ship. These precautions were directed against piracy by Chinese soldiers. Piracy on the coastal runs was carried out so often by bandits, who would come aboard disguised as passengers, that the ships plying to Hong Kong or Tientsin had each deck and the bridge shut off by steel gratings. On the River this had never been necessary, but soldiers had seized one ship; the Admiral was determined they should not seize another.

One night, while we were anchored in Chinkiang, I saw a launch come alongside, and several soldiers clamber aboard. I lost no time reporting this to the officer of the watch, who used a flashlight to signal a nearby British destroyer. Within ten minutes she had grappled us and was rushing a boarding party, complete to steel helmets, across the railings. To our chagrin, the *Tuckwo*'s chief officer, abruptly wakened by the commotion, had not waited for an explanation; he had kicked the trespassing soldiers back on the their launch, which slipped away, leaving us nothing to show for the alarm. These soldiers, panicky witnesses disclosed in a high-pitched bedlam, had got wind of several wealthy Chinese passengers and had sneaked aboard in a brash attempt to kidnap them.

Theirs was a private venture. The Communists were subtler. At Kiukiang[31] a petty officer from *Wild Swan*, a ginger-haired sailor known up and down the Yangtze for his alertness, brought me a package of Chinese books.

"What are these?" he asked.

One glance told what they were – volumes describing the Third Internationale, pictures of Lenin and Karl Marx, copies of a magazine called the "Hung Ch'i" or Red Flag, and, oddly enough, books on birth control illustrated by explicit diagrams.

"There are more than two hundred of these parcels stowed on the main deck, he told me.

On investigation I learned that they had been put aboard as "pidgin" cargo at fifteen cents a package, paid to a crewman. Every package was stamped and addressed to some agent. Since Chiang Kai-shek's break with the Communists, they could not be mailed in Shanghai and so were being dispatched to Hankow, whence they could be sent (through a still undivided postal service) to every part of China.

The problem was what to do with them. The British Consul's first plan, to burn them on the Kiukiang foreshore, proved impracticable. Inflammatory though they were, they were not inflammable. Dumping them into the river between the pontoons was no more feasible. So completely did they choke the narrow space that Chinese coolies soon were walking across them and fishing out the many packages still intact. Ultimately we tossed them overboard after we had departed for Hankow. Our wake looked like the trail in a paper chase.

Kiukiang was always providing incidents. We generally drowned three or four passengers each time we arrived from Hankow. Chinese, who can measure time by centuries, are a recklessly impatient people when it comes to measuring minutes. Whether by ship or train, their arrivals and departures always rocket into pandemonium. No sooner had we turned to face the current off Kiukiang than sampans by the dozen would hook alongside, and their coolies start grappling for fares. The passengers were in no position to refuse their solicitation: cumbered with baskets and pigskin boxes they had a footing on the deck's narrow ledge insecure enough even without rival sampanmen attaching themselves to each arm and struggling to pull their prize into two separate boats. If a passenger tripped and slipped into the river, nobody bothered. Down he went, while the sampan men pounced on their next victim.

One passenger rushed up to the bridge, frantically entreating the captain to turn his ship around in a try at saving his brother. The captain refused; not only was it too late but, where the Chinese are so callous about their own people, one cannot blame the ship's officers for being hard-hearted. These tragedies had become commonplace.

The Chinese attitude also had its logic. Refusal to save a drowning man, they believed, was only common sense. The water spirits would not forget nor forgive having their prey snatched from their clutches. No matter how many years they might have to wait, they would bide their time until they could seize his rescuer. For men who made their living on the water this risk was too inescapable to chance.

When our ship tied up at the hulk, sampans were put to other uses. Manipulating a long single scull, their owners would sneak in with bundles of firewood to be shipped as "pidgin" cargo to Shanghai, frequently running the gauntlet of the ship's hoses and even taking this drenching with a smile as they laughed at the ship's officers who were amusing themselves with this diversion.

A more profitable business was to tie their craft astern and play host, during the ship's stay, to the wealthier Chinese passengers, selling them space under their matshed to smoke opium, an indulgence forbidden aboard ship. The moment the *Tuckwo* gave the signal for departure, the smokers scrambled back to her decks; they brought the poppy's sweetish fumes with them.

In other ways sampans were a necessary adjunct to the steamships at Kiukiang. Out of them came much of the cargo on which the steamer depended. When Communist soldiers began commandeering sampans tied up at the company pontoons, I was sent to interpret for a small naval detachment in demanding their release. One soldier in a boat offshore had been at the point of seizing a Standard Oil sampan, a fancy craft painted white, when he chanced to look up; what he saw made him abandon this seizure in a hurry. A sailor aboard an American gunboat had a rifle leveled on him and was waiting eagerly for the soldier to lay one hand on the craft. With a disappointment we all could understand he put down his gun.

The soldiers whom we were to accost had come into the open water between two pontoons and taken possession of several sampans from which we had been loading. But the mere sight of our naval platoon instantly cowed them. In language considerably more tactful than the curt orders I had been given to translate, I told them to free their captives and get out.

They were all apologies, all deference, frantically ready to withdraw – but they voiced one fear: would the *Wild Swan* fire on them as they pushed out past the destroyer. No assurances on our part would convince them. Insistently they argued for a promise from the destroyer herself that they would be allowed to go free.

It was a hot morning, and the walk from the pontoons ashore, then down the Bund and out to the pontoon where *Wild Swan* was tied up did not appeal to any in my party. I suggested that one of the sailors pretend to wig-wag to his ship, and then report that the soldiers' safe-conduct had been granted.

Action of this kind had every element of the comical which British sailors love. The man chosen performed his role with genius. He flapped his arms in a series of uncouth gestures fit for a constipated sea-gull. So vastly did he enjoy his imposture that his gyrations, prolonged in contorted agony, mocked the dynamic ferocity of a modern ballet. Soberly we watched him, repressing an impulse to grin almost uncontrollable when he came back to me and, his own mirth under tight control, announced, "*Wild Swan* reports she will not shoot, sir."

* * * * * * * *

The terminus of our voyage from Shanghai, which the nightly anchorages had lengthened to six days, was Hankow. At this inland metropolis, six hundred miles from the sea, Communism held ruthless sway. Here the Russian sympathizers who had broken with Chiang Kai-shek were making their stand. They were a motley lot. Most conspicuous was the Foreign Secretary, Eugene Ch'en, native of Jamaica and son of a Chinese father and Negro mother. He could be seen walking the Bund with his children.

Back of Eugene Ch'en loomed the portentous figure of his Russian advisor, Borodin, and among his fire-brand helpers were a red-headed American girl, a University of Chicago graduate, and a young Chinese graduate of Princeton who, after malignant denunciations of Britain, ended by fleeing down river aboard our British ship. To keep his get-away secret he had an American acquaintance buy his ticket. When the latter taunted him over seeking refuge in a British steamer this glib young man exclaimed, "Oh, there is no nationality in economics."

If there was no nationality in economics, there was the virulence of class hatred emphatically proclaimed in the huge banner strung across the street before the American consulate. "Workers of the World, Unite," it shouted in bold English lettering. Quite understandably this manifesto, glaring at him all day through his windows, upset the digestion of the Consul-General. I listened to him, on an afternoon visit, as he denounced in irascible speech both the Communists and his own Secretary of State, Kellogg. This official, who had hoped to go down in history as co-sponsor of the Kellogg-Briand pact, an ingenuous document obliging its signatories to renounce war by a simple pen-stroke, the Consul General derided as "Nervous Nellie."

At the moment Hankow exhibited more graphically the nervousness of the British Foreign Office. The once flourishing British concession had been surrendered without a blow and was now overrun by boys and girls, dressed alike, in grey uniforms, who exuded self-importance as they hurried on mysterious errands. All this the foreign community took in their stride. They could not spare time to be nervous: after all, the horse races were being run at the Club. Revolution had to take second place.

Under cover of these races I did a most unsporting thing. Jardine's Hankow office looked with suspicion on the institution of pursers, a low scheme – they were convinced – which the Shanghai office had devised to cut into their commissions. When I presented myself with my assistant to handle the ticket sale, they dismissed us. They would manage this; they didn't want Shanghai prying into their books.

But I had my revenge. I went to the office on a Sunday afternoon when every loyal Englishman was off to bet on the horses. In an office serenely deserted I copied all their vouchers, a record I carried back to Shanghai. On our next voyage the Hankow staff gave me a desk – and a shroff to test with his teeth the silver dollars which we insisted on for passage.

In demanding silver we were counting on *H.M.S. Hawkins*, the British flagship anchored in mid-stream, to preserve us from the headsman's sword. By local regulations, anyone who declined the paper money rolling off the presses, pretty currency worth more pictorially than fiscally, was liable to execution. But we got our silver, got it in greater quantities than we could accept, silver smuggled into the office under the long gowns of merchants and gentry, all frantic to escape the Communist reign of terror.

So desperate were these men that often my room-boy would summon me from a siesta to ward off petitioners who had come to the ship. Kneeling in the hot sun, they would kowtow, beating their heads on the pontoon's steel deck as they pleaded to be taken aboard. It was a sad business refusing them, but I had no option. The Royal Navy had limited us to eight hundred passengers, a restriction we eased a bit by taking aboard eleven hundred! More than this we dared not accept.

Before we departed, each trip, a naval guard – as at the way-ports – combed the ship. They would start with the First Class Chinese section, then seal its exits with sentries, while continuing in the same way through other areas, and eventually to the steerage. Although their chief purpose was to rout out any Chinese soldiers who might be aboard, they ended by uncovering stowaways – not as in Shanghai where men were seeking a cheap passage but political refugees running from the Communists. To make their escape – which for some spelled life or death – they braved unbelievable hardships, hiding under boxes and baskets stacked against the boiler room, whole families sweltering on May nights when temperature and humidity were both in the nineties. Already, in 1927, the Communists had worked out those tactics of terror which, two generations later, were to intimidate whole continents as they intimidated Hankow's hapless citizens. Even then, to us who lived in China, Communism was a portent too menacing to be shrugged off. We had had frightening glimpses of the passions that seethed beneath China's usually placid surface, the white hot lava swelling up against the thin crust of Western might, of Chinese tradition, and awaiting the opportune moment to surge into scorching eruption.

My immediate concern, however, the never forgotten aim in adopting this purser's career, was some opportune moment to salvage my possessions. Each time we passed up or down river I could see my house, its sturdy red-brick walls tantalizing me by their undisturbed appearance, a bare five minutes' walk from the Bund. That walk seemed longer than the distance to Shanghai. On our first voyage our Wuhu stays were too brief, too uncertain to make even the most hurried visit feasible. But a morning came when the Captain promised me two hours in port. Instantly I was ashore and walking a road which no foreigner had trod for two months. The Chinese acquaintances I met on the way eyed me as if they were seeing a ghost.

I was soon face to face with one detail I could not see from the river – a Chinese sentry slouching outside the house. But formidable though he looked with a bayonet fixed to his rifle, he did not hinder my unlocking the front door and entering the musty hall, nor did he follow me despite a placard that claimed the house as property of the army then occupying Wuhu.

Almost as soon as I had entered, my servants were on the scene. They had done a remarkable job, a job which testified poignantly to their loyalty: almost everything of value they had crowded into my study and barricaded the room so staunchly that no casual looter could have broken in. Upstairs, looters had been active, wantonly active. They had torn mattresses apart, snowed kapok over the floors, stolen utensils, cut the square centre out of a rug to carry their plunder. But my really irreplaceable treasures they had not reached.

This happy circumstance I owed not only to my servants but to the fact that a general had chosen the large house on the hill above mine for his residence. It was no regard for my property that had caused him to post sentries at my front and back doors; he simply did not relish soldiers occupying a house so close to his own. No Chinese officer, least of all a general, felt comfortable at too close quarters with his men; they could be stirred too quickly to mutinous outbreaks.

This good luck, however, I dared not press too far. No sooner did I reach Shanghai than I hurried to Jardine's. The time had come to resign. My next trip upriver, I told them, must be as a passenger so that I could rescue my belongings before the general decided to move.

Jardine's proved how richly it deserved to be called the Princely Hong. "Why go as a "passenger?" they asked. "We can put you aboard one of our intermediate ships which makes Wuhu its terminus. There you can stop off for a week, get your stuff down to the hulk, and bring it to Shanghai by the next ship. "Of course," added my boss ("boss is too crude a word for a Jardine manager!) " we don't really need pursers aboard these intermediate ships, but you might as well take the job, if it will help you."

They actually were paying me to salvage my own property, munificence which reminded me of the generous action of another Scottish firm, some ten years earlier, during the First World War. This firm, Butterfield and Swire, had long carried the insurance for all the buildings erected in China by the Episcopal Church. The latest of these was a church in Wushi[32], near Shanghai, one of the largest and most beautiful churches in the entire Mission – and one of the first in which electric lights were not an afterthought. To make sure that everything was done properly, skilled electricians had been imported from Shanghai to install the wiring.

This was challenging the spirits! Within six months the church burned down. A short circuit in the much vaunted wiring had set fire to the altar boys' cottas, starting a conflagration that left the brick walls a smoke-blackened shell. To underline the irony, it turned out that this, of all the buildings in a mission extended over much of the Yangtze valley, from Shanghai to Ichang Changsha, this church alone had not been insured!

It took a supposedly tight-fisted Scottish firm to acknowledge a moral obligation where no legal one existed. Butterfield & Swire responded to this dismaying fire by paying four-fifths of what the church would have been insured for. Only a clerical oversight, they conceded, had caused this negligence, negligence of which they declined to take advantage. If it had not been war time, they explained – and a most critical stage of the First World War it was – they would have made up the loss in full!

In similar vein Jardine's let me earn my way back to Wuhu, although their prediction that I would have little to do was amply confirmed. After the thousand and more who had jammed the *Tuckwo*'s every deck, the stowaways by the score whom we had had the sad task of putting ashore, a passenger list of twelve certainly did not merit the exalted offices of a purser.

My new ship, the *Kiangwo*, of course was smaller. But not long before she had been the unwilling conveyance for five thousand soldiers. She was the ship famous both for being seized by a Chinese army and for the exploit by which, without a shot fired, she had been recovered, and her pirate horde dumped ashore at Kiukiang.

Her captain had his own claim to fame, a claim others had to make for him since he always brushed aside the report that he, in what was still known as The War, and flying one of the rudimentary seaplanes of the conflict, had shot down a Zeppelin off the Dutch coast. He was as charming as he was modest, a very pleasant man to travel with. When he heard that I was an Anglican priest, he exclaimed:

"Now at last I have something to write home to Mother. Pulpit to Purser – a parson earning an honest living!"

* * * * * * * *

If I had known that this voyage was to be my farewell to China, I would have watched with pensive absorption the unrolling landscape I knew and loved so well, the pagodas, proud pillars spearing the sky's blue vault with their brazen spires, the villages, drab grey in winter but now luxuriating in the puff-blown green of their many willows, the mountains, their outline broken into massive crags, a misty serrated horizon while slowly, tranquilly, no longer confined to a convoy, we pushed upstream away from the Yangtze's flat, reedy delta. Hot June sunshine polished till it glistened the great River's sinuous brown turbulence. The war was withdrawing northward; out from hiding had come huge fleets of junks, crowding the far reaches like a flock of sea-birds.

The resumption of peace-time activity overtook us in Wuhu. No sooner had we tied up than we received word that with the convoys discontinued, there were to be no more intermediate ships. *Kiangwo* was ordered to Kiukiang to load tea.

This materially altered my plans. Since I could be of use in Kiukiang, where there were certain to be many passengers, I felt it my duty to stick with the ship, a decision that allowed little more than a day to shift my furniture to the riverside godown, and to bring aboard everything that was readily portable. In this I had noble aid from the few foreigners still lingering in Wuhu; they scoured the Club for empty beer and whisky crates. My servants also rallied to the task.

But when we brought a preliminary load to the Bund, we were stopped, a hundred feet short of the ship, by the Bund-Coolies Union. To transport my goods this last hundred feet was prerogative now reserved to this new, fly-by-night organization. Their demands, of course, were exorbitant, but unless I could make terms with them I saw little hope of getting the next day's heavy shipments into the *Kiangwo*'s baggage room.

At this juncture I remembered a policy I had used often when taking pictures in China to set up tripod and camera was sure to draw curious crowds as inevitably as honey draws bees. At such times I would pick out the heftiest and most intrusive of the mob, invite them to look through the ground glass, show him some of the camera's workings. From that moment self-importance converted him into an ally. He would keep the people back, clear the scene I was seeking to photograph, receive my grateful commendations with the knowing smile of a colleague. We photographers must stick together.

The method worked now. Communism had not yet got rid of China's ancient regard for "face." One of the Bund coolies had shown himself an outstanding nuisance by his glib, loud-mouthed talent for extortion. This noisy malcontent I invited on board. Slipping him a dollar, I complimented him on his leadership, praised his administrative ability. He was exactly the man I needed, I told him, to manage the large shipment of goods which I would be bringing to the Bund the next morning. If I could secure his help to oversee this job I would count myself fortunate, and of course would pay him well.

This was not mere flattery. He was worth every cent and proved his efficiency by the smooth dispatch with which he got everything across those critical hundred feet. No union rules impeded my servants. When the *Kiangwo* cast loose late in the afternoon I said good-bye to my new assistant as cordially as to my loyal retainers."Tsai chien, tsai chien – see you again," we repeated, although we all knew this good-bye was final. This bodily removal of my goods and chattels I suddenly, reluctantly, realized for what it was: I had pulled up stakes. I was taking my home with me.

Among the things brought aboard were several decanters filled with wines or spirits. These had been prepared for a naval tiffin party which never happened. It had been set to coincide, unluckily, with the day Wuhu joined the revolution. At the exact moment when we awaited our guests, they had been called to action stations. My problem now was to empty these decanters so that I could pack them. But when I looked for help from the *Kiangwo*'s officers I discovered to my amazement, that none of them drank. Perhaps never in the long history of the British Merchant marine had this wonder occurred, a ship staffed entirely by teetotalers! The only tippler aboard was a missionary, for the necessity of emptying these bottles was making me a secret drinker, determined each day to consume my allotted portion of liquor.

Perhaps I should make a slight exception. The Captain, at rare intervals could be coaxed into taking a drink, but he had to be on guard, he declared, because it made him too generous. During our subsequent stay in Kiukiang we entertained Jardine's agent and with him the skipper of *H.M.S. Woodlark*, a tiny gunboat tied alongside. Here was one occasion when our own Captain felt constrained to drink with his guests – very modestly, it must be recorded, but enough so that at dinner he presented the *Woodlark*'s skipper with the 2d Engineer's dog.

Next morning I challenged him.

"Do you know what you did last night, sir?" I asked him.

"No," he admitted. "Nothing dreadful, I hope."

"You gave away the 2d Engineer's dog to the *Woodlark*'s skipper."

"Did I?" he exclaimed. "It's damned lucky I didn't give away the ship!"

This stay in Kiukiang my last trip upriver, was an experience nostalgic to recall, a last extravagant sample of the China we never should see again. The *Kiangwo* chugged into port on the eve of the King's birthday, too late to join the celebrations wherewith the foreign community, attenuated though it was, put up a brave show. As the royal birthday was also a British holiday, we spent it swinging idly at anchor. The following day, Saturday, was the Dragon Boat Festival, a Chinese holiday. Whitsunday too was a holiday, and Whitmonday – four successive days during which we could do nothing but watch the muddy Yangtze pouring past us in the hot June sunlight. When at last we prepared to up anchor and shift to our berth, the *Wild Swan*, alerted by rumours of trouble ashore, moved in ahead of us. Not until Wednesday, nearly six days after our arrival, could we begin loading our precious tea.

Despite these delays I was reluctant to see the little *Kiangwo* point her nose downstream. For years I had lived within sight of the Great River. I had watched the familiar steamers passing daily, seen the stream thick with the bamboo-ribbed sails of lorcha and junk, I had heard the pulsating drums urging rivermen at their long sweeps as they guided their log rafts on a crawling journey to Shanghai. The Yangtze's current coursed through my blood.

My brief career as purser had deepened this acquaintance with the River, bringing me a set of experiences I would not have missed. Pursering was still adventure, a matter of blithe improvisation – and for the present it was still honest. My fellow ship's officers had been skeptical as to how long it would remain so. When the Office first broached the plan to one of them, he objected cynically, "It will be one more finger in the pie." What he meant I did not fully perceive until two years later, after I had left China and returned only to pick up the furniture still stored in the Wuhu godowns.

In the *Kutwo*, aboard which I had booked passage, I was surprised to find my erstwhile assistant installed as purser. There were other changes: Jardine's had accommodated its ships to the declining income of many once affluent foreigners by putting in an intermediate class on the deck below First Class European. Naturally, I was curious to see the new cabins, and my friend obliged me by unlocking one that happened to be empty. It looked both neat and comfortable but when, pursuing my curiosity further, I pulled out a life preserver from its ceiling rack; I was so startled by its unexpected weight that

I dropped it with a thud on the floor. It was filled with smuggled salt. Whose "pidgin" this was I was too tactful to enquire.

This of course was two years later. In those two years the pursers had thrived. This I had not expected. At the time when I resigned Jardine's was becoming less princely. Not content with selling passage, the management was considering a plan to sell berth and meals and to invade the feudal domain of the compradore and his ninety teaboys. My comment was that any purser who attempted this had better make out his will.

Quite evidently this issue, like all issues in China before the Communists' more drastic rule, had been compromised. Everybody was happy – and that one more finger was in the pie. But short though it was I was proud of my river-faring career, proud enough to prepare a voluminous report on how pursering on the Yangtze could be improved. I hope somebody read it. For me the wrench of packing my gear and going ashore for the last time was a sad one. It was not only farewell to the River, to all its sights and smells – which I have only to read about (as in Thomas Woodroof's River of Golden Sand) to smell again in my nostrils the pungent mixture of odours I sniffed familiarly aboard a Yangtze steamship; it was good-bye to China, good-bye to fourteen happy years in a country I loved dearly. China had taken me, a raw boy of twenty, and – I hope – made me a man.

THE EMPRESSES

During the "Sunrise Years" Vincent Gowen (VHG) made six trips to the Orient. His favorite ships, were the Empresses owned by the Canadian Pacific Railway that departed from Vancouver.

.
".. on a few thrilling occasions I saw one of the ships in the sunlight, the famous white Empresses, Empress of India, or China, or Japan, sister ships shaped long and sleek with a yacht's clipper bow." (p.10)

EMPRESS OF CANADA
(right) docked in Vancouver. B.C.

EMPRESS OF RUSSIA *(below) leaving port*

"Into the hill-girt bay came to anchor a towering white liner, the Empress of Russia, promising home and swift escape from lands to which we would be forever strangers.(p.19).

EMPRESS OF RUSSIA *(left) at sea.*

139

STOPOVER IN NAGASAKI

THE BELLE VUE HOTEL

A stopover here in November 1913 allowed VHG to connect with the Poltava for his onward leg to Shanghai. (Photo courtesy of the Nagasaki Foreign Settlements Research Group.)

Belle Vue Hotel, Oura, Nagasaki.

"Our hotel, its rose-garden still flowering forlornly in November, was a stopping-place where the lost souls of Joseph Conrad's novels might have yawned and drunk stupidly to ease their homesickness. (p.19)

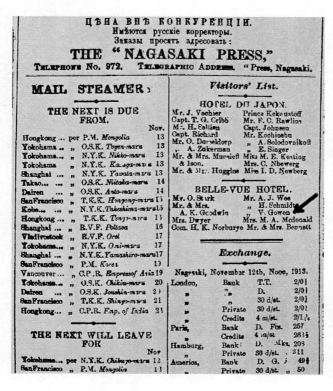

THE NAGASAKI PRESS *an English language daily that published the names of guests at the local hotels.*

VHG's name can be seen in the right-hand column of the listings for the Belle Vue Hotel. (Photo courtesy of Brian Burke-Gaffney, Faculty of Human Environment at the Nagasaki Institute of Applied Science.)

SHANGHAI, THE BUND *(two views)*

"A city reckoned by the millions, Shanghai's smoking chimneys made foreigners rich. Along its Bund stood buildings so substantial that their empire of alien commerce promised to last forever." (p.20)

JUNKS ALONG THE YANGTZE

Endlessly fascinated by the vitality of life along the Yangtze, VHG captured many images on film over the years. These are three of junks that he recorded.

Moving from Anking to Wuhu he traveled by junk, with all his possessions. "What the river steamers traveled in a night took us a week". Soon, however, the "outside world of newspapers and mail had disappeared across a horizon almost shut out by the high banks of a stream that had receded to its mid-winter low" (p.82)

". . .the junks moved in stately procession or spread across the broader reaches like a flock of huge-winged birds. . ." (p.83)

PEOPLE OF THE YANGTZE

VHG was equally fascinated by the people of the Yangtze, working endlessly to make a living. These are three from the many images he recorded.

WOMEN WASHING CLOTHES *(left)*

MAN FISHING WITH CORMORANTS *(right)*

MEN POLING RAFT *(right)*

ARRIVING NANCHANG

THE TRAIN TO NANCHANG FROM KIUKIANG *(above)*

"Eighty miles south of the Yangtze, Nanchang was reached by a train which took most of a day to travel those eighty miles. . . At the end of this tedious journey the train still stopped short of Nanchang which was separated by the mile's width of the Kan River. . .across which passengers had to be transported by sampan or barge. . ." *(p.68)*

SAMPANS AWAITING TRAIN PASSENGERS FOR NANCHANG *(below)*

SIGHTS OF NANCHANG

"Nanchang was not a spectacular city to approach. Its walls were low, its houses a ramshackle clutter roofed with grey tile. But it was a proud city, a rich city. . . (p.69)

WALL AND ARCH *(above)*

BOATS, EAST LAKES *(above)*

"Through the city. . . extended a string of lakes, the Tung Hu, or East Lakes.. .[which had] their own beauty, especially in the pearl-grey of early dawn. . . (p.69)

RAFTS AND RAFT MEN *(below)*

STREET SCENE
(above) and Tei Chin Gate.

"I liked best the streets where furniture and chests were being made of camphor-wood. Their fragrance over-powered the smell of open drains. . .(p.69)

145

NANCHANG FRIENDS

MR CH'EN, A.C.M. *(above)*

"Even to look at them, one saw in the kindly, disciplined restraint of their faces the inner harmonies of a life well lived." (p.75)

THE SHEN FAMILY *(below)*
Shen lao-ye, Shen t'ai-t'ai and their grandson, Shen Ch'uan-ling and his young bride. VHG tutored the grandson and his bride, as well as the three children of a neighbor, the T'sais, for two years, 1921-1922.

FAMINE RELIEF

UNLOADING RELIEF GRAIN *(below)*

Famine relief, funded by the Red Cross, was supervised by missionary volunteers. These and other photos recorded Fr.Gowen's stint the summer of 1921 at a relief distribution centre near Yung-ching, located about 50 miles south of Peking.

"Spindly-legged scarecrows staggered in from ten or eleven miles away. . . The were a sight to weep over, so thin that I would not have been startled to see daylight shining through the stark framework of their ribs." *(p.59)*

GRAIN DISTRIBUTION *(left)*

147

THE MING TOMBS

STONE CAMELS *(above)*

". . . I passed between pairs of elephants, camels, horses, immense figures, and between warriors and statesmen, a silent company stationed here five centuries ago to watch greatness go to its grave." (p.65)

"This temple was upheld by pillars of laurel, eighty feet tall, hauled from Burma, and still as sound as when they were erected sixty-odd years before Columbus discovered America. (p.65)

STONE WARRIOR *(above)*

YUNG LO'S TEMPLE *(left)*

OTHER SIGHTS OF CHINA

PAGODA AT ANKING *(below) "Anking was proclaimed for miles up and down the Yangtze by its towering pagoda, the river's most impressive." (p.79)*

THE GREAT WALL *(above) Looking down toward Pu Tu Li "The same keenness of sensation was awakend by the spectacle of the Great Wall."(p.66)*

BRIDGE AT THE SUMMER PALACE, PEKING *(below)*

FRIENDS AND FAMILY

BURGOYNE CHAPMAN, *(p.29)* **ALAN LEE, VINCENT AND MARY GOWEN** *(left) at the Gowen's Wuhu home.*

ANN GOWEN *(below) VHG's mother, known to children and grandchildren as Muzzie.*

In the summer of 1923 VHG's mother and two sisters, pictured here, visited Wuhu.

ALAN LEE, *VHG's oldest and dearest friend in China.*

JOYCE GOWEN *(left) VHG's younger sister*

SYLVIA GOWEN, *(right) VHG's youngest sister, in Chinese costume*

150

THE WUHU HOME

WUHU HOME SEEN FROM THE EAST *(left)*

WUHU HOME, INTERIOR *(above)*
View across dining table to blossoms.

"There is an art to blending the several ingredients with the rice so as not to swamp it with too much liquid or salt it disagreeably by pouring in too much soy sauce; this art can be practiced only with its proper tools, with chopsticks. It is an art worth learning. (p.58)

EATING CHINESE FOOD *(left)*

151

SACRED SPACES

ST. MARK'S CHURCH, WUHU *(left)*
where VHG was assigned during his Wuhu years, 1922-1927.

ST. MARK'S CHURCH INTERIOR *(right)*

FOREIGN CEMETERY, WUHU *(below)*

MISSION ACTIVITIES

ST. LIOBA'S CHOIR, WUHU
(above) VHG at left in vestments

**CONFIRMATION CLASS,
ST. LIOBA'S, WUHU** *(right)*
*The confirmation class of the
spring of 1926*

**ST. AGNES GIRLS DANCING,
ANKING** *(below)*

153

KIU HUA SHAN, SACRED MOUNTAIN AND MONASTERY

VIEW FROM ABOVE *(above)*

"Kiu Hua Shan, towering to an outline as sharply serrated as a giant's jawful of teeth, had all the components of a Chinese painting, abrupt cliffs entwined by a scarf of mist, mysteriously disappearing valleys, the day's last sunlight picking out furrowed glens and loitering on the peaks. (p.86-p.89)

TOMB *(above) of Chin Ti-tsang*

LARGE MONASTERY *(right)*

154

PEKING
ANCIENT STRUCTURES

VHG visited Peking (Beijing) many
times during his China sojourn. On
this and the next page are a few of the
images he recorded.

"Even Peking is not ancient by European
standards. A drum tower and a bell tower
remain from the time of Kublai Khan;
among the city's tallest structures, they ...
were erected not to exceed 99 Chinese feet
in height lest they impede passage of the
good spirits, whose domain commences at
a hundred feet." (p.64)

BELL TOWER *(above\)*

BELL IN BELL TOWER *(above)*

DRUM IN DRUM TOWER *(above)*

155

PEKING, THE TEMPLE OF HEAVEN

TEMPLE OF HEAVEN *and passageway.(above)*

"In Peking itself a score of palaces and temples witnessed to this simple statement of a greatness unchallenged for all time. The noblest is the Altar of Heaven" (p.66)

"Many great buildings serve the [Altar of Heaven], outstanding among them the Temple of Heaven, its round conical roof glowing a deep fathomless blue. ." (p.66)

INTERIOR OF TEMPLE OF HEAVEN *(left)*

TREATY PORT, GUNBOAT

VIEW OF PORT OF WUHU *(above). View from near the Gowen residence. Customs tower can be seen on the far right of the waterfront.*

"Wuhu was a treaty port; ocean liners came three hundred miles up the Yangtze to moor alongside its crumbling banks and load the rice which it exported in larger quantities than any other port in China." (p.79)

"In demanding silver we were counting on H.M.S. Hawkins, the British flagship anchored in mid-stream, to preserve us from the headsman's sword." (p.132)

H.M.S. HAWKINS, *(below) flagship of the British fleet, seen from the Customs Tower, Wuhu,*

YANGTZE STEAMERS

Except for Nanchang, the main cities of the lower Yangtze River valley, from Shanghai to Hankow were reached by Yangtze river steamers, most run by the British trading firms Jardine Mathison or Butterfield & Swire.

S.S. TUCKWO *(above) seen from Sue Huo Shan, site of a temple that VHG visited in 1923. Four years later he was hired by Jardine Mathisen, its owners, as its purser.*

"River travel had been always my delight; to be paid for this indulgence was an unexpected luxury." (p.124)

M.S. KUTWO *(below) owned by Jardine Mathison. Six years after this 1921 shot VHG made his last Yangtze voyage as a China resident on this ship, bound for Shanghai to leave for a new post in The Philippines.*

Part II

The Philippines, 1927 — 1942

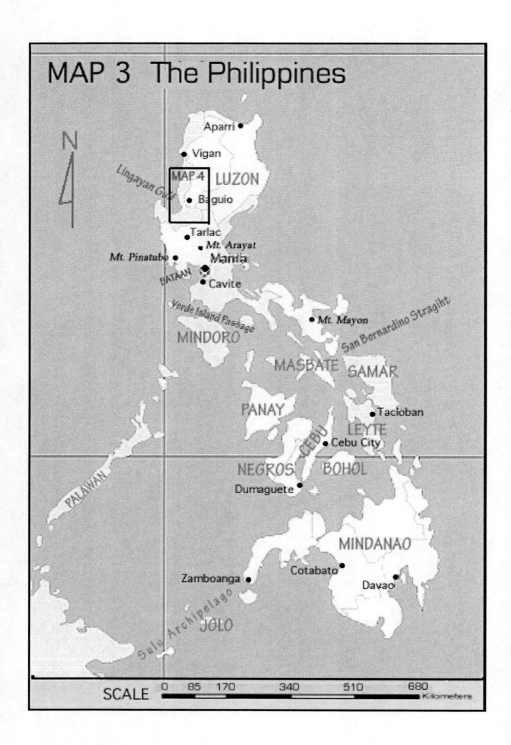

MAP 3   The Philippines

N

Aparri

Vigan

Lingayan Gulf

MAP 4   LUZON

Baguio

Tarlac

Mt. Arayat

Mt. Pinatubo

Manila

BATAAN

Cavite

Verde Island Passage

Mt. Mayon

San Bernardino Straight

MINDORO

MASBATE

SAMAR

PANAY

Tacloban

LEYTE

CEBU

Cebu City

PALAWAN

NEGROS

BOHOL

Dumaguete

MINDANAO

Cotabato

Zamboanga

Davao

Sulu Archipelago

JOLO

SCALE   0   85   170   340   510   680

Kilometers

160

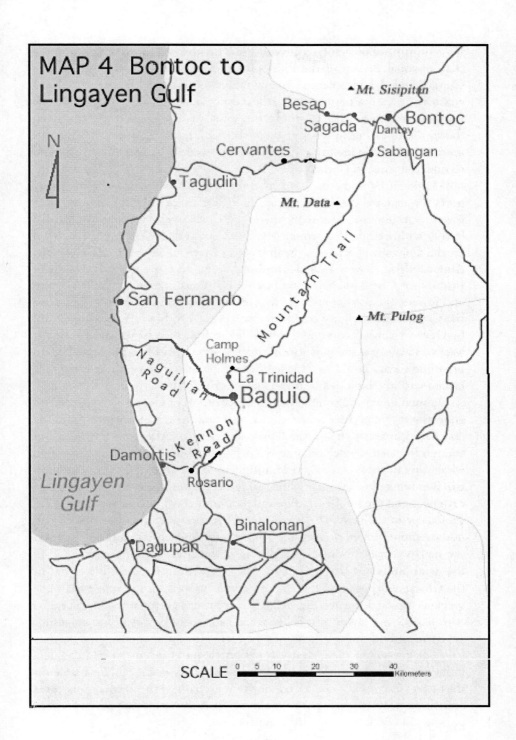

MAP 4 Bontoc to Lingayen Gulf

N

Mt. Sisipitan

Besao

Sagada

Dantey

Bontoc

Cervantes

Sabangan

Tagudin

Mt. Data

Mountain Trail

San Fernando

Mt. Pulog

Camp Holmes

La Trinidad

Naguilian Road

Baguio

Kennon Road

Damortis

Rosario

Lingayen Gulf

Binalonan

Dagupan

SCALE

0   5   10   20   30   40
Kilometers

LATE IN JUNE of that fateful year, 1927, I embarked for Manila. From the Episcopal Bishop of the Philippines[33], a personal friend and one-time China hand, I had accepted an invitation to work in his diocese. That I was leaving China permanently still did not occur to me as I watched the Empress of Asia's wake churning the muddy Yangtze, and the low-lying shores disappearing in a fringe of reeds. All I intended was to savour this unexpected interlude in the tropics until – certainly within a year – I could resume residence in China.

Manila itself took me into another world. Unlike the China treaty ports it antedated the 19th Century. From the Empress's deck, as we glided toward Pier Seven, supposedly the longest pier in the world and regarded locally with a pride that would have been extravagant had it been lavished on the Colossus of Rhodes, the one object that looked out of place was the American flag. It was an anachronism flying above the mediaeval walls of Intramuros. These walls, the stout bastions at every corner, the church domes and towers, the ponderously buttressed bodegas built of adobe still recalled the Castilian sovereignty transferred so abruptly to brash American control by Dewey's famous command to Gridley to fire when he was ready. This at least was history through whose hysterical excitement I had lived as a boy. In my mind's eye I could see, spelled out in coloured chalk on our first grade blackboard, the famous slogan, Remember the Maine.

As soon as we had completed the sticky ordeal of Customs, however, and gone ashore, I could see how far advanced was the transformation from the lazy-paced Spanish city to the febrile urgencies of American business. But enough lingered to enchant a newcomer – tortuous, narrow streets through which tiny European taxis and a multiplicity of the American cars popular in the '20's honked incessantly while trying to squeeze past erratic horse-drawn carretelas and the lumbering two-mile-an-hour crawl of carabao carts.

Except to fill in its moat and convert it to a golf course, America had not attempted to modernize the Walled city; only fire could do that. Yet she had not been unmindful of her new Imperial role. She had called in the great landscape designer, Frederick Olmsted, famous for his layout of the Chicago Exposition of 1893, and commissioned him to make Manila a spacious capital. Olmsted did well. He surrounded cold cramped Intramuros with parks, with lawns, playfields, trees; he laid out boulevards and sites for government buildings. Whose was the blame for the use made of these sites I do not know. On them were erected public buildings in blurred concrete imitation of Washington's classical architecture, as inappropriate a style for the tropics as could be conceived, one that exchanged the overhanging eaves and sliding, oyster-shell paned walls of Spanish design for pseudo-Greek pillars, and windows unshaded from the sun.

I am certain that Olmsted was not responsible for these follies. They were monuments to bureaucracy, whether American or Filipino I never gave myself the trouble to find out. But it was an American Government architect, just a few years later, after the inauguration of the Commonwealth, who designed the High Commissioner's residence to include central heating: he built it, moreover, on filled land jutting into Manila Bay, where its west windows sponged up all afternoon the blinding reflections of the sun. This was a building better suited to New Hampshire than to a city fourteen degrees from the Equator. Yet when, in substitution for the discarded furnace, the High Commissioner requested air conditioning, Congress balked. To make at least four rooms habitable, all that he could afford, the High Commissioner had to air-condition them out of his own pocket.

I arrived, fortunately, before Commonwealth or High Commissioner had been thought of. The Philippines still were administered by the greatest of their Governors-General, Leonard Wood[34] whose sense of duty had overstayed his prudence. He had just gone home to die.

Politics concerned me less at the moment than admiring the breathing spaces which Olmsted's plan had given the old, cluttered city. The plan had preserved and enlarged the esplanade of the Luneta, a gathering place and park luxuriant in lawns, palms, magnificent scarlet-flowering flame trees. Here, central to patriotic reverence, stood a monument to the Philippine hero, Jose Rizal. Under this monument the martyr's bodily remains were entombed.

Rizal had been entombed twice. In an era when the irresistible momentum of a people pressing toward freedom had not been sidetracked into demagoguery or despotism his two graves were a parable. They argued the futility of opposing man's will to grow, the gross futility of hoping to silence by the guns of a firing squad a voice as articulate as Jose Rizal's. Rizal was no homespun insurgent; he was a man of the world, doctor of medicine, doctor of philosophy, the brilliant product of Europe's most famous universities. Paris, Leipzig, Heidelberg, Berlin, each in its turn had contributed to his education but, like many upper class Filipinos, he had taken his basic studies in Madrid. He was versed in Spanish culture and, initially, sympathetic to Spanish ways.

This sympathy the Spanish blunted, turning a man who might have been their colleague – and a colleague of superior integrity – into a powerfully effective opponent. Rizal's sharpest weapons were his writings, particularly his novel, *Noli Me Tangere*, which earned Spanish condemnation by its frankness in laying bare the general misery of life under Spain. Even to hint that *Noli Me Tangere* does not belong with the world's supreme classics was greater blasphemy to Filipino ears than downgrading the Bible, but I must

163

confess that I never could read it through. For that matter, nothing could drag me through Uncle Tom's Cabin! Whether books of this sort are works of art is of little account; at the right moment in history they proved to be masterpieces of propaganda. The Spaniards shot Jose Rizal; they could not shoot his books.

They buried him in the Paco Cemetery, a resting-place withdrawn into the shady stillness of the frangi-pangi, whose heavy-scented, waxen blossoms strew its walks. To make Rizal's grave inconspicuous, the initials on his tombstone were reversed. There I used to see them, spelled backward, R.P.J., and a little bird extracted from the pages of his novel to watch in stone over the grave his body no longer occupied.

Paco Cemetery was Old Manila. Over the door of its round-vaulted chapel the Castilian coat of arms remained. Everything about the cemetery seemed round, the chapel, the enclosing walls, even the old caretaker's bald head – as smooth and shiny as the chapel dome. In the circular wall were niches, a sepulture less permanent than under the chapel floor, for the dead put in these niches had to renew their rent after five years. If the rent was not renewed, their bones were tossed into a charnel pit hidden behind a wall carved with skull and cross-bones. "Blessed are the dead who die in the Lord," was inscribed in Latin across the archway to this abandoned cemetery; to this should have been added, "More blessed are they who pay their rent" - although I doubt if many graves deserve to be kept up longer than five years.

Past this quiet enclave rolled an avenue of Olmsted's planning, Taft Avenue, a highly useful thoroughfare; but the avenue which served as highway for my happiest recollections of Manila was Dewey Boulevard. Nobly enclosed by colonnades of royal palms, Dewey Boulevard was resorted to, every afternoon, by a throng intriguingly mixed but all intent on inhaling the sea breeze and shaking off the torpour of the hot siesta hours. There came friars in their brown habit, nuns steering a double line of schoolgirls primly clad in black, Englishmen with pipe and dog briskly pacing their measured miles, bare-legged children, American, British, Filipino. Groups of young people, gesticulating animatedly, scrambled over the breakwater to watch Manila's green and gold sunsets. The west wind quickened, livening air that had been sultry and languid, the palm fronds rattled in a sound as evocative of the tropics as Sibelius's shuttling rhythms call to the hearer's mind the forest of his native Finland, bright waves splashed across the rocks. Back and forth, back and forth, from tea-time until time to shower for dinner, people rode in their cars, asking no other excitement than to see and be seen, while the western sky faded and swift twilight enveloped them in darkness.

The Bishop, the only man I have known to dignify a Model T Ford with a chauffeur, loved this excursion as did I, but my developing relish for Manila, on this first arrival, was soon curtailed. I had come to work although exactly what I was to do I did not know. The Bishop presented me with two choices. He did not describe them beyond saying that one would be easy, the other difficult. Faced with such a choice I could not be anything but heroic. I chose the harder assignment. This, I then learned, was to take me to Besao, a complex of Igorot villages situated some three hundred miles northeast of Manila in the central Cordilleras of Luzon.

The Igorots at that time were truly out of this world. A year earlier, a very sketchy motor-road had been built from the coast to Bontoc, the Mountain Province capital. Little by little a second road was being extended north from the hot weather resort of Baguio. This followed the route of the Mountain Trail, a pathway which through most of its length could be traveled only on horseback. Whether the Bishop included several days in the saddle among the difficulties he had projected I do not now; to me it was the most formidable of all.

To reach Baguio, our first objective, we had the Manila North Railway, a line built with British capital but operated by the Philippine Government with a government's indifference to improvement. The 1st class car was of 1904 vintage, and looked it. Its compartments offered two crosswise seats upholstered with khaki cloth; khaki the traveler did well to wear. Although this car was hooked up close to the engine on the theory that the soot would alight further astern, passengers emerged at the journey's end gritty with cinders and, in the dry season, streaked with the dust continually being sucked in through the open windows. Air-conditioning had not yet been thought of. Some years later, this improvement was installed, but not in the dining car. After sweating through lunch at 90 degrees Fahrenheit, one came back to risk pneumonia in a chilled compartment.

I soon learned how tedious this ride could become, especially when Manila bound. Hour after hour I would look out only to see the volcano Arayat still with us. It seemed to keep pace with the train; sometimes I thought it was outdistancing us. It was a handsome mountain, a tapering cone rising monumentally from hot, flat plains, but to the traveler, impatient to sluice away the journey's grime under a hot shower, Arayat was a bore, a landmark he would have bartered gladly for a cold drink.

On my first trip, however, I was too new to the tropics to complain about the train's discomforts; indeed I was too fresh from China where nobody expected railway travel to be comfortable. The rainy season had dampened down the dust. Clear sunshine polished trees and fields, bamboo, palms, papaya, mango, rice, the budding sugar cane, the young tobacco leaves, till all glistened like burnished enamel. The people too were a colourful contrast to China's drab blues. At every station, summoned by the locomotive's banshee shriek, they crowded the platform, men in flower-embroidered *camisas*, women trailing raspberry-hued skirts below blouses with winged piña-cloth sleeves whose billowing ampleness gave the fly-away buoyancy of butterflies in concourse.

Before arriving at Baguio we had exchanged the torrid (or, one of my Chinese schoolboys once wrote, the torpid) zone for the temperate We also had exchanged the train for a 'bus which shot boldly up a steep gorge and along ledges hewn from stony precipices until, in a breathlessly melodramatic flourish, it zig-zagged up a last gigantic slope into the cool pine groves of what then was called the Philippine summer capital.

Since April and May, the Philippine summer, had passed, the fashionable season was over, the town quiet. So widespreading indeed were the pines that we were slow to guess just how much town there was. A bulky cathedral, a tall firetrap barracks of a hotel, a street of Chinese stores, and the expansive roof of a market were all we could see. Much of Baguio's favoured population lived in wooden bungalows hidden beneath the trees, such a bungalow as we occupied that night, rejoicing in a fire of pine logs to keep out the chill of the clouds that enveloped us. We were a mile above the sea on the southern edge of Igorot territory. The Igorots might get along in gee-strings; we needed sweaters and blankets.

Few Americans nowadays are privileged to step out of the 20th Century and to drop back not just a hundred years or so but several millennia to a world before history. My journey from America to China had been an exchange of civilizations; there could be lively argument as to which was preferable. This further journey into the heart of the Igorot country was into a region which – in our sense of the word – never had been civilized. Until barely twenty years before, it had kept civilization at bay.

The Spanish had made a few sorties, only to retreat. Chinese traders had penetrated these mountains: an Igorot's intrinsic wealth was measured by the Ming dynasty medicine jars, the *gosi*, in which he matured his liquor; his dances were performed to the beat of *gansas*, brass gongs imported from China. Beyond these the Chinese had left no mark. The same can be said of the Japanese reputed to have settled in these mountains. Traces of intermarriage can be discerned but Japanese settlers, as a body, were expelled by the Spanish in retaliation for the expulsion of Christian missionaries from Japan. Even intercourse with lowland Filipino had been scant; to the Igorot, "Cristiano" was a term of abuse, a synonym for cheat and scoundrel – pregnant commentary on how the Igorot had been victimized in this intercourse.

166

Only the Americans, soldiers, scientists, and missionaries, had succeeded where others had failed. By kindness, honest dealing, compassion they had won the trust of a people whose instinct was not to make friends. So highly did they regard the Igorots that they sought to fence them apart from the world until they could meet its challenges. There had been breaches in this policy. In her first flush of excitement over an unexpected colonial possession America had exhibited the Igorot as a sideshow, sending him to expositions at St. Louis in 1904 and Seattle in 1909 to be gaped at, but this policy American good sense soon reversed. Such measures to maintain the Igorot's isolation had been instituted as the refusal to let him leave his ancestral territory except with a passport.

At the time of our arrival this isolation had nearly run its course. The paternalism which dictated it was to break down after the discovery of gold in these mountains and the need of cheap, readily available labour. We were just in time to see the end of an era, to see villages still without reading or writing, without medicine, without money, and to witness the breathless pace with which they had to ferry across four thousand years of history in one generation.

* * * * * * * *

The Mountain Trail[35] was a suitable gateway into the yesterdays of Igorot life. It was leisurely, it was lonely, it wound along sunny ridges, one moment in the damp tropics of the west slope, a hundred yards farther in a region that could have passed for California, dry, grassy uplands whose only trees were pines. It penetrated a no man's land, empty of villages, a strangely vacant country which, eighteen years later, by one of history's most curious ironies, was to stage the final collapse of Japan's epic bid for empire. On a remote, steep-sided spur, jutting off from the Mountain Trail, General Yamashita, Singapore's conqueror, was to be cornered with no protection, no chance to fight back, no place to go – except to prison and the gallows. Years afterward, the rusting wrecks of Japanese staff cars strewn beside the road were punctuation marks to a story that was tragedy both to victor and vanquished.

As we set out along this twisting road, it looked the last place to make history, slumbering in an unawakened dawn on the world's dim edges – like the Solomon Islands or New Guinea! Few Americans of the "roaring "20's" could have located any of these on the map. Our first stage, however, was modern enough to be done by car. We could ride by car as far as the government rest-house at kilometer 59. So tortuous was the road that there was seldom more than a hundred yards of straight driving. Since cars had no room to pass,

167

one way traffic was enforced by gates, planted eight or nine kilometers apart. At each we halted while the gatekeeper telephoned ahead, making sure that the next stretch was clear before allowing us to proceed. No large cars could inch around the sharp curves. Traffic was restricted to vehicles with a 120" wheelbase, a regulation that gave the Chevrolet a monopoly, unchallenged until Ford adopted gear-shift and Chrysler manufactured Plymouths. The models in use were the still prevalent touring-car. The drivers were a breed apart, men hardened to plunging through ruts so deep that mud grazed the axles, and to poising at the extremest edge of a rock-slide, six inches from eternity. After a few miles of this I looked forward eagerly to the horses.

It was the rainy season when travel on the Mountain Trail was a race to reach shelter before the skies fell. In topography as varied as the Philippines observations on climate apply only to where one happens to be; the dry season on the west coast will be the rainy season on the east. All depends on whether the northeast or the southwest monsoon is blowing, but individual valleys may still have their own private seasons. On our western slopes of Luzon the rainy season was characterized by mornings brilliantly clear. By noon clouds were gathering for the afternoon's downpour. By sunset, quite generally, the sun again was shining. This time-table, as regular as clockwork except during a typhoon, governed our arrivals and departures.

The first rest-house, at kilometer 59, which we reached just before the afternoon's cloudburst came crashing down on the iron roof, was typical of these convenient stopping places. Staffed by lowland families, the active operation usually depended on the voluble "bamboo English" and the infectious giggling of the 'teen-age daughter delegated to meet the guests. It was a happy welcome to saddle-sore travelers; the rest-houses were scrubbed white, their beds invited a deserved siesta, their *salas* glowed from a roaring log-fire. The best of these government managed inns, Governor-General Harrison's one-time hunting lodge, even offered individual suites with a sala and hearth fire attached to every bedroom.

But the meals were the operators' special, beaming pride. They were gargantuan, a huge tureen of soup, a mountain of hot biscuits, platters laden with corned beef, baked beans boiled potatoes, cabbage, even carrots and turnips, and the inevitable pie cased in armour-plate crust. The tradition as to what to serve must have been handed down from early days of the "Empire" when the caretakers catered to military appetites. The dining tables were set permanently, and invariably for a dozen guests, and the food cooked for the same number even when advance word from the gatekeepers reported but two or three travelers on the Trail. It didn't matter; the caretaker could count on a swarm of relatives in the kitchen to eat up the surplus. Much of this food, of course, was emptied from tins, but the rest-houses prided themselves on their gardens. Most temperate zone vegetables they grew in abundance, and in December luscious strawberries.

That initial afternoon at 59 put me under a spell I never wanted to shake off, the joy of easing travel weariness by a long siesta while the rain burst like surf against the roof, the relaxing episode of tea in a mountain cabin insulated against all worldly cares by the clouds that shut us in, the drowsy, inattentive fumbling through a stack of old magazines, then dinner, and no excuse for not going to bed by nine.

Our companions on the first trip, however, were devoted to bridge - still the older game of auction — a pastime that suited our carefree situation, but when the caretaker, learning that two of us were Anglican priests, brought a child to be baptized, we were hard put to explain why we had playing cards but no prayer book! The theology as well as the wording of that christening we simplified.

Next morning I met my horse. A sturdy beast, he was inured to novices. He had sized me up before I had finished crawling into the saddle. He knew exactly how far it was to the next rest-house, and exactly how long he intended to take getting there. Nothing I could do would hurry him.

We had made an exhilarating start, breakfasting before dawn and mounting our beasts just as the sun was painting vermilion the limestone summits of the mountains west of us, mountains rising precipitately from a valley which still drowsed in darkness like a man lapsing into a few more minutes' sleep before he throws back the covers and leaps from bed. These mountain mornings seemed to dawn dewy fresh in a world just created.

Within an hour or two our party was spread so far apart that for much of that morning in the saddle I travelled alone, often over a trail so faint as to breed doubts; only the kilometre stones, indicating with splashed red numerals how far we had come from Baguio, reassured me. My sole companion was my chow dog, brought from China. Water running wild he never had seen; at each stream he stopped, barking fearfully. Pigs running wild were a novelty even more exciting. When he attacked a litter of wild boar I had to dismount hastily and put him on a leash; any moment I expected an infuriated sow to come charging out of the thickets. The rest of the way I continued on foot, the dog under restraint, the horse following. We made better time than with me deposited like a sack of rice on the horse's back.

Day after day the rest-houses passed: next after 59 came 84 – which had been 88 in the directions given us and next year was to be 82 as bends in the Mountain Trail were shortened – then Mount Data, this last attained only by a taxing climb through deep pine forest and past the first of many leaping falls and eventually by a path gouged out of living rock. Each noon we clambered up the rest-house steps barely minutes before huge splashing drops announced the afternoon's deluge. Last to straggle in were the *cargadores*, their backs glistening wet as they put down the baggage, baggage wrapped in yellow oil-cloth – or "coli," as the *cargadores* called it.

For me the magic of this trail never paled – air exhilarating as wine, the lavish spectacle of fern-trees fifteen feet high upsoaring amid the pines, a solitude delicious to a refugee from China even without the unaccustomed drone of wind in the forest, the rumble of pouring streams. But from Mount Data onward we saw arresting signs of the Igorot. We began passing clusters of grass-roofed huts. We saw the first tiny rice terraces, tracing with mirrored reflections of cloud and sky the mountainside's grassy undulations.

These terraces were as yet but a small hint of what they would enlarge to after we had descended to the Chico Canyon at Sabangan. At its highest the Mountain Trail had scaled eight thousand feet; Sabangan's altitude was three thousand. This little town was a junction; here the Mountain Trail merged with the first motor-road to give access to the Igorot country, a road completed – if its ruts and treacherous fords merited such flattery – only a year earlier. In many features more startling than the Mountain Trail it came directly from the coast. Following the zigzags of an ox-cart route it climbed dizzily to Bessang Pass, a mile above the sea, then dropped to 1800 feet at the sleepy town of Cervantes, climbed again nearly to the five thousand foot level and back to three thousand feet where we joined it at Sabangan.

It was a road I was to travel oftener than the Mountain Trail, but in its earlier years it was no highway for a weak heart. In the Cervantes valley and even down the Ilocos coast, where Spanish league posts still measured distance, it encountered several streams without trouble, but in the wet season they could only resort to a bamboo raft. Whether hitched to a cable or poled across, it was a frail, hazardous conveyance which required adept gauging of the river's turbulent current as it was swept down to the landing opposite. Two cars were ferried at a time. On one occasion, near the sea, the rain was pelting so violently that we could not even see the car parked next to ours on the raft. We recalled tales of rafts swept into the breakers at the river's mouth, but the boatmen straining at their long poles always got us across, feeling their course by a sureness of instinct over which we could but marvel and breathe a hearty thanksgiving.

Needless to say, we hired car and driver for such trips. The roads often were as perilous as the fords. To be caught on these mountain roads in a thunder shower was a fearsome business, to watch rocks tumbling down ahead and behind and expect every minute that we should be engulfed by a slide. As frightening as the roads were the cars, third and fourth-hand vehicles which had outlasted their usefulness in the lowlands and been sold to the guileless mountaineer.

My worst experience was in 1935, eight years after my arrival in the Philippines. I had taken the front seat in a jitney which was travelling the Mountain Trail, by then converted to motor traffic; scarcely had we begun the daylong journey to Baguio when a series of catastrophic bumps nearly jolted me out of my seat. A rear wheel had come off. Mustering what bolts he could find and hammering them into place to the rhythm of lurid Spanish oaths, the driver put back the errant wheel into place. Next, the front shackles slipped. Such ominous symptoms of falling to pieces did the car give that, each time we stopped, I practised opening the door and testing my alacrity in jumping out.

Somehow – perhaps the oaths helped – we rattled on until, half way to Baguio, the wheel again dropped off. This time not enough bolts were left to fasten it. All the driver dared do was wire it on and limp at reduced speed – full speed on the Mountain Trail was 25 miles an hour – to the gatehouse at kilometre 60. Here, in a cramped shed, our carload of passengers had resigned themselves to passing the night, but since, to their surprise and the driver's, the wheel had not dropped off again, we crawled along to the more commodious rest-house at 52 (once 59, our 1927 stopping place). It was lucky we did. That night, the gatehouse at 60 burned to the ground.

I could have used some warmth from that fire. The month was January and the rest-house 7350 feet above sea-level. A bitter monsoon wind whistled up through the wide cracks between the floor boards. Even if the fire on the hearth could have coped with the monsoon, it could not cope with the rest-house keeper's ten children. Singly they came to gape at me, for now that the horse-trail days were past, few Americans stopped overnight. Each child left the door open when he came in, left it open when he went out, but the exercise of closing it twenty consecutive times could not keep me warm. I went to bed fully clothed and with every cover, even to my poncho, piled on top – and still I shivered. Next morning, I noticed a fringe of ice edging a pond outside.

The crowning irony of this hapless journey was to have an old Igorot, clad only in grey cotton blanket and flimsy red gee-string, grunt in English, as he watched the driver improvising repairs, "1935 model!"

But I have jumped years ahead of our initial entrance into the Mountain Province. In 1927 we still were riding horses. On that first journey as often out of the saddle as in it we were like the sea-sick voyager who vowed that if he once got to land, he would never, never, never go to sea again. I decided that the three hundred miles between me and Manila would have to remain exactly that. Nothing short of furlough, I vowed, would tempt me to repeat this journey. The vow was short-lived. We were not only three hundred miles from Manila, we were a hundred and fifty miles from a doctor.

To get an ailing wife[36] to Baguio I could not even secure a jalopy but had to make do with a truck, a truck twelve inches too long for travel on the Mountain Trail. This involved, first, a visit to Bontoc and a permit from the district engineer. The permit did not solve all our difficulties. The truck, although new, was hampered by a choked fuel line. This defect so delayed us that we were still on the road past the hour when traffic was required to halt for the night. By then we had done all the bad places. Every sharp, tricky curve, however, we had negotiated without even having to sidle around them. Baguio's lights, and a clear road, were in sight.

Yet at this stage a gatekeeper came out with a measuring stick to inform us that our truck was too long to have come over the Mountain Trail. The fact that we had come, and with a permit, made no headway with him. It was a physical impossibility, he insisted, obstinately prepared to hold us up all night while he argued that we hadn't done what we had. Only our promise to present the truck at Constabulary headquarters and have this miracle vouched for did at last mollify him.

Such emergency trips were not lightly undertaken; it was too debatable whether the medical aid at the terminus was worth the ordeal of getting there. If a man was sick enough to risk the journey, he was undoubtedly too sick to endure it. But pain leaves no choice. I fell ill one evening with some obscure stomach disorder which kept me in agony till daylight, when I got hold of a nurse at Sagada, across the ridge, to allay my pain as best she could with morphine. The relief was barely temporary; beneath my dulled senses the throbbing persisted, pressing to flare up again.

It happened luckily that the Governor-General's aide had been visiting Sagada and was setting forth that morning for Baguio. He volunteered to take me in his car.

Huddled in a blanket I was too miserable to do more than tick off the hours until I could be in bed at the Baguio hospital. Every kilometre was torture. Instead of the Mountain Trail we were proceeding by the Coast road; after the precipitate down-up-down travel to the sea at Tagudin we could make time through the flat coastal provinces, Ilocos Sur and La Union, and climb again to Baguio by the Naguilian Trail. We had gone through Cervantes, forded the Abra River, zigzagged up the Coast range to Bessang Pass when, after a sharp turn around a bend, we came abruptly face to face with a log slung across the road. A new gate had been installed at the Pass.

Captain Knight applied his brakes; he could not halt soon enough to avoid this unlooked for barrier. It caved in the top of the car and threw the automobile to one side with a violence so impetuous that we had no time to appreciate our danger; only after it had stopped and we were preparing to get out did we discover that the right hand doors opened on a six hundred foot drop. According to our precise measurements we had escaped eternity by six inches.

This fright cured me. My pains disappeared. In complete comfort I continued the several hours' journey to Baguio. Having come this far, I entered the hospital, but I felt like a fraud. After two nights and a day during which the doctors could find nothing wrong I returned home, sheepish yet glad to have been so drastically healed.

My explanation, vouched for by no medical men, is that the jolt had dislodged something – perhaps "p'i-ch'ai," the Chinese cabbage I had eaten – that had got caught in my stomach. Since physiology is a subject I have shunned, it may be just as simple to attribute both my sickness and recovery to the spirits, the *anito*!

The Igorots would have had no diffidence about accepting this. They held the *anito* responsible for sickness and accident alike – a fact brought home graphically when, on one of my trips, the Baguio 'bus stopped at a particularly risky stretch of trail so that an old woman might sacrifice to the *anito*. Several days earlier, a car in which her daughter was riding had gone over the cliff at this point. The driver was killed and her daughter so gravely hurt that recovery looked doubtful. The mother had come on but one errand, to implore the local spirits to let the girl live. While the 'busful of passengers looked on soberly, she kindled a little fire beside the road and offered rice-wine and food, all the time singing a plaintive chant as she knelt at the fire. After some ten minutes of poignant invocation, she climbed back into her seat – and we re-entered the 20th century.

The Igorot country which I entered for the first time was still empty of history. A primitive community, of course, is not the naïve, pastoral idyll imagined by writers like Rousseau. It had its tensions. It lived chained by fear. Yet in a world all too swiftly aping our drab pattern I cherish the memory of an enclave which had no history, no time, which did not even trouble even to devise a calendar nor to check off months and days. I think of it echoing to but one sound that could be called seasonal, the throb of the brass gongs, the *gansa*, summoning its villager to immemorial observances, the wedding feast or *dawak*, or to *obaya,* to days of rest, not calculated at regular intervals like the Sabbath but called when the old men, seized by an unpredictable impulse, saw fit to call them.

* * * * * * * *

Sagada – Besao – around these names my life for the next fifteen years was to revolve. Of the two, Sagada was famous; it was known and talked of in New York and Chicago and San Francisco, even in Seattle. Besao was

173

its poor relation, a cluster of villages across the mountains five miles to the west, a place nobody had heard of – but it was to be my home, so deeply the centre of my affection that, even after years of separation, no other home can supplant it in my heart, in the love I feel for its people.

Sagada was a dramatic town to come upon, as we learned from our first sight of its grey, stone buildings. From Sabangan we had ridden on a shelf of rock between the overhanging walls of the Chico Canyon. Below us a foaming river poured over boulders toward Bontoc. We were traversing now the narrow motor road we had met at Sabangan. Bontoc, the Mountain Province capital, was its terminus, but traffic at that time was so inconsiderable that all we had to watch out for was the mail truck which departed every morning for the coast at Tagudin. To warn the driver of our approach we had telephoned from Sabangan; when we saw the car coming around one of the innumerable bends, we had time to dismount and turn our horses' heads so that they would not panic over this monstrous contraption.

From the Canyon we soon were climbing straight up formidable slopes and by zigzags across huge shoulders of rock until at last we had entered an upland of red clay and blue limestone spires, gnarled outthrusts of what, ages before, had been ocean bottom, but heaved to this hot, sun-bright eminence a full mile above the sea. Through a corridor of Nature's gothic carving we came suddenly face to face with Sagada.

Sagada was an engineer's dream, dream of the engineer turned priest who had chiselled out of stubborn wilderness this assemblage of massive stone buildings. He had founded his mission at what in 1904 was the crossroads of the two trails that penetrated this aloof region of the head-hunters. One was the Mountain Trail, the other an earlier path followed by Ilocano traders from the coast and, centuries earlier, by the Chinese. Here, helped by Japanese foremen, he taught the Igorots both to quarry and to cut stone, and to build a church and houses of masonry staunch enough to outlast earthquake or typhoon. On the backs of cargadores he had had transported the machinery of a saw-mill so that he could utilize the falls at Fidelisan nearby to cut from almost impenetrable pine forests the lumber he needed. He had installed a printing press, organized a clinic, even opened a store to stimulate Igorot incentive, kindling in them a desire for novelties which they must first work to buy. John Armitage Staunton, Father Staunton, as everybody knew him, was a dreamer gifted with a practical genius for making his dreams take solid form.

But other engineers had outwitted him. Bypassing the old trails, they had built their new road through the Chico Canyon, three thousand feet below, and left Sagada – which had been placed to burst upon every traveller's sight like the City of God – now stranded high and dry in what had become just a back eddy of Mountain Province traffic.

We at least, emerging from five days' lonely travel, saw Sagada in the full boldness of the imagination that had planned it, a metropolis sprung from a blue print and planted like a giant's ponderous fortress in a steep valleyful of grass huts. People were pouring out from Mass as we rode the last half mile past fissured limestone cliffs to the open plaza in front of the church.

Of this church one could repeat that it was unique. It certainly was not beautiful; in blasphemous moments we compared it to a fire-hall, but its impact was crushing, an engineer's church built to outlast eternity[37]. Inside, the broad, bare, stone floor spread past a series of altars, monastic altars set side by side each in its stone partitioned alcove to allow every priest his separate mass, until we gazed irresistibly not at the high altar nor its tabernacle nor even the lamps honouring the Blessed Sacrament but at the giant statue of the Virgin Mary for which altar and tabernacle were but a grey pedestal. For this high altar the famous American architect, Ralph Adams Cram, mediaevalist and devout Anglo-Catholic, had contributed a design. It told much about Father Staunton's sternly dominating assurance that he had discarded Cram's plan in favour of his own. By the time of our arrival Father Staunton had been gone two years; a disappointed, angry man, he had fought his bishop once too often, but the building which he had shaped from a mind epic in scope remained, unwieldy as a mastodon's skeleton.

Our destination was humbler, a school five miles farther west, beyond the ridge which shut off from Sagada the setting sun's rays and hemmed in the monsoon's chill mists. This was the difficult place which the Bishop had offered me, but at Sagada it had been implied that my sojourn there would be brief: a place soon would be found for me in their proud centre.

My first visit to Besao made me hope that the sojourn could be cut even shorter. Rain and mist obscured the site of my new home. All I could note was a sprawling wooden building of which the priest's quarters were two long, unfinished rooms, the lower room giving access by an interior stairway to a second story bedroom so squeezed by three dormer windows that headroom was a case of dodging rafters. Furniture was negligible, plumbing absent. Along the cross beams of the unsealed walls was lined up a regiment of empty chocolate tins; they betrayed the one self-indulgence of the priest whose job it had been to visit this outstation. If I had to live long in these forlorn quarters, I thought, an array of empty whisky bottles would be my monument.

Yet there were echoes of life. Beyond the thin walls the steady, drenching rain could not muffle completely the clatter of classes in progress. Balconies looked down on a *sala*, an all-purpose *sala* that could serve (I was soon to discover) as classroom, chapel, or dance-hall. In earlier days, the formidable

175

little English deaconness[38] who had founded this mission and, uncowed by priest or bishop, ruled the L-shaped building she called, with cockney aspirates, her "little h-ell," had utilized these balconies to house the girls in her charge. They had addressed her as "Ina" – Mother. She was dead now, buried in the Campo Santo under a stone cross visible from the upstairs windows when the mist cleared. Her spirit lived on. It pervaded the chattering informality of a building more home than school, filled it with her deep personal concern for her Igorot children, with love that spread out to the village, to the old men and women whom she petted or cajoled or scolded with a salty vigour they respected and adored.

There are many graves like hers scattered through the Orient. I remembered the two English priests, victims of the Boxer rebellion, buried among their flock at Yungching. So intimately had they been identified with their adopted people that their headstones bore only their Chinese names, not their English. Such graves do not speak of loneliness or exile but of men and women who have made their home, not just been born to it. Little more than a year later I was to add a grave of my own to this Besao Campo Santo, the grave of the wife who had come with me from China. In her last illness, brought on by a grave accident, by the collapse of a sodden trail under her horse's foot, her thoughts roamed over these mountains. She had known them so briefly yet with a joy that surged through her words even when mind and speech wandered. Her last coherent sentence, spoken with a sudden calm from the midst of delirium, was, "I came in trusting; I go out trusting."[39]

To such trust these graves witness. The time was to arrive when the dearest privilege I could think of was to call Besao home, and to have its people welcome me as one who belonged. If I could have had my wish, at no other place would I more gladly have laid down my life than on its sunny slopes where quiet, enclosing the thatched villages, the deep gorges overhung by cliffs of blue stone, the ravines penetrating mysteriously into forests haunted by *bozo*[40], spread over them its golden patina till all life seemed halted by a spell whose outpoured, glowing radiance nothing had changed since the world began. Cocks from the village crowed strangely and drowsily in mid-afternoon, and were answered by wild cocks in the jungle.

The casual visitor, surveying this scene, might question our right to be there at all. Why trespass on this primeval enclave which had endured, isolated and self-sufficient, through millennia it had, happily enough, no calendar to record? It was not we who trespassed; it was the 20th Century, rudely smashing a gateway into these silent valleys. Whatever misguided missionaries might have done elsewhere, we did not cajole the inhabitants of these valleys into adopting the folly of Western dress. We preferred to leave them comfortably undressed, the men in skimpy gee-strings, the girls in the *tapis*, the brief skirts, striped red and white like a peppermint stick. Gee-strings and *tapis*, like the blankets the Igorots wrapped themselves to ward off the evening's chill, were products of the looms which women set up outdoors between stout mango trees; the dyes, blue, red, orange, yellow, even green, were dyes which the tropical sun could not outstare. Beautifully in their stripes they repeated conventional patterns; always the python was conspicuous, sometimes with a man's head disappearing between his jaw. Down a narrow blue strip of fabric he writhed, hemmed in by crimson borders. This great snake was the chief ornament of Igorot heraldry; his bleached vertebrae were the beads which women twined through their hair as the badge of motherhood.

Here at last was the school I had wanted, small, intimate, eager, simple. At the moment, of course, all I could see was the opportunity, a prospect as fair as the sun-warmed landscape to which I woke the next morning.

Besao's more than twenty villages sprawled across a vast complex of mountains, mountains that slid downward from the pine-forested upper ridges, from peaks with mellifluous names – Tinangdanan, Kalimogtong, Sisipitan[41] – to disappear into rock-walled gorges so deep that, though I could hear the rumbling of rainy season torrents, their foam-flecked yellow streams could not be seen except far down the valley. Only from that distance, miles away, three thousand feet lower, a glint of sunlight sparkled back from their crest as they surged into the swift, smoothly eddying Abra beneath the western Cordilleras. The voice of many waters was ever audible at Besao, even in the dry season, but now it was July, when the afternoon rains fell hardest, perhaps six inches between noon and sunset. Across the widest valley a water-fall plunged a hundred feet down a cliff; steering headlong toward the ravine's hidden depths, cascades, just emerged from the wooded uplands, glistened over huge boulders.

The villages, spread up these slopes, were peaceful to see, steep-pitched roofs of thatch hemmed in by thickets of coffee, by cane-brakes and plumes of bamboo, and overshadowed by pine and mango, the latter trees like huge globes of dark, glossy verdure.

But what made the whole uniquely spectacular was its terraces. July, I learned, was harvest time, when the second of the year's two crops was being garnered. Some fields already were stubble; in others, tiny figures still moved slowly forward lopping off with their bales the heads of golden rice. How many tiers of terraces there were I could not count; I guessed eighty. Bolstered by dykes six, eight, ten feet high, whose stones, though without mortar, were so skillfully fitted that they had kept their place through the battering of centuries, these terraces gave the mountain slopes an ever breathing, ever changing vitality. They fanned out like a luxuriant river delta across the mouth of every valley; water-smooth, they were mirrors to the clouds in daylight, to the stars at night, until the rice growing drew a veil across their surface. In their two thousand foot ascent from stream-bed to gloomy forest they scaled the precipitous slopes like gigantic stairways, yellow against the green mountainside in the rainy season, green against brown in the dry. Immediately after each harvest they lay freshly flooded with water while the next season's rice was growing emerald bright in patches of seed-bed but soon the women were at work wading ankle deep through the water as they transplanted the seedlings. On misty mornings the terraces became thin pencillings traced in green to define the contour of the mountains till, higher than the clouds, their lightly stencilled skein dissolved in fog.

Yet bold as had been the engineering which constructed these terraces, Igorot culture was stagnant; its magnificent landscapes lay embalmed in the preserving clarity of a sun whose morning brilliance we counted on as surely as we expected the clock to strike. Under this primeval calm lurked fear. It inhibited all progress; it stifled thought, letting men's minds fossilize, letting their bodies wrinkle before they had finished being young; it stultified them with the mysterious terrors of witchcraft, and kept them paralyzed by fear of poison. Beyond the tyranny which fear itself exercised was the tyranny wielded by those crafty enough to manipulate its terrors to their own use. The real tyrants were the old men; they held the villages in thrall.

The Igorots themselves knew this: they had a saying that it is always the man with the fattest pigs who is threatened with disaster. To him the old men were sure to come; they would warn him of some impending misfortune which nothing less than the sacrifice of these prize pigs could avert. Ostensibly the pigs were slaughtered to nourish the *anito*, the spirits – but the old men took the meat!

Igorot diet at that time was meager – rice and *camotes* (or yams, a sweet potato which had never learned to be sweet). Until the Mission school encouraged its pupils to plant cabbages, this diet seldom included green vegetables. Cows as well as pigs were raised, though not for their milk, but except at sacrificial feasts they were seldom killed. Occasionally, the circling of hawks would lead men to the carcass of a steer which had fallen over a cliff. No matter how long he had been rotting in the sun, the Igorots would salvage his remains, fetching the green, putrefying mess to the village. Once, while climbing the hot, steep ascent from a ford, I encountered two men bearing such a load, so decomposed that even the head of the defunct beast was barely recognizable.

This trail, its heat reflected oven-hot from the cogon grass, usually exhausted me. I would stagger a hundred yards and then stop for breath. But the dead cow expelled all thought except a frantic need to get beyond range of its stench. Since the breeze was blowing the stink toward me, I climbed that trail with an alacrity a marathon runner would have been proud of. If their craving for meat could drive men to devour this putrid mess, I did not wonder at the old men's asserting their authority to extort a tastier diet.

Their iron sway over the village, however, boded other consequences far more ominous. However stubborn their resistance, the 20th Century was seeping into their remote, inaccessible valleys. Soon it would burst all barriers. When that time came, the younger generations might sweep aside not only this despotism of the most ignorant, bigoted part of their community but make garbage of all their inherited traditions, good and bad alike. Revolutions as harshly abrupt as this had destroyed many primitive peoples just as they could cut the Igorot hopelessly adrift from his ancestral moorings.

To prevent this was the purpose of our schools, to substitute <u>Do</u> for <u>Don't</u> in their thinking. In a single generation we had to ferry these Mountain people across four thousand years. We did not intend by this process to create imitation Americans. We did little to raise, or to interfere with, their standard of living. Undoubtedly the change would come, but it must come of their own volition, and no sooner than they were able to support it. We did not wish these students to turn their backs on their own past, nor to accept without discriminating judgement the novelties – often the most uncultured novelties – of Western culture. They must choose their own destiny.

In the process they were encouraged to examine their own customs, to appraise them, and determine what should be retained, what adjusted, what discarded. Similarly, they were to figure out what customs from the West could be valuable, what harmful. Only clear-headed, unbiased teaching could help them make these decisions prudently. It had to help them also to a community of interest with the villages beyond their own valley, villages that up to now had been automatically their foes, proper subjects for the head-hunting forays from which every young man had to bring back his own trophy before he could ask a girl to marry him.

Education keyed this new attitude, education in the largest sense, directed to build character as well as train minds. Scholastically there was little to build on. The Igorots had existed since the dawn of time without reading or writing; they had not devised even the crude rudiments of medicine but had gone on wholly content to treat sickness as a visitation of the *anito* which only a sacrifice could turn away. Their language, a Malay dialect added to by a few Spanish words borrowed from the Lowlands – *mistro* for teacher, *kabayo* for horse, *iskuela* for student, *misa-an* for church – had a subtly inflected structure strangely reminiscent of Greek, but no abstract terms. Its vocabulary was overweighted with words to describe the stages of boiling rice, or the swift changing gradations of dawn, but it was a blank when describing truth or justice or pity. Even the phrase for "Thank you" – *Dies tinag ngina*, god reward you – had been copied from the Ilocanos.

Under such limitations our medium for instruction had to be English. English indeed was the language of all Philippine schools, used thus not only for the practical reason that it provided the necessary text-books but to carry out the American Government's policy of a common tongue in the hope of unifying a people diverse in custom, in dress, in manners, a people scattered over the islands of a huge archipelago and split up by perhaps eight major dialects, as distinct from each other as French from Spanish, Spanish from Portuguese, Portuguese from Italian.

By this accident I could begin teaching at once; I need not wait on protracted language study but could be immediately useful in exactly the school I wanted. It was not much to exclaim at – simple wooden buildings crudely furnished. Its pupils slept, wrapped in cotton blankets, on their dormitory floor; they cooked their own meals of rice and cabbage, flavoured occasionally with mongo beans and, very rarely, with meat; they contributed to their own support by growing vegetables in their individual plots. They composed that most prized of all institutions, a school without rules, where each breach of discipline could be dealt with, as in a family, on its own merits.

From the start I caught that accent on family. Despite the cheerless impressions of that first rainy afternoon, the neglected, attic-like confusion of my quarters, the lack of ordinary conveniences, the bath-tub unattached to any pipe and propped up on four blocks high enough so that it could be drained with a pail, despite having to anchor my socks out of reach of rats, I knew, even while the rain dripped at the windows, that I was home. Not only would I refuse the chance, if offered, of removing to the stone-girt comforts and society of Sagada, but I began to doubt whether I would ever return to China. In unbelievable fullness the years ahead confirmed the rightness of my choice.

* * * * * * * * *

"Another walk after Vespers to see the mountains transfigured by golden sunlight and the intense voiceless peace of dusk: dark shadows already give the glen which winds up toward the forest from Agawa a deep brooding mystery; the rampart of cliffs between Sisipitan and Kaligmogtong turns amethyst; infinite blue is the sky, the tiny crescent of a moon almost dissolved in its unfathomable depths. Earth and heaven are so tranquil at that hour that description only disturbs their serene glowing content; the men who come by, driving *carabao* or carrying logs, the old women and girls with baskets of

180

camotes poised on their heads, accent this feeling of peace as they go home, their day's work done."

This paragraph, written in 1933 when life in Besao was no longer a novelty, I copy from my diary. It comes from one of the few volumes of a journal, kept day by day since prep school, which survived the war. This excerpt reveals the quality of Igorot life as it impressed us during any of the fifteen years we spent in their mountains. It cannot be dismissed as the idealized impression of a visitor looking for the picturesque, nor is it a violet-tinted memory from many years afterward. It records how I felt at the time.

The "we" in this passage is key to a second marriage. After Mary's death in 1928, I was permitted home-leave ahead of schedule. While crossing the Pacific in my favourite *Empress of Russia* I received a telegram from my father, founder and head of the Oriental Department at the University of Washington, a wireless request that I relieve him for a quarter so that he might conduct an Oriental tour. The University's president, he told me, had approved my appointment as a Visiting Lecturer, and the two subjects to be taught were in my line (more his opinion, it turned out, than my own!). the message left me no option.

"Wire acceptance immediately."

In sequel to this acceptance, I had been home three weeks when my father handed me, one morning at breakfast, an old envelope on which he had penciled some titles. "These," he informed me, "are the headings of your lectures."

"Oh, yes," I commented. "I have intended to ask for your notes so that I can get started."

His answer nearly paralyzed me, "I have no notes."

That winter I spent immersed in the University library. One course, History of China, I was prepared for, but the other, Religions of China, India and Japan, buried me deep in books. Again, of China and Japan I had some knowledge, but India was a pitfall, and most formidable a lecture entitled, The Six Orthodox Schools of Hindu Philosophy. I had trouble understanding them. As I told my classes, "The last time I was here, I was trying to hide my ignorance from the professors; now I am hoping to hide it from the students."

They survived, and so did I, but it was during my brief tenure as a professor that I became engaged to Frances Olin, a close friend of my sister's, and herself a senior at the University, though not in my classes. Whether this engagement increased the fervour of my teaching is debatable; it certainly impeded my preparations. On my first involvement with Frances I was three weeks ahead of my class; before my last lecture on Shintoism, I led them by a scant twenty minutes.

Frances came out to be married in October, 1929, bravely facing the ordeal of a wedding at six-fifteen in the morning, and the deterring grimness of a shower so violent that she required a taxi to ferry the fifty feet of flooded road from Bishopsted to the Cathedral. The Bishop, noting her youth, her inexperience, her gay liking for jazz and its concomitants, predicted (by his later admission) that she would last perhaps two weeks in the solitude of Besao. He was wrong by thirteen years. It took war, in fact, and the Japanese to remove her. In Besao she created her own gaiety. In its mountains and among its people she found satisfying happiness, a happiness sobered by the loss of her first child, an infant daughter, Mary Millicent, but shared by two more children, Geoffrey and Ann, who like her were to respond to the enfolding peace of the mountains and to feel at one with the Igorots whose land this was.

Within a few weeks after I had settled in Besao we had our first typhoon. The mountains broke up the full scope of the wind so that the extreme gusts, so far as I could guess, did not exceed sixty miles an hour, but it proved enough to shake the house to its roots. To withstand gale and earthquake, the building was of exceptionally supple construction: beams, joists, rafters had been dovetailed, and their jointure was spaced irregularly to forestall any one line of breakage. Under the wind's impact the house swayed till we could imagine we were at sea, an illusion quickened by the roar of rain slapped against wall and window, and by the deeper, more ominous grumble of torrents cataracting through the ravine two thousand feet below.

This rain frightened me more than the wind. Perched as we were close to the edge of the ridge, I could only pray that the builder had planted us on solid ground. The gale was forcing the rain between the window frames and their many square panes, driving it so fiercely that it sprayed the rooms several feet from the window. Hour after hour the downpour continued, never slackening, never abating. Except for brief intervals we lived in a grey fog nearer night than day. In the rare moment when the clouds tore free in tattered shreds we confronted an astounding spectacle: from the highest ridges the mountains were running white water, a vast raging cataract plunging down, down, to ravage the streambeds and tumble ten-weight boulders like pebbles.

"Are all typhoons like this?" I asked the Igorot houseboy.

"Yes, Father," was his blithe reply.

"How long will it last?"

"Perhaps three days, Father," and he laughed again.

Fortunately he was wrong on both counts. Igorots, I discovered later, were never reliable predictors of their own weather. Next morning dawned brilliantly clear; wind and rain had gone. But their fury had left its scars: the horsetrail was gouged out in pot holes five feet deep; on the mountain slopes I counted more than a hundred slides. Yet the rice terraces stood unshaken, scarcely a stone dislodged.

This first typhoon was my worst. The rainfall had been measured at Sagada at twenty-six inches for twenty-four hours, still far short of the record set, sixteen years before, in Baguio. That storm, measuring forty-two inches, dissolved mountains.

We had other typhoons which registered as high as fifteen or eighteen inches in a day but – my houseboy to the contrary – they were not usual. Most typhoons were no more than spells of clouded or rainy weather, noticeable only because they interrupted the normally sunny morning. Innocuous though they might be, I was never comfortable when they threatened. Mindful of our exposed site, I would note the signals from the Manila Observatory, signals numbered to indicate both force and direction, but my main reliance was the surveyor's barometre which I kept on my desk. My imagination was too active; it suggested such dire possibilities as waking to hear the shingles ripped off the roof or the house trembling to the first ominous movement of a landslide.

In mountains one cannot assume that what hasn't happened won't happen. Mountains are shaped by disaster; typhoons wield a potent chisel. Across the ridge east of us two villages which had lived secure for centuries were buried too deep even to salvage the bodies when a night saturated by rain brought half a ridge down upon them. There were two slides, half an hour apart, just long enough for rescuers to start frantically digging for the first victims ere they too were engulfed.

What good it would have done me to know that I was being buried alive I never debated. Sometimes almost to dawn I would sit at my desk fumbling wearily through an interminable round of solitaire. I would brace myself to the coming impact as the gusts shrieked down the slopes like an express train. I would walk to the windows and try vainly to peer through the impenetrable blackness of the rain. Hour after hour I watched the little barometre. Not till it began inching upward did I dare go to bed.

Yet the typhoon I remember best for the insouciant spirit it bred. It was characterized by an Igorot boy who reported,

"The roads, they are destroyed, Father."

That destruction, by confining us to our isolated ridge, cut us off from all care. The outside world had vanished. Telephone lines were down; the mails could not get through; the school due to convene after vacation, could not

183

assemble. Best of all, we had congenial guests who could prolong their stay without a qualm and help us enjoy days that had no schedule, no time-table. Daylight was so little brighter than night that we gave up living by the clock, going to bed or getting up with total disregard of the hours by which we are accustomed to mete out our existence. Our entertainment we improvised to fit this unrestrained mood, preparing and acting out scenarios from the old-fashioned formula that had been popular before "talkies" superseded the silent movies. Our villains were out-and-out villains; they couldn't be excused by Freudian theories. Our heroines were modeled in the ringletted innocence of Mary Pickford. Although we had no piano to syncopate a stirring accompaniment, we did have a member of the cast whose passion for realism impelled him to rap out with his knuckles on the floor the horse's hoof-beats while the heroine seated supposedly in a buggy beside her swain rode to Friday night supper at the Baptist Church.

That typhoon, I forgot to watch the barometre.

* * * * * * * * *

The ferocity of typhoons we might tame to social entertainment. The Luzon thunder storms we never tamed. In the rainy season they were almost a daily visitation, but there was no getting used to them. There was no predicting what they would do. In our complex of valleys they might follow any of a dozen courses, rounding on us when we thought their threat had fizzled out, dissolving in sun and rainbow just as we waited breathless for the heavens to crash down on our heads. Hypnotized, we watched the shattering approach of their rain-clouds as they reached out for each silent glen and clutched the wooded upland dales in their grey tentacles. As suddenly as they came they would depart, leaving a screen of raindrops to build up double rainbows zenith-high and to frame Mugao, the sacred mountain, aglow like an emerald while the late sun pierced to the red soil beneath its dripping pines.

What we could not put out of mind were the afternoons when the lightning picked us for its target. There were fearful moments when every nerve was jumpy as we ticked off the seconds between flash and thunder, hoping the next interval would be longer and the storm would move away. My upstairs study was particularly vulnerable. In it was installed the telephone, instrument of the private line that kept us in touch with Sagada. In thunder storms this telephone was a menace, compelling me to evacuate my study and take refuge downstairs. Although there was a switch to disconnect it and, theoretically, to ground any intruding bolt, the switch did not prevent one bolt from knocking splinters out of my ceiling. The only omen I trusted was the rainbow.

Even at night there were rainbows, too pale for colours but hanging ghostlike over villages where no light shone. These were dry season rainbows created on the shredded fringe of the northeast monsoon. They never seemed believable. Like the nights in these mountains they breathed witchery.

Igorots did not venture far at night. For an hour or so after the brief twilight they could be seen holding aloft their pitch-pine torches while they climbed up and down the slab-stone trails, imperiling with sparks the flammable grass roofs of the village. Their activity soon quieted. Only in March, near the end of the dry season, were their nights bright with movement, for then the ripening of the harvest needed water.

The year's two seasons alternated drought and cloudburst. By March, water often had to be conveyed two, even three, miles in split bamboo conduits, carried from remote springs through newly dug ditches or supported on a spindly trestle till it could flow to the terraces and pour down from tier to tier, making each field a pond for the young rice; hundred of pools there were, open mirrors to sun and sky and at night to the stars.

This irrigation was a communal affair; every field was entitled to its portion. To make sure that no one stole their water, the owners camped all night by their terraces, their vigilance displayed in countless torches whose flickering light had changed the usually deserted slopes into a metropolis.

The Igorot's dependence on Nature was as real as the Chinese, and closer because swarming cities had not crowded out these portents of wind and rain and sun which, almost from day to day, ruled his existence. Although back of his consciousness loomed a beneficent god, Lumawig, his mythology was vague. Igorot nature worship lacked system; it venerated mountains, trees, boulders much as a Catholic might kneel before the Blessed Sacrament, feeling behind these phenomena a whole range of powers too mysteriously formless to be thought of as a person. This worship, which had no priests except the old men, it is impossible to disentangle from the corrupting effects of spirit worship, much more immediate, much more dreadful, in which he asked only to be left alone, to be free from the petulant interference of the dead. Lumawig was well-disposed, but far off; the dead were too close for comfort.

In the Igorot's concern with fertility there were, of course, attitudes and practices common to all primitive peoples, and tinged with the same somber veneration of the Earth on whose inscrutable will depended life itself. Among some tribes, this seems to have been the principal cause of head-hunting, requiring that a head be planted in a field at seed-time to ensure fair harvest, a custom like the sacrifice of the king in pre-Hellenic Greece or the annual

185

death and resurrection of a god in some Mediterranean cultures. In the same class was the *ngilin*, the fast at time of planting when the villages were quarantined by barriers of reeds at each outgoing trail.

A similar fast, lasting but a day, was the *obaya*, an observance like the Jewish sabbath – with the one vital exception, that it was not kept at regularly stated intervals. Its originating impulse appears to have been the same – man's need for a day of rest. But whereas the Jews' great discovery was the importance of ensuring that this day of rest could be counted on, week by week, the *obaya* could not be predicted. Its occurrence was dictated by a psychic impulse that would seize on the old men, moving them when or why they could neither foretell nor explain. Early some morning they would be overwhelmed by the mystic conviction that an *obaya* was needed. Before dawn I used to hear them announcing its observance in sounds that to my drowsy, reluctantly awakened senses were like the shrilling of cocks.

Soon from village to village the cry was repeated, and measures instituted for keeping the fast properly. These stringently prohibited work, at least work in the fields. The barriers of reeds and sticks across the trails warned that no one might leave or enter the village. Throughout the day people sat idly outside their huts. To make sure that they were there, young men patrolled from house to house: if they found a family absent, they collected a forfeit, pigs or chickens which the owner could not reclaim unless he had an excuse acceptable to the village elders.

The barriers also excluded outsiders, a rule that could work hardship to travelers. Since the main trails led through the villages, passers-by had to pick a rough path of their own around the quarantined settlement. I met one wayfarer who had circumvented the tabu only by leading his horse up and down a steep, rocky mountain, a long and troublesome detour imposed to prevent his importing any malign influence. Such a restriction, however, they never enforced against me, exempting me – and other Americans – with the highly flattering excuse that we brought only good. *Obaya* or no *obaya*, they expected me to come and go as I chose.

The importance of fertility in fields on whose yield the people depended needs no explanation. Despite their teeming superfluity of rain and sun, the Igorots had suffered lean years when hunger compelled them to peddle in the lowlands a local stone, picked up from the stream-beds, which could serve as a whetstone. Against these lean years each village had granaries, erected on its outskirts to be safer from fire.

The importance of human fertility was less obvious. Compared with China their family ties were tenuous. No surnames preserved the continuity of such kinship. At ten or thereabouts – the Igorot was sketchy about his exact age, numbering neither years, months nor years – boys and girls left home to live in their respective dormitories, the *dapay* and the *ebgan*. This move was almost necessary, for the grass huts provided no accommodation adequate for a family. The ground floor was just that, earth trampled flat; the walls were too flimsy to screen out wind and rain. On platforms within the steep-pitched roofs, perches hermetically sealed against fresh air and ghosts, the family slept, and stored their food.

The dormitories set the children free not only to manage their own lives but to contract their own marriages. This system, which never failed to intrigue tourists with lurid anticipation, was far more decorous than prurient minded visitors liked to imagine. The boys, it is true, visited the girls; if the girls found them congenial, they mated. Some degree of promiscuous alliances was inescapable but when a girl became pregnant, she was in little doubt as to who had fathered her child. Pregnancy certified their union; without it there could be no marriage.

This should be amended to no marriage in the village sense, a union asking quite different sanctions from those of State or Church. By Igorot custom a newly married couple might live together for several years before their marriage had met the standards set for village approval, an approval granted only when they had offered the sacrifices of pigs and cows insisted on by the old men. However long they might try to postpone this outlay, eventually they had to meet these demands. Very onerous they could be, often putting the couple in debt for years to come. All the bride and groom got out of it was to sit fasting for thirty-six hours on the doorstep of their hut while their guests danced and feasted and drank in front of them. This was their marriage rite. The guests, it was true, brought gifts of food, but each gift was recorded so that it could be repaid in kind when the guests were celebrating wedding feasts in their own families.

In Besao, these feasts (or "*dawak*") were celebrated twice a year, at which time all pending marriages were solemnized – if the word "solemn" can be associated with the raucous merrymaking for which they were the pretext. Scattered through the village there might be a dozen weddings in progress, signalized by the incessant beating of the *gansa*, the brass gongs, and by the trooping of villagers and visitors from house to house. Brimming refreshment of *bassi* and *tapui*, drinks fermented from sugar-cane or rice, soon frenzied them till people were – as the old English phrase has it – "well dronken," and the old men so many degrees past that stage that they could barely stagger in their maudlin pilgrimage up and down the slippery stone steps of the village trails.

So extravagant was the cost of this orgy that for Christian newlyweds I tried to institute on their own *dawak* under Church auspices, suggesting that all who had been married within the half year contribute to a jointly shared

187

and much less expensive feast. My efforts were in vain; the grip of the *dawak* was too strong, and the old men had no mind to relax it.

One year, when its celebration was attended by sickness that spread with the feasting from village to village, I used every argument I could muster to get the *dawak* postponed, all without success. The Igorots often were victimized by the lowlander's acuter business sense; in this case, they had bought tainted pigs in the Ilocos provinces, pigs condemned during a clean-up week but more profitably sold to the mountain people than destroyed. These pigs soon infected the local swine and caused an epidemic of food poisoning among the feasters who ate them.

When I appealed to the old men to check its spread by halting the *dawak*, they laughed at me.

"You say this sickness is caused by germs," they retorted. "Show us a germ!"

Not able to pull one out of my pocket, I lost the argument.

"We know what causes disease," they maintained. "If we neglect the *dawak, the anito* will be angry, and the sickness will be much worse. But these germs you talk about: they are just an American superstition."

* * * * * * * *

Thanks to the equable climate, to the uncrowded isolation, to a life spent largely out of doors, the Igorot was generally healthy. His isolation indeed had preserved him from the childhood diseases which are an expected scourge of every American community. Yet death lurked at every corner. Ghosts were everywhere. I met a young man who told of encountering warriors fighting ancient battles at Bannao, the sacred lake on the ridge between Besao and Sagada. This small pond, little better than a carabao wallow, was enshrined in local legend. To its muddy shores men from Besao and Sagada resorted to consult their ancestors, and, one panicky morning, even the Bontocs appeared, stalwart, naked warriors, clashing their spears against wooden shields as they strode defiantly through Sagada and on up the hill. Before the lake, yellow and smooth like a snake's unblinking eye, they explained to their forefathers how the constabulary men, trailing their grim parade, had prevented their taking a Besao or Sagada head in atonement for one of their men murdered at the mines.

Ghosts did not belong only to the past. They could be very recent. One of our schoolboys, after watching a much-loved father die, came back to the school screaming; on the uphill trail he had encountered this same father, changed already to a fearful enemy, a spectre that might drag him too to the grave. Not infrequently at nights I would hear the schoolboys shout from the upper windows of their dormitory: they were scaring off a ghost which some one had seen lurking in the play ground. I myself was mistaken for a ghost and hailed with screams as I moved through the garden with a flashlight, nipping between thumb and forefinger the flying cockroaches that were chewing the rosebuds.

Ghosts lured the souls of the living, the Igorot's only explanation of any thing, whether sickness or accident, that might cause death. Sacrifice alone, not medicine, could avert such a threat. But if death overrode these precautions, the old men were more than ever in the ascendant, thriving on the people's natural dread in their attempts to allay the spirit of the deceased. If the dead man had been christened we kept our own death watch from the Mission, and I was expected to assume the role of Christian body-snatcher. To break the spell of inherited fear I had to insist on his right to be buried in consecrated ground, in the Campo Santo. The old men used every wile to outwit me.

Children they buried inside the home under the earthen floor, adults just oustide the hut. In some cases the corpse, wrapped in a black and white striped blanket was set up in a chair inside the hut; there it remained in grisly eminence while the village crowded in to keep a three nights' wake. Needless to say, the atmosphere soon was stifling. The heat generated by many people packed into a tiny space combined with heat -- and smoke – from a highly unnecessary fire to hasten decomposition. To smells the Igorot seemed impervious but on one occasion, when I was reading the Burial Office over a body too ripe to be brought into church, even the mourners stuffed their nostrils with grass to keep out the stench.

In my time this custom seemed happily on the wane, and only in the remoter villages was it tolerated by Christians. It was still practised, however, for the old men; they were outside my province. With their beliefs I did not tamper. But to be old was to be stamped with sanctity. What more convincing proof of virtue could one ask for than the sheer feat of escaping unscathed death's omnipresent pitfalls? When an old man died, his putrefying corpse was carried to the caves -- man's oldest burial ground – in the same chair which it had occupied during the wake. This was no decorous procession but a frenzied relay during which the young men took turns not only at carrying the chair but jostling it in hope that fragments of the deceased, the quite noticeably deceased, might spatter them as they ran, and thus convey to them the dead man's good fortune in having lived so long.

My debates with the village elders, however, concerned bodies too quickly buried. Whenever a Christian was known to be dying our Igorot teachers and catechists kept their own lookout; the moment they saw the funeral fires lighted, they were on the scene. Even this vigilance was not always prompt

189

enough. By the time one sick woman died, her grave had been dug, and I was met by mourners objecting, quite understandably, that to dig another grave in the Campo Santo would leave the first grave unfilled, greedy for some other victim. Since this woman had left but one child, there was no doubt whom the *anito* would seize on. Their reasoning was too heart-felt, too plausible, to be shouldered aside; compromise was the only decent policy. I blessed the grave already dug, and buried the woman there.

There were times to make concessions, times to be adamant, times indeed when my Igorot advisors were adamant for me. Our most fervid argument with the village elders occurred over a man who had been killed in the mines. His body, expensively but very cheaply embalmed, had been brought home by 'bus. When we began planning his funeral, the old men were voluble with objections. Wrinkled old sages, clad in skimpy red gee-strings, they squatted in a circle around my study, impassive figures, pulling on their guava root pipes as they huddled beneath the striped blankets which they clutched across their shoulders. To the unpractised eye they might be savages, but there was no subservience in their demeanor; they had pride, they had dignity, they upheld a tradition for which they felt no need to apologize. I was the barbarian.

Our council was long, lapsing often into silence. In consulting with Igorots, the art of knowing when to be silent was one which Americans, generally, were too impatient to learn. When an old man did speak, I was never quite sure who was talking. From somewhere in the circle came sounds, low-keyed, reflective, never blustering, enunciated and listened to without the smallest flicker of excitement in any face.

Yet their argument was obdurate. To bring the body to the church, they told me, would necessitate taking it past a new house, a house still being built. To underline their objections they pointed out that this was not a hut which could be thrown together between sunup and sundown but a home up-to-date in style, constructed of sawn lumber, with wall, windows, doors, and almost ready for a corrugated iron roof. Yet substantial though it was, if a dead man were carried past, the owner would have no option but to tear it down and build it anew on another site.

Their words carried force. Just recently, as I knew, a new house even more solid had been torn down because the builder had heard the bleat of the "kolling" a speckled hawk whose appearance the Besao people looked upon as the most ill-fated of all their many omens. In the present case, however, the old men's arguments had a weak link: while taking the dead man's body from the 'bus to his home, they already had carried it past the new house. How, I asked, had they contrived this without incurring the calamities they so stubbornly predicted.

"We took him down at night."

"Very well," I suggested, "bring him back at night."

"No," came the reply, "we can fool the *anito* once, perhaps. We don't dare try it twice."

At this stage, the Igorot teacher who had been interpreting our colloquy assured me that the old men were bluffing. On his own forthright initiative he delivered an ultimatum: by two o'clock the body must be brought to the church. If they buried it in the village – a procedure admittedly illegal and under a ban which, like all such prescriptions, they dismissed as "lowland law!" – the *Apo Padi* would come down with a spade and dig it up.

"And you'll have to do it, Father," he warned, almost gaily.

I was not gay. Anxiously I kept walking to the edge of the hill to scan the rail up which the cortege must come. Just as the clock neared two I saw it, the long procession winding through the pines, skirting the rice terraces. Past the new house the mourners came, not once halting until they had laid the crude coffin at the chancel steps.

We had the funeral, we aspersed the coffin, we moved on the grave newly dug in the Campo Santo. For the first time I used a translation of the Burial Office which we had just completed. At the grave were some old men who had come to perform rites of their own after our departure. Gravely they listened to this service spoken in their own language. When we had gone, one of them spoke out, "What can we say? What can we do? The *Apo Padi* has said and done everything we could do."

So they abandoned their rites.

Next morning, I looked out to note whether the builder of the new house had begun to pull it down. He was putting on the roof.

* * * * * * * *

It is a cheap trick, of course, to parade all that is odd or repulsive in a primitive people's recoil from death. The more one compares their attitude with our own, the less we can muster any right to condescend. We Americans have become so expert in packaging everything that we even dare to package death. Between an Igorot burial and an American "mortician's" obsequies, I would not hesitate a moment in choosing the former. The Igorot – I am speaking of him in his pagan days – could not understand death, but he accepted it as a grim fact. He did not call the corpse a "patient," nor lay it out in a "slumber room." A coffin was a box hurriedly nailed together – how many times I have heard that hammering! It was not a casket, padded with nylon, extravagantly casing the deceased in polished woods and shining metal – if his sorrowing relatives can be deluded into wasting money on

191

this spurious panoply. Such heathen customs would have puzzled the Igorot. No matter how artistically the undertaker apes the dead man's picture with rouge and powder, a corpse still is only a corpse, the empty decaying shell of a man no longer alive; it is not an ornament to be embowered in flowers, and no prissy use of words can disguise the fact that he is dead.

With such pretence the Igorot does not fool himself. I have seen the old men stand on the coffin lid, pushing it down like a college boy trying to shut an overstuffed footlocker, and laugh as they did so. The procession up hill to the Camp Santo was almost gay as the men edged their burden around the bends of a narrow trail, chuckling, chattering while the people behind them kept up blithe gossip. Their topmost concern was to make sure that the dead man stayed dead. Into his grave they tossed the broken fragments of his chair; they gave him too a bottle of *tapui*, and tobacco for his pipe. On the Eve of All souls – Hallowe'en, we call it – if they were Christian they came back with pine torches flaring and let them burn out on each grave in bonfires of remembrance.

This Christian use of All Souls was imported by the Spanish, alien conquerors who never asserted more than tenuous hold on the Igorots. Like the Moros in the South, and mountain people in all the larger islands, the Igorots stayed outside the pale, lumped together condescendingly as the Non-Christian Tribes. The Filipino attitude toward them, when Filipinos began taking over from the American sovereignty an ever larger part in local government, was colonial. I have had Filipino officials and their wives, who I met at a Government House ball in Bontoc, ask me how I could endure living "in the provinces!" The Igorot was a cousin of whom they were ashamed. Picture postcards of tribesmen doing their wild dances were confiscated in the mails. They gave, the Filipinos declared, a false impression. The Filipinos, proud of their borrowed European culture, elaborately and colourfully dressed to perform the *rigadon*, their traditional dance, graceful old-world figures as intricate and as sedate as the minuet, did not relish having the world judge them by savages in g-strings.

To the American missionaries who worked among them this was false shame. The Igorot needed no apology. He had his own pride, his own dignity; his candour could be startling. Riding horseback over a rough and treacherous trail, I exclaimed to the Igorot boy who was accompanying me,

"Camilo, it will take me a hundred years to ride as well as you do."

"Yes, Father," he replied, unhesitatingly.

I cannot fancy any other Oriental blurting out the truth so frankly.

"Look at me," said an old Igorot whom we tried to convince (unsuccessfully) that he should leave his boy in school. "Look at me: I am rich" – he had many rice fields – "yet I never went to school."

He was shrewd as a Yankee farmer arguing against "book-l'larnin'," perhaps the same farmer who scoffed at his son's academic degrees as B.S. (defined from the compost heap), M.S. (more of the same), Ph.D. (piled higher and deeper).

Fanatically independent the Igorot was, yet he could not live for ever shut off from the cultural destiny of the Malay kinsfolk, the Ilocanos, the Pangasinese, the Tagalogs, whose island he shared. Spanish words, Spanish customs, long naturalized to this remote tropical scene, had sifted up from the Lowlands. We used them where we could, as with the bonfires on All souls, so that he would not remain a people apart, but we added as well an infusion of American vigour, hard-headed American insistence on progress, lest he relapse from one spell to another, from primitive torpour to Spanish lethargy. What we hoped the Igorot would learn was to value life, value the potential of manhood.

How unlimited this potential actually was we were to see proven over and over again in the record of individual Igorots and their dynamic, transforming effect upon their own society. They needed, however, this stimulus from outside their native culture. Roussseau and Diderot and other Encyclopaedists – not to omit our own Thomas Jefferson – put their savages back (although they would have resented the metaphor) in the Garden of Eden, a view they had borrowed from Bougainville and other explorers' reports from the South Seas. Man, as they typified the Polynesian, was by nature good, and primitive life completely joyful in its innocence and its simplicity. The snake that corrupted their happiness was a trespasser from the West, the adventurers, whalers, missionaries, misguided intruders who considered themselves the product of superior culture, yet whose legacy was to be disease, guilt, slavery, and a bigot's catalogue of invented sins. Ours was the culture to be ashamed of, claimed Diderot and other apostles of the Enlightenment, a culture poisoned by Church, State, and Society. Man's sole salvation was to get back to nature, back to Eden.

Whether Polynesian life was as idyllic as they reported I do not know. That it was invaded to its detriment in the name of commerce and religion and unreasonably alien concepts of justice I do not doubt. The missionaries probably did as much harm as the whalers. But what I can vouch for is the absence from Igorot life, a life certainly as primitive as the Polynesian's and not much less favoured by Nature, of the gaiety, that innate happiness, the Encyclopaedists would have expected them to exult in. My strong suspicion is that the Polynesians suffered from similar tyrannies, the tyranny of the old men, all the more arbitrary because it was rooted in ignorance, and the kindred tyrannies of superstition and witchcraft.

193

Besao confronted witchcraft country. In the sunny hills to the west were villages so notorious for their potent spells that the first Igorot physician, a man who had studied at the University of Michigan, once confessed how, despite his western training, he would not have dared help himself even to a *camote* while passing through their fields.

Besao itself had its witch-doctors and its seeresses. The latter, when called on to predict the future, fell into trances like the priestesses of Apollo at Delphi, and babbled prophecies as fateful if not as historically significant as the oracle whom kings came to consult. The witch-doctors were greatly feared; one boy in our school, fortunate enough to have a notably powerful witch-doctor for his grandfather, bloomed under the protection of his grandfather's fame. Nobody dared quarrel with him or cross his wishes. One can guess what our child specialists would have predicted for him yet, instead of being spoiled or self-willed, he turned out a boy of singularly sunny disposition and, in contradiction to the laws of probability, became a Christian priest.

"Witch-doctor," of course, is an inept term, a term for which no adequate substitute has been invented. It demeans by its savage connotation, the role of men who are honoured as deeply as they are feared. In a society where no legal code regulates justice, the witch-doctor has the prestige of a judge; he claims the respect given by other communities to a sheriff. The magic he wielded checked and punished crime. To him came victims of theft, and the redress they got was stern enough to dismay any wrongdoer.

I remember one old man from another village, Agawa, whose spells were so redoubtable that on one occasion he was called to a distant town to deal with some flagrant stealing. He went the two days' journey, invoked his spells and, within a few hours, frightened the culprits to death, culprits whose identity was not known until their corpses were found and, in their huts, the stolen property.

To see this man, no one would have guessed his sinister powers. My first meeting with him occurred when he brought his two sons to school. Although his village was one of the last to admit a public school, holding out obstinately for years against the suspect intrusion of books, this man, the very picture of stubborn backwardness, saw that to the educated man belonged the future.

I met him, another time, on the trail. We were resting, some schoolboys and I, on a sharp-sloping mountainside and shading our tired, sweaty bodies against the afternoon's glare. He joined us under the pines, setting down his bundle of faggots. His wrinkled face enlarged to a smiling network and while he talked he used his woodcutters bolo to pare his toe-nails. A stranger would have exclaimed that here was the eternal savage, immured in a stagnation which no change could ruffle – but his words rebutted the primitive rudeness

194

of his appearance. Naked except for the usual red wisp of a gee-string and the woven belt from which he hung his wooden scabbard, his feet thickly callused, his hair straggling unbrushed under the basket cap that served as a pocket for his pipe, he was the last person we should have expected to talk as he did. Like all parents he wanted assurance that his sons were making headway in their studies, but he looked beyond, to their sharing a community certain to outgrow, to outlive, the spells, the witchcraft, on which his fame had depended.

He was a shrewd prophet. The changes he welcomed with foresight as magnanimous as it was exceptional we saw come to pass.

On this arduous hike up and down slippery trails and through the shallows of streams which an afternoon's thunder storm could bloat to rock-tumbling turbulence I was headed toward what we called, almost fearfully, the witchcraft villages. Although on clear days their thatched huts were visible from my study window, they were a region into which strangers dreaded to intrude.

The schoolboys accompanying me set the keynote to our approach as they discussed, in matter-of-fact tones, our chance of being poisoned. Later while we were staying in these villages. Lodging in whatever hut was offered us, I noted how watchful they were to pick up the peelings of the pineapples they had eaten. Not one scrap would they leave lest it be made the physical basis of a curse. I did not laugh at their precautions. Never had I stopped in a place so sinister.

All evening I argued, to no point, with a group of old men. We met on the raised floor of the village's best house, and I was accorded the honour of a chair while the rest squatted on the wooden boards, a posture they had assumed not from humility but from preference. I was an intruder to whom they conceded a hearing but most decidedly not a welcome. There was no pretence of courtesy. If a man grew bored – as several did – from proceedings which threatened to drag on till dawn, he pulled himself to his feet and, without apology or farewell, walked out. Envy their bluntness though I might, I alas had to stay. I had lapsed into a coma of inattention when suddenly, unbelievably, moved by no conclusion arrived at nor by any spoken agreement, all the lingerers stood up and departed.

It says much for the potency of education and of the positive spiritual thesis undergirding it that in a few years these villages no longer seemed sinister. Their oppressive atmosphere had been dispelled by the simple expedient of enlisting a few of their boys in our school at Kiniway. The first recruits came diffidently. In a few weeks they ran away, too homesick to stay, but next year some were back, until soon they were making up a stable part of our student body. The friendliness acquired through participation in school activities with boys they had once shied away from as hereditary enemies transformed the attitude of their home villages. On subsequent visits we were greeted not with suspicion but with a glad welcome. Our own boys from Besao were no longer fearful. They could laugh at spells and omens. Even when, after leaving Besao, we encountered the dreaded hawk, the *kolling*, they could make light of its evil boding. If a traveler heard the *kolling*, they told me, he must do two things – rest, and turn home. As we had heard this bird's beeping cry while we were relaxing on a sunny, grass-blanketed slope, we already were taking our ease; this was rest enough and, they reminded me further, we were on our way home. The *kolling* could not hurt us.

Yet, mock the spells as we might, no one who had seen their effects dared deny their power. Even in the comparative sophistication of Besao I had seen strange things happen. One rainy afternoon, as I came on horseback from Sagada, I encountered a man writhing in a muddy ditch beside the trail. My summons brought the sanitary inspector, who helped him to the Presidencia. He soon recovered and, within an hour, was able to set out, accompanied by two fellow townsmen, for his home village some ten miles away.

I had assumed that his trouble was epilepsy but our inquiries did not support this theory. No fits had he suffered before his seizure, which came upon him just as he and his friends started over a short-cut to meet the trail beyond the wooden tract they were crossing, a tract – we learned further – on which a spell had been put because a thief, as yet unknown, had helped himself there to some sawn timber. From the instant he entered this tract the man (whose visit had been to purchase *carabao*) had begun leaping and shouting, and had shaken off all pursuit until he fell, his mouth foaming, to the ground. Unable to restrain these mad antics, his friends had gone for help.

What made the case mysterious was not the spell – these were common enough – but the fact that its victim had not known the tract was bewitched. To deepen the puzzle, only one man of the three had been affected.

Although this particular instance defied explanation, I gradually convinced myself that the secret of these phenomena was the expectancy of evil so commonly found in primitive society. Fear bred its offspring. It was a psychic obsession matched only by its complementary attitude, the expectancy of good. Both are powerful, both draw on spiritual sources too elusive to be explained scientifically, yet I have do doubt that both are responsive to what we describe loosely as the laws of nature. Where expectancy of evil can produce witchcraft's eerie phenomena, expectancy can produce the miracles recorded in the New Testament, both results reasonable though beyond what our present experience permits us to define.

In the sophistication of our Western culture we have lost this expectancy to so large a degree that witchcraft and miracles alike are rare. We have taken up the unscientific position of denying them. Of regarding them as a freakish interference with Nature, confusing the supernatural with mere superstition instead of admitting that their only "unnatural" feature is their reliance on influences as yet outside our normal experience. In time they will be seen to have just as natural a basis as the once incomprehensible laws that enable us to record and transmit scenes, features, and voices which we watch on a television set.

Not so many years ago a radio broadcaster brought on a panic in 20th Century America from a populace gullible enough to expect an invasion from Mars. In Nanking I remember the city buzzing with hysterical rumours of a "paper man" who snatched children and mutilated little boys. If expectancy can rise to faith, it can sink ignobly to credulity.

Interwoven with the Igorots' fear of the *anito* was an inherited fear of tribal enemies. Feuds are a primitive man's only history. They are the villager's substitute for patriotism, and as sadly tainted by bigotry as in countries that call themselves enlightened. Nearly two years after the Armistice that ended the First World War I heard Parsifal sung very limply in English because the New York public would not tolerate its performance in German. A few months earlier, the great violinist, Fritz Kreisler, had been howled down in Chicago for the heinous offence of doing his duty as an Austrian officer. In this spirit the Tukukan old men compelled a schoolboy in our Bontoc school to kill a schoolmate because, forty years before, the grandfather of the murdered boy had killed his own grandfather. To accomplish this, he invited his intended victim to come home with him on a visit to Tutukan and, ignoring the fact that he was his friend, slew him on the way.

The Bontocs had printed the terrible memory of their raids on the Besao and Sagada people. More warlike, they were also more vengeful. Not many months after my arrival in the mountains I was setting out, in the brief December twilight, to ride from Sagada across the pass to Besao. Barely had I climbed into the saddle before a schoolboy exclaimed at my temerity in starting so late in the day.

"This is the time of the year," he warned me, "when the Bontocs come up the trails."

Other boys agreed, but one of the group laughed at their fears.

"They won't take his head," he scoffed. "He's an Americano."

I laughed with him, giving my horse a prod, but the farther I rode on my silent climb toward the pass, the more intently the warning preyed on my mind. *Carabao*, looming black and immense in the near-darkness, slid down the slopes in front of me. They frightened my horse, making him jumpy till at every twist of the trail he shied as if from savages lurking in the shadows. How would they know I was an American, I wondered. Bad enough it would be to lose my head, sadder still to lose it by mistake. The Bontocs were notorious for moving swiftly, for loosing the grey lightning of their spears without preliminary palaver. The wrong victim was preferable to no victim. Of course, to kill an Americano would have been an embarrassment, but an embarrassment which I would have felt even more keenly than they.

Absurd though these fears sound, they had built up to actual panic by the time I had crossed the pass and could look westward to the last glimmer of sunset, to a vast, empty panorama of blackly silhouetted mountains. Mercifully at this moment, when I was afraid to go on, afraid to turn back, there resounded from the school, two miles away, the first deep tones of the Angelus. Calmly across the intervening darkness its tones rang forth. They stilled my panic, dispelled the unreasonable folly to which I was falling prey. I rode on confidently now, picking my stony way along the cliffs, fording a stream, circling the rocky slopes of Mugao, till the lights of the Mission drew me home, home to the dinner table and all the dear, trivial occupations that hold at bay the dark night world of ghosts and feuding tribesmen.

The bulwark against this night world was the school. Slowly, steadily, its influence embraced the outlying villages. In the earliest years, naturally, the influence was the American priest's as he went the round of these villages, but an American's visit was only a temporary measure anticipating the time, still a generation or two into the future, when Igorot priests would minister to their own people.

Few Americans could cope adequately with the rigours of the trail. I always went reluctantly, though no more so than the horse I used, a wily beast who for the first kilometer or so would pretend to limp till he realized that I really intended to go through with the ordeal. He knew all our stops and would turn in at the first village regardless of my plan to continue further; when I reined him in, he would twist his head accusingly as if to say, "What! Are you going to neglect these people?"

Eventually my journeys included villages which were inaccessible to horses; they had to be attained by teetering progress along the dykes lining the ricefields or down the projecting stones that served as steps to a lower level. One careless step, one displaced stone, and we landed knee-deep in mud. There was trouble too at the fords. Streams that barely trickled through dry boulders, when we crossed them first, could swell during a night's deluge to torrents, devastating freshets that tumbled these great stones like billiard balls. One horse we nearly lost at what usually was a viable ford; only the agility of the Igorots, reaching out from a slippery perch on the rocks to grab his mane and tail, kept the panicky beast from being swept away.

I learned not to trust the legend that these mountain ponies were too surefooted to bring their riders to harm. While I was pausing to make adjustments to my camera, one horse backed me off the trail. As he went down, I jumped, landing by good fortune in a Japanese sunflower bush, a shrub springy enough to yield as he rolled over on top of me. Like the notorious burro, these ponies picked the trail's outer edge where, however sure-footed they may have been, they did not reckon on the trail's being undermined by a rainy season downpour. Twice I saw it give way under their weight. On the first of these mishaps, the victim was Mary, the wife who had come with me from China, who suffered the internal injuries which led, several months later, to her death. The second was my new bride, Frances, making a first – and only – tour of the villages. This time there were no casualties; though he dropped fifteen feet, her horse landed upright.

Yet the fascination of the villages overrode the hardship of getting to them. Their names – Bantey, Sumadel, Masla, Luben, Tambuan – were as poetically inviting as the first view of their drowsy valleys which we paused to admire from the heights above. Always I entered these valleys like an intruder venturing upon an enchanted region, a region that had lain spellbound from before men reckoned time.

Time indeed meant nothing to them. The habit of naming days and months was an imported custom to which they paid but casual heed. To a place where so little happened my arrival was like the appearance of a circus. Boys and girls crowded the little hut where I lodged, a hut that did multiple duty as dining-room, dormitory and church. Some time they chattered, often they stood in a hushed circle gaping at my outlandish ways. From the girls my little steel shaving mirror provoked giggling excitement. Eagerly they passed it from hand to hand. Some of them were seeing themselves for the first time and could hardly credit the faces that laughed back at them. A few were schoolgirls, too sophisticated to betray such naïve surprise though equally ready to handle and examine every stitch of my belongings. Only one pertinacious schoolboy, however, ever overstepped mannerly bounds. Coming, going, returning, staying until late at night, he was impossible to get rid of. Whereas the other products of the local school were tongue-tied, he ached to air his English..

What these visits accomplished was hard to assess. I had no doubt that these villages needed a new, livening impulse if they were not to be engulfed by the 20th Century, by a secular submersion as fatal to them as to the American Indian. Such a submersion from which only their isolation had sheltered them, the infrequent appearance of an Anglican priest did little to check. His ministry could be no more than shallow - baptism into what few of his adherents comprehended, confession of sins that rolled lightly off the tongues of his penitents because in their minds what they confessed were not sins at all but merely things recited to satisfy the missionary. Mass said in English, as incomprehensible to an "ili" (or village) convert as Latin to a Roman Catholic.

The villager liked having his house blessed or the graves of his dead sprinkled with holy water; any incantation against the *anito* was worth trying. When the priest had mounted his horse, however, and headed down the trail, the village whose placid apathy he had ruffled for a few brief hours would revert to its time-tried sacrifices; its old men would chant all night under the *patapatayan*, the sacred tree, and seek auspices for the future from a chicken's entrails.

I arrived just when the Mission had reached the borderline between old and new. The inadequacies of the past had grown glaringly apparent. What I could perceive was the entry my predecessors had won; their conduct had made certain that we would be welcomed as friends. They had secured us at least a hearing, a friendly hearing from a people disposed to resent the stranger. It was an achievement to be proud of.

All too obviously, however, their long practiced procedure was out of date. Early in the morning the catechist, little more literate than his fellow villagers, would make the rounds of the *ili*, ringing a dinner bell to announce Mass as he climbed up and down the town's stony paths. Thus summoned, the people crowded into the grass-thatched hut where the priest had shoved into a corner his now folded camp cot, his washing utensils, his cans of Vienna sausage and baked beans, and cloaked riding breeches and khaki shirt beneath the black folds of a cassock. The altar on which, overnight, he had disposed his clothes to keep them beyond reach of the rats – they loved to feast on socks and shaving brushes – had now been decked with a frontal. Crucifix, candles, chalice, paten, missal, mass vestments had been extracted from their basket, from the church "tampipi," as it was called. While confessions were being muttered – "beans, camotes, cabbage," *ili* confessions were seldom subtler – the congregation, squatting on a rough board floor, chanted the Rosary. Through most of the Mass they squatted. Those who made their Communion handed the catechist one of the four perforated tickets given them after Confession; on these he scrawled their names. If the Bishop were present, the catechist pushed his way through the crowd examining the baptismal certificates they were expected to bring. Whenever he discovered one of these grimy cards still unsigned by the Bishop, he shoved the holder forward to be confirmed. This, with a sermon translated by an interpreter was the time-honoured procedure.

The routine disclosed startling gaps. Children baptized in infancy grew up ignorant of the names assigned them. The Igorot at that time had not

200

yet taken on a surname; he was not likely to be exact about Christian names. Some times the public school, assiduous in their name-giving as the Church, attached an entirely new name to the child when he entered school; sometimes an echo of the original name lingered in altered form. Epifania became Estefaria, Lorenzo appeared as Florencio. In either case, the child, with no identifying surname, quite often was baptized again. As to Confirmation, many seemed to believe that if it was efficacious once its value could be doubled by repetition. Canvassing our register with a corps of knowledgeable Igorots to help me in a task that would have stretched the ingenuity of an archaeologist, I eventually ran down a host of multiple baptisms and confirmations.

Our crowning discovery was a boy who had been baptized twice and confirmed by three successive bishops. This was more grace than any single individual could assimilate. He died*!*

* * * * * * * *

My activity was centered, as should be clear by now, in the school. I saw small value in tackling older people, the illiterate villagers whose minds had fossilized before they were out of their thirties. Such efforts, if they attracted an adherent, attracted him only because he hoped for some premium, as with the old man, slightly bibulous, who kept volunteering to be baptized in exchange for a ticket to Manila. In Manila, he told me, everybody was rich. He knew as little about Manila as he was capable of knowing about the Christian Gospel. To baptize the old or aging Igorot simply meant encouraging him to perjure himself in two religions.

The school held hope for the future. It proved that the Igorot mind was as receptive to knowledge as any. There was the quota of brilliant minds to be looked for in any school. I expected great things of the boy who, in an English composition, could compare a man's pock-marked face to a cabbage eaten by worms. What I valued most, however, was the entirety of this school life, an association more family than school. We were happily independent of outside control, accessible only by trails so rugged that the Bureau of Education inspectors came seldom and departed soon. They were experienced men, sensibly ready to make allowance for shortcomings in our equipment. How long officialdom would refrain from vexatious interference we dared not predict. The public schools were under tighter, and often absurd, surveillance. I had two girls who had transferred from a nearby public school. When called to recite, they stood blankly mute, their faces contorted with embarrassment.

"Didn't you recite in your former school?" I asked.

201

"No," they admitted.

"But what was your teacher doing?"

"Oh, he always make lesson plans to show the Supervising when he come."

We skipped lesson plans and the paraphernalia of modern pedagogy, but we educated our youngsters – a fact so thoroughly recognized that when the Philippine Commonwealth, to save money ostensibly for defense, shortened its curriculum to seven primary and three secondary grades, many students rejected this short-cut and transferred to our eighth grade to get the fuller instruction which their common sense told them they needed.

In agreeable contrast to China, where mission schools and government schools were ready to fly at each other's throats, our relations with the public schools were happy. When it was Besao's turn to hold the district's academic and athletic contests, we gladly lent the public schools our more adequate buildings and ampler playgrounds. Every room in our house swarmed with children, all except the guestroom, where the Bishop, worn out by outstation trails, was trying to sleep. These pupils even parked chickens on the stairs, live props for one of the plays whose excited, eager-faced actors we had helped costume.

At the academic contests I was sole judge, an honour made awkward when the Besao principal came secretly to say how important it was that the Besao schools win. Naturally I bent backwards not to favour the local contestants but, by a lucky accident, Besao won by a single point. No one believed that I had not contrived this. From friend and foe alike this chance outcome brought me unmerited praise for my tact! Not only had I done my duty in assuring victory for the home team, but I managed this (so people believed) by so close a margin that the runner-up felt no soreness in defeat.

On another occasion, when I shared the judging with two Filipino colleagues, I attempted to lay the ghost of Patrick Henry, whose "Give me liberty or give me death," was the backbone of Philippine oratory. For the reading selection I chose a passage which could not be declaimed. Although our Igorots bothered little about Independence – schoolchildren had been taught by their lowland teachers to declaim as dramatically as their Ilocano cousins. The paragraphs I picked seemed proof against melodrama: they were the factual description of a pine tree.

One girl read this passage factually. She got my vote; she did not get the prize. I was overruled by the other teachers. Their choice was a boy who extolled the pine tree with the fervour of Mark Antony praising Caesar. "De pine – it grow upon de mountainside" – his throat vibrated a clarion call to action, his gestures were a legacy from the long-deceased schoolmarms imported to the Philippines in the U.S. Army Transport Thomas[42]. Had he been swathed in white muslin, he would have matched the illustrations in old-time elocution books, the females, long-haired and frantic, rolling their eyes heavenward in attitudes labeled "Defiance" or "Entreaty" or "Despair."

This was the single occasion when my opinions, unfashionable enough, were not deferred to. In China I had had deference of another kind. As Headmaster of St. Paul's Middle School I had been installed as Chief Judge to pass on calisthenics and drill exercises in which all Anking's numerous Government Schools competed for the prize I was supposed to award. Through the whole of a Sunday morning I sat in eminence closely flanked by long-gowned officaldom. I took my duties stringently, making notes of each performance. I could have spared myself this trouble. My judgements were never asked for. Flattering though my post was, it was purely ornamental, entitling me to be guest of honour at a feast given subsequently by the Commissioner of Education, and to hear my fairness and discrimination extolled in words smoothly stimulated by haohsing wine a hundred years old. I had gained "face," my school had gained "face;" a great pity it would have been to upset this glory by an expressed opinion on the merits of the contestants.

Filipinos did not practise this finesse. They were polite but in a matter as sacred as Declamation their teachers would not dream of violating the principles bred into them any more than American pedagogues of the between-War generations would have questioned the all-wisdom of their prophet, John Dewey.

Our schools escaped the pestilence by omitting Declamation. We never taught our pupils to rant but – as I was to observe in a visit long after the War – we did teach them a better patriotism, a patriotism courageous in war, sensibly constructive in peace. We achieved this in Besao, I believe, because St, James's was more family than school. For years, church, dormitory, classrooms, *sala*, and the rooms we occupied were under one roof. School noises penetrated through thin walls into our home, yet seldom harshly. Although our door was locked only at night, and pupils were allowed unrestricted access to my study upstairs, only once was this freedom abused.

For several days I had been absent in Manila. When I returned, I chanced to notice that a gold pocket-watch was missing from my desk. It had hung suspended from the tusk of a bronzed elephant.

A brief investigation would soon have discovered the culprit. I preferred to stay ignorant. Consulting the Igorot principal, a man with whom I had been privileged to work for at least a dozen years with never a whisper of misunderstanding, I explained the situation: the watch, I was certain, had been taken on impulse. Could he contrive its return in such a manner as to make it appear that the watch had never been stolen.

Not more than a day later, my small daughter came, voicing a reproachful tale, to her mother. Her doll, Heidi, was the thief. She had found the lost watch in Heidi's lap! Naughty Heidi!

Heidi was a solemn-faced rag doll, best beloved of a whole array whom Ann kept on a long seat in her bedroom. Since this seat was exactly under a window that looked down into the school *sala*, a window usually propped open, it was no feat for a boy to climb up the exposed framework of the walls and drop the watch in Heidi's lap.

Heidi never repeated her one misdeed. She lived through years of concentration camp and, like her small mistress, had to be fumigated with DDT by our Army rescuers to depopulate her of bedbugs. She was brought home, dirty and disheveled, to an honourable retirement. If we blamed her unfairly, it was in a good cause.

* * * * * * *

St. James's was spoken of quite generally as "a happy school." It cherished the diversions that made it so, the dances, the plays, the softball games, the hikes, which flavoured an otherwise humdrum routine.

Softball was our one interscholastic sport, and games with other schools were played only at their annual fiestas or at ours. The chief of these encounters was Sagada. Ours was a small school; we had no hope of holding our own against such opponents as Sagada and Bontoc until, one autumn, I undertook to give our players systematic coaching. Every afternoon, following classes and the singing of Vespers, we practiced. The game bore but faint resemblance to what in America became fastball. On a playfield gouged out of the mountainside anything smaller than a 13-inch ball would have chased the outfielders fifty feet downhill to retrieve a long fly. Our training too lacked the deadly concentration of American teams preparing to die for dear old Rutgers. Blithe is the only word suitable to describe these practice games played in the late afternoon sunshine, sunshine often tempered by gusts of the northeast monsoon sweeping briskly down from Mugao's pine-wooded slopes. For the first time in their lives, the Igorots learned the fascination of batting averages; each evening before supper they trooped to the bulletin board to decipher the day's box-score.

They were sportsmanlike players. A game was always a game, not to be cried over in defeat nor magnified in victory. But it was nonetheless satisfying when little St. James's startled its opponents at Sagada and merited an ovation from the fiesta crowds by winning the championship, gained it by a unique device, the use of a left-handed pitcher. The word "southpaw" joined the Igorot vocabulary. A southpaw was our secret weapon.

Soon our rivals copied our methods, but never again could Besao be discounted. The St. James's teams continued in the running year after year until that heart-stopping day when war brought games to a sudden end. Word had come not only of Pearl Harbor but of an attack more terrifyingly immediate: Baguio had been bombarded. At any moment enemy 'planes might come hurtling through the blue skies just as, not knowing what they were, we had heard them, concealed by early morning cloudiness, pass over our heads that same morning. We could not risk letting the fiesta crowds invite a further attack. The merrymakers were dispersed; the teams sent home.

But there is no use rushing on to the War. It came soon enough. The years without history are those on which my mind lingers, years the Igorots now numbered A.D., but as eventless in the swift alternation of dry season and wet as the earlier years before the Mountain people learned to tabulate. They were a cycle of contentment.

Once a week there was a dance. Upstairs in my study I awaited the usual summons, a knock at the foot of the stairs and a boy's voice telling me,

"The girls are here, Father."

Some were school girls in gingham frocks, others village girls clothed in blouse and red-and-white striped *tapis*. Only on superfine occasions did any of the dancers wear shoes, and then, after two or three dances, they would kick them off. For music the boys carried out from my living room a heavy orthophonic phonograph. Our records were an assortment, three or four hundred, which kept alive popular tunes from 1922 up to the first war year, 1939. I played them chronologically, starting the series with an ancient favourite, Three O'Clock in the Morning, and continuing, week by week, till we reached the Two Little Fishes. That marked time to begin the round over again, fox-trots and an occasional waltz, their melodies strident above the soft shuffling of bare feet.

Sitting by my Victrola, I never tired of watching these dancers, especially the village girls who, on the instant the music stopped, broke from their partners and ran to their chairs, bending as if dodging through a hut's low door. Very pretty in youth's brief bloom, their black flashing eyes, their trim, slender figures mingled coquetry with the shy wariness of a jungle deer. Sophistication had not yet dimmed their mirthful simplicity. Except when surprised by an American, who – so the schoolmarmish tradition had taught them – scowled on their graceful nudity, they were not ashamed to bathe at a roadside spring as they came homeward from the fields. Often they crouched under a tap back of the school; their wet, glistening bodies showed a middle zone more lightly tanned where their skirts had kept off the sun. They were not embarrassed to have the boys see them as they washed. Mixed bathing beside the trail had been their custom. But the dance was another matter, an occasion when it was proper to be coy. Theirs in fact was the distinction an American girl draws between being stared at in a bikini and observed in pants and brassiere. Clothes or lack of them are universally a woman's weapon, whether she grows up in a thatched hut or adjusts the length of her hem, before a floor-length mirror, in slavish deference to Paris.

Our schoolgirls generally wore western dress; it was less expensive. The story is always the same, cheap machine-sewn goods ousting the honest, colourful excellence of native handicrafts. Whether students gained status from wearing western cloths I was never sure. In the Lowlands the starched white suit, the neatly pressed white frock were a badge, like the Chinese student's long gown and overlong sleeves, a badge which parents waded ankle-deep in rice paddies to earn for their literate offspring. In the Igorot country, schoolboys and girls had not elevated themselves as yet into a caste.

Whatever influence I could exert was bent toward keeping these youngsters well rooted in their past. To let fox-trot and waltz supersede the traditional dances was certainly not my intention, and there were times when I was explicit about their wearing the traditional costumes. I was not purist enough to require, as did the Bontoc schools, that our softball players wear gee-strings. In the flurry of a quick-moving play an infielder risked fielding a yard or two of his gee-string along with the ball, for the gee-strings donned for gala events were not the wisps of red cloth that sufficed for every day use; generally woven of blue cotton thread and embroidered with a cross-stitch border of bright yellows and reds, they were long enough, both in front and back, to reach the knees.

On school hikes native costume was the style. These parties we organized to explore the fringes of untravelled wilderness which extended northward from our valley. This wilderness had no villages. The very few passers-by who dared its exiguous paths went well armed, for its only inhabitants were the *boso*, the savages, lurking to ambush any unwary traveler. Late in the 1930's they had murdered two hunters from Besao and taken their jaw-bones as handles from which to suspend their brass gongs. Such agriculture as they practiced was the rudimentary method known as *caingin*, a system in wide use by Philippine aborigines. First burning off a piece of land, they would plant their crops, mainly *camotes*, in this crude clearing. Actual cultivation was a nicety beyond their skill. When the soil wore out, they fired another stretch of forest.

Our sorties into their domain was strenuous, taking us up two thousand feet to the seven thousand foot level, at which altitude we pursued a well-defined trail for a further ten or eleven miles. Since the path followed the contour of the ridge, we were continually exchanging climates, tropical and temperate. At one time we would be winding through a ravine overshadowed by great trees, smooth boles sixty feet to their lowest branches. In the ravine's darkness, kept moist by the stream that cascaded across giant boulders, fern trees flourished to two and three times a man's stature. The lesser shrubs which we grazed with our bare knees, fought us with leeches.

On the outer bend of each ridge, however, we came back to the temperate zone, to pine trees and waist-high grass, to a vast panoramic survey of valleys cleaving their knife-sharp chasms toward the sea. Here we did not look for leeches; we looked for pits dug to snare the wild boar. Six feet deep they were, lined with stones and armed with sharpened stakes. So cleverly were they roofed over that anyone less sharp-sighted than the boys and girls accompanying me might well have stumbled into the trap.

The *boso* who made them were camouflaged with a skill just as baffling to my untutored eyes. Almost at our goal we came upon three of these savages, two men and a woman. Though they could not have been a hundred yards distant, it took the schoolboys several minutes to point them out to me. They wore gee-strings or skirt of bark fibre, perfect blend with the shrubs that so nearly concealed them. How many others had shadowed our progress we could but guess. Always we had the eerie sense of their surveillance as they slipped noiselessly through the trees hoping to pounce on some straggler. To one overt mark of ill will they gave vent, setting fire to a fallen tree across which we had to clamber on our way home.

Our goal was Bwasao, a stream of almost legendary repute. Broad and shallow, tumbling over pebbles from one limpid pool to the next, it must have strayed from the Rockies. It did not belong in the Philippines, where rivers in the mountains are torrents or trickles, in the lowlands deep, sluggish, mud-laden. On its shoals the girls gathered crayfish while the boys swam underwater in the pools, protecting their eyes with goggles in order to shoot with bows and steel rods such fish as flickered into sight.

Bwasao flowed unsuspected through its lofty forest, boundary to a world which maps had not yet claimed. More conspicuous was Sisipitan, a landmark that for years had tantalized me not only because it was the highest mountain on our horizon, a pyramid of rock jutting out from jungle at an altitude close to eight thousand feet, but because around it had gathered legend and history in an improbable mixture.

Up our valley, I knew, had fled Emilio Aguinaldo, escaping from the American soldiers against whom he had led an unsuccessful revolt. What I could not credit was the local report that the American troops had fortified Sisipitan – certainly an oddly static mode of pursuing an *insurrecto* already on the run. Nor was there any sense in setting up a fort there to pacify the surrounding country. For one thing, this was not a region friendly to

207

Aguinaldo; the Igorots were not his people. Even had they been friendly, who would have been lunatic enough to establish an outpost on a barren, waterless peak isolated from supplies and reenforcements by miles of impermeable jungle, by mountains so rugged, so steeply exposed to stifling sunshine that to keep lines open would have taxed relief parties beyond what heart and lungs could endure? Until we had solved the mystery of Sisipitan, however, we could not lay these questions to rest.

The mountain we reached only by sending ahead twelve boys, each with a bolo, to slash a path through the forest. Long before, when Sisipitan was still an object of sacrifice, paths had led to its peak both from our side and from the hostile Bontoc side to the east. But even the men from the nearest village, Mai-init, had abandoned their one-time pilgrimage to the mountain they venerated. Mai-init was not a community with whom the Besao people cared to have dealings. Immemorial feuds still kept them aloof.

How our schoolboys ferreted their way was to me a mystery. For an hour or more after our initial climb to the ridge out of which Sisipitan towers, we had been immersed in jungle, immersed in an atmosphere as hot and humid as it was gloomy. The trees, jostling us, prevented any chance to take our bearings. Steadily, grimly, we plodded upward, an ascent relieved only by a few downward passages into ravines from which we had to clamber still higher, ever higher. Amid the densely crowding branches neither up nor down was visible. The headache that split my brain at every step, the lagging exhaustion of my legs, alone told how sharply we were climbing.

Just when I knew I could go no further, an exultant shout from the boys ahead announced that they were at the summit. Spurred by their outcry, I staggered a few steps more and, to my surprise, came suddenly out of the jungle. I was at the base of the ultimate pyramid. A short scramble pulled me to the top.

The view I remember not because of the vast, fissured panorama of mountains to the west, a spectacle we could admire any day, though not so loftily, from our own windows, but for the somber, unexplored forests eastward. More black than green, they opposed a sullen, inhospitable barrier to trespassers, haunted by soft-treading *boso* who kept inviolate an existence that had gone on and on, barbarously fearful, since man's bleak dawn. In the dark trees coiled pythons thirty feet long waiting to swing their bony heads like catapults and strike senseless any living thing, pig or deer or even man himself, that came within range.

Python were so common in these mountains that married women wound their vertebrae through their hair as a mother's badge instead of the elongated, unglazed white beads worn by unwedded girls. I have been given these vertebrae while still so fresh that cockroaches were making a meal off their sinews. The Igorots wait until a python has made and swallowed his kill; after this surfeit the huge snake sleeps for a month or two, and can be surprised. If he has killed a deer, he can squeeze into an assimilable mass everything except the horns. These he must wait to rot off. When pursued in this handicapped state the python can be entangled in bushes and slain.

I once met an Igorot who claimed to have stepped on a python. Mistaking it for a log. My inquiries never brought any authentic report of a man killed either by these constrictors or by the poisonous snakes, particularly the adders and the unhooded cobra common in this region. I have had a snake which the schoolboys promptly declared to be poisonous squirm across a classroom window sill, just as I have had a tarantula hop down on to a bench beside a schoolgirl; many distractions could divert the humdrum of an Igorot classroom – an earthquake, a lunatic, a rabid dog.

As to pythons, I read in an East African paper a missionary's advice on what to do when encountering one. "Don't run," he warned. "The python can outglide you." His recommendation was to lie down and hold one's body so stiffly against the ground that the python could not push his head under his victim. After some ineffectual nuzzling the snake would turn next to swallowing its prey feet first. All the man need do then was to wait until it had reached his knees, at which moment he could draw his knife and slash the python's throat. Who had tested this theory the missionary did not state!

Our concern at the top of Sisipitan, however, was not pythons, not even the *boso*. We were too many to worry about snakes or wild men. What we had come to examine was fortifications. We found none. The only evidence that Americans had occupied this remote peak was a hole in the rock into which it was plain that a metal socket had been inserted. Bit by bit we pieced together the clues. Although the Mai-init tribesmen, long ago, had stolen the socket, at one time, as far back as 1902, it had held a flagpole from which waved not the American flag but a red flag, a triangulation flag set there by surveyors. To learn this we need not have climbed Sisipitan, but we had to dispose first of the mythical fortifications before we could construct from village hearsay this reasonable solution of our mystery.

* * * * * * *

Romantic though these expeditions were, our real romance centred within the crude, unpainted pine-board walls of the school itself. This was the romance of boys and girls taking on their shoulders, in a generation's brief span, the burden which Western peoples have accustomed themselves to through the slow, often barbarous climb out of years reckoned not by hundreds but by thousands. Valiantly these Igorot youngsters did their job – and had fun doing it. Education was more than a chore; it was privilege, adventure, a quickening of every vital interest. It gave new dimensions to friendship, to family life, it burst the cramping restraints of feudal hatreds. To every student his graduation was a solemn promise. There were tears; there was also laughter.

No teacher should underestimate youth's capacity for dedication to a great hope. Young people, if we give them a fair chance, can remake the world. They must be taught to enjoy doing it. However solemn our Igorot graduations were, they were first gay.

Aside from the timeworn cycle of feast and fast, school doings offered an Igorot village its major entertainment. Broadway, Hollywood, were telescoped into the school plays which preceded graduation. Such plays as were available in Western text-books did not fit our requirement. Since a large part of the audience did not understand English, the language in which the Philippine government then insisted that all its pupils be taught, examined, granted diplomas, effective drama demanded pantomime to make its dialogue intelligible. After searching vainly for plays that would do this we ended by writing our own.

We had always two, a faery tale, culled from Hans Christian Andersen's treasury, and a comedy imagined from incidents in Igorot life. The faery tales have universal application. Unversed through they might be in the ornate affairs of prince and princess, the Igorot audience understood and applauded, avidly watching their sons and daughters gallivant in the outmoded finery of the 1920's. Brief skirts, remnants of my wife's trousseau and once dear to the flapper, were unstitched to make capes, the shapeless sack dresses hung with rhinestone jewelry to look regal.

The plays supplied also that pleasantly unreal element of blood-and-thunder which our TV addicted generation looks for in Westerns. Like the Westerns, they incited to violence. Our small son, Geoffrey, having attended all rehearsals and memorized every scene, was stirred to prodigious threats.

"Maria," he spouted to his amah, "I hate you. I will kill you, and cut you into little bits, and put you in the toilet – and I will plush the toilet!"

The other plays, based on Igorot life, were frankly didactic, but the moral, the value of education, wore humourous disguise. One play, for instance, dealt with the Philippine Government's substitution of orange-backed for the traditional green-backed one peso notes. From this change sharpers reaped a harvest cheating back woods folk who thought that they were getting, for the palay they sold not these one-peso orangebacks but the five-peso yellowbacks. This plot was a natural: the schoolboy, whose literacy his crafty old father had pooh-poohed – "I had no education, and look where I am!" – proved the ability to distinguish F-I-V-E from O-N-E was worth more in pesos and centavos than the old man's down-to-earth cunning.

But graduation did not end on this whimsical note. It ended in tears. At the close of the Sunday Mass the graduates knelt before the high altar for a final benediction and then, with the congregation, stood to sing, "Lord, dismiss us with thy blessing." This moment was holy in their lives, a moment that hallowed all they had learned to the good of their people. No wonder they wept, the priest wept, and all the people with them.

How truly their promise was to be kept I saw with my own eyes, some fifteen years after war had forced this school abruptly to close its doors. During that war their part had been valiant. In the peace that followed they had done even better. They had taken on their own shoulders the rebuilding of their community, and managed it so effectively that hope had supplanted fear, wisdom replaced ignorance. However much remained to be done, they had become a people proud of their future rather than mournfully regretful for their past. For once, a primitive people had made the insistent transition. Clear-eyed, thanks to the inspired leadership of these boys and girls, they had crossed an unrecorded history's treacherous pitfalls without sinking victim to gaudy innovations from the West. Barely a generation removed from head-hunters, they had planted their feet firmly in the 20th Century not as glossy imitation Americans but as Igorots.

That brief visit, fifteen years after, showed me a dream come true[43].

* * * * * * * *

Years ago I was booked to speak on the Philippines at a fashionable girls' school in Minnesota. Before my talk, the headmistress asked my to show her exactly on the map where the Philippines were so that she could introduce me more intelligently. On a later visit to the Mid-West, this time to Ohio, I related this incident to illustrate how little many educated Americans actually knew about their trans-Pacific dependency.

From the audience a girl came to me afterwards and demanded,

"Was the school you mentioned St. Mary's?" I admitted that it was.

"And the headmistress was Miss M.?"

"Yes."

"I knew it," she exclaimed.

"I was there. It made me mad that she didn't know how to find the Philippines."

She had reason to be mad, for she had grown up in Cebu, where her father, a one-time United States Army colonel, had been Collector of Customs.

Even those Americans who could spot the Philippines on the map may be excused for knowing almost nothing of the luxuriantly varied beauty of the islands included under that name, or of the greater, even more picturesque differences of the peoples whom we lump together as Filipinos.

How fascinating were these differences I myself did not appreciate until I began taking vacation trips through the Southern islands, visits to such intriguingly named towns as Cebu, Dumaguete, Zamboanga, Jolo, and Cotabato.

The ship I traveled by, the *Kinau*, had been the maritime pride of the Hawaiians back in the age, fabulous now, when they were better known as the Sandwich Islands. Built in 1883 at Cramps' famous Philadelphia shipyard, she was the first steamship in the Pacific to boast the glamourous novelty of electric lights. But this glory she had long outlived. No longer able to meet Hawaiian standards of inspection, she had been sold to eke out her final years in the Philippines.

No tourist would have sought out the *Kinau* for the luxury of her accommodations. Her staterooms were narrow cells, their walls crusted with so many layers of paint that it was doubtful if dry rot had left any wood under it. If I hung up my coat too sharply, down it would drop, hook and all. At night I could hear the cockroaches rustling beneath by bunk, their active foraging noisily audible even against the click-click-click of mahjongg counters slapped down endlessly, day and night, by Chinese merchants in the saloon below. The ship had no bathroom, only toilets wedged over the stern; to reach this rudimentary plumbing across the feet of sprawling deck passengers was an expedition.

Yet one voyage in the *Kinau* always inspired keenness for another. Her captain alone was worth the ticket. Like many Philippine skippers he was a Basque, fluent in languages, forthright in speech, but he wielded arts of entertainment that would have graced the commander of a Cunard liner. His quick mind, his wit, his broad range of interests held his passengers enchanted through every meal. His mate we did not meet; he apparently was delegated to exercise his charm on shore, keeping himself in trim from the aphrodisiac leaves of a plant which grew on the bridge. How much of this activity was for pleasure, how much by way of business, was a moot point. Some of the *Kinau*'s most important shippers were widows. A wise navigator set his course by Venus.

The *Kinau*'s larger life was enjoyed on the top deck. Here, shielded under a wooden awning, we lounged, read, talked, ate our meals. My custom was to come up before dawn in pyjamas and drink the coffee my roomboy brought me while I watched daylight boiling up behind the mountains and splashing, saffron and purple, across the sea. Sunrise drove me back to bed for an hour's dozing before I essayed a sponge=bath and shave and came up again clothed for breakfast, hungry to dip spoon in the golden sweetness of papaya or mango.

From this top deck we watched the islands drift by, some of the jungle to the water's edge, or mangrove swamps haunted by crocodiles, enlivened by monkeys, but others tamed to coconut plantations, to colonnades of palm trees unrolled mile after mile. So slowly did the *Kinau*'s ancient engines propel the little steamer that the islands seemed to outrun us, but gradually, before our drowsing eyes, one island dropped behind, another was overtaken. All were mountainous, none more spectacularly than Negros, rising in a long, imperceptibly steepening line from sea level to its final ridge, six thousand feet skyward, or Mindanao's craggy peaks, first sighted through the enamel-bright arc of an early morning rainbow.

Our first stop, however, was Cebu. This was Magellan's last stop. Just across the narrow channel he was slain by hostile natives, but too late for their freedom. He had put their islands on the map, given Spain claim for the sovereignty which she was to cling to for almost four centuries.

Cebu, smelling sickly sweet of copra, still remembers Magellan. The wooden cross used at his first Philippine Mass it had sheltered under a canopy near the city's bustling quay. The canopy may soon have to be lifted higher or the cross will thrust through its roof; according to local legend it has continued to grow and, when I last saw it, was an unwieldy ten feet tall.

Another Magellan memento was the Santo Niño, a figure of the Christ child which is brought out in procession at the Epiphany. I was fortunate that my several January visits coincided with this festival of the Three Kings, by Spanish reckoning the true Christmas.

Ahead of the Santo Nino were other sacred mages, each on a float flanked by panels of solid silver. The floats had gone modern, and were illuminated by the electric globes that shone from massive candelabra, but the hundreds of men, many of them friars, and the long, double line of white-clad women and girls who escorted the holy figures all carried candles. As the procession approached the Cathedral, rockets flared, cannon resounded, a garish din which continued until the paraders had disappeared within the great church, vanished in clouds of incense, in a celestial starburst of light seen far within the wide-flung doors.

But Cebu to me was memorable for other less dramatic reminders of holiness. On one of our voyages the *Kinau* had among its passengers Colonel Reasoner, head of the United States Army's Medical Corps in the Philippines. Colonel Reasoner had just won some money on the stock market. Unlike most people lucky enough to squeeze a profit out of Wall Street, he considered this money not his own but expendable for some worthy cause.

213

The worthy project was ready to hand in the Cebu Leprosarium. His wish was to brighten the lives of the hundred and twenty young people quarantined there, and to do so not by outright charity but in such a way that each youngster could feel he had deserved his prize. In carrying out this plan he asked from the Jesuit in charge a feat of tactful contrivance any lesser man would have declined as impossible: he wanted games and academic contests to be arranged so skillfully that every single one of these hundred and twenty children could win a prize. The Army thinks big, but the Jesuit director, even without a general staff to help him, promised big. He guaranteed that on our return, one week later, the field day would be ready for our approval. It was.

Colonel Reasoner enlisted the entire passenger list to give the occasion face. Each of us was assigned a job. Mine was to judge compositions in the academic contest, less exciting than judging foot races and games but poignant in what it revealed of the normal aspirations these children cherished. Their normalcy made their plight sadder.

I was brought up in the days when leprosy still emanated its antique horror. As a boy I was afraid to look at magic lantern slides of the Hawaiian leper colony at Molokai, slides which my father used to show. I tortured my imagination into believing that I could contract this ghastly disease from a pictured glimpse of the houses in which lepers lived. In China the Sisters had had me put on a surgeon's gown and rubber gloves to baptize a leper, more perhaps to allay any lurking worry in my mind than in theirs. That the disease was not easily contracted was, by that time, well known. This Chinese leper, some years after his disease had been diagnosed, had married, and engendered children; so far as we knew, neither his wife nor children had been infected. To avoid the slightest chance of contagion, however, he was isolated at the church services and required to sit outside on the porch. Leprosy in its most gruesome shape had the run of Chinese streets and often could be met with in beggars whose lips and nose had been eaten away until they were suppurating holes.

The leprosy we saw at Cebu had few of these grim associations, though it had not yet been disguised under a new name, Hansen's Disease – a curious quirk of modern medicine which has substituted more complicated names for ailments we used to know as grippe, palsy, infantile paralysis, as if it were hoped that by new labels they would sound more curable. These Cebu youngsters whose contests we judged were still called lepers, yet none of us laymen would have recognized them as such. A few reddish blotches on their faces or some healed scars on their legs were the only signs of disease, and generally so inconspicuous that we should have passed them off as a passing skin infection. Except for more advanced cases with ulcerating sores, the old-time precautions had been waived. We were given no rubber gloves to handle

214

their English essays. These children even were permitted to go home once a month and to enjoy a week-end with their families.

How the disease is contracted was still a mystery; the theory at the time was that, with rare exceptions, it could be caught only in infancy, perhaps by skin contact with an amah. Since leprosy can take as long as twenty years to incubate, the source of contagion was often too remote to trace.

Equally, no cure was in sight. The best hope of arresting the disease was by use of chaulmoogra oil. Yet this treatment, painful and prolonged, frequently held out hope only to dash it in the moment of victory. Those who took chaulmoogra injections could not be released even tentatively until they had shown themselves negative to leprosy for twenty-four months. Two of the inmates we talked to had come near making it; they were a young man and a young woman, each a teacher, each about twenty-one years old. One had gone for twenty-two months negative; on her twenty-third test, she recorded positive. The man's disappointment was even harsher: he came safely through all but one of his required twenty-four test; the last month undid the process. Like the girl, he had to start again the whole tedious, excruciating series and hope, with an optimism less resilient, for better luck the second time – two years later.

Yet they both mustered the heroism to smile. Laughter indeed characterized all these youngsters, the laughter, I suppose, of youth which helped them believe that they had time on their side. To us their laughter was sadder than tears.

* * * * * * * * *

Before America had grown callous to the novelty of ruling her own Oriental dependencies, two names echoed in flamboyant song her first imperial excitement. One gained ribald currency from a ditty sung by the precursors of the doughboy and the G.I., the blue flannel-shirted soldiers who sweated through Mindanao jungles in chase of the elusive Moro. The other bloomed in the title of a musical comedy once as popular as its author, George Ade. Time has erased both, but I grew up to the tuneful music of the Sultan of Sulu, even if I was too young to catch the lilting implications of "The monkeys have no tails in Zamboanga." Little did I imagine that I should make the four hour voyage from Zamboanga to Jolo and meet in person George Ade's same Sultan of Sulu, hero of as many wives as Solomon. America's only colonial exhibit to be placed alongside Britain's fabulous Indian princes, he nearly outlived our brief Empire, although he had been converted to democratic imposture by his appointment to the Philippine Senate. Legislative deliberations in Manila were incongruous with the fierce piratical people over whom he and his forebears had held absolute rule, the rule of the sword, the ripple-bladed kris, the only domination the Moros respected.

Moroland begins at Zamboanga, a town seldom wracked by storm and flowering breezes that preserve its verdant peninsula from cloying heat. Zamboanga looked southward toward equatorial seas. It turned its back on the hot bustle of Manila and Cebu, on the intrusion of American energy, the strident demands of American commerce. Stretched between palm trees and beach, the drowsy town was an enclave where Spanish still was spoken. Its colour, however, the flamboyantly mixed hues of its women's dress, lightning shot through a rainbow, bannered a culture the Spanish never could subjugate and which, in the transitional years when I visited Zamboanga, the Filipino seemed unlikely to curb. This culture the Spanish had termed Moro, paying its fierce proponents the compliment of naming it after the Moor whose prowess Spain had age-old cause to respect.

The Moros were the last wave of Malay invasion to oversweep the Philippines. Just as Celt and Teuton, Greek, Roman, Slav, had pushed impetuously across Europe, driving earlier invaders ahead of them, compelling Irish and Scots to make their ultimate stand with backs to the Atlantic's stern barrier, so Igorot, Ilocano, Pangasinese, Tagalog, Visayan, Moro had pushed each other steadily northward through their archipelago. Some had gone farther, crossing the sea to mingle with the aborigines of Formosa and the natives of southern Japan. The Igorots, first comers, had made the mountains of Luzon their fastness; the Moros, the latest comers, just as skillfully at home on water as on land, fastened their grip on the islands of the south. At Zamboanga the women's dress seems to scream the bravado of this reckless dominion.

Like the slit-skirted Chinese girls in Hong Kong, Moro women matched colours which the staid canon of Western taste declared impossible, indecent, irreligious. That was the 1930s when the Puritan tradition still taught that God had created all men drab. Since then, we Westerners have escaped our prim slavery to dull browns and greys. Englishmen still go to the office carrying rolled umbrellas but in America we no longer are shocked by a President whose seaside shirts outglared a technicolour sunset. But Moro women, in their loose silk pantaloons, aquamarine, lightning emerald, electric azure, their pale blue bodices fitted close to the rising curve of the breasts and archly fastened with tiny gold buttons up to the gently sloped valley between, their plaid sarongs rolled over one shoulder and across the opposite hip in a slash of yellow and scarlet more clamative than the noisiest 'Scottish tartan, these anticipated the polychromes of a seedsman's catalogue. They brightened the

216

streets with a garden bed's profuse hues, with the bold pastels of zinnias, the subtly delicate tints of the sweet pea.

Other things about Moroland I learned in Zamboanga. I soon was warned that we were in a country spurred by passions as spectacular as its colours. Here men ran amok, made running amok a habit. Walkers in the streets had always to be alert for the panic cry, "*Juramentado!*" This cry gave the alarm that some fanatic was slashing his path to heaven with sharp-edged *kris* or heavy-bladed *barong*. Brooding over some slight, malcontents would consecrate their anger by a vow, duly sworn, whereby they engaged to kill as many nonbelievers as Allah put in their way before they themselves were cut down. To make a more thorough job of this wholesale homicide they wrapped their bodies, their arms and legs, with rattan. So staunch was this protection, and even stouter their determination that outlaws thus armoured have made a frontal assault on the soldiers guarding Army headquarters and pushed their way, seemingly impervious to bullets, within grabbing reach of the sentries' rifles.

In the frequency of these murderous forays, however, Zamboanga took second place to Jolo. Off to the west, close to the Borneo coast, we came to this long-notorious pirate capital, seat of the Sultans of Sulu. Our approach was melodramatic. The full moon, silver white, was rising as the sun set. Dark between them, on a low shore backed by hills, squatted the town, a foreboding place, grimly sinister. Spain had never truly subjected it; the Filipinos as far away as the north coats of Luzon had studded the shore with round watch-towers to give warning of Moro pirates. If the striped sails of their *vintas* hove above the horizon, the villagers did not linger to resist the marauders, but snatched up wives, children, what goods they could carry, and fled to the hills. Only to the Americans, in the person of General Pershing, had the Moros surrendered, making their grudging acknowledgement of an enemy who had outfought them.

It was a peace punctured often by violence. Few years passed without some outbreak. To keep these in check the American army and now the Philippine Constabulary maintained garrisons in Jolo's back country. We could not forget how impulsively treachery had bloodied the Moro's history nor banish from our minds as we went ashore that evening, the ever-lurking risk of being sliced by a *juramentado*.

My guide on this first excursion ashore was a one-time captain of the U.S. Marines. He impressed me at once with the prime precaution for walkers in Jolo streets: never let anyone approach too close behind you. It seemed almost as dangerous to let a Moro approach too close in front. On the trip preceding my next visit, two years later, one of the *Kinau*'s passengers, an American Army officer traveling with his wife, had been attacked while bargaining outside a shop on the Chinese Pier. On this long, ramshackle structure where for safety's sake the Chinese merchants had during two centuries lived and sold their wares, a Moro suddenly drew his *kris* and lunged at the startled tourist.

The officer owed his life to the old-fashioned pocket watch he was wearing in what then was known as the fob-pocket, a pocket which wrist watches have made obsolete. By the luckiest of chances the watch deflected the knife from his groin. Before the assassin could stab him a second time, bystanders had seized him from behind and pinioned his arms.

My marine captain had himself just missed a hazardous encounter. At the one time when he had neglected to strap on his revolver he had been startled, in the Jolo Market, by the outcry of "Juramentado!" He looked for a store to dodge into, but he was not quick enough. With a celerity no one could have believed possible the Chinese shop-keepers had pushed into place the cumbersome boards they used to shut up their open-fronted *tiendas*. Left alone outside this barricade of solid wood, the captain braced himself to encounter the desperado. The Marines never retreat, he reminded himself. Fortunately, the outlaw ran off in another direction and saved him the ignominy of putting this slogan to a test.

On the evening he showed me Jolo, he made sure of his gun. We walked streets haunted only by moonlight till we reached the Sultan's mosque. Across its white walls spread the shadows, inky black, of palm fronds. Every pointed branch the moon traced in fantastic outline. But from inside the mosque's open windows flared the scarlet fezes of worshippers gathered to anticipate Friday's holy day. We could hear the imam chanting sentence after sentence and the congregation shouting responses as frenzied as a war-cry. Their voices vibrated with an agitation so baleful that we hurried to get clear before the doors opened and this swarm of true believers emerged.

Yet my three visits to Jolo were peaceful enough. The nearest I came to mishap was dropping my favourite Dunhill pipe overboard one morning as I spent the last idle minutes before breakfast admiring the pearl-fishing schooner that had tied up next to the *Kinau*. In sudden dismay I saw my cherished briar sink slowly out of sight. I had chanced, however, on the one place in the world where such an accident could be salvaged. A diver aboard the schooner caught my distress. Down he plunged and, a minute later, was clambering up the *Kinau*'s side to hand me back my pipe.

This tiny incident suited Jolo's knack for the unusual. The town had no outward distinction except the tottering landmark of the Chinese Pier - a landmark of shacks patched together so crazily with odd bits of lumber that a tourist, stamping heavy-heeled across its planks, half expected to tilt the quaking structure into the sea. The buildings on shore were innocuous –

drab, grey edifices. Yet never did I visit this island without becoming uneasily alert to the accrued violence of centuries. Jolo was a chapter out of Conrad. Drama quickened the faces of the people, drama annexed the countryside for its ominous setting.

In a car lent us by the Constabulary I accompanied an Army friend to the island's furthest outpost. Over the unpretentious road hung the memory of savage fighting, of ambushes sprung between narrow hills, of hatreds as predictable of the future as they had been rife in the past. The truce made with the American Army did not cover the Philippine Constabulary. In this back country there had been bloodshed within months of our visit. The police station on which we called had the air of a garrison planted in enemy territory.

Its site was amazing. It edged the lip of a crater, a bowl whose sides sloped steeply down through jungle to a lake, perfectly round and bluer than the sky. While we gazed, a flock of white parrots scattered across its surface and disappeared into the dense blackness of the trees.

Only a thin barrier separated this lake from the sea, a wedge, jungle-clad like the rest of the lake's encircling slopes but so narrow as barely to dyke back the encompassing waters of the Celebes Sea. This final margin of the Philippines looked south, looked away indeed from the Philippines, from Manila and its borrowed politics, to the enchantment of the South Seas. Across this watery expanse whose currents glistened in the sunshine no land intervened until the craggy peaks, the fetid, half-drowned mangrove swamps of New Guinea. The blue distances beckoned, and Sulu, like its companion islands, strained at an insecure anchorage. As I looked I fancied that they were already adrift and moving toward a world still mysterious, a world which war had not yet scarred with landing fields nor left to sink back into primeval dotage amid the rusting relics of discarded bull-dozers, shattered airplanes.

Off one of these companion islands we anchored, late one afternoon, to load cattle. Their owner swam out to the *Kinau*, his revolver strapped to his head. He was a young German, an aviator in the First World War. In Germany he had met and married the daughter of a compatriot, Jolo's leading merchant, himself wedded to a Mora princess, and so successful in a dozen money-making enterprises the he had sent his children back to the Vaterland to be educated. As if to the South Seas born, the young flyer now managed much of his father-in-law's business and was overseeing this dispatch of livestock to Manila.

To bring the steers aboard, the *Kinau*'s crew launched the lifeboats. They would have been a sorry safeguard in emergency, having baked too long in the hot sun. No sooner were they dropped into the sea than they swamped and, except for the air tanks at bow and stern, would have sunk.

This did not perturb the crew. Sitting waist-deep at their oars, they rowed the boats close enough inshore so that they could herd the unfortunate cattle into the water and fasten each beast by his nose to the rope that hung down from the gunwale. When they could squeeze no more horned heads alongside, the sailors headed back to the *Kinau*, compelling the cows, barely able to breathe, to swim with thrashing desperation until crewmen could affix belly-bands under them and signal winch and boom to swing them inboard.

Ashore there were other hazards. At sunset all work stopped, awaiting moonrise. Moonlight was needed to spy out the crocodiles lurking in a lagoon through which the steers waded thigh-deep on their way to the beach. Sharks and barracuda the sailors did not seem to fear. Brilliantly the loading lights shone down on ship and sea as they struggled past midnight to get their panicky cargo stowed flank to flank in the foc's'le. Knowing how notorious was the Sulu Sea for both sharks and barracuda, I watched expectantly, but never a fin did I see. As for the steers, they soon permeated our ship with barnyard odours. Thinner and thinner they waned during the ten days' voyage still ahead of them, and not a few died, choosing perversely to depart this life just as we had returned to Cebu, where port regulations did not permit carcases to be dumped overboard. Dead cow was disagreeable enough, dead cow bloating for twelve hours under a tropical sun gave us more local atmosphere than we could stomach, an atmosphere nauseatingly blended with the sickly sweet coconut candy fumes from the copra stored below decks.

No one should live in the Orient, however, if he objects to smells. The air, when I came home to America from Oriental ports, used at first to seem tasteless, like meat without salt – but we are catching up. We now admit the divine right of pulp mills, smelters, oil refineries, and a million automobile exhaust pipes to stifle our breathing with smog, a compound not as rich to the nostrils as Oriental scents, but more deadly.

* * * * * * * * *

The German aviator climbing aboard clothed in bathing trunks and revolver was but one sample of the picturesque characters the time-worn *Kinau* attracted. He stirred us to the ever-present hazards of life in the Moro country. He could never let down his guard. When doing the rounds of his cattle domain he kept his eyes ever alert scanning the horizon. A single sail, he told us, he could ignore; two sails traveling in company boded trouble.

This need to size up a situation promptly and accurately was instanced by another passenger on another voyage, an American who filled the lonely post of school superintendent for all the islands between Zamboanga and Borneo. His most critical moment came when he was attending an academic programme in rural hill country back of Jolo.

Squeezed with a throng of pupils and parents into the meager shack of a school, he felt not only hot and uncomfortable, but uneasy, for he was sitting beside the principal on a platform barely raised above the crowd facing him. The room had but one exit, a door at the back completely blocked by the crowd.

"What a perfect place for a man to run amok." He thought to himself.

Even as he mulled over this bleak possibility, his attention was hypnotized by a fierce-faced man whom he saw drawing his kris from its scabbard. The man had fixed his gaze intently on him, and was staring with glittering, excited eyes while all the time he stroked the wavy-edged blade, testing its keenness. Then, to the superintendent's horror, he stood up; with stealthy paces he advanced, keeping the long, sinuous knife pointed directly at him.

"I will let him come two steps nearer," he resolved, "then I will have to shoot."

But just before his assailant reached the critical zone, the American suddenly observed that the man's eyes were not directed exactly at him. Checked by split-second judgement, the Superintendent held his fire, as the Moro lunged forward and, with a stroke too swift to follow, impaled a centipede on the post behind his head.

On such hair's breadth decisions hung the success or failure of education in Jolo.

Our most illustrious passengers, in my several voyages, were the Sultan of Sulu himself, and his brother, the Rajah Muda. Contrary to our expectation they were not the most impressive. The Jolo pier at sailing time bustled like a New York pier before the departure of a Cunarder. On this night there were two steamships ready to cast off, the *Kinau* and a rival Maritima vessel, a double attraction which brought out a fiesta crowd. The gayest part of this crowd were what we assumed must be a choice selection from the Sultan's innumerable wives, pretty girls, chattering, laughing, outdazzling in their brocaded silks a garden-bed of zinnias. So brilliant was their mirthful display that we did not observe the sultan when he slipped aboard; the crowd's deference was paid not to Sulu's saturnine little ruler but to a *hadji*, a one-time pilgrim to Mecca, who boarded the Maritima ship opposite us.

An instant hush signaled this holy man; the crowd parted to let him pass. Tall, wearing a white turban, white flowing robes, barely leaning on his staff, he walked like an ancient prophet. He was not modern potentate gesturing to his populace, but looking neither right nor left, accepting their awed silence as his due while he strode, majestic and self-absorbed, toward the ship's gangplank. Even after he had disappeared within his cabin the crowd was slow to resume its babble.

Our fellow passenger, the Sultan, we did not see until later in the voyage. He did not appear on the awning deck but established himself at a table on the narrow deck below. He heeded no outsiders and, except for playing chess with his secretary, engaged in no social activity. Guarded by four well-armed retainers, who squatted at the corners of his table, he sat aloof. Supposedly he was keeping the fast, for the month was Ramadan when no Moslem is permitted to swallow even his saliva until after sundown – a custom that sends Moro schoolchildren incessantly to their classroom windows to spit. No sooner had the *Kinau* paid its last visit to Zamboanga, however, and turned north, away from Moslem territory, than the Sultan shocked us not only by eating breakfast but – as my trips aft to the latrine gave me close chance to observe – by improving his breakfast eggs with the ham his religion forbade. Allah had conceded jurisdiction to the Holy Trinity, so the sultan, well fleshed under his wrinkled white duck suit, put off the religious leader and put on the politician, the Philippine Senator.

His brother, the Rajah Muda, was more engaging. He was his brother's heir. Destined soon to succeed him as sultan and to die abruptly, victim – it was reported – of poison after a reign as brief as the old sultan's had been long. But no anticipation of this grim outcome clouded our shipboard acquaintance with the rascally, talkative crown prince.

Nimbly interpreted by the sultan's secretary, himself a half-brother of the sultan of Perak and connected with much Malay royalty, the Rajah Muda held forth genially in the *Kinau*'s tiny smoke-room. His reminiscences were from the far past; they centred in what evidently was the epochal experience of his life, the visit which he and the Sultan paid to President Taft in 1912.

The stay in Washington, however unique its role in glorifying our republic with tributary kings, paled in the Rajah Muda's memory beside his adventure en route to the White House. He could still wax exuberant over the hospitality proferred the travelers at Singapore, where the British Governor, Sir High Clifford, donned Malay dress in their honour and talked Malay glibly while feasting them on Malay food.

This feast was his only respectable memory. The rest of their journey, by North German Lloyd via Suez, was commentary on the brothels he and his brother contrived to visit. Of this very thorough sampling, Naples took top honors. Paris he recalled with bitterness. He had retired with an attractive partner to her room where she undressed, as did he. Before proceeding to the evening's prime activity, however, he made the mistake of putting a gold coin on the night-table beside the bed. This coin the girl instantly picked up and then, donning her robe, excused herself for a moment. She never came back. After twenty years her defection still rankled.

Washington and the United States proved a dismal anti-climax for the two Sulu princes. So closely were they restricted, so carefully chaperoned, that they had to behave. After all, they were State visitors, and their paternal Government made sure that no prying reporter should hunt out the nation's only live sultan in a whore-house.

The two dignitaries concluded their all too pure sojourn by embarking at San Francisco. This provoked their journey's most baffling puzzle: they had started their travels sailing west; how could they return to the Philippines by the same westerly course! America must be tricking them.

The closer their steamship pursued the setting sun, the more surely they smelt betrayal. They resolved on one last desperate act; they would run amok. Rather than be slaughtered like cattle they would take with them the Americans who had fooled them.

Luckily their American advisor got wind of their scheme. By much argument he persuaded them to postpone their sortie. The transport had passed Guam; within a week, he promised, they would anchor in Manila. Things turned out, concluded the Rajah Muda, exactly as he had predicted: within a week they came to Manila. All this had happened twenty years before, but amazement still echoed in the genial old chieftain's voice as he related this astonishing fact. Little did he say about New York or Washington or the spectacle unrolled before his eyes in the long railway journey across the American continent. What clung to his recollection was this marvel that they could have crossed an infinite expanse of oceans, Indian, Atlantic, Pacific, and come home, as they set, still headed west.

* * * * * * * *

The *Kinau* ended her half century not, as her romantic career merited, on a coral reef in the South Seas. She sank in Manila Bay, an outworn old hulk not worth the cost of raising. My last trip south was in the *Lanao*, more modern, more comfortable, but with no awning deck I could ascend to watch dawn erupt from crimson clouds, no outdoor table where I could spoon out my breakfast papaya as we sidled past jungle-dark shores, no long chairs in which to drowse through afternoons when ship and island drifted southward together in currents as sinuous, as glassy smooth, as a serpent.

The *Lanao* visited other ports. Its destination was Davao, southeastern most of the Philippines' important towns, but thriving more from Japanese than native enterprise. So large were the holdings which Japanese had acquired for producing hemp that Davao was almost a Japanese colony. What they might make of this colony was a theme for bad dreams at the time I visited it.

The time was January 1941. For a year and a half we had been living in the shadow of this heart-chilling question, What will Japan do? The United States, when we sailed through the Golden Gate in 1939, had been at its summer gayest. It was celebrating man's optimism in the two great expositions, at Flushing Meadows in New York, at Treasure Island in San Francisco. The first of these I had attended on its opening day and heard Albert Einstein, in heavy Germanic accents, expatiate on the wonders of science before he triggered the impulse from a remote star to set the Fair's illuminations blazing. The star, I believe, was Arcturus, and the beam which ignited all this man-made brilliance had started across space before man existed[44]. This indeed was wonderful, although the beam arrived ten minutes late because (as was explained – not by Einstein!) it had come by way of Philadelphia. What caused me more wonder, however, was how the great Einstein managed throughout his long speech to keep dangling from the corner of his mouth an unlighted cheroot.

San Francisco's fair had entranced me even more than New York's. Its polychrome courtyards gave pattern to the sunshine. Full though the newspapers might be of threats and ultimatums, we would not believe that the madness they boded could seize a world so luminous with promise. We ought to have paid more heed to the July afternoons when fog rolled in to make these courtyards spectral. Worse than fog was soon to obscure the happiness of every man living.

Far across the Pacific, just as we were passing Guam, we heard that Hitler and Stalin had come to terms. Quite suitably we had run smack into a typhoon. Over the bow of our Dutch freighter towered waves so massive that they loomed like the Rockies. I still can see the lascar crewmen lined up across the whole front of the *Bengalen*'s top deck, staring at this foamcrested mountain range. Their attitude dramatized their awe, awe for seas that soon rose to lash these windows into splinters, but it conveyed more than awe; it was dazed worship of the typhoon's monstrous threat.

A week the typhoon delayed us, yet we came out of it. The storm of human violence which we heard building up over the radio we did not escape so soon. It was to engulf the ends of the world, places once regarded as below the human horizon, Borneo, New Guinea, the Solomon Islands, by-words for savagery but, alas for them, not inaccessible to the cyclonic devastation stirred up by the so-called civilized world.

During the storm the *Bengalen* had signaled the Japanese held island of Yap for information on the typhoon's course. Yap did not answer. No one answered. Hitler and Stalin's compact meant war. Japan was Hitler's ally.

Her destroyers, lethal, soot-grey wolves, already would be prowling the high seas. Later, in Manila, an acquaintance from the Weather Bureau told me of the sudden silence that had left his station groping. One night, seventy ships were reporting the data his bureau relied on to compose its predictions. The next night, the whole seventy had disappeared; they were taking no risks on what Japan might do.

They were ready for Pearl Harbor two years too soon. The question of what Japan might do was still unanswered when I took my last vacation trip to the Southern Islands. She had begun moves against Indo-China and Thailand, but by that time our fears were concentrated on Europe. Poland, Norway, Denmark, Holland, Belgium, even France had toppled. The *Lanao*'s captain, a Basque like the *Kinau*'s, was emphatic in denying Pierre Laval's right to be called a Basque. Our hopes had found their champion in Britain, in Winston Churchill and a Royal Air Force that was repeating against the Luftwaffe what Drake had done to Spain's Armada. We were trying to believe that Japan had waited too long. In June, when Russia declared war on the Nazis, we were seven parts certain that Japan had waited too long. Germany and Russian would destroy each other, and all would be well.

1941 is not an easy year to think back into. All our guesses were wrong. At Besao, in the late months of 1940, we had entertained an American editor who for years had declaimed against Japan; from his Manila office he had issued, month by month, fiercely worded warnings against the Nipponese thrust to all of Asia. On this visit, however, he allayed our fears of any real danger to the Philippines. The American Army, he assured us, was saying little, but it had taken precautions which would blunt any attack on the Islands. Since he of all men had most to fear from Japanese invasion we gulped down his statements with confidence that he knew what he was talking about. If we were that safe in 1940, how much safer we thought ourselves in 1941.

My interest had been absorbed by the building of a church, St. Benedict's, a beautiful church reared in stone which we quarried from a mountain slope close by. Eagerly I watched the sturdy pillars take shape, the round arches complete their span, the squat tower occupy the ridge like a fortress. It was an edifice that compelled adoration by its strength, its grace, the scintillating warmth of its stones, blue, white, golden tan, the faintest flush of pink. Its high altar was of stone, its chapel altar of stone, its baptistery roofed with a half vault of stone. Under its arches several hundred worshippers could squat on the little square stools which they stacked at the back between services.

From a ten foot cross above the altar the triumphant Christ held out His arms. The figure had been covered with gold leaf, face, hands, feet, the vestments polychromed in crimson, green, and blue which the underlying gold made translucent. On the darkest night they glowed. At sunset they

225

flung back the glory of the western clouds. At dawn they were as coolly serene as the morning's primrose sky. These walls brooded eternity; they matched the mountains' tranquil strength; they signified peace[45].

Difficult it was to imagine the unleashed savagery of war breaking in upon the timeless quiet of a region where sun and stars, wind, rain, lightning, the alternating changes of the rice terraces from mirrored fragments of the sky to steeply won footholds of golden abundance, were life's major events. Which, one asked, was the more rudely primitive, the fields of Europe plowed by shell-bursts, by crunching tank tracks, or this network of terraces laid fallow by wooden ploughs behind mud-coated, clumsy *carabaos*?

Yet the War insisted on intruding. Russia's entry had not resolved the puzzle of what Japan would do. Crisis following crisis hastened intervention like the momentum of a great stream moving ever faster toward the precipice.

In late October the Bishop[46] came to dedicate St. Benedict's. The High Commissioner, Mr. Sayre, also came, a visit which threw the *capataz* of our local road into panic. I had warned him that the High commissioner might come; he did not believe me. These roads were kept up by tax labour, most Igorots preferring to work ten days instead of paying their *cedula*, their poll-tax, in cash. But the year was nearly ended; the job of filling in rainy season ruts and clearing away slides had exhausted 1941's tax rolls. The *Capatas* had hoped to postpone further repairs until January. To his dismay, that October morning, a telegram announced not just that Mr. Sayre was coming but that he already was on his way; he had started from Baguio at daybreak.

The cardinal rule of Philippine road maintenance was that no high official must ever guess how rough the trails could be, nor suffer the tedious waits that held up ordinary travelers at the gates. Smoothly, swiftly, expeditiously, he must glide, nerves unstrained, eyes opened only to the matchless scenery.

Whether the *capataz* fooled Mr. Sayre by such deception I doubt, but Mr. Sayre had deception of his own to think of, and reluctantly to practise. Those of us with families were anxious to extract his knowledgeable opinion on whether a Japanese attack was really imminent. Should wives and children be sent home? We were certain, of course, that Luzon would be secure. The Japanese, if they did attack, would aim for Mindanao and their foothold at Davao. They would not be foolish enough to beat their heads against American strength at Manila. Yet without doubt there would be a blockade. From six months to a year we might be cut off from the States. Against this eventuality we were laying up stores. A siege, nonetheless, is a siege. Before we were relieved we might have to adjust our diet, live off the land, smoke native tobacco. We should breathe easier if wives and children could be spared this ordeal, if they could be sent home while there was still time.

Mr. Sayre kept his counsel. He was friendly, smiling, evasive. Only after he had been smuggled home in the War's first months did the truth come out that he was under strictest orders not to disclose the actual gravity of the situation. If American families were precipitated into a mass flight from the Philippines, the State Department feared the damage this would do to Filipino morale. It might panic the islands into surrender. To preserve the fiction of Philippine security American women and children, when evacuated from China and Japan, were sent to Manila instead of to the United States. Total warfare was given a new slant. Civilians were planted unsuspectingly in a danger zone to support political strategy.

Crisis and alarm were so recurrent in the autumn of 1941 that we grew hardened to them When hostilities did irrupt, they caught us by surprise. We were as incredulous about what was happening as the sailors on week-end leave in Honolulu. In our mountains we had crowded into Sagada from every adjacent town and village to celebrate the annual Fiesta. For nearly forty years, a long time in Mountain chronology, its prestige had been unrivalled. Little did one think it would not follow its usual lively course of games and dances, of sacred and secular ceremony so magnificently combined that one was hard put to tell which was the Fiesta's supreme moment, the Solemn High Mass in the ponderous stone fortress of a church, or the equally solemn performance of the *Rigadon* when Filipino and American and Igorot, in courtly style, all essayed together this far, far cousin of the minuet.

But this year the shimmering-hued mestiza gowns, stately in their long satin trains, their stiff butterfly wings of embroidered piña cloth, were doomed to be laid aside unworn. The High Mass was as far as we got. Our procession, emerging from church, was soon disrupted by portentous whispers, whispers of Pearl Harbor, closer still, of Baguio – only a hundred miles away – which had been bombed in the same way, abruptly, ruthlessly, without heed to the old chivalric amenities of war-making.

That morning, as I ate breakfast, after saying an earlier Mass, I had heard 'planes flying through the clouds which, till the sun came up strong, used to swathe Sagada. I had noted them, of course, as American 'planes, routine evidence that our army was keeping up its guard. But they were not American; they were Japanese, and oddly enough had chosen to attack the militarily impotent Camp John Hay, a vacation post used for escape from hot weather in the Lowlands. They had bombed it at the same time that they surprised and sank the Pacific battle fleet at Pearl Harbor[47].

How deadly had been the Pearl Harbor assault none of us then knew. Even while we were trying to grasp the bare fact of war, another attack, equally deadly in its completeness, was destroying at Fort Stotzenberg the Air Force we had counted on to protect Luzon. That disaster we did not hear about until weeks later. We still thought ourselves safe, although there was the chilling reminder that we now occupied a far and gravely exposed salient of American's battle front.

When I telephone Frances, however, to tell her that war had come, she exclaimed,

"Oh, that's nothing. I've had burglars!"

She had elected, this year, not to attend Fiesta, a decision she soon came to regret. Everyone, family, school, servants, neighbors, departed, leaving her completely alone. After dark she grew nervous. The monsoon, blowing up at sunset, was making the wooden building creak, as it always did, but from the study at the top of the stairs she became sensitive to noises the monsoon could not account for. As she listened, she suddenly caught a whiff of native tobacco.

Picking up a flashlight, she went down the dark stairs to investigate. In the living-room its beams revealed two strange men.

"What are you doing?" she demanded

"None, mum," came the answer.

Before she had time to estimate her peril, the intruders bolted toward a French window that opened on an outside porch. The lock baffled them. For several panicky minutes they struggled with it, then turned, blinded by the flashlight, to push past her and duck through the hall into an adjoining guest-room.

This, quite evidently, had been their way of access. Although the room's one window was screened, the screen had a panel which could be opened to permit hooking the Venetian blinds. Out this small square squirmed one of the burglars, but the second, in his fright, got caught in the narrow opening. Their panic emboldened my wife to pick up a blackthorn stick from the hall and belabor the man's backside till he screamed. In a desperate surge of fright he squeezed himself through, and escaped.

Not till she had bolted the window and made sure the doors were locked did Frances have time to be afraid, time to wonder whether she had been heroic – or foolhardy. The intruders were lowlander; undoubtedly they carried knives. But they had been too confident that the house was empty; they could not adjust themselves to this unexpected light dazzling them out of the darkness.

The rest of that night, quite understandably, Frances was too fearful to sleep. Compared to an experience as perilous as this, Pearl Harbor, Camp John Hay were anticlimax.

* * * * * * *

War is an astounding fact to get used to, whatever the degree of one's participation. Every trivial detail, all ordinary pursuits, are darkened by unproven immensities, by the aching reminder that nothing now can be called ordinary.

As we struggled home from the cancelled Fiesta we tried to remind ourselves that this trail, zigzagging on the ridge, passing Bannao, the sacred lake, meandering around the most sun-scorched valleys on the mountains' west slope, this trail familiar to every footstep was familiar no longer. Danger lurked in the afternoon's unclouded sky. At any moment we might hear the drone of hostile 'planes. Although we could not believe that they had bombs to waste on us, our scattered procession of men, women, and children dared not take this immunity for granted.

But the skies remained quiet, the sunlight shone on country tantalizingly peaceful. At home the wartime precautions we resorted to seemed so curiously out of place.

There was first the blackout. Since we had too many windows to darken we ate supper in the hall where but one window needed to be curtained. Soon after the brief twilight the school subsided into silence. No fires burned in the village. We tried to re-order our life to premature bed-time or to hearing music in the dark.

None of these precautions were in the least necessary. Never once did we hear Japanese 'planes at night. We were unwilling, at first, to concede that the 'planes we saw in the daytime could be Japanese. We soon learned better. With no radio of our own, we depended on a battery-powered instrument in Sagada for what little news could filter through an atmosphere jammed by the enemy's deliberate bedlam. Sagada passed on the grim news that the eighteen 'planes we had seen fly over in ordered formation had gone to destroy Cavite[48]. Back they came over our heads, all eighteen, still in formation, unruffled, unscarred. We had prided ourselves that only the United States had an accurate high altitude bomb-sight. The Japanese 'planes that wrecked Cavite's naval base flew too high to be touched by anti-aircraft fire, yet their aim was deadly.

At a moment when so many improbabilities needed to be explained, our isolation, our paucity of news were tough to cope with. No matter how faithfully our Sagada friends relayed what little their inadequate radio could out of the din, their information perplexed more than it enlightened. Each told of new enemy landings, landings minimized by Manila as ineffectual. They could be easily disposed of; the situation was well in hand.

"The situation is well in hand" – how many times we heard that assurance! At every new landing the situation seemed to get better in hand. If these invading forces were so paltry, we asked ourselves dumbly, why didn't our soldiers drive them back into the sea?

Only by degrees did we learn the actual scope of the disaster that had befallen us. Temporarily we had been cheered by the resumption of mail service, by the arrival of eagerly expected newspapers from Manila. But what comfort they brought, what flimsy assurance that our remembered world was still active, these were dashed by an eye-witness account of that fatal day of war. We got the story from a mining friend who had brought his family to Sagada as a safer refuge than Baguio.

On the day war broke out, while he was returning from Manila to Baguio, his car had been commandeered at Fort Stotzenburg[49]. He was still arguing this seizure when Japanese 'planes returned in force to bomb Clark Field. Into a ditch he tumbled and, from this lowly observation post, watched our air strength in the Philippines reduced to a shambles of twisted junk, smashed and bleeding bodies.

This calamity, quite as drastic as Pearl Harbor's and even less excusable, has been handled charily by the critics. Morison, in his naval history, puts it up to the Army to explain; the Army, naturally enough, has done its explaining in small type. No excuses can shake the fact that, only a few hours after Baguio had been bombed, bombed within earshot and almost within eyeshot, our airmen were so trusting as to park their 'planes wing to wing while they retired to their quarters for lunch. Their sole provision against attack was reliance on some Filipino telegraph operator who had been instructed to report any more enemy 'planes he might see approaching the Philippines.[50]

The 'planes came, but no report. Within minutes they wiped out the Philippines' aerial defense, destroying 'planes and pilots in one concerted holocaust. My friend saw it all. After the bombardment he took back his car – no one was in a mood to challenge him – and continued to Baguio.

These doings we were still digesting, struggling to catch up with events already two weeks old, when current events caught up with us, caught up even more fearfully. The Japanese had landed in force, landed unopposed. Baguio residents had crowded their hill-tops to watch the deadly spectacle. They could count the ninety-odd transports[51] swarming the Gulf of Lingayen to unload into small boats an army against which scarcely a shot was fired. There was no disguising the truth now: the situation was out of hand.

In our hearts there was room for but one thought, that we – and all northern Luzon – were cut off from Manila. It made ice in our veins. The news of Manila soon proved still more chilling. We knew nothing of the strategy which surrendered the capital without a battle and shifted the American and Filipino forces to Bataan. All we knew was that in three weeks the Japanese had gained mastery of Luzon, the island guaranteed too staunchly protected to fear frontal attack. This incredible debacle stirred afresh doubts which many of us had entertained about the military competence of Douglas MacArthur.

How unpopular MacArthur was with his former colleagues I was surprised to note as early as January 1936 when I sat down one evening to dinner with two majors at the Army and Navy Club. I had been delegated, as a canon of the Episcopal Cathedral of SS. Mary and John, to plan with them a memorial service for the late King George V. This service the United States Army was sponsoring, just why I cannot remember except that the Army did these affairs with an impressive style no one else could match.

Our chief problem that night dealt with protocol. In the first flush of semi-independence, the Filipino leaders seemed confused as to who was top man, Quezon, the Commonwealth President, or McNutt, the American High Commissioner. Perhaps their confusion was intentional, but at a dinner the High Commissioner checkmated a prior toast to Quezon by a bold reminder that he, as representing the President of the United States, still took precedence. These niceties of status, however, did not long detain us. In sketching their seating plan for the Cathedral the two majors soon had the two rivals suitably placed. What absorbed them was where to put MacArthur. Their whole evening's preoccupation was how to seat him so that he would know that he was being slighted, yet have no comeback.

One major suggested putting him well forward, as his rank required, but behind a pillar.

"No," argued the other. "We can't do that. After all, he was Chief of Staff."

This weighty question I don't believe was settled to anybody's satisfaction, but I was more interested in how McNutt and Quezon would manage their separate departures. Would they stand on the order of their going?

For a moment they rose to face each other across the centre aisle. Quezon faltered, his look a quizzical smile, until the High commissioner, in a masterly gesture, took the Commonwealth President's arm and walked out with him side by side. Whether Douglas MacArthur made his exit before or behind the U.S. General commanding the Philippine Department I was not alert enough to observe.

These peacetime jealousies persisted. When war came we blamed General (no one remembered to call him Field Marshall) MacArthur for upsetting, as we imagined, the plans for defence prepared by General Grunert. MacArthur, some months before, had been given command of both Philippine and American soldiers, the USAFFE, or United States Armed Forces for the Far East. We blamed him for a situation about which we knew very little.

231

Actually (as I learned later from the Army's official history of the War) the plans which he did upset were plans to sacrifice the Philippines in the interest of more pressing commitments across the Atlantic. To these he would not agree. By the vehement weight of his protests he compelled Washington to change these plans, and to provide for holding not Luzon alone but the entire archipelago. He infected the General Staff with his own belief that, in the limited time at his disposal, he could convert the Philippine Army into an effective fighting force. Key to this hope was the Flying Fortress, the B17 bomber.[52] It would shield the Philippines while his new armies were molded into shape.

If MacArthur is to be blamed, it should be for encouraging the expectation that new armies could be molded so quickly. Events were moving too fast. America had no up-to-date equipment to furnish such armies, too few professional soldiers to train them. These deficiencies made MacArthur's hopes extravagant. Pearl Harbor and Clark Field dashed them with murderous finality. On the same day, the first day of war, the bombers which were to shield the Philippines and the fleet which was to relieve them were wiped out.

* * * * * * *

These large events we could read about, and try to understand, afterwards. Smaller things had more direct impact. To one small family, precariously isolated in a war zone, these opening weeks of conflict were measured in poignant attempts to lull ourselves, and especially our children, into sustaining a domestic normalcy. No matter how disturbing the news, we found ourselves getting used to it.

Christmas was the hardest to face. The restoration of mail service, suspended again almost as soon as it had been resumed, had not brought the gifts ordered from home. Our children were still so young, a boy of ten, a girl of seven, that it was harrowing to confront them with empty hands. There was no Santa Claus to visit them Christmas Eve, there were no packages to be unwrapped, no stocking to be hung beside the stone fireplace. The blackout precluded even the candle-lit magic of the Midnight Mass. The holy day dawned in the vacancy of hot, clear sunshine.

But in mid-morning the telephone began ringing. Hastily we answered it. The message we received was incredible. Santa Claus was wearing khaki instead of scarlet, but he had not deserted us. A friend, we learned, had gone down to Bontoc. In the post-office, abandoned by its staff, he had found heaps of undelivered mail, and among it our packages. These he had brought to Sagada where they awaited our messenger to fetch them to Besao.

232

The packages converted Christmas into an authentic festival, a festival whose antiphon was the noise of roller skates going round and round the school sala. We had missed the angels singing across the midnight sky, but the gleeful laughter of children announced its own prediction of a happier world. It dispelled the appalling silence of the Christmas sun.

Through the weeks afterward the war stayed so far away that we could almost dismiss it as a bad dream. Igorots arrived from Manila. One brought a message from the Bishop that he was applying for a pass to visit us. The Mission people, from this man's report, were free not only in Manila but in Baguio. Part of his journey he had made with Japanese soldiers; he spoke highly of their discipline and contrasted their training, their equipment, with the slipshod organization of the Philippine Army. From what he had seen he even anticipated that the Japanese might give the Mountain Province a more orderly government than it had received from the lowland Filipinos. Similar testimony from other travelers quieted the rumours of enemy atrocities, the overheated gossip which ballooned each bit of hearsay to horrendous dimensions.

Our only news was still such broadcasts as our Sagada friends could piece together through the din of enemy interference. They came from the Voice of Freedom, an itinerant station that had followed the Army to Bataan. Unfortunately, the will to believe played an undue part in interpreting its messages.

I was stirred to exhilaration by word that the USAFFE had interposed an army of 120,000 American troops between the Japanese and their Manila base. This was what we had looked for, a masterpiece of strategy that could at last drive the invaders back into the sea. Down to the Presidencia I hurried to proclaim the tide turned. Out of a fertile imagination I deduced the plans that now assured victory. We congratulated one another over this glorious release from the tension that had preyed on us so dismally that we hated to wake in the morning to a new day's aching fears.

My exultation was short-lived. Next morning when American visitors came over from Sagada, I exclaimed over the joyful upturn the news of this large American force had produced.

"What force?" they asked.

I repeated what I had heard.

"Who told you that?"

"X."

"Oh, X!" they pooh-poohed, dismissing my authority with a shrug. "The way the rest of us heard it, there were 120,000 Japanese troops, not American."

233

We were amateurs groping our way through military reports, military contradictions. There was less excuse for the credulity of military men themselves, the American sergeant, for instance, a career man from the regular Army, who drifted into Sagada on some errand in January and cheered its residents by predicting that "every Jap will be out of the Islands by the end of February."

The next such prediction we heard in February itself, and after we had been raided by Japanese patrols. The deadline had been amended: "Every Jap will be out of the Islands by April."

An American colonel, who stayed with us in March stamped out that hope. The Japanese, he told us, were solidly established. They would not be pushed out in months, nor would he guess how many years the job might take.

In January we had not yet confronted this stark disclaimer. Only an infrequent enemy 'plane disturbed our peace. As if to strengthen our hope that the war would never penetrate our quiet valleys, a scattering of Chinese refugees, handsome youths, pretty girls, lively children, had come all the way from Manila to find asylum in our midst. The days drowsed by in hot sunshine; cocks in the village, replied to sometimes by cocks in the jungle, kept up their peculiar habit of crowing through the afternoons. Theirs was no clarion but a call to sleep. Nothing else, not even human voices, disturbed the somnolence of barrios, sunk deep in the shade of their mango trees, where they seemed to have lapsed into perpetual siesta.

To preserve this calm against some trigger-happy aggressor, the Presidencia ordered us to take down our flag-pole. It was a pole we were proud of, glistening in a new coat of aluminum paint. But this pole, we were advised, might cause Japanese 'planes to mistake our school for a military outpost.

Down came the pole, while our ten year old son added, unintentionally, his ironic comment by playing the Star Spangled Banner on his mouth organ.

* * * * * * * *

Late in the evening of the 1ˢᵗ of February 1942 a car drove down the hill toward our home. Wondering who could be coming at that hour, I hurried outside to confront a friend from Sagada. He brought ominous news: the Japanese had occupied Cervantes in the great Abra valley west of us. Other detachments were approaching by the Mountain Trail. But the threat from the Cervantes was the grimmer, for this sleepy old town not only lay astride the road to the coast; it was connected directly with Besao by a horse-trail over the intervening hills. While we were talking, a small body of Constabulary

234

arrived, intending – we were told – to contest any enemy approach by this shortcut. They bivouacked at the Presidencia.

Only at this juncture did we realize how strongly we had counted on the Japanese not invading our region. We had been confident that they would not spare troops for an area destitute of any strategic advantage.

Our one immediate comfort was the presence of a woman transferred, not many months earlier, from Japan. Born in Japan, Nellie McKim spoke Japanese with a mastery far more fluent than this statement can suggest. She was completely familiar with the several class levels to which the speaker must adjust his idioms if he is to give the Japanese he addresses the social status to which they deem themselves entitled. It is a tricky business, for these differentiations can be employed to flatter or to insult. Adept as she was, however, Miss McKim still shrunk from close contact with the Japanese Army. Unlike the Navy or the mercantile classes, its ranks were drawn from the peasantry, for a class that had known little of Westerners at first hand. Ignorant, bigoted, fanatical, the Army was notorious for the brutal disciplining of its own members. How they would treat foreigners we did not like to imagine.

Despite these fears we refused Sagada's urgings that we abandon our home and join their larger group across the ridge. The decision was harrowing. Suddenly, abruptly, the war had brought us lonely eminence – one small family left to encounter an unknown but too explicitly rumoured adversary. Citizens though we were of the world's most powerful country, and living in a land under American suzerainty, American protection, our nationality now amounted to nothing. Wholly helpless, with the welfare of two young children burdening our hearts, we faced the armed might of an Empire vainglorious over victories so swift, so easily won, that we could neither believe nor explain what had happened. Every likelihood boded horror.

All these likelihoods we conjured up through a night too agitated for sleep. Of the war's overmany crucial times, that was the night I would most shudder to live over. Its one comfort was that we came through its dark hours unharmed. Daylight showed at least that the Japanese were not coming our way. We had escaped the ordeal of watching khaki-clad figures crawling like ants along the path that gashed the terraced slope opposite us, a path suddenly become sinister. So far we had been spared the suspense of waiting for them to come up our hill, waiting, staring, to see their guns bristle around each nearer bend of the trail.

The Constabulary, having got word that the enemy were proceeding, after all, by the motor road, soon withdrew, abandoned in fact their only warlike gesture, and disbanded. They showed as little disposition to be heroes as the policemen in The Pirates of Penzance, but, alas, they were comic without

235

being entertaining. Their most aggressive exploit had been to lead a Bontoc mob in sacking Adachi's, the Japanese-owned emporium on whose books, doubtless, many of the looters were carried in red ink.

Our next days were a perpetual sifting of rumours. All we could be certain of was that the Japanese had reached Bontoc. At our Presidencia Miss McKim had listened to them talking to gate-houses along the Government telephone lines; their voices, she told us, sounded gentlemanly. This was a very thin straw to clutch at, though we clung to such straws as if they had been logs.

Our own private telephone line to Sagada had picked out this emergency to become inoperative. We could not call each other; the bells would not ring. We arranged, however, to pick up the receiver every hour on the hour, and oftener if events seemed to demand it. Only once did human agony compel the balky instrument to override the laws of physics. One afternoon, a day or two later, the bell startled us by its strident summons.

A woman was calling, a refugee whose husband, long manager of a saw-mill on the Mountain Trail, had sent her to Sagada while he joined the Army.

"The Japs are at Dantay," she screamed, "they are starting up the road to Sagada. Pray for us over there!"

Whatever magic her anguish had summoned to turn this trick, no one else could make that telephone ring. But when we picked up the receiver fifteen minutes later, we were reassured by the calm, dry accents of another friend. The Japs were not coming, he said. Some one had mistaken a group of Igorots for hostile troops, and panicked.

These false alarms were to be frequent. Villages, first said to have been burned because the invaders found them deserted, later were reported unharmed. A grass fire had been mistaken for arson. Rumours and their denials ran neck and neck. Yet eventually the Japanese were certain to come. Our puzzle was how to prepare for these visitants, how to anticipate the temper in which they might appear. Our one bit of authentic news came from our Bontoc Mission. Its members had been treated with encouraging tolerance. Their only warning was that the Japanese did not like to see a house stripped. Such distrust hurt their feelings.

Our problem then was not to let our distrust be evident. Reserves of food we hid in walled compartments under stairs or wherever they did not invite attention. Some special treasures, such as an eight-panelled Chinese screen, we gave to Igorot friends to hide in their granaries. We did the same with passports, baptismal and marriage certificates, and other private papers. Before parting from it, I memorized the dates and number of my certificate of Derivative Citizenship. My thousands of photographic negatives, many depicting scenes, Chinese and Philippine, which never again could be caught, a boy concealed for me in the church. Putting up a ladder, he inserted them in crannies where the roof met the top of the stone walls.

For several years I had been entrusted by a doctor, formerly resident in Sagada, with his grandfather's journal. The doctor, descendant of one of South Carolina's oldest and most illustrious families, had lent me this journal to edit for publication. Leather bound, stamped in gold lettering, its eight hundred pages described in long hand a voyage around the world which the grandfather, Louis Manigault, had taken after graduation from Yale in 1850. It described a record clipper passage – 89 days – from New York to Canton, and gave fascinating details about Hong Kong and Shanghai in their infancy, a graphic account of the Philippines under Spain. From the Orient its story continued across the Pacific in a Peruvian barque, a stage during which the passenger worked out the Grand Circle route for his skipper, who was short on navigation. Its culminating scenes were from San Francisco and Sacramento during the gold strike, pages in which Manigault was hard put to decide which was worse, California or its rascally inhabitants. California he set down as the most miserable region on the earth's entire surface – he made Sahara sound balmy by comparison – while he labeled its population, particularly its Yankee overlords, as mankind's vilest scum.

Although the book hinted at romantic adventures in Peru and Chile, these were summarized with the intention of granting them fuller treatment in another volume. So far as I could ascertain, that volume never was written. What intrigued me was the contrast between the fire-breathing belligerence of its South Carolinian author, aching to settle accounts with the North, and the slow remorseless way in which the War he had prayed for eventually ground down his spirit. Across one of its final pages was scribbled a pathetic notion that he had consigned the book to a faithful slave to save it from Sherman's army, then advancing on Columbia. Thanks to this precaution it escaped the fire which destroyed the Manigault plantation. Up under the church roof we now stored it to outlive another war.

My own journals I concealed less satisfactorily between the upstairs ceiling and the roof of our home. Back in 1908, while still at a boys' boarding school near Tacoma, I had been carried away by a flurry of diary writing that blazed like wild-fire among the pupils and died as quickly. My interest, however, did not cool. Throughout the ensuing thirty-four years I had omitted only one day, and that by accident. Now its disposition haunted me. It contained no state secrets, nothing incriminating, but to a people as suspiciously curious as the Japanese it would have been a prize. If I hoped to see it again, I had to keep it out of their hands.

Up to the attic it went, leaving a great vacancy in my life, since I had been accustomed to reviewing each morning what had happened on that date. Taking a fresh notebook I now commenced what purported to be a war journal. Needless to say, I wrote cautiously, making no mention of the guerrillas with whom we soon were to have contact. Yet no matter how discreet I might be, I did not count on this new diary's enjoying more than a brief future. It survived more durably than I could have hoped.

The many volumes hidden in the attic did not fare so well. Late in the war our house was bombed by our own 'planes, needlessly as it chanced, though our flyers could not have known that only one wounded Japanese was left within its walls. On hearing, after we had been repatriated, that our house had gone skyward in flames, I kissed thirty-four years of my life good-bye. Yet to my great mystification, three years after the war, two volumes were returned to me, packed among other things that had been preserved; on a visit to the Philippines in 1956 I picked up still another. How they survived, who found them, where they were kept, these remain unanswered. All I know is that the Igorots took pains to disperse many of our things for safekeeping, and that we might have got many more things back but for the unfortunate misjudgement which led our own 'planes to destroy friendly villages after the enemy had evacuated them. As we often were to hear from Japanese lips – War is war!

* * * * * * * *

While we fumbled through the precaution of hiding what we could, and that pitifully little, our experience of war still lurked in the future tense. Each morning we woke to a nightmare, to the thought that this day the Japanese will come. Every attempt to picture what that encounter would be like gave me a chill, a spasm of nausea, at the pit of the stomach.

Still, we had one reliance. We had Miss McKim and her inborn ability to speak and understand Japanese. Sagada envied us her presence. Since the enemy, if they came from Bontoc, must come to them first, they put a car at her disposal, stationing it at Besao ready on a minute's summons to bring her to the rescue.

When the summons did come, however, the driver could not be found. He was unearthed at last pursuing his own entertainment in the village. By the time he had been hustled back to his car, the Japanese had reached Sagada; they had, we were told, their own interpreter. Dike-san, a long-time friend of the Mission and the contractor for many of its buildings. Although too late to do the introductions, Miss McKim's ride still was not wasted; she had ample opportunity to greet the newcomers. Her telephoned report lifted a load from our hearts. She had met with the utmost friendliness. Beyond requisitioning rice from the municipality, the Japanese had made no demands. They had not even troubled to enter any of the American homes, and Besao they could not spare the time to visit. Their considerate, courteous behaviour made mock of every evil rumour. Her spirits lifted to the seventh heaven, Miss McKim came back to regale us with every glad detail. The Japanese had lived up to hopes she scarcely had dared count on.

So completely did this first visit dispel our fears that when, four days later, we heard the clatter of a truck and saw it coming down the hill bristling with bayonets. We went without qualms to meet the invaders. I had been having a lesson in sixth grade fractions with a son who taught me more than I could teach him. To make my appearance dignified, I paused just long enough to don a white cassock and thus walked down with Miss McKim to the Presidencia, where the Japanese were clambering out of their truck.

Miss McKim, hurrying forward, addressed their captain but, instead of showing pleasure, or even surprise, at being spoken to in his own language, he cut her short.

"Don't speak till you are asked," he told her.

This was not the courtesy we had been expecting. Nor was there anything amicable in these soldiers' actions. No sooner had they arrived than they posted men with machine guns on a wide perimeter. And they lost no time herding our little group inside a ring of bayonets. Here for almost an hour we were harangued by the captain. His subject, interpreted by Dike-san, was the iniquities of an American which, "under Lincoln or Roosevelt?" – the interpreter said, "Lincoln" – had fought to make the negroes slaves.

Our ears were full of other noises. Dimly we tried to grasp threats that our home and its contents were to be seized and we transported as prisoners to Baguio, but even these ominous words could not compete with the tumult around us. They were spoken to the percussive accompaniment of rifle-butts battering down doors, smashing windows, as soldiers ran from house to house unchecked in their greed for loot. I could remember only that Frances had remained in our kitchen when we came down to the Presidencia. Frantic dismay poisoned every moment of the captain's long-winded tirade as I thought of her confronting this violence alone.

Before he concluded, the captain did temper his threats. His soldiers, he now said, were to take what things they needed, a fact already obvious although less drastic than the confiscation he had held over our heads. He was turning even more amenable as he accompanied us to the house, but not till I saw Frances waiting for us, evidently unharmed, could I feel relief.

"These are not the same men, dearie," Miss McKim told her.

"Don't I know it!" she exclaimed.

239

Hers had been a chilling ordeal. While we were held at bayonets' point, a soldier had pushed his way into the kitchen. Bruskly he had expelled our Igorot cook and then snatched my wife's watch from her wrist before gesturing her to open the oven door and pull out the rhubarb pie she was baking. In his greed he grabbed a handful and stuffed it into his mouth before considering how hot it would be. Angrily he spat out the mouthful and then sought to cool his tongue with what he mistook for wine, a tart swallow of vinegar. Worse yet, he was growing amourous, slobbering over her with his thick lips, when she managed to divert his interest to loot. Upstairs he plunged to ransack her bedroom for the jewelry she hinted at, leaving her to escape outdoors.

At this juncture we arrived with the captain, whom we attempted to mollify further by serving him tea in the dining-room. He had become almost mannerly, thanks to Miss McKim's facile politeness, but he was still wholly insensitive to the depredations of his troops, who trampled through the house, pulling out drawers, dumping their contents, sounding for all the world like heavy-hoofed cattle as they stomped across the floors in their hob-nailed boots. By degrees he became so conciliatory that, when he heard of Frances's stolen watch, he ordered his men to return it. They did bring back some costume jewelry, quite valueless. The watch, they declared, had been lost. When the captain went to Miss McKim's cottage and saw how it had been devastated, saw tins of food punctured by bayonets, he even had the grace to put his hand on her shoulder and say, "I am sorry."

* * * * * * * *

Our raiders departed in mid-afternoon, having feasted first on a concoction of tinned foods plundered from local stores as well as from our pantry. They mixed the stuff in one huge mess and commandeered our stove, among others, to prepare it. This brought back the victim of the rhubarb pie who warned us that we were to make no further complaint about the stolen watch. If we did, he would come back and burn our house. He had spared us, he said, because we looked pathetic.

There were other episodes, as when a moon-faced soldier, perfect picture of a Mongoloid imbecile, prodded me upstairs ahead of his bayonet. What he wanted I could not understand. I had visions of murder only to discover, in farcical anti-climax, that he had taken two pieces of three flashlights and now was demanding that I fit enough of their parts together to make one useable torch. The beam I brought to life was almost too feeble to be seen, but it satisfied him. The children had borne the day's ordeal better than their elders. Geoffrey even struck up friendship with one man, formerly a barber in

240

Baguio, and spent some time showing him his stamp collection. While they turned the pages, other soldiers kept barging in, and each in turn picked up the Brownie camera from his desk. Each time, the barber, elevated to medical attendant, took back the camera and replaced it. But when our visitors at last cleared out, the camera had vanished.

Despite the strewn, chaotic state of the house, an inventory disclosed fewer things stolen than we had thought. Except for the watch, the articles looted were not valuable but common place, practical things – candles, towels, soap, toothpaste, toothbrushes. Such losses, of course, were not negligible. They could not be replaced. A theft even more serious, was the pilfering of eye-glasses off my desk. Luckily I had a second pair. Miss McKim was less fortunate. Her only pair was taken. She had to make do with a lorgnette which the soldiers, sweeping through her cottage like a grass fire, had been too hasty to observe. My glasses I was fortunate enough to recover, brought back by the wife of a Sagada schoolteacher. They had been dropped in her home which the soldiers were ransacking as frantically as they ransacked ours.

Although we had got off lightly, the effect of this raid cut deep. We could not shake off a feeling that the house had been defiled. Every drawer bore evidence of the grimy hands that had pawed through its contents; the rooms still resounded to the wooden clop-clop-clop of the soldiers' boots trampling down all we held sacred. Too stunned were we even to try exorcizing the house of this evil seizure, of the devils whose malign visitation haunted it as it haunted our hearts.

Our marauders, we learned, were a fighting unit which had come in a bad humour after being attacked by tribesmen further north. They behaved probably as well as most soldiers in their case. Despite my love for the Chinese, I would have dreaded much more keenly falling into the clutches of Chinese soldiery. Where Japanese troops were brutal, Chinese would have been cruel.

But the strain told. We had no resilience left to meet another incursion. The mere rumour, two days later, that the Japanese were on their way back revealed almost sickeningly how tense our nerves had been strung. This rumour was disproved almost as soon as we heard it but, after yet another two days, just when we believed that we were regaining poise, the rattle of a truck descending the hill hurled us into panic. My heart might be pounding, my knees striking sparks, as I flew to don my white cassock, but my blood froze, my mind turned faint; I was without plan, without the hardihood to confront this ordeal a second time.

This panic too was wasted. What we heard was a rattletrap car which a local merchant was bringing back from its hiding place. The enemy, he assured us, had gone, and would not be back. They had burned the Government buildings in Bontoc, and in them (so the story ran) not only their dead but the wounded whom they could not take with them.

The next day brought stories even more positive, stories from a new set of visitors – this time American. They belonged to the guerrilla bands rapidly being organized, and brought news that the Japanese patrol whose return we dreaded had been wiped out to the last man. How this had happened, and where, or even whether it had happened were never confirmed. We believed the report; we wanted to believe it, just as we grasped at their prediction that every Jap would be out of the Islands before May. We had the prudence, nonetheless, to start dispersing our provisions, to send a trunkful of clothes to what we called our "country home," a village a steep distance away which had offered to conceal us. By great good luck the Japanese had not discovered our small stock of liquor. Numberless times they had passed the door to our walk-in cupboard, thinking it led to an adjacent hall. We did not tempt our luck again. Our supply of beer and other beverages we hid in the rafters of the school *sala*, our last bottle of whiskey behind a loose stone in the garden wall.

For the ensuing weeks we occupied a No Man's Land. While the Japanese were still in the neighbourhood, American guerrillas kept dropping in. Most were mining engineers who had taken temporary commissions, but some were regular Army. Quite plainly the Army had not anticipated fighting a war in the Mountain Province. The only maps these men had were post-card size, the kind given out to travelers at the province's handful of gas stations. They showed its few motor roads, but told nothing of the skein of foot trails connecting the many villages, nor even of the old established horse trails that for generations had been the merchant's means of ingress from the Ilocos coast. When we were interned we saw how contemptuous were the Japanese of even our lowland military maps; these they used to line rice sacks. Their own maps were more accurate.

The guerrillas who first came to us were trying to fill out the lamentable gaps in the Army's knowledge of our topography by following the trails on foot to see where they led. Heart-breaking work it was, down crumbling paths perhaps two or three thousand feet to the stifling depths of a gorge, across a mountain wilderness which could outlast their endurance.

Plucky men they were, assigned to a job they never should have been asked to undertake. Of the perhaps twenty-five we met I doubt if more than five survived the war. One sergeant, a lanky Texan, had to be left behind by his two companions; he was burning up with malaria, too sick to continue. Ill though he was, he kept us in stitches by his droll account of his hardships. He had climbed so many mountains that he expected one leg to be permanently shorter than the other. He told of how he and another American, each attended by two or three Philippines Scouts, were attempting with two machine guns to block Japanese progress up the Mountain Trail. After some desultory shooting, he realized that no noise was coming from his comrades across the road. The Scout whom he sent to investigate came back breathless.

"They are not here, sir," he reported.

"Then we are not here, either, " he announced, hurriedly evacuating their futile outpost before the Japanese engulfed them.

The moment his fever relaxed we had to hustle him away. Our house was too conspicuous to shelter him long. We secured a retired sergeant of the Scouts, the Philippines' best-trained fighting corps, to hide him more securely. Treachery from the Igorots we did not fear, but there were fifth columnists infiltrating from the Lowlands against whom we had to keep up our guard.

Proof of this we had shortly afterwards when we were visited by an officer, then a lieutenant, who was to become one of the most aggressive and successful of guerrilla leaders, operating inside Japanese lines throughout the war and maddening the enemy by his brilliantly punishing raids. When we met him next, after our rescue in '45, he was Lieutenant-Colonel Barnett. His talk went back to that earlier visit, recalling how Frances had greeted him with,

"Do you wish coffee or beer?"

"Both," he replied.

Accompanied by an enlisted man, he had come to our door-step just before dusk. Dinner we served them in a darkened room, for a Japanese foraging party was staying overnight in Sagada, only five miles away. The meal ended, our guests did not linger but slipped away into the night.

Next morning two Lowlanders approached me while I was writing outside.

"We have a letter from Captain Scholey for the American soldiers, they informed me.

"What soldiers?" I asked.

"The soldiers who were here last night."

"I don't know any soldiers who were here last night."

They persisted, begging me to sign a receipt for their letter, while I refused to sign anything until balked by my stubbornness they withdrew. They did not go far. I could watch them deliberating before they returned to renew their plea that I accept the letter and sign for it. Despite my disclaimers they even came back a third time, still in vain.

Some weeks later, I met Captain Scholey. He had sent no letter.

* * * * * * * *

The long, tragically hopeless resistance at Bataan stayed further Japanese forays into our district. Guerrilla resistance was making such invasions unhealthy. We were encouraged to reopen our school. This the public schools had not attempted. Many of their pupils as well as our own crowded our classrooms, eager to take up again their neglected studies. With the gay chatter of youngsters echoing in our ears from dawn to sunset we could forget, for a spell, the incredible intrusion of war.

This same oddly peaceful interim gave me leisure also to do things I had never found time to do. The twelve stout, closely printed volumes of the Cambridge Modern History had long reproached my neglect. One by one I plodded across their desert of facts, their barren wasteland of man's folly and futility, till I arrived at their concluding chapters. These were completed in 1911. They made strange reading.

There would never be another great war, they declared, colonial expeditions, perhaps to subdue jungle tribes, but never again full-scale conflict between civilized nations. For one thing, man had grown too sensible; the people now controlled their governments. They would not let their countries be sucked into a war which they themselves must fight.

A further safeguard was international trade. All nations had a vested interest in commerce so profitable that none could afford to see it disrupted. Aside from this fact, modern instruments of combat were too costly for prolonged fighting. If war lasted beyond three months, the wealthiest powers would be insolvent, and compelled to make peace.

Yet suppose, continued these the most expert historians of their day, suppose war did come. Men could rest easy. Warfare now had its conventions, its rules. They had extracted the sting of battle. These humane ordinances would protect civilians and control the combatants. They would make violence antiseptic. No doubt there would be inconveniences, but the old bad days were gone, gone forever.

So predicted the men who had made a science of history. They belonged to the generations that expected salvation from giving everybody, even women, a vote, salvation from sending every child to school. Man was his own saviour. All he required was to know what was right in order to do it. Almost automatically the world would improve and, in Tennyson's words,

"Freedom slowly broaden down
From precedent to precedent."

In 1911, still under the 19th Century's complacent spell, men could believe these things. In 1942, as I finished these optimistic chapters, I went outside

244

and from our garden terrace I could see, far to the south a sky reddened by the glare of burning villages. After two world wars and a harrowing Depression, this was the 20th Century, the era of Progress's acid commentary.

The guerrilla bands supplied their own vigourous commentary. In Besao we had frequent reminders of the damage they were inflicting. Some of our men were enrolled in such enterprises under the command of Captain Cushing, a leader whose almost foolhardy courage attracted a fearless response from his men.

Cushing, half Mexican, half American, was a mining engineer who had just got his own little gold mine working when the enemy destroyed it. Careless of a life thus abruptly ruined, he had but one motive – revenge. His tactics were hit and run. After each smashing raid, he would disband his Igorots, sending them home with orders for the next rendezvous, perhaps ten days later. His daring made him a living legend. From his own men I heard how he would reconnoiter the Japanese, even peering through the windows while they were carousing in the Cervantes rest-house. His attacks were as bold as they were fierce. He would toss in a hand grenade at one door, then race to the opposite exit to shoot his quarry as they scrambled to escape.

His most notable exploit was the ambush he set for two carloads of high Japanese officers as they drove up the coast road to install a government for Ilocos Norte. So complete was this raid that for days the enemy dared not travel this highway, a main artery, after dark. We had gaudy evidence of this victory in the Japanese gold braid which local Igorots were flaunting as their spoils of war.

Much of this warfare was too informal for the taste of the Army's professional heads. Late in February we were visited by the officer who had been in command at Baguio[53]. This man, a lieutenant-colonel, had not succeeded in carrying out General MacArthur's orders for a juncture with the main army. Instead, he had come north to consolidate the several guerrilla detachments, a command the latter did not welcome. Like Cushing, they were miners, and, like him, bent on fighting the war Indian fashion, whereas their official commander seemed equally determined to fight it in World War I style. For a final stand he was reputed to have ordered that trenches be dug, trenches in a valley chequered with rice terraces. There, with a handful of men and one machine gun, he planned a last resistance quite as if the Japanese did not overlook his futile defences from ridges a thousand feet higher. They were not fools enough to waste men on a frontal attack through rice paddy mud when they could lob howitzer shells into his position with complete impunity. The mining engineers were having none of it. They ignored his orders.

Our visitor was a likeable man, a genial guest, pleasant company, but not an officer in whose management we could put much trust. If anything, he exemplified the easy-going methods that had pervaded the Army in the Philippines during the many peaceful years when their duties were more social than military. So lethargic had been their tempo that even the imminence of war did not appear urgent enough to arouse them. By common, perhaps libelous, report, their working day ended at ten, after which they could devote themselves seriously to golf and the Army and Navy Club.

Whether unfair or not, this impression jibed with what we learned of how the Baguio garrison had met the war's emergency. Bridges whose destruction could have impeded for days the enemy invasion were not blown up, suspension bridges on the Kennon Road, Baguio's principal approach, that carried the road across canyons hundreds of feet deep. To have blown them up was a simple business, but the men sent down by twos or threes to do the job had a knack of arriving just as the Japanese, in overwhelming numbers, were starting to cross.

Our visitor confessed mournfully to having destroyed all his code-books and some thirty-odd truckloads of equipment, including the Christmas dinners he and his men had hoped to eat, only to learn afterwards that he could have moved them all to Bontoc. Not till they had pushed all these trucks over a cliff, even his own faithful Buick which he patted on the hood in poignant farewell as he sent it rolling to its doom, did he get word that the Mountain Trail was still open, open for five more days. Throughout his residence in Baguio, so far as I could gather, he never had travelled the Mountain Trail, never had the curiosity to see where it led.

From Besao he was attempting to reopen communication with MacArthur. His sole means of making contact was a private radio station set up at a mine a two days' hike to the north. It was slow work. Messages were brought, messages dispatched, by runners loping over a tortuous, slippery trail.

Before there could be even this limited contact with headquarters, the colonel had first to identify himself. Luckily, he could recall to a friend on MacArthur's staff a spicy bit of Schofield Barracks gossip to which they were both privy, some innuendoes about an Army officer's wife. To re-establish the basis for code messages he now turned to me for a book so commonly used as to be available anywhere in the Philippines. I gave him a third grade reader.

By such contrivance did he put in a request for guns and ammunition, all to be air-dropped in nearby rice paddies. These were to replace the equipment prematurely destroyed. The colonel had large plans: he expected to organize new regiments, blow up bridges, induce landslides. All these he discussed in voluble detail at the dinner table, even handing me Captain Cushing's dispatches to read aloud. None of this were we eager to hear. If the Japanese returned, the less we knew the better. But the colonel was not to be silenced. Since he talked just as freely at the Presidencia, his plans were soon public property. It was not enough for us to know in large detail what he proposed to do; we heard with equal fullness on what dates the bridges were to be blown up, just when the landslides were to block the roads.

Undoubtedly the Japanese knew all this too – and lost little sleep over it. MacArthur had no 'planes to air-drop the needed equipment. Before it could have been used, the companionable colonel had obeyed General Wainwright's order to surrender.

His chief worry, during his stay with us, was not his perilous state but the slight notice which General MacArthur gave to his operations on the Voice of Freedom broadcasts.

"Why do you want notice?" I objected. "The more that's said about your work, the more the Japanese will feel obliged to wipe you out."

My remonstrance made no dent. To him the exigencies of war did not weigh against his fear that a rival lieutenant-colonel, conducting a campaign of his own on the Cordillera's opposite slope, might win his full colonelcy first.

One thing, however, we could credit to our guest. He did not parrot the Army's prediction of "every Jap out of the Islands by the end of April." He knew the score, knew the desperate nature of the Bataan resistance, and shattered any further confidence in our own propaganda, which had deluded us into believing that the USAFFE could not be defeated.

"I wonder that they have held out this long," he told us.

Even during his stay came a dispatch, relayed as usual by messenger from the hand-to-mouth radio station at Balbalasang. It was official, put out by the Navy Department at Washington.

"Expect big push October 1943," it read.

To us in March 1942, October 1943 sounded as remote as the end of the world – or even after.

We subscribed to the sentiments of the signalman, who had received and forwarded this message.

"Optimistic bastards, aren't they?" he appended.

* * * * * * * *

Despite successive blows, Singapore, Java, Bataan, and then, inevitably Corregidor, we struggled to nourish our local optimism. Our hopes centred in the rains. The Mountain Trail, we knew, had been blown up at several points; if the rainy season could break early, we counted on its provoking expanded slides. Even when the roads were in good repair, storms sometimes blocked them for days. "The roads they are destroyed, sir," was a familiar Igorot refrain during typhoons.

Calling on intuition, I picked a date exceptionally early, the 5th of March, for the first downpour. My guess was not far off. On the date I had chosen a few token drops did fall. Within a week we were enjoying cloudbursts. But the rains, though weeks ahead of schedule, were sporadic. They would live out their cycle, then give way to spells of disheartening sunshine. Our prayer that these mountains be made too inaccessible to be worth the trouble of further enemy invasion was doomed to disappointment.

Yet our mood, like the weather, had its ups and downs Guerrillas continued to drop in. The most interesting were a trio of mining engineers led by the Captain Scholey whose supposed letter the fifth columnists sought to inveigle me into acknowledging. He and his associates came flushed with success. They had just completed a notable exploit, having destroyed the copper mine at Lepanto.

In the war's first panic this mine and its mill had been abandoned while still in working order; large stocks of ore, already mined, had been left ready for the grabbing. Copper was a metal which the Japanese needed urgently, and this Lepanto mine, far richer in its deposits than the pre-war surveys had indicated, was the only source of copper available to them in all their far-flung conquests. Ready though it was for their use, it was a prize of which they had failed to take immediate advantage. The patrols that first inspected it were too small to occupy Lepanto; the roads had to be mended.

Scholey's party came in the nick of time. Barely hours before the Japanese returned to seize the plant, they flushed the ore into the stream and destroyed the mill. They could see the lights of the enemy column picking its way down hill as they slipped off into the darkness.

Such visits bolstered our courage. They did not prevent the Japanese from returning. Corregidor had not yet fallen when rumours heralded a new advance, this time from two directions. American prisoners from Bataan, we heard, were being used as porters, as *cargadores*. But there was such baffling discrepancy in the estimates of how many prisoners were being thus used that after the first shock we dismissed them as more of the wild stories to which we were inured. There were 150 prisoners by one reckoning, then only three, next a dozen, and from another source – none!

Of the exact number we were never certain, but the rumours proved dismally true. This was a death march from which I have not heard that any survived, a death march infinitely more harrowing, if possible, than the more notorious march which prodded and pushed the Bataan defenders from their grisly peninsula to confinement at O'Donnell, Cabantuan, Bilibid. These later victims were herded up and down mountain ranges under a glaring

248

tropical sun. Racked by dysentery and malaria, they staggered, human beasts of burden, beneath loads that made every kilometre hopeless, agonizing travail.

One American soldier I did meet who escaped this ordeal. While traversing the shelf of road cut from the rock walls of Chico Canyon, he had stumbled and fallen, too exhausted to pick himself up. Bayonets could not prod him further. He lay senseless to punishments until the Japanese guards kicked him over the cliff and left him supposedly broken on the boulders below.

But he was not dead. Igorots recovered, him, took him to a village near Sagada, nursed him back to health. When I encountered him, a meeting too hazardous to be more than brief, he was with a guerrilla party led by an erstwhile Filipino school teacher, a friend of long standing whom I was not surprised to see exhibiting gay courage as a bold and skilful officer. The recovered prisoner said little. He had vowed that never again would he be captured. His name I forgot to enquire – in meetings of this sort there were so many important things we were too hurried to ask! – and I know nothing certain of his fate. Long afterward I heard conflicting stories, both of them tragic.

Such encounters did not keep our own existence from being lulled almost to forgetfulnes that the enemy had occupied Bontoc, only an hour's drive distant. What we heard of their attitude was reassuring. Dike-san, our old contractor, married to an Igorot wife and bound by friendly ties to Sagada and Besao, had been appointed governor. His messages promised a minimum of interference.

Money was a problem. Earlier in the spring the Sagada Mission, under the Filipino governor's direction, had printed 100,000 pesos' worth of currency. Its backing was the several million pesos which the province had kept on deposit in Manila. So long as the Japanese occupied the Philippines this money was out of reach, but the local population were confident enough of final victory to accept their unique currency at par. They paid little heed to the Japanese proclamation that anyone using, or even possessing, these emergency notes was liable to be shot.

Collector's items these notes would have been, if we had dared save them; with the Japanese once again at Bontoc, we hid our contraband currency. At the back of our minds lurked always the expectation of the next enemy raid. How, when would it come? Dread of this inescapable crisis preyed on our hearts, despite the continuing lull. Tantalizing it was to gaze northward to the vast uncharted forests, knowing that no foe could find us in that wilderness but also that, if the *bozo* did not finish us, disease and starvation would. On other, smaller islands people did hide out. In our huge mountains no one succeeded. The few civilians who tried this eventually were rooted out. Methodically the Japanese hunted out their source of supply; they shelled the villages suspected of befriending American refugees, machine-gunned their inhabitants. This treatment we foresaw. Grateful though we were for Igorot pleas to conceal us, we could not inflict such drastic penalties on their hospitality.

If we could not hide ourselves, a lesser but gnawing worry was how to hide the belongings we held dearest. Our first concern, naturally, was food. In dispersing our stock we entrusted several cases of provisions to a family to keep in the grass shelter they used to watch their rice-fields. It was visible, several hundred feet below our house. One Saturday, at noon, we heard shouting. A boy rushed in to tell us the shelter was on fire. Helplessly we watched it burn, watched the flames ruining supplies that could have kept us for months.

This was our second fire within the week. Several nights earlier, Frances had roused me in my downstairs bedroom with word that the house was afire. Geoffrey had knocked on her door complaining that the smoke was choking him. Not for a moment or two could she grasp what he meant by "the smoke." In ever denser clouds it was rolling through the upstairs rooms. When she stumbled to the hall below she came face to face with a glare so livid that it daunted the children, who huddled on the stairs, afraid to follow her. It daunted me too. I gave up the house for lost, and even felt a twinge of relief: we need worry no longer about how to hide our treasures from the Japanese.

A second, more careful examination catapulted me into action. The glare was shining through the hall window. The fire was outside; it was burning the shingled wall of the kitchen annex.

Grabbing an extinguisher, I ran bare-footed through the garden and began spraying the flames. The issue looked hopeless, but I worked the heavy extinguisher until my arm was limp. Slowly, as I directed the stream down the wall, I saw that I was checking the blaze. By the time that I had shifted to a second extinguisher I had it controlled.

It was a lonely fight. Frances, I knew, must be summoning help, yet I could hear no sound except the crackling shingles. No one came. In ordinary times we should have had a dormitoryful of boys scurrying to our aid – and no people are more sensibly adept at subduing fire than the Igorots. This, however, was wartime. Only two boys remained at the school, sleeping so soundly, so snugly insulated by the blankets wrapped around their faces that Gabriel's horn could not have pierced their slumber. Frantically Frances shook them, pulled at them, shouted in their ears; they moaned and clutched their blankets tighter. Not till after many wasted minutes did she wake them.

When once they had opened their eyes to the fire's eerie light, they needed to further prodding.

Out they stumbled, screaming, "Apui! Fire!"

Still no help came.

People in nearby houses heard the shouts, they saw the flames, but instead of scurrying to our aid, they scrambled together what belongings they could snatch and started running to the hills. "Apui! Fire!" they had mistaken for "Japon – Japanese."

Only after they had steadied from this first panic did they gauge the real trouble. Back they hastened, and soon we had no lack of helpers. By this stage, however, I had the fire almost extinguished. All that was left to them was to pry out the few places where it still smouldered, where it was creeping under the eaves and making inroads into the corners I could not reach.

This fire, subdued so much more handily than we could have expected from its first appalling flare-up, was the result of war-time economy. To save fuel we had eaten a cold supper and, in a further frugal mood, the servants had cleaned out the stove, and put the ashes in a box for use in the garden. The school-boy who did this had been less than cautious: taking it too quickly for granted that the ashes were dead, he had left them, still in their wooden box, under the steps that led from kitchen to garden. There they smouldered till the night wind fanned the embers back to life. Yet for all the alarm the damage was negligible. We had still on our hands a house bright with old Chinese treasures – and the question of where to hide them.

In the end we did nothing. A few things we had sent out earlier to be hidden in granaries, but to have buried porcelains and brasses would have invited curiosity, indeed marked them for plunder. It seemed safer to let them remain in the house, especially since the latest word was that the Japanese might leave us undisturbed. Dike-san, in his role of civil governor, had renewed his kindly assurances.

To celebrate this hopeful relaxing of tension, a Sagada friend came to spend the night with us, the first time he had felt free to enjoy this little diversion. The time was ripe for opening my last bottle of whisky. It proved hard to find. Although I thought that I remembered where I had hidden it in the garden's rubble wall, when I searched for it, all the stones looked alike. For a few drab moments I saw myself pulling down the entire wall, stone by stone. But before I had quite begun this prodigious labour, I discovered my prize.

It soothed the evening, helped us forget the war, enlivened us to indulge in a musical debauch. Three symphonies we listed to, the Beethoven Third, the Brahms Fourth, the Sibelius Fourth and strayed through excerpts from Iolanthe and the Gondoliers. So carefree were we that we stayed up to

251

midnight, extravagantly late after the weeks wherein we had been doling out kerosene too sparingly to keep lamps burning later than nine.

Next day the blow fell. From Bontoc, relayed through Sagada, came Japanese orders that within four days all of us at Besao and Sagada were to report at Bontoc for internment. Had these orders come when we were resigned to them, we could have borne them better. To receive them just when tension had relaxed was an event of such mocking irony that we could not grasp it. We still snatched at the hope that internment would be brief. Dike-san, we knew, had gone to Baguio. When he returned he would send us back again. Little did we realize that Dike-san's influence already was on the wane. However they might have utilized their expatriates in the Philippines, the Imperial Army now was taking charge.

The saddest part of this irony we did not know, that our internment was reprisal for what America had done to her Japanese residents, reprisal for the war distemper that had dispossessed and imprisoned not only Japanese nationals but American-born Japanese, inoffensive Nisei whose constitutional rights as citizens of the United States had been swept aside in ruthless disregard of what America's sovereign law supposedly guaranteed them. We were victims of a lawless, vindictive folly so inexcusable that the Supreme Court, long after the war, tried too late to redress an acknowledged wrong.

One single day was our allotment for squeezing a home into suit-cases (repetition of my doleful experience in China), one day must suffice to terminate work that had spanned nearly a generation. For months we had been debating how to encounter this emergency. When the decisions were shoved at us with no time to dilly-dally, they proved simple, too simple, indeed almost as blunt as the renunciation for which a death-bed grants no postponement. It was better, we found, not to linger over things we loved but to cherish in their place tooth-paste and soap and socks and razor-blades – and the poems of John Milton, not because I was particularly fond of Milton (I hadn't read him in years) but the book was small the contents long-winded, ideally suited to internment. I might even get through Paradise Regained.

Our Paradise, for the moment, was lost. We said good-bye next morning in tears. Many girls and women, after Mass, had used the church for a wailing wall. This was our home; these were our people. They had received us as their own and now did all they could to comfort our departure.

Before us was a long walk, five miles to Sagada, where we were to stay overnight, and then fifteen or sixteen miles to Bontoc, yet more volunteers than we needed offered themselves as *cargadores* to carry not only our suit-cases, camp-cots, bedding, but boxes of supplies in response to the Bontoc Mission's urgent request, "Bring food." What they were offering was more than the transport of baggage, though this was burdensome enough; they were venturing into enemy-held territory where they risked being impressed as labourers for the Japanese Army. This risk no one could appraise; it presented direful uncertainties.

When we left Sagada, after watching the Americans there go through the same melancholy ordeal of farewell, our procession took on the dimensions of a migration. One or two of the Sisters were carried in chairs – there were nuns from two Orders, St. Mary's and St. Anne's; the rest of us were on foot. Even our two children, Geoffrey, ten, Ann, seven, insisted on walking. We were part of a parade that wound down the sunny mountainside like an uncoiled snake.

Just before the main highway, which clings to the Chico Canyon's rocky, perpendicular walls, we all halted, Igorots and Americans alike, to eat lunch and to exchange our last free greetings. What opportunity we should have later to thank our helpers we did not know. A few hundred yards ahead we expected to meet the Japanese. By tacit agreement we all shrank from that unpredictable encounter.

As things turned out, the Japanese barely noticed us. The few who did responded affably to Miss McKim's greetings. They were busy building up with stones and gravel a temporary detour through the river until they could restore the bridge across the Amlusong gorge. One Japanese engineer, talking with Miss McKim, laughed uproariously as he praised the expertness with which this bridge had been dynamited. From its towers hung empty cables. Under it the Fidelisan river rushed pell-mell to its confluence with the Chico.

How we were to cross was a puzzle. Although the Fidelisan is a narrow stream, few of us dared follow the cargadores across slippery planks from boulder to boulder. The Chico was broader, shallower, narrower. A bit of reconnoitering, however, discovered fords only knee-deep. Most of the women were taken across in chairs; the more venturesome doffed shoes and stocking and, holding their skirts high enough to satisfy the patrons of a burlesque show, splashed through to the opposite bank.

The rest was straight walking. Threatened though we were by untimely thunder showers, we came weary but dry to Bontoc's one long street. In sad-eyed wonder the people of this isolated little capital watched us from their windows. No Japanese met us or took us in charge. Without escort we pursued our way through the Mission gate. Nobody ever went to prison with such scant formality.

The compound was in a flurry. That same day the school dormitory where we were booked to stay had been commandeered by the Japanese. Only kitchen and dining-room did they leave us, but they granted the useful assistance of a cook and a houseboy. Contact with other Igorots was forbidden with a single exception of the resident Igorot priest. All these instructions were transmitted second hand. Our captors evinced no recognition of our arrival. Had we been able to compare our experience with that of other prisoners we should have appreciated how nearly luxurious was our treatment. For the moment, however, we were too weary to be cheerful. The thought of our homes deserted, abandoned to enemy plunder, lay like a dead weight on our hearts. In our makeshift, crowded quarters we saw nothing but their inconvenience, camp cots for beds, suit-cases for chests of drawers, bathrooms unavailable except by running the gauntlet of a rainy season downpour. Only one of our bewildered group refused to be despondent.

This was our daughter, Ann. The Bontoc women had made her a doll, a rag doll which they had been unable to send on her birthday, some weeks earlier. Holding up her new gift by its limp arms, she exclaimed, "Hasn't this been a happy day!"

* * * * * * * *

THE COAST ROUTE

RAFTING TRUCK ACROSS THE AMBARAYAN RIVER *(above)*

The Coast Route ran from Tagudin through Cervantes to Bontoc. It was the main access to the mountains in 1928 when these photos taken.

ROAD TO BONTOC SEEN FROM BESSANG PASS NEAR CERVANTES *(below)*

POLING RAFT *(above) An automobile was aboard,*

THE MOUNTAIN TRAIL ROUTE

These photos were taken the winter of 1930-31
Shortly after the Mountain Trail had been com-
pleted to Bontoc

VIEW THROUGH TREES NEAR MT.DATA

CLEARING SLIDE ON MOUNTAIN TRAIL

"For me the magic of this trail never paled – air
exhilarating as wine, the lavish spectacle of fern-
trees fifteen feet high upsoaring among the pines,
a solitude delicious to a refugee from China even
without the unaccustomed drone of wind in the
forest, the rumble of pouring streams." (p.170)

MT. DATA REST HOUSE *(right)*

256

THE CONVENT AT SAGADA *(below)*
Both Mary Millicent and Geoffrey were born there.

CHURCH OF ST.MARY, VIRGIN (SMV) *(above)*
The road to Besao cuts across the hill in the background.

"Of this church one could repeat that it was unique. It certainly was not beautiful; in blasphemous moments we compared it to a fire-hall, but its impact was crushing, an engineer's church built to outlast eternity." (p.175). Sadly the church did not outlast World War II and American bombs. It has since been completely rebuilt with a different design.

BISHOP MOSHER, FATHER ROSE AND SOME MISSION STAFF
(below)

From left to right:

Mrs. Mosher, Miss Weiser (superintendent, St.Luke's Hospital in Manila) Miss Griffin (Mission Treasurer) Bishop Mosher, Father Rose, Miss Whitcomb

257

GETTING TO BESAO

THE SACRED LAKE BANNAO *(below) located on the ridge between Sagada and Besao*

"This small pond, little better than a carabao wallow, was enshrined in local legend." (p.188)

THE ROUTE UP TO SAGADA FROM DANTAY *(above), The road climbs 3000 feet, much of it in switchbacks up the mountain that can be seen here. (This photo taken late 1929)*

RIDING TO BESAO *(left). At this time, 1928, Besao was not accessible by road. The riders are Mary Gowen and Mrs. Mosher. They are probably on or near the slopes of Mugao, the sacred mountain near Besao.*

258

VIEWS FROM BESAO
(These photos probably taken in 1928)

LOOKING EAST
Rice terraces below morning mists.

"Bolstered by dykes six, eight, ten feet high, whose stones, though without mortar, were so skillfully fitted that they had kept their place through the battering of centuries, these terraces gave the mountain slopes an ever breathing, ever changing vitality." (p.177)

RICE FIELDS NEAR BESAO

MORE BESAO VIEWS

KINIWAY FROM MT. PADANGO-AO. *(above) Kiniway, is the Besao village where St. James Mission was located. Its building appears as a white speck on ridge near tree at extreme left.*

RICE TERRACES TO NORTH OF THE MISSION *(below)*

AMONG THE IGOROTS

The photos on this and the following two pages are a sample of many taken of Igorots and other mountain people, mostly between 1927 and 1931.

VILLAGE OF PAYEO *(right)*
Another of the villages that comprise Besao.

MAN ON CARABAO *(below)*
Rice terrace walls can be seen behind. Their height – six feet and more – is evident.

WOMAN CARRYING BASKET *(above)*

261

AMONG THE IGOROTS

VILLAGE OF MASLA *(left) To the South of Besao and inaccessible by car, Masla was one of many out-staion villages visited once or twice a year for baptisms, confirmations and religious services.*

"...the fascination of these villages overrode the hardship of getting to them. Their names – Bantey, Sumadel, Masla, Luben, Tambuan – were as poetically inviting as the first view of their drowsy valleys which we paused to admire from above." (p.199)

THREE GENERATIONS *(above)*

GIRL WITH BABY *(right)*

MEN IN CELEBRATION

IGOROT DANCE *(above) Sagada, 1927.*

KALINGA TRIBESMAN DRESSED FOR BETRO-THAL FEAST. *(left) Bontoc, 1928.*

ST. JAMES MISSION

**ST.JAMES MISSION
FROM SLOPES TO EAST**
*(above) Houses of Kiniway
can be seen below and to left.*

WEST SIDE OF ST.JAMES MISSION *(above)*
*The steps accessed the Gowen family residence. Classes
and services were held in the portion of building to the far
right. VHG's study looked out from the central gable.*

MARY ANGELINE GOWEN *(right) in front of the
residence. VHG's first wife, she came with him from China
in June 1927 shortly before this picture was taken. A year
later she died and was buried in the Besao Camp Santo.*

MISSION ACTIVITY

MAUNDY THURSDAY PROCESSION *(below)*
Frances Gowen and Ann can be seen in foreground.

FR. JAMES BOLBOLIN KOLLIN *(left) in a postwar photo after he was ordained. Before World War II he was principal of St.James School and VHG's assistant.*

MASS AT ST. JAMES'S CHURCH *(below) November, 1939 with VHG as cele-brant. This space was also used for classrooms, dances and other secular activities.*

265

ST. JAMES STUDENTS

ST.JAMES GIRLS' SOFTBALL TEAM *(left) December, 1937. They are wearing red and white uniforms designed by Frances Gowen and made by the girls themselves.*

CAMPFIRE GIRLS AND THEIR MOTHERS *(above) at Christmas Party, 1930.*

ST. JAMES BOYS' CHAMPION SOFTBALL TEAM *(left) December, 1937*

266

FAMILY

VINCENT AND FRANCES GOWEN
(above) with cat Pollux, Besao, 1931

FRANCES WITH MARY MILLICENT *(above).*

Their first child, Mary Millicent was born Jan. 31, 1931. She died less than two weeks later on the way to St. Luke's hospital, Manila.

ALTAR OF MORNING CHAPEL, EPISCOPAL CATHEDRAL OF SS MARY AND JOHN, MANILA *(right).*

Frances and Vincent were married by Bishop Mosher before this altar, Oct. 7, 1929. Mary Millicent was buried at right corner of altar, Feb. 9, 1931. The Cathedral, including this chapel, were completely destroyed during the Battle of Manila, 1945. (See Map 6)

CHILDREN

ANN AND HEIDI *(far left) Heidi survived internment and the Battle of Manila and returned safely to the U.S.*

GEOFFREY *(near left) proves his Igorot heritage.by wearing a G-string*

ANN'S SECOND BIRTHDAY *with friends (left.) April, 1937*

LOOKING WEST *(right) This photo was taken in 1940 and used on the Gowen family Christmas card*

ST. BENEDICTS'S CHURCH

ST. BENEDICT'S UNDER CONSTRUCTION *(below)*

CARRYING G.I. SHEET FOR THE ROOF OF ST. BENEDICT'S *(above) St. James mission is in the background.*

"I watched the sturdy pillars take shape, the round arches complete their span, the squat tower occupy the ridge like a fortress." (p.225)

ST. BENEDICT'S COMPLETED *seen here from hillside to East. St Benedict's was dedicated by Bishop Norman Binstead in October, 1941.*

ST. BENEDICT'S CHURCH

ST. BENEDICT'S CHURCH, ANOTHER VIEW *(above).*
St. Benedict's, unlike St. James Mission building, survived World War II. This photo was taken in 1971

"It was an edifice that compelled adoration by its strength, its grace, the scintillating warmth of its stones. . . (p.225)

ST. BENEDICT'S CHURCH, INTERIOR *(left) This photo was taken in 1941*

Part III

Internment: 1942 - 45

FOR THREE WEEKS we lingered in Bontoc, slowly subsiding into a routine as placid as it was dull. Perhaps because we had Miss McKim, we were visited by several Japanese, but always sociably. Without doubt it was her facile command of their language, her understanding of their thought, their viewpoint, her subtle deference to their social habits, that made their visits entertaining. Although they teased us by predicting victory marches up the streets of Washington and New York, they did not display the curt arrogance for which the Japanese Army was notorious.

Even the private soldiers who wandered into the compound from time to time were amiable. On my first morning one soldier did help himself to a basket of bananas, an Igorot gift I had not yet learned to store out of sight, but he paid me for it, declining to accept it as a gift. I was dubious about the value of the military peso he forced into my hands. It was my first introduction to what later we called "mickey-mouse money," too pretty a piece of printing to look real. Without serial numbers, without any backing except the credit of the Imperial Army, this money eventually became our barometre of how the war was faring. At the moment, Japanese credit was riding high; their pesos circulated at par.

There were moments in our daily boredom when I envied convicts at home; they knew the terms of their imprisonment whereas we were plagued by the puzzle of why we were confined, how soon we should be released. I scaled my expectations by Miss McKim's. At first optimistic, she bent more and more to the opinion that our internment would be long. We were given a half dozen explanations of why we had been brought in, but any hope of early release smacked against the obdurate fact that our fate was in the hands of too many conflicting agencies for any one official to assert authority over us. Dike-san, when he heard of our internment, came hurrying back from Baguio only to discover that there was nothing he dared do. What did appear certain was that we were being held for scrutiny by the Kempei-tai, the dreaded military police.

Military movements outside our compound continued to confuse us. Soldiers were pouring into Bontoc by the hundreds. Many were quartered in our compound at the boys' school, there to survey the situation though what situation there could be to require so many troops in a backwater like Bontoc we could not guess. The people were ordered to celebrate the general's arrival with a *cañao*. All evening the *gansas* clanged, and then as suddenly ceased. Instead of letting their new subjects dance all night, the Japanese shut down their festivities at midnight. To the Bontocs a *cañao* curtailed by the clock must have been sacrilege.

Japanese were not the only soldiers who came and went. There were Americans too. A few were survivors of the unfortunate group pressed into servitude as *cargadores* when this Japanese expedition invaded the mountains. We passed them sitting under the trees as we went to and from meals. Any talk with them, of course, was forbidden, but some did manage gestures of recognition, a smile a wave of the hand. Others sat stolidly indifferent to our nearness. Their faces were blank, their hair bleached almost white. In a perpetual stupor they slumped, their minds gone.

A more cheerful set of prisoners were the chauffeurs. Japanese officers were not comfortable with their own men as drivers. Anyone who has ridden in Tokyo taxis will not need this explained. Since all the high brass of the Japanese command traveled in American cars, Cadillacs and Lincolns snatched new from Manila's show-rooms, their natural course was to pick competent prisoners both to operate them and keep them in good repair For the prisoners this was a welcome assignment, affording better treatment, better food. Only toward the war's end, by which time the Japanese were running their cars on alcohol, did they revert to drivers of their own race. According to the story we heard, an American driver, grown tired of life, had taken his vehicle and all its passengers over a cliff. To the Japanese, with their aptitude for suicide, such a death was so gloriously proper that they must have wondered why their captives did not resort to it earlier. Once the example had been set, however, they took no chances of its being copied. If they must risk dying in a crash, better to be slaughtered accidentally by their own countrymen than deliberately by their foes.

One fact we guessed from the arrival of these cars: the Mountain Trail must have been repaired. So lethargically had we lapsed into the doldrums of internment, however, that we forgot how this could affect us. When we heard quite casually that we were to be moved to Baguio, we heard it in one ear and out the other. The rumour was confirmed by the sudden appearance of a Japanese civilian, Nakamura[54], sent to convey us, and considerably annoyed to find that we alone had not been informed of our transfer. Yet this fitted, after all, the Japanese genius for being abrupt: Nakamura arrived in the evening, we were to be moved next morning.

Despite the formidable tales we had heard of the camp to which we were destined, our journey to Baguio proved surprisingly cheerful. Up to the last, our stay in Bontoc had been oddly free; whatever control we may have been subject to remained invisible. No officer asserted charge over us. No secret police examined us. Our transfer was just as informal. We did have a boss, Nakamura, but he was a genial soul, little inclined to make show of his authority.

From Bontoc's populace our departure excited a display of emotions as flattering as it was indiscreet; they wept and waved as we passed. At Amlusong the newly restored bridge was in use. American prisoners were at work here, some of them men we had seen in the compound. They did not seem downcast, and even squeezed out snatches of talk with us while we were halted. We renewed acquaintance also with several of the Japanese who had visited us in Bontoc. Again they rallied us on the victory parade they soon would be holding in New York. Ticker tape they did not specify but it was on this trip, to the best of my memory, that we heard their astounding claims to have established a beach-head on the coast of Wyoming. We took care not to advance, in rebuttal, what had been whispered to us before we left Bontoc, news of the American victory at Midway.

Our chief surprise was the admirable condition of the Mountain Trail. A well-built road is not easily destroyed. Even at Mt. Data, where the narrow shelf of road cut from tall cliffs had been dynamited, the enemy had not been balked long. They had requisitioned square-cut timbers from the mines, and built a wooden highway jutting out from the supposedly impassable precipice, a cheap, quickly erected substitute for the original road. There was not dynamite enough in the Philippines, we now realized, to put the Mountain Trail effectually out of commission. The job called for a typhoon, a typhoon of the first magnitude.

Late in the afternoon we attained our goal, Camp Holmes, a Philippine Army post in Trinidad, Baguio's cabbage-growing suburb. Since our time-table was better known to its occupants than to us, we had a welcoming committee awaiting us. Many of these people we had known before the war, but so strange was their appearance that we felt like Gulliver suddenly thrown into contact with some eccentric tribe whom geographers had yet to discover.

What startled us first was the beards. As beatniks since have demonstrated, the surest way to look unkempt is to sprout whiskers. These beards, black, red, grey, even white, made their wearers' faces topheavy. They had sprung up like a garden gone to seed.

Equally unkempt were the clothes. Even when they were clean, they looked dirty. No one was self-conscious about the fit of his garments or their state of repair. Like ourselves, the earlier inhabitants of Camp Holmes had entered captivity with the few things they could carry. Unlike ourselves, they had been denied *cargadores*, and herded, men, women, children, old and young, into a march much shorter than ours but without the assistance we had benefited by, so exhausting that some had discarded their baggage while struggling to keep up the pace which their captors enforced.

By now, six months had passed; their wardrobes were in tatters, faded misfits. Many of the men had gone so long wearing only ragged shorts that their backs were burnt a deep mahogany, but there was one mysterious figure, a man in knee-breeches and black silk stocking fit to attend the Court of St.

James. He was busy. Everybody was busy. The purpose of their activity eluded us. They woke memories of an insane asylum (outdated word!) which used to attract me and other boys of the prep school we were attending; situated about two miles distant, it drew us like a magnet to watch its denizens – the harmless ones – masquerading in their rococo fantasies as they roamed the asylum gardens. Their variety of picturesque careers ranged from the woman who imagined herself as Queen Elizabeth, and wrote cheques on the Bank of the World, to the demented prospector who panned the asylum creek, day after day, for gold.

But we were to learn soon that Camp Holmes's queer pursuits were under rational direction. They kept in working order a community intelligently improvised to meet and triumph over a situation no one was prepared for. In the fame or notoriety of larger camps, Camp Holmes has been lost sight of. Its members, a bare five hundred, were few compared with the thousands in Manila's Santo Tomas. They were spared, to a large degree, the cruelty of the military camps, O'Donnell, Cabanatuan. Yet for its resolute spirit in coping with hardship, the consistently high level of its morale, Camp Holmes made a record to be proud of. Little did we appreciate, as stiffly we climbed down from our truck that June afternoon, how we would value, like graduates of a notable university our enrolment in this bleak outpost. We would not foresee our share in demonstrating how Americans, free, stubborn individualists though they be, can discipline themselves to meet the worst and by courage and self-control emerge the stronger for this experience.

I don't wish to overdraw the picture. Camp Holmes had its quarrels, its enmities; it was split at times by dissension. It had its blowhards, its malingerers, its thieves, its suspected traitors. The curious fact, in the long run, was how little they mattered; never were they able to disrupt the truly practical unity which helped the camp organize itself and, by its elected government, government by committee, rested on the voluntary compliance of the governed. Its authority, its methods were those of the first New England town meetings. Its position, however was more difficult: whatever power the internees might grant their committee could not disguise the fact that actually it had no power. The supreme authority was the Japanese who at any moment could ignore the Camp Committee, or wipe it off the map. Not till the final year did Japanese take real cognizance of this body or utilize it as an intermediary. So prudently had it balanced its precarious functions that it upheld the Camp's chance to live its own life as a working democracy and, in the face of a ruthless enemy, to secure its own survival.

* * * * * * * *

Camp Holmes introduced us to the Japanese control which up to this moment had been remote rather than immediate. Guards were on hand to inspect our baggage. This would mean good-bye to my new Diary, little more than four months old and so discreet in its omissions as to be innocuous, yet still a record I did not wish to lose. Opportunely, I noticed that there were two piles of baggage, one heaped with articles already inspected. I saved much trouble by putting my suitcase and *tampipi* on the inspected pile – a first lesson in what we all were quick to learn, that no matter how many rules the Japanese made, they could be circumvented.

Camp Holmes was the second site of (to use our official designation) the Imperial Japanese Army's Internment Camp #3. Originally, its inmates had been herded to Camp John Hay, a vacation and recuperation centre set up in Baguio, years before, for U.S. Army personnel. During their occupancy of John Hay, which began just after Christmas 1941, the prisoners had done some effective looting of medical and food supplies, and possessed themselves of electrical shop equipment and a variety of tools, all of which they contrived to transfer to their new quarters in Trinidad.

In that first stage of internment, nevertheless, food had run short and the prisoners came uncomfortably near starvation. As with us in Bontoc, the Japanese had made no provision to feed their captives. Long before our mid-June arrival the Camp had shaken down. The initial exigency had passed and people had developed the routine which was to serve them for nearly three more years.

Although a mixed group they were more homogenous than the huge Manila camp at Santo Tomas. Their nucleus was Baguio's American residents, with a scattering of British subjects. Added to this nucleus were people from the gold mines adjacent to Baguio, and a considerable number of refugees from Manila, and even from China. Eventually, the Japanese rounded up what locally were known as "squaw men" or "beach-combers," veterans of the Spanish-American War and the Philippines Insurrection. These were the ultimate back wash of the Western migration that had swept across the United States and, in the volunteer forces of 1898, even across the Pacific to the final limits of American sovereignty. They were the recalcitrant souls who could not tolerate authority nor, for that matter, work. Too lazy to go home, they contracted unions with Filipina women and devoted their lives to sitting under coco-palms or waiting for bananas to drop into their laps, dozing away the years while their "wives" supported them. Their indolence they brought with them to camp, indolence that kept some from washing and most from undertaking any job which they thought might benefit anybody else. No sooner had they finished eating than they settled down on a long bench outside the mess-hall, waiting to be first at the next meal. The only thing benign about them was their flourish of white whiskers; the few who made the mistake of shaving unmasked their native meanness. In their case, westward the tide of empire had fizzled out[55].

These free-loaders the Camp carried. Most of its population was more obliging. The two predominant groups were mining engineers and missionaries; both used the name of God – but in different contexts! One large missionary group consisted of new arrivals to the Orient who had been studying Chinese in Peking. Their removal to the Philippines had been designed to escape the Japanese. Although they included some excellent men, humility was not the trademark of this group. Their knowledge of all things Oriental was in inverse proportion to their experience. Another missionary group evinced an acquisitive knack, a knack for hoarding Camp tableware and similar equipment, such as contradicted their heavenly pretensions. On the whole, however, what might have been dissident factions contrived a tolerable truce. Secular and religious worked together not merely in careful amity but often with mutual respect and even warm friendship.

The solvent factor was the generally high standard of education which both the mining and missionary communities could claim. A large proportion were college graduates. But the chance of ever going to college was a problem that beset another large sector of the Camp's population, the children. In all there were some hundred and twenty children, children of all ages. Their elders might settle down in torpid acceptance of three years' stagnancy; for the children time could not stand still.

Among the Camp's earliest concerns was the continuance of their education. A school had been started, largely staffed by the Brent School faculty and equipped with text-books salvaged from that school. These classes had not lasted long. Barely had they begun than they were shut down by the Camp's first commandant, Dr. Mukaibo, whose Ph D., ironically enough, had been procured at Harvard[56].

Dr. Mukaibo, in more ways than one, was an enigma. Not only had he done graduate work at Harvard, but he was also a Methodist minister and, reputedly, head of a Methodist divinity school in Japan. Neither of these distinctions brought any easement to the lot of his prisoners. Just as he had confiscated the dearly preserved school-books, sweeping them aside as American propaganda, so for several months, he had banned religious worship, not permitting any public service until Easter and, thereafter, acceding to repeated requests for Sunday observance only a week or two before our arrival. Sermons he restricted to commentary on a Bible selection, and required that this commentary be typed and submitted to the guard-house for approval.

I was the first to preach an uncensored sermon. As a newcomer, I pretended to be ignorant of these restrictions. Since no one challenged me, all subsequent speakers followed this precedent, a precedent we might not have established so successfully but for the happy chance that Dr. Mukaibo had removed to Baguio, and been replaced in the Camp's actual supervision by Hayakawa, an inoffensive member of Baguio's mercantile colony.

Dr. Mukaibo's most sharply resented prohibition was what he termed "commingling." This hit us from the day we arrived in camp. A reception committee had made ready for us an early dinner. As we sat down, these friends gave us the bitter news that this was the last time in which men and women, even husbands and wives could eat together. The Camp's ugly brown barracks were apportioned, as we knew, between three groups – single women, mothers with daughters and small children, men and boys. Such an arrangement was understandable, but Dr. Mukaibo had not stopped with this; he had proscribed all communication between husbands and wives, except for an hour's stroll cross the parade grounds on Sunday afternoons. In an emergency he did permit them further converse across barbed wire fences strung some ten feet apart. American women, he declared were not to be trusted. Give them leeway and they would begin kissing!

His edict did not prevent this deplorable habit. Husbands and wives met freely behind the barracks and even dared kiss each other good night. Under such restrictions marriages which had been close to dissolution before the war now took on new life. As one husband commented, it gave marriage such a pleasant sense of the illicit.

That first afternoon, we could not rise to the more humourous aspects of internment. We were too glumly sensitive to what seemed unreasonable limitation on our behavior, on our rights as human beings. The feeling persisted. Never did we quite adjust ourselves to the notion that we had no rights. We could not slough off habits of freedom.

Comparing our lot with that of other camps, we can now admit that our treatment was mild. Brutality was infrequent; we were not subjected to brain-washing, we were given marked latitude in managing our own affairs, yet always there was latent resentment that our privacy, the privacy even of our thoughts, should be open to invasion. It gave me a sinking sensation, touch of spiritual nausea that first day, and this feeling, set throbbing at every new instance of petty interference, was to find in this pettiness the worst indignity of our imprisonment. Not till much later could we recognize that the Japanese, when it came to the art of thought-control, were rank amateurs. Never did they display the finesse which made the plight of our prisoners in Korea so intolerable. Beastly they could be, and savage, but they acted on impulse rather than policy. Seldom did they match the bland, smiling cruelty in which the Chinese were to prove themselves masters.

Despite the welcoming committee's attempt to ease our initiation, we soon were introduced to other bleak facts. The breakup of our existence as a family was signalized by assignment to places in our respective barracks. I had Geoffrey with me in the men's barracks. All we were allotted was floor-space, and precious little of that. The barracks already was overcrowded. As newcomers, we had to nudge our way in. Little could be done to make us comfortable. Such furniture as there was had been apportioned months before. We lacked chairs, stools, even wires from which to hang our clothes. I did have my camp-cot on which I slept elbow to elbow with a genial army sergeant. Geoffrey's pad and blanket were on the floor beside my cot. To find room for my feet, when I got up, I had to roll back his bedding.

Our final assignment was jobs. Quite differently from Santo Tomas, where people were paid for their work, Camp Holmes claimed the right to exact work from every able-bodied prisoner. This was managed by the General Committee, nine men elected every four months. Each member of the General committee supervised some specific area – health, sanitation, food, entertainment, education, religion; among these several departments, none was more important than the oversight of labor details. The Japanese took no part in this; it was the Committee's responsibility to keep the Camp wheels revolving. So far as possible, people were assigned the jobs for which they were best fitted, doctors and nurses to the hospital, teachers to the school, men skilled with tools to the shop, a corps of young, vigourous men to the wood-gang, or to garbage disposal. My first job was waiting on tables.

This was not exactly what I had been trained for, but the schools were still in abeyance, awaiting Dr. Mukaibo's permission to resume classes. My work began next morning. Meals, served in a long, dingy mess-hall, were dished out in separate shifts to men, children, women. Each shift was announced by a gong. I was responsible for two tables, first the men, next the women. The duties, though simple, kept me stepping lively since all plates were filled at a counter. Fortunately, the menu offered scant choice; my chief care was to make sure the Seventh Day Adventists were given beef instead of pork. Since the meat, cooked in a stew, did not lend itself to those fastidious distinctions, they risked going to hell through my carelessness. Within a week, however, the system was changed to cafeteria style; whether they chose pork or beef now depended on their own conscience, not mine – and on the acuteness of their sense of smell.

After the dire reports we had heard about people starving in Camp, we were surprised that the food was so ample. Provided we did not inspect it too closely nor balk at an occasional cockroach trapped in the stew, it was even palatable. In those early months the Japanese were allotting a specified sum for each prisoner and allowing the head-cook to make his purchases daily in the Baguio market. So long as the Japanese had victories to brag about, their currency bought things at par. This soon changed. Inflation began to overtake the ebb tide of their over-extended conquests until their per diem allotment could not be printed fast enough to keep pace with mounting prices. Eventually, the Imperial Army had to send in our provisions, provisions scantier month by month and day by day. In the earlier months, however, we were eating, if not luxuriously, at least sufficiently to maintain weight and energy. We were receiving, so our doctors assured us, a balanced diet. Our first day's meals I recorded in my diary. For breakfast, we ate rice with syrup, coffee with sugar, and a banana. Lunch brought a bowl of soup and a cold scone or slice of cornbread garnished with camp-made marmalade. At dinner we again were given a banana, beef or pork with rice, beans, and gravy, tomato and cucumber salad. Although this could not be termed sumptuous living, it surpassed what many camps were receiving.

Two year later, on this same date, our meals had shrunk to the following menu: breakfast – rice and Japanese tea; lunch – rice; dinner – rice, stewed cucumbers, baked *camotes*. Even this, in retrospect, was a banquet, looked back on enviously when, for a time, our daily rations had been reduced to one tablespoonful of mouldy corn-meal for breakfast and another for supper.

"A banana" was a regular item in the bill-of-fare published each day on the bulletin board. "A banana" did not specify the size; some were of dwarf parentage. So certain were the squaw-men that they were being cheated, even though the dispenser drew them out at random, that to soften their complaints, a woman finally was appointed to hand them out. Her gentle manner did not conciliate the old-timers. When one bearded pensioner threw his banana on the floor and stamped on it, the kitchen staff resorted to automation. They had a wheel prepared, miniature replica of an old fashioned water-wheel, with box-like compartments into which the bananas were inserted; in whatever size they chanced to tumble out – medium-sized or small (there were no large ones) – no recipient could cry favoritism. He took what fate gave him – and still grumbled.

Shortages soon developed, shortages annoyingly enough in the things which the Philippines produced most abundantly, margarine, sugar, coffee. Coffee, indeed, went through several phases, first, second, and third "submarine," labeled by the number of times the grounds had been sent down. Third submarine was so faint a dilution as to ease our transition to mornings when the menu announced only "hot water." An ingenious kitchener named Frost did improvise from parched rice a substitute named, more in derision than gratitude, Frostina. No one invented a substitute for salt. With us, "Wherewithal shall it be salted?" was uncomfortably pertinent, but when salt came back to the tables it gave renewed relish to meals we had scoffed at as tasteless.

Children were nourished on banana milk, and bananas were the basis for a yeast substitute, a clever attempt to supply us with vitamins. For vegetables we could choose from several tropical items, none of which I recall without a shudder. Some were concentrate slime yet, slippery though they were, they stuck in the throat, provoking an incipient regurgitation that threatened to bring up not only the offensive vegetable but the rest of dinner with it. Other vegetables were so innocuous that boiled newspaper would have been tastier. What I dreaded most, however, were black beans; their effect was like swallowing a string of firecrackers.

Many of us soon would have been skinny as scarecrows but for baskets of special provisions sent in weekly by local storekeepers. Because we were known in Baguio, we could arrange credit from merchants who trusted us to pay after the War. They were, I fear, over-trustful. Few ever bothered to settle this debt of honour. This privilege of baskets sent in each week, baskets generously filled with eggs, meat, fruit, coconuts, was granted us only during the mid-year of our captivity; without it many could not have endured the stringencies of the final year.

Food obsessed our casual talk. My mind was haunted by the stacked tables I had seen in an Oregon logging camp. Like other husbands I used to help out my wife in the chore, shared by all women, of picking out from the rice dumped on a long table the stones, bits of coal, worm's nests which threatened teeth and digestion. These were gossipy sessions, as each woman worked off her allotted hours, but their subject always veered to food, to the delicacies they would rush to regale themselves with in the blissful future they spoke of constantly yet had such trouble picturing.

We were like the child beguiled with descriptions of the happiness in store at her grandparents.'

"Mummy," she said, "at Grandma's when do they have roll-call?"

Irksome as was this rice-picking, the days when there was no rice to pick were harrowing. Nothing else supplied the stamina we got from rice. Corn could not take its place, particularly since such corn as we were supplied looked like the scourings of a garbage can. Not only was it mouldy but so infested with weevils that we probably drew more nourishment from the insects than the grain. It deserved the Camp motto: See no weevil, smell no weevil, taste no weevil.

As the months of confinement dragged on, Camp Holmes wives developed special ingenuity in palliating its shortcomings. Little by little, the Japanese had relaxed their rule against men and women eating together. The change

281

started with permission for families to share their meals – but outdoors only, where they could be watched from the guard-house and kept in line with Japanese notions of propriety. In the rainy season and in the cold, blustery monsoon such meals were so uncomfortable that families, tired of lugging plates and table to a matshed's leaky shelter, began venturing the bold course of eating together in the women's dormitory – by now a rabbits' warren in which each wife had walled her brood with Red Cross sheets to ensure some tiny semblance of privacy. This was illegal, of course, but the Camp, happily, was more adept at breaking rules than the Japanese in enforcing them.

This segregation into cubicles led to private cooking. Catering to the Camp wholesale, the kitchen did what they could to make their product palatable; no woman offered to take over their job. But the housekeeping instinct was too ingrained not to impel many to improve on kitchen fare. In addition to recooking what they got from the mess-hall, they had to cook the materials bought from outside. Even after the Camp improved matters by raising its own livestock, it could not supply pork-chops or pineapples or strawberries or coconuts. When very infrequently the kitchen did manage a Camp-wide distribution of eggs, the recipients soon learned that these were least offensive scrambled.

By the middle year few were the wives who did not collect their family's rations, stews grey in appearance, drab in taste, and convert them to dishes more appealing. They did so under prodigious handicaps. They had but one small iron stove, set back of their barracks and so limited in cooking area that the space allotted each woman had to be measured by inches while the time apportioned them was restricted to fifteen minute periods. From early morning until late evening there were claimants for each precious bit of space, and arguments if anyone tried to usurp more room or time than her pots and pans were entitled to. Only by a rapid increase in home-made hot-plates was this situation eased. These hot-plates, one more proof of the technical skills available among our mixed population, eventually became so necessary to our housekeeping that, like modern Americans accustomed to their electric kitchens, we could not remember how we had done without them. They helped us cope with an economy perpetually driven to improvise substitutes for the staples we once had thought necessary. Such was our pride in the queer things contrived from these substitutes – apple pie made from papaya rinds, *gabi* salad, bread from every imaginable and unimaginable grind of flour – that we used to boast, "This would even taste good outside!" That boast none of us has put to the test.

The ludicrous expedients of this cuisine came to life in a menu for Chocolate Cake (it was like naming a novel before it was written), which Frances set down in orthodox cook-book phrasing:

282

"1 ½ cups cassava flour
1 cup rice flour
½ cup velvet bean flour
½ cup coconut oil
1 small ball panocha (native unrefined sugar)
1 teaspoon native salt
1 scant teaspoon soda
1 or 2 native eggs
1 cup sour bean milk

"If no cassava flour available, use all rice flour (but add 2 mashed bananas to hold mixture together). If no panocha is available, use 2 cups dining room syrup boiled down to 1 cup, and leave out bean milk and add 1 tablespoons pineapple vinegar or calamansi juice. Eggs may be left out, but if so add 2 extra mashed bananas.

"If no coconut or peanut oil is available, ¼ cup pork fat will be good, but if no fat of any kind is available, Albolene (a face cream) will work, though not very rich. When bean milk is not available, water may be used, but add a little vinegar or calamansi juice. <u>Caution</u> Don't use too much velvet bean, as a little gives fair chocolate flavour, but too much makes cake bitter. Don't use bananas with cassava flour as mixture will be rubbery.

"In case <u>no</u> fat, sugar, or eggs are available, mixture may be steamed in tin for brown bread, in which case substitute corn flour for cassava flour. If this mixture doesn't rise properly or is gummy, add a little corned beef and garlic and bake it for spoon bread."

Stave it off as we might, the time was to come when even substitutes failed us. Of that period the most heart-rending reminder is a note still embedded in my Diary for the autumn of 1944. Pencilled at bed-time on a tiny scrap of paper, it read simply,
"To Mummy I am hungry Is there anything to eat love Ann."

* * * * * * * *

Returning to the excitement of our entry into Camp, I can recall much that bewildered and depressed us, and some ordeals that proved less fearsome than we had expected. Always at the base of our minds had lurked the inevitable examination by the Japanese secret police. But the dreaded Kempei-tai never bothered with us; our examination, conducted by the genial Nakamura and one of his aides, did not even prod the sensitive points of our contact with guerrillas. So perfunctory was it that we anticipated a second, more searching inquisition – which never came[57]. Without any close prying into subjects about which dumbness was the only prudence, we were allowed to merge with the anonymity of the Camp's five hundred occupants.

Anonymity describes our status. My number, 494, I wore in the usual pattern on a piece of cardboard, safety-pinned to my jacket. Some of us later replaced this dog-eared identification with aluminum or copper badges, but these were ornaments, the neat handiwork of the shop crew. As the cardboard tags wore into tatters, the rule requiring their display fell into disuse. Japanese edicts did not pretend to the permanence of the laws of the Medes and the Persians.

We had entered camp late enough to escape the officious intrusion of earlier months. Whereas the guards had once made offensive patrols through the dormitories, and especially the women's, our contact with the Nips (as we called them) was fast becoming minimal. Enlivened by sake they might attach themselves to a bridge game and ask about clubs and spades and the inexplicable mystery of no trumps. One guard, genially intoxicated, attended a birthday party and sat next to the guest of honour, a little girl much doted on by her parents, who was being congratulated by a distinguished selection of her elders.

When the guard withdrew, she cried to have him back.

"Oh, you don't want that damned old drunken guard," remonstrated her father.

"But I do want that damned old drunken guard," she wailed.

The guards, seldom more than six or seven, were changed every few weeks. By that time they had grown actually friendly with their prisoners, perhaps too friendly to suit the higher command. Even the most hostile seemed to soften by acquaintance with Americans. That they had been briefed beforehand to dislike and resent Americans was evident, but we were not the monsters their briefing had described. Some went so far as to drink with their captives and to engage in a convivial party whose raucous echoes, resounding through the barracks, woke righteous indignation from the many who were not invited to this orgy.

Our most regular contact with our guards was at roll-call. This tedious formality went through several phases. In our first months it was called without fail at breakfast time; we responded "Hai" to our names and bowed low to the East as we gave our captors the morning greeting, "Ohai-o gozaimas." As much by carelessness as design our slovenly demeanour was the daily despair of the soldiers. Occasionally the sergeant would kick together the heels of some man who offended his sensibilities but never did the guards secure the military stance and precision so dear to the Japanese mind.

The ludicrous casualness of these roll-calls led, indeed, to their abeyance. Even when our last commandant, his own appearance slovenly enough to disgrace a recruit, insisted on these line-ups with what seemed vindictive fussiness, his staff often sought an excuse to omit this irksome requirement. One morning we were startled by heavy gunfire, perhaps naval guns on the coast.

"What's the use?" exclaimed the officer. "Too much noise!" – and dismissed us.

On another morning, after looking about him cautiously to make sure that the commandant was not in sight, he dismissed us again. A bellow like the outcry of a wounded bull shocked him to attention. In his casual survey of the parade grounds he had not noticed that the commandant was standing so close behind him as practically to breathe over his shoulder.

Seldom were these roll-calls operated meticulously enough to be a real check. One man, who made a habit of visiting the guerrillas at their secret headquarters not far from Camp Holmes, was answered for by his friends for two days without being missed. Whether the Japanese had spies in our midst, spies supposedly of mixed American and Filipino parentage, was never proven. One morning some occupants of the men's barracks were startled to observe Hayakawa sleeping in the bed of a *mestiza* who was absent on one of his occasional errands with the Camp truck. Except for some fluent profanity, he probably learned little, and if he had his supposed spies, they must have been deplorably inefficient.

At no stage did our guards inspire much respect for the Imperial Army's martial qualities. They were as shabby as their flag, which through all weather they kept nailed to a bamboo pole until the red circle, the "fried egg," as we called it, had become nearly indistinguishable from the dirty grey of its once white field. They did try renewing once with red paint, but that dissolved in a shapeless blotch in the first rain.

The poverty of Japanese resources was most evident in the medical neglect of their men. As a boy I had heard admiring tales of how their armies, when fighting the Russians, reduced casualties by dressing their soldiers before battle in clean underwear, a hygienic precaution not yet thought of in the West's supposedly more up-to-date forces.

Our contact with the Japanese disclosed no such enlightened practices. Quite to the contrary, their soldiers were left to shift for themselves. Particularly was this the case with venereal disease. Our observation, of course, was limited, but with surprising frequency guards used to beg members of the Camp for sulfa drugs. They were under two delusions, first,

285

that these drugs, then a medical novelty, were a panacea capable of instant cures for both syphilis and gonorrhea, and secondly, that every American kept his private supply of these magical remedies. Many favours in money and food they would offer for the round white tablets, explaining their need in the adequately succinct sentence, "Prick sick!"

Japanese soldiers were notorious for abusing women in the countries they overran. Earlier anxiety on this score, however, had been lulled long before our arrival at Camp Holmes. Our guards were more worried over our morals than we over theirs. In American 'teen-agers they met their match. Try as they could, they never succeeded in stifling the camaraderie to which American boys and girls were accustomed. On permitting the school to reopen, they specified that boys and girls walk to classes in two lines, fifty feet apart. This rule was ignored from the start. Other sporadic efforts to enforce Nipponese notions of decency succeeded no better. Occasionally individual guards would arrest 'teen-agers whom they surprised joking together, and hale them to the guard-house for an angry lecture. One guard even knocked down a boy, breaking his ear-drum, because he had talked openly to a girl outside the mess-hall. Threats were made to cancel the Camp's few privileges, to restrict, for instance, the right to play bridge until nine o'clock. The threats were breath wasted. Youth won out. Week by week, month by month, censorship retreated until eventually the Japanese so compromised their principles as to drag in a piano – "that damned piano," many soon called it – and to sanction dances.

On one edict they insisted, the ban against liquor, yet here too they had setbacks. Among the Camp's population was an authentic bootlegger, a Tennessee[58] mountaineer to whom moonshine was second nature, and luckily blessed with a skull which mayhem could not dent. Once the guards caught him and beat him on head and body with a baseball bat, blows that would have killed any ordinary man. Two days he spent in hospital, by which time his cannon-ball cranium and muscle-bound trunk were enough healed for him to take up again what the baseball bats had interrupted.

Brutal though this was, his punishment probably was less damaging than the liquor he sold. Where he got it or what were its ingredients we could only guess. One suggestion – furniture polish – seemed as likely as any. I tried the stuff once. I was standing at the time beside a double-deck bunk in a section of the men's barracks commonly derided as "The Country Club." No sooner had I drunk the poison than my chin began to float past the upper bunk as if I had been changed into a balloon. The rest of the drink I poured out lest it burn holes in my canteen.

Our guards, it can be gathered, troubled us little. We lived our life, they lived theirs. The cruelty visited on the military prisoners we were spared.

Cruelty there had been in the first months of the war, cruelty which we latecomers had the good luck to miss. Long afterwards, cruelty was to irrupt again, sequel to the escape of two men who skipped camp to join the guerrillas. That episode, however, does not belong at this stage. What we did feel from the beginning and never ceased to feel was inner resentment over the pettiness to which we were subject, the incessant prying into our thoughts, our hopes.

This found shape in an endless series of trivial restrictions, small-minded regulations thought up as if for but one purpose, to irritate us. Just when a tranquil balance had been obtained, we would be confronted by a new questionnaire, but asking the same old irrelevancies. Yet there was sport in figuring out the motive behind each mimeographed sheet. Always there was a joker inserted amid the usual repetitious inquiries about age, sex, birthplace, etc., etc. Sometimes it stood out like an inflamed thumb, as when we were asked to name our favourite sports.

Correctly we guessed that what they wanted was outdoor sports, a clue to who were able-bodied and eligible for work on the docks or in the mines. This question the Japanese staff could have answered for themselves by copying the roster of the wood-gang or the garbage-disposal crew, but this was a method too original for the Kempei-tai. They wanted papers to compile and tabulate in sound bureaucratic style. What they learned was startling. Not one man at Camp Holmes had any taste for able-bodied sport. Our preferences in recreation ranged from chess to writing poetry.

* * * * * * * *

To many of the Camp's inmates their internment was three years stolen from their lives. They existed; they did not live. Naturally their attitude depended on the work they had to do. No towering inspiration could be expected from digging garbage pits or cleaning out cesspools. Men thus engaged or women on hands and knees scrubbing perpetually muddy floors could not be blamed if they grumbled, although those who worked the least grumbled most. I was exceptionally fortunate, after a short spell as waiter, in being assigned a job which, war or no war, had to be done, a job permanent in its value. It was, moreover, congenial to my whole training, the job of teaching boys and girls.

Camp Holmes had perhaps 125 children. Their educational background varied widely, Brent School, the American School in Manila, Roman Catholic schools, and (for some pupils of mixed race) the Philippine public schools. Whatever their background, it was acknowledged from the start that their education would not stand still. The students were as eager as their parents

287

that their classwork continue. They were haunted by dread of emerging at the war's end, unfit for college, overgrown infants whose lost years could never be recovered.

Dr. Mukaibo's obstruction killed the first school. By the time we arrived in June its backers were ready to try again. The Camp's dynamic leader, Dr. Dana Nance, a man never hesitant to face up boldly to the Japanese or, as often was necessary, to his fellow-Americans, had wrung permission for classes to be resumed. So glad were the students, after weeks of inaction, to be back in class that one girl celebrated school's opening with a party.

I too had good reason to celebrate. For the first time in my teaching career I was teaching American pupils, pupils, moreover, who were reciting in their native tongue. My Chinese and Igorot classes had first to overcome the difficulties of a language foreign to them before making it the vehicle of their learning. The text-books they required were available only in English or some other Western language.

As for Camp Holmes, I had not been teaching long before I was given charge both of the school and of the Camp's entire educational system. I was high school principal and superintendent in one, and overseeing a curriculum that reached not only from first grade to twelfth but even further into adult education, offering a catch-all of subjects, flower arrangement, contract bridge, ballet, and – most unlikely yet most popular of all – navigation. On this mountain ridge, with its tantalizing, far glimpse of a sea whose only ships were enemy destroyers, transports, cruisers, men and women escaped prison charting the course of imaginary vessels across an imaginary ocean.

Our schools did not stray so far afield. They held fast to what we hoped was still the course prescribed by the College Entrance Board. To do so demanded the surmounting unique handicaps. Of equipment we had almost nothing. Our science laboratory was put together from odds and ends improvised in camp or salvaged, under Japanese chaperonage, from such wreckage as looters had left at Brent School. The books too were from Brent, and generally in such short supply that we rationed them out, half an hour at a time, to each pupil. Chalk I almost slept with, doling it out like a miser's gold.

In one respect we were lucky, Camp Holmes had been a Philippine Army post and copied with meticulous mimicry the pattern set by the American Army, but whatever the American Army did, the Philippine Army did one better. If the Americans required reports in quadruplicate, the Filipinos filled theirs in quintuplicate. Thanks to this bureaucratic contagion we had paper enough to last us through most of the war, mountains of discarded files, court-martial findings, medical histories, bulletins checked name by name by the Camp's vanished hierarchy. Mimeographed on but one side, these records gave us quantities of scratch paper and, for the teacher plodding through compositions, much spicier reading on the opposite side. Yet prolific though these records were, they too began to run short. I had to dole out paper as I had doled out chalk, limiting each high school student to one and a half sheets of paper for a week's work (in four subjects, not just one) – and making him sign for it as if he had withdrawn money from a bank[59].

So parsimonious did this experience make me that I never could adjust myself, when teaching in an American school after the war, to its pupils' prodigal ways. I would wince each time I watched a boy write three or four words on a clean sheet of paper, then crumple it up, and toss it in the waste-basket. I could not forget how Camp Holmes pupils conserved paper by writing their letters so small – three lines where we would write one – that today I need a magnifying glass to read my few surviving samples of their work.

Our schools were housed as meagerly as they were equipped. The grade school used a converted chicken house which Camp Holmes men had carried bodily from a nearby farm[60]. The high school was quartered in a shabby, paint-worn cottage near the gate. Study-hall we installed in a basement almost windowless except for the tiny cubby hole that served as office. Early in my internment I had acquired a stool. This I carried to school daily, but even more important was the loan of a battered alarm clock by which I regulated classes. Most precious of all was the desk I secured for the office. Almost as large as the office itself, it was no treasure to look at, but it provided space for files, and a surface much battered and weather-beaten, yet flat enough to write on. It was the school's only desk; classrooms and study-hall made do with tables and benches.

Whatever Camp Holmes High School lacked in equipment it compensated for in curriculum and staff. The curriculum, it was true, had its official limitations. The Japanese, as promoters of the East Asia Co-Prosperity Sphere, had decreed that no history be taught. Like all dictatorships they swept into the dust-bin everything that man had done or attempted prior to their glorious regime. For a similar reason they banned our teaching geography in the grade school. Their conquests had made earlier maps obsolete.

To these prohibitions we paid little heed. History we disguised as Biography, geography as physiography. Ancient History was Biography II (II looked more professional than I); Mediaeval and Modern History was Biography III. For these subjects we had obtained texts; on the rare occasions when a Japanese inspector hove in sight, the girls had been drilled to conceal the textbooks under their skirts. Biography IV was a more critical matter. This was American History, a course so emphatically proscribed that I could not ask any teacher to conduct it. Since we had but one text, smuggled into camp at some risk, I had no option but to make this a lecture course. Our classroom was uncomfortably public; it opened directly on the outdoor steps, and gave much too ready access to unannounced visitors. As we had no books to hide, this was still the safest arrangement. My class had been well trained to evince no surprise if suddenly I switched the subject of my lecture. Not a smile did they crack, not an eyelid blink when, interrupted half way through a disquisition on Ben Franklin, I shifted to Ben Jonson.

These were the only limitations to a prospectus such as few American high schools could boast. In language it was, Name it, and we have it. We offered Greek, Latin and in modern languages French, German, Spanish, Norwegian, Chinese. Had any pupil asked for Sanskrit or Hebrew, we could have obliged him. One other language we were compelled to offer – Japanese, but we had no takers. One boy expressed the consensus:

"Aw gee," he protested, "Do I have to study another dead language!"

Camp Holmes might have confuted the modern school boards who pour money into buildings and skimp teachers. We could have echoed James Garfield's tribute to "the value of a true teacher," continuing, "Give me a log hut, with only a simple bench, Mark Hopkins on one end and I on the other, and you may have all the buildings, apparatus and libraries." At our disposal were so many excellent teachers that they came near outnumbering the student body. Let anybody fall behind and he was assigned a tutor. The test of their work came after the war when Camp Holmes graduates were accepted at colleges throughout the United States, accepted on the basis of our report cards. One boy[61], whose senior year was broken up after the initial weeks by the convulsions that were propelling us to freedom, took the New York State Regents examinations, after his return home, and passed at the head of all that year's applicants.

Though it lacked all the elegant superfluities so dearly cherished by American schools, Camp Holmes High School became a real school, and an excellent one – a statement equally true of the grade school. The grade school staff were heroic in the compensations they devised, the aids so essential to capturing the attention of younger children. Under the devoted direction of Miss Cordy Job and Mrs. Phyllis Gibbons (later, young Arthur MacArthur's governess in the years when his father directed Japan's post-war occupation), they wore themselves to the bone, day after day, week after week. Much more than I they deserved the compliment I received from a Japanese visitor, "You are like Robinson Crusoe; you make much out of little."

As for the high school, it did prove that only one activity is necessary to a school – education. It got along without interscholastic games, without dances, without clubs. Classes were the daily interest, small classes conducted in seminar style and generally with excited discussion. Seldom have I looked forward to anything with livelier eagerness than to these classes. They could be gay as in an assignment I once gave to the girls, asking them to write a letter congratulating the friend who is marrying the man "you hoped to marry." They made practical use too of the war to sharpen their gift for expression; since the Japanese sometimes had prisoners broadcast to America how well they were being treated, they imagined themselves given such an assignment, and prepared radio talks subtle enough to describe the Camp life accurately without running afoul of Japanese censorship. Our captivity indeed could not be forgotten. Its ever oppressive fact made sacred even those pages of American history filled with political quarrels which historians recount for their sordid warning. We envied a fatherland that permitted men to quarrel over politics.

The Spirit of this school I tried to frame in a song, a song reserved for such state occasions as commencement.

"We sing our Alma mater,
    We hope it won't be long
Till there is nothing left of her
    Except this fleeting song.
And history o'er her emptied halls
    Shall knell a last ding-dong.

"For ball and chain we're wearing,
    Our teachers wear them too,
Our uniform is Sing Sing stripes,
    Our colour's mostly blue,
We're fellow convicts in one jail
    Condemned to meatless stew.

"But when we're back in freedom
    We'll not forget these days,
Upon our dingy classrooms
    We'll look with tearful gaze,
And see our Mother School, Camp Holmes,
    As thro' a golden haze."[62]

In more ways than one this song was prophetic. Long before we were free there promised to be "nothing left of her." Late in 1943 the Japanese requisitioned our high school cottage to house an augmented guard. In measures that inconvenienced us the Imperial Army could be very prompt. On no preliminary notice we were told to get out. We were thrown into a hapless flurry struggling to salvage and safeguard our dearly collected equipment.

Less prompt were the Japanese in finding us substitute quarters. Their promises were large. From cottages in Baguio which they were wrecking they would build us a school. They approved magnificent plans drawn up by a Camp architect. We should be complete even to school toilets and our own cesspool. Magnanimously they offered to pay everybody who worked at erecting the school – an offer we declined; our impatience to get classes started again was an incentive more than sufficient.

Only on paper did that school take shape. After two months' suspension we were directed to utilize the Camp bodega, a warehouse made of concrete and galvanized iron, and so resoundingly empty that it magnified every whisper. To summon classes there was like assembling inside a drum. No partitions separated them nor confined their din, nor did they separate us from the bodega's other use as a slaughter house. Slaughtering, of course, was not an every day occurrence – the Camp did not own that many pigs – and it was held in abeyance until the school's dismissal at 12:30, long enough for all but the morbid to get back to the barracks. One day, however, a dead pig forced on us a holiday. It had died from hog cholera, but those in control of ex-pigs, as enterprising as they were thrifty, overruled our plea that it be buried. All day the carcass hung, waiting to be converted into soap and tainting the air with a scent just putrid enough to corrupt our academic atmosphere.

Within weeks the Japanese disputed our tenancy of the bodega. All we could do now was take our tables and benches outdoors where, until the rainy season, we held classes. Protecting ourselves against the mounting sun with what shade the acacia trees provided, and suffering dramatic interruptions, as when a tarantula hopped down beside a girl in my English class.

The rains, starting to spatter before noon, pushed us indoors. Gladly the grade school foreclosed their term and let us take over their chicken house until we could move into the fifth and last of our premises. We had been promised an academy; we were given a shack. For this frail structure the Japanese themselves apologized, although they tried to brave out its inauguration with tea and cookies and a dynamic exhibition of the sword dance.

We were lucky that the sword dances did not stamp the building down. It was an overgrown matshed, roofed with second hand iron full of nail-holes that had to be plugged with tar, a job our schoolboys undertook, to keep out the rain. So skimpy were the eaves that we could prevent the rain splashing through the unglazed windows only by letting down the shutters. This kept out not rain alone but light. The *sawali* partitions between the classrooms were removable, and taken down every week-end to convert the school into church. My office, happily, could not be dismantled. On week days, through its thin wall, I absorbed the school's whole curriculum, on Sundays, assorted sermons. My ears grew ecumenical.

Whatever the handicaps, school morale never faltered. Even when gnawed by hunger, boys and girls plugged away at their books, still passing them on from pupil to pupil, half an hour's use apiece, and sharing too the 40 watt bulbs which ranked high in the Camp's hoarded treasure.

Reading in semi-darkness did harm to our eyes; it did not darken our spirits. The School indeed carried the Camp to one of its greatest moments when it presented Thornton Wilder's Our Town. For this play we had fifty-three rehearsals. We used every member of the student body, including two Seventh Day Adventists, who waived doctrinal scruples to take part. If influenza or dysentery had crippled our cast we should have been in a quandary; nobody was left to understudy, and already we had drafted the school principal to play the Stagehand.

The performance confounded our expectations. Not only were the pupils so completely versed in their lines that never once did they need help from the prompter, but they were inspired. The love for a country some of them were too young to remember, love for American ways, the homely American friendships, the habitual American freedom, welled up in acting as natural in its persuasive ease as it was incandescent in fervour.

The whole Camp, all but the toddlers, who had attended dress rehearsal, laughed and wept with them. Long before the play began, people had queued up for admittance, even the Japanese guards, who shuffled along with the rest. The mess-hall was the theatre, its tables the stage, army blankets the curtain. Although this long, narrow room was anything but suitable for dramatic performance, the audience gave such rapt attention that every word carried with vibrant clarity to the far back, to the kitchen counter on which sat several spectators.

The evening was an emotional catharsis best described by James Halsema, later an A.P. correspondent, in a full page review. Mr. Halsema had been publishing the *Camp Holmes News*, a paper which he typed daily on the blank back-side of the Philippine Army records, and posted on bulletin boards outside the mess-hall and in the hospital. In this most valuable activity only once did he resort to a second page, the review of our Town. Addressed in letter form to Thornton Wilder, it apologized for our performing the play without paying royalties. All we could offer, he explained, was perhaps a hand of bananas, and these no longer were easy to come by.

"So perhaps," he wrote, "you will be satisfied with our thanks and you might like to know how we did it. Last year we started a high school here for all the children who had been going to one before the war began. Books were scarcer than taxis on a rainy day in New York. As a matter fact, there wasn't much of anything except some good teachers and some willing and able students. They've been studying for quite a while now, and tomorrow they will be graduated. Of course they wanted a school play before commencement. What little we have left in the way of possessions and traditions we cling to.

"The principal of the school is a Canadian-born Anglican priest named Gowen. Someone said last night after the play that the reason 'Our Town' went off so smoothly was that he had his own ideas about what he wanted and after seven weeks of almost daily rehearsals he got them. Father Gowen never saw your play produced on stage or screen because he has been a missionary up in the mountains at a place called Besao. (A lot wilder mountains than the ones in New Hampshire, Thornton – although the kids play baseball as enthusiastically as George Gibbs, their parents aren't above a bit of head-hunting on occasions.) But you would have liked to have seen his version.

"This wasn't any stilted, awkward high school play with some embarrassed children reciting a lot of rigmarole they don't understand. Nobody was awkward and you didn't see anyone strained or scared. No, they went at it like they knew the people in Grover's Corners as well as the Stage manager did. . .

"Sometimes we don't get along with each other too well here – we've been together too long without an opportunity to see other people, but there's a lot of co-operation and help, and a lot of people who know how to do things in this camp. . . .You wanted to show people a thousand years from now how the people in Grover's corners really lived, 'the way we were in our growing up and in our marrying and in our doctoring and in our living and in our dying.' Well, we're not living in 1900, we're in 1943, but it's mighty fine to know that's about the way our own people are. You see, living in a concentration camp all these months sometimes makes us wonder if anyone still lives a normal life any more. And 'Our Town' is good medicine for that.

"We had a good time last night. We depend on ourselves for our entertainment, these days, you know, and it's not very often that we have anything quite so worth while as your play. Even sitting on a hard bench for two hours wasn't difficult then. We had permission to have the lights on after 9:30. After we got out of the dining hall we looked at the moonlight lighting up the mountains and the pine trees around here and it didn't seem quite so hard to wait...."

* * * * * * * *

Camp Holmes High School graduated three classes. Two, the classes of 1942 and 1943, received their diplomas together at exercises to which Our Town had been an illustrious prelude.

My puzzle was how to tie up these diplomas. Since we had no ribbon, we could not follow the practice then current in American schools. As a substitute, I asked Mr. Fabian Ream, who was manufacturing many useful things in the Camp shop, to make us balls and chains. His response was ingenious as it was willing. For this first graduation the balls were hardwood, turned out on the lathe, but the next year he made them even more handsomely out of star coral. For chains he melted Philippine silver coins and beat them into links. So greatly prized were these emblems wrapped around each diploma that one boy, who would have been graduated in 1945, voiced a hope that the war would not end until he had earned his ball and chain.

Happily for the rest of us his wish was not granted. By the time the class of 1944 was graduated, study was competing with hunger. The two months' suspension while we hunted for classrooms had postponed the ceremony from August to October. Our search for another play had comparable disappointments. Our Town had been a natural; it was available, moreover, in the one text-book, *Adventures in American Literature*, of which we had been able to salvage copies enough from Brent School's ransacked buildings. Apart from text-books, our only recourse was to the Camp library.

This collection we scoured in vain. It was a hit-or-miss assortment brought in by various people, a library valuable in many respects, for it offered readers, blessed by infinite leisure, the whole of Dickens and several of Walter Scott's ambling novels. Hopefully I had begun internment by borrowing Southall Freeman's four volume *Life of Robert E. Lee*, confident that if I picked out the longest-winded work in the collection I might not finish it before I was freed. Vain hope! Had it been on the shelves, I could have read *Gibbon's Decline and Fall of the Roman Empire* ten times over. But of plays worthy to succeed Our Town I found none. I was driven back to the text-books.

My eventual choice was Percy Mackaye's *Gettysburg*. It left much to be desired, principally because it gave scope for but two characters. By 1944, however, transfers to Santo Tomas in Manila had made inroads on our student body. Our graduates were reduced to three.

If it could not rival *Our Town*, *Gettysburg* nevertheless proved so moving, so poignantly accordant with the times, that Yamato, the Japanese censor deputed to watch our doings, actually apologized for being present. He had not realized, he said, that this was a sacred occasion.

Simple though its theme, a Grand Army veteran reliving on Memorial Day the great battle which turned back the high tide of Confederate strength, and diagramming for his granddaughter, as he sat paralyzed, the several stages of a conflict she had heard often enough to prompt him if his memory faltered, the play surged with our own swelling certitude of victory. We could not supply the band which the play called for, a band accompanying Memorial Day rites in a distant cemetery, but we substituted the grade school children. Off stage and unseen, they began singing very softly "The Battle Hymn of the Republic." Little by little the tone mounted, ascending to a fortissimo exultant enough to fill the building as the young voiced declaimed the last refrain,

"Glory, glory, hallelujah,
His truth goes marching on."

Like the veteran, throwing down his crutches, we were swept by its momentum into tearful ecstasy.

With this song the Camp Holmes schools could be said to have come to their end. For some weeks all school work was suspended in order that the pupils might do their part in the gardening project which our Japanese commandant, much too late, imposed upon every able-bodied prisoner. Although eventually a new term was begun, it was barely started before it had to be stopped. Our fortunes were too deeply involved in the war's accelerated development to leave room for books. Soon, as we had sung, "there was to be nothing left of her," but if the Camp Holmes schools disappeared, if their hard-won equipment became trash and firewood, and their meager building a heap of ashes, the school still asserted its proud existence in the hearts of its pupils. Fellow-wearers of the ball and chain, they boasted a distinction no other school could match. Long afterward, I had letters whose writers looked back with envy on the classes they had shared. I too envy the dedication, the gaiety, the sincerity of those classes, the honest work done by teachers and pupils alike in an accord such as one may teach for a lifetime yet never see equaled. Their truth, indeed, "goes marching on."

* * * * * * * *

The Camp Holmes schools were but one feature of the resourcefulness whereby some five hundred Americans girded themselves to cope with conditions which this resourcefulness alone could help them meet and shape.

Early in the war the Camp had recognized that the conflict would be long, and that as important as feeding its people was the task of sustaining their health and morale. Its accomplishment in both was amazing. Again, thanks to the adroit leadership of Dana Nance, a hospital had been set up and staffed by the Camp's doctors and nurses. Of these there were ample supply. They too did much with little. Prudently they husbanded the stock of medicine which they had brought from Camp John Hay, but thrifty though they were, this stock was almost gone when, on Christmas Day 1943, one of the six Red Cross shipments, the only one, sent us from America was allowed to reach its destination. This shipment, however, brought puzzling reminders of what our isolation was costing us. Not only were we cut off from a sufficient supply of medicines but, in these drugs we did receive, we realized how drastically we were cut off from the knowledge of how to use them.

Outside our barbed wire fences the medical world was undergoing revolution, a revolution begun shortly before the war by the introduction of sulfa drugs. So recent were the sulfa drugs which reached us in 1943 that our doctors could only guess at their use. Some things, like blood plasma, they dared not guess at. Yet despite these handicaps, despite temperamental differences natural to any professional group but aggravated by too close confinement, our doctors managed their problems so capably that the death rate at Camp Holmes was no higher than it would have been, had we been free.

With equal success the Camp's morale was upheld. Never once, even in moments of extreme peril, did it crack. To this result the most diligent contributor was Mr. Sidney Burnett; single-handed, he inaugurated a series of entertainments, at first twice weekly and, later, weekly, that was to continue to within a few weeks of our rescue.

How Sidney Burnett achieved this was a miracle, for tact and finesse were never his forte. With indomitable persistence he browbeat, cajoled, flattered his victims into contributing their talents to his varied programmes – lectures, dramatic readings, vaudeville turns, satirical farces, imitations of the then popular Major Bowes's amateur shows, much of it spiced with singing commercials on behalf of an imaginary sponsor which, by a ribald slip of the tongue, he called – instead of Rice Incorporated – Rice Incopulated.

This series was just getting underway way at the time of our arrival. It was a lively symptom of the newer freedom which the Camp, after months of boring repression, was nerving itself to seize. Early in the series I was asked to speak on evacuation experiences in China and to underscore the parallels between a refugee camp in Shanghai and an internment camp in Baguio. To my own surprise I succeeded in provoking a groundswell of laughter so compelling that I gained instant acclaim as a humourist. Whether the talk would have sounded so funny under other conditions I have no surviving notes to indicate but, on the testimony of many people, it spurred the first good laugh they had enjoyed since they were dragged into camp. It was laughter they needed. The hilarity which this talk sparked, and later talks in a vein similarly facetious was probably the chief factor in securing my election, shortly afterward, to the august ranks of the General Committee, and to supervision of the Camp's entertainment, of the Saturday night programmes which loomed so large in the Camp's narrow opportunities of amusement.

Amusement was not their sole function. Information on many subjects was interestingly available, thanks to the Camp's many gifted people, and to the world-ranging experience which many of them had known.

No experience, however, was of acuter interest than our current servitude. What we craved was some hopeful yet expert analysis of how and when we should be set free. Such was the gullibility of the Camp's old women, male and female alike, that as far back as 1942 their tongues had American forces landing in Mindanao. By afternoon these forces had advanced several hundred miles to the Visayans. By evening they were bombing Manila.

The staggering obstacles of trans-pacific strategy meant little to these people. "America cannot let us down," was their repeated assertion. To their infatuated souls there was no absurdity in picturing President Roosevelt and his Chiefs of Staff specially met to give their plight top priority, and scratching their heads over how to rescue five hundred civilian captives from their Luzon mountain ridge. So violent was their obsession that they impugned the patriotism of anyone who dared doubt whether it was worth sacrificing thousands of soldiers in order that these grumblers might resume their comforts and fatten on three palatable meals each day.

Fortunately, we were not left to the mercy of rumour-mongers. We could squeeze better guesses as to how the war actually was shaping from the Japanese broadcasts, which some listened to daily outside the guard-house. We learned even more when the radio broke down. In these emergencies the guards called on a prisoner to mend what they could not repair. This man, a retired Navy signalman, had more than mechanical talent: he had a mind trained to memorize long messages, memorize them to the last detail.

At times his memory was tediously perfect. He could reel off for twenty minutes the latest provisions for ex-servicemen's pensions. But even though he added as an afterthought word of victories off Midway and in the Coral Sea, we were grateful for these crumbs, grateful to know that the National and American Leagues still were playing baseball, and that the miraculous could happen in a pennant won by the St. Louis Cardinals. These fragments the Japanese themselves would supplement. Their favourite topic was John L. Lewis and his coal miners' strikes, while with gleeful exultation they let us know that the manufacture of refrigerators had been banned.

Our signalman's method of gleaning news was clever. He would put on earphones and fiddle about with wires for a day or two while absorbing Treasure Island's broadcasts, and each time his repairs were contrived with such inexpertness that within a fortnight he was summoned back to do more mending. Eventually the Japanese must have grown suspicious. They stopped sending for him.

A more dangerous means of securing news was confined to a very few initiates, who operated a receiving set in a hospital cupboard. On Jim Halsema's advice they listened to the B.B.C. instead of Treasure Island; unlike the San Francisco station, it took pains to distinguish between a skirmish and a battle. Only a few were informed of the news thus obtained. The risks were so great that long before the end of our stay at Camp Holmes this radio was dismantled.

Our final source of news was the guerrillas. One of my closest friends, Douglas Strachan, slipped out of Camp dozens of times for brief visits to their headquarters. One night, he had to lie low in shrubs so close to the barbed wire fence that a sentry, patrolling his beat, just missed stopping on him. The news he brought he divulged to but a handful. He used to whisper bulletins to me as we played chess, or go out with me to the middle of the parade ground – and often in the dark – to make sure that no eavesdropper overheard his words. Never could we be certain that the Japanese did not have informers planted in the Camp, nor could we control tongues more voluble than discreet. Gossip, enlarged and distorted, could reach enemy ears and alert the Kempei-tai to evidence that we knew more than Tokyo Rose deigned to tell us.

What the Japanese wished us to accept as news was published in their English language paper, the *Manila Tribune*. Many of us subscribed to it, not so much for its contents but because it was the most convenient substitute for toilet paper. For that purpose it was a bargain; as an official publication, the Tribune could not countenance inflation, but had to be sold at the price first set, when the military peso, scenic and prettily printed currency, was circulating at par.

The *Manila Tribune* should have fooled nobody versed in English to read it. Its target was the educated Filipino, but any faintly intelligent reader could discern from its pages the war's relentless progress. Its pattern never varied: first, the advancing American forces were destroyed at sea; next they were destroyed at the beach-head; finally, they were destroyed on the air-fields which, despite having been twice wiped out, these ghostly warriors had constructed. A few weeks later, this triple destruction would be repeated, but with a significant difference: each series of exterminations occurred several hundred miles nearer the Philippines.

The *Tribune* headlines were equally entertaining. Across the front page, for example, bold print would proclaim, Ten Enemy Planes Shot Down Over Africa, while tucked away at the bottom of a column, a terse statement announced that enemy forces had occupied Tunis.

Even more farcical was the Tribune's complaint about "American Ambiguity." It was criticizing the formula for American casualty lists – so many killed, so many wounded, so many missing "to date." What did this vague phrase, "to date," mean? It asked with heavy-handed emphasis, before concluding that "to date" was a meaningless evasion. Yet the same column which ridiculed these casualty lists as ambiguous went on to tell of an American air-raid in the Gilberts, then Japanese held. It ended with the statement, "our forces suffered some losses, more or less." So much for ambiguity!

An enlightening feature of the Saturday night entertainments was Jim Halsema's periodic lectures on the war's progress. Using only the Japanese reports, gleaned from the Tribune and the Tokyo broadcasts, he demonstrated almost as graphically as though we had the *New York Times* to read each morning just what was happening in Africa, in Europe, and in the Pacific's far-probing battle zones.

His analyses became too accurate. Japanese suspicions were provoked. Prudence advised him to abandon these lectures lest the Kempei-tai institute inquiries in which it was as dangerous to be innocent as guilty. The time came, indeed, when our jailers dared not let us read or listen to their own propaganda. Our subscriptions to the *Tribune* were cancelled, the guard-house radio silenced. In April 1944 the *Tribune* stopped arriving; in May we were told that we might receive our copies again from the 1st June except on such days as the news was "bad!" It must all have been bad; when June came, Yamato, our official translator, told us that no more Tribunes would be forthcoming because – as he put it – he did not wish us "concerned about social occurrences outside." He wanted, he explained further, to make this "an exemplary camp." Henceforth, ignorance was to be our bliss.

He could not keep us ignorant, alas, of the swift rise in prices, a rise ever accelerated until rice cost thousands of pesos a sack and even the lowly peanuts sold for a peso apiece. Clearer than words such rapidly swelling prices told how the war was going.

* * * * * * * *

Within two months of our arrival I was elected to the General Committee. I cannot claim that I deserved this honour. My chief qualification, probably, was my newness. No camp like Camp Holmes could convert several hundred civilians from the independence and comfort of peace-time life to the exigencies of internment without recrimination and bitterness. It was remarkable that this organization had been managed without deeper dissension. What truth there was in the accusation that some of the organizers had treated themselves too liberally, appropriating from the original foodstocks more than their due, we latecomers had no way of judging. We at least were clear from earlier scandals and, at a time when inmates were weary of hashing over outworn topics, my Saturday night talks introduced a novelty of subject matter refreshing enough to win me an election I neither sought nor expected.

To be elevated to the General Committee was, indeed, startling, for I had regarded its nine members as enthroned on an eminence to which a mere waiter might look up as mortals once looked up to Olympus.

This deference was not unreasonable. Its members were able and devoted, and their accepted ascendancy was just tribute to that gift for political stability which characterizes English-speaking peoples. It was in stark contrast to the passive submission to their fate out of which the Japanese civilians, in their earlier but brief turn at being prisoners, made no attempt to struggle.

Except for the first eight months of 1944, my service on the Committee continued until our release. The Camp's initial organization provided for an election every four months, an election preceded by a primary. There were no formal candidacies, no speeches, no platforms, but politics there was a-plenty, politics at times heated and even rancourous. Quite naturally the Camp divided into two parties. Conservatives and liberals they could be termed, although often they might better have been labelled the "Ins" and the "Outs." Whatever they did, the "Ins" laid themselves open to criticism, yet the composition of the committee changed but little. Occasionally some member suffered a loss of favour, but the chronic malcontents which, in Camp Homes as in any community, talked much but did little never achieved the revolution they always were fomenting. Blocs there were and deals, and a tricky practice of politics by many of the young missionaries from China, the migrants from the Peking Language School, who displayed a civic sense truer to Tammany hall than to the Gospel. By no means did this describe the entire group. Some missionaries had a friendlier affinity with lay people than with their fellow preachers. Nevertheless, it was noticeable that some, children of light thought they might deem themselves, were not above worldly accommodations; one election was swayed by what Jim Halsema dubbed the "Beer and Bibles party," a coalition temporarily tied together to work off personal grudges.

The General Committee's major change was effected not by ballots but by the transfer of Dana Nance to the new camp at Los Baños. For well into two years Nance had been the Committee's chairman. He was the right man whom a crisis sometimes brings to the front, able, prompt in decisions, boldly aggressive, never afraid to stand up to the Japanese nor to promote necessary but controversial policies among his fellow prisoners. He insisted on schools in defiance of those who wished to snatch classrooms for living quarters. He presented a newly devised judicial system to the Camp at a public meeting, defending its need with logic so irrefutable that not one of the grumblers who had vowed to move a vote of no confidence even opened his mouth. He led the General Committee to reject a much debated proposal for Woman's suffrage but not until the issue had been submitted to the Camp in plebiscite, a plebiscite which the next year's Committee, in an even more hotly argued question dared not call lest the Camp vote down the policy they favoured.

It seems ironical, in retrospect, that the Camp should have been so reactionary as to deny the Woman's Suffrage which, a year later, they were to accept on Japanese insistence – a lesson in democracy from our totalitarian foes! Certainly, in 1943 woman's suffrage was no startling novelty. The plebiscite, however, gave no strong lead. The men's vote was predominantly against change, the women's vote only narrowly in favour. Our reasons, perhaps, were no better than those that lead American legislators to resist reapportionment of their districts; we were reluctant to tamper with the status quo, to introduce any unpredictable factor into our improvised government. In this vein, many women were more outspoken that the men; they did not care to vote. A considerable number ignored the plebiscite. So it remained for the subjects of the Sun-God to recall us, forcibly, to our principles as free Americans, and to prove from this experiment that, though there were more votes to count, the status quo was still the status quo.

Only one woman was elected to the committee; no others bothered to be candidates. Nellie McKim joined the Committee because the Japanese demanded her inclusion, having decreed that at least one member must speak Japanese. Her inclusion was valuable; all of us benefitted from her presence at meetings, but I doubt whether she gained any larger prestige or influence than she had earned as chairman of the now superseded Women's Committee. Hers were qualities of judgement and courage and innate knowledge of how to handle the Japanese such as no man in Camp Holmes could excel. Her talents had been potent from the start; they continued potent to the end.

General Committee met at least once a week in Dr. Nance's hospital quarters. Here the Committeemen seated themselves as best they could and, stimulated by a cup of coffee, the one perquisite of their high office, struggled over problems that multiplied faster than they could be dealt with. Once or twice they had to approve such police measures as an unannounced raid on the barracks to recover – as it turned out – but a fraction of the Camp's vanishing cutlery. A Camp store was set up and rules laboured over to ensure that all purchasers had a fair chance at its inadequate stocks. The Camp had no constitution; its ordinances could not anticipate situations but were put together to cope with ever worsening conditions. Over every meeting hung the problem of food, the hopeless effort to stretch our per capita allowance to meet our barest needs. Even when we could persuade the Japanese to increase our allowance, it was always too late. Our overlords could not print their "mickey mouse money" fast enough to meet expanding prices.

Dana Nance's departure left us with weaker leadership[63], a leadership which the Japanese themselves soon subjected to more stringent rules of their own. Instead of tolerating the Committee while giving it no formal recognition, they now made it an adjunct to their system. They altered our scheme of elections: these were to be held every six months instead of every four. Candidates no longer could file at large but for the particular department they sought to administer. Women now voted; the Committee had obeyed their order to instal a Japanese-speaking vice-chairman. The next step could be predicted – a Japanese censor present at its meetings.

This unwelcome visitor was Yamato, the interpreter. Competent though he considered himself in his knowledge of English, this meeting staggered him. He had studied Shakespeare; he had not studied American slang. The idiom he listened to that afternoon, an idiom purposely and mischievously distorted, kept him knitting his brows in bewilderment. He did not come again!

The Committee's most violent crisis was the result not of greater Japanese strictness but greater leniency. The old prohibition against "commingling" had been relaxed. Families now ate together, first at the edge of the parade ground and, later, in the married women's barracks, where within cubicles curtained by sheets they enjoyed meals more palatable than in the mess hall. Many now had hot-plates constructed in the Camp shop, constructed of odds and ends but serviceable and prized by camp wives as, in the expanded days of post-war America, they would prize their completely electrified kitchens. Miracles of cuisine they contrived on these rusty, rudimentary stoves.

But when the Japanese let down the bars still further and said that families not only might eat together but sleep together, their generosity tore the Camp apart, provoking the most divisive issue of our entire internment. At this time, in the spring of 1944, I was among the "outs," having fallen victim, with other more important Committeemen, to the Beer and Bibles coalition. When I was elected again to the Committee in September, the issue had been settled, settled – as many of us felt – by a high-handed refusal to submit this controversy to the whole Camp's decision.

The argument against co-habitation was in equal parts emotional and practical. Many couples thought our condition too unsuitable for decent married life. Temperamentally, they recoiled from even the pretense of intimacy under the inevitable restrictions, the furtive privacy which was all they could expect from the sheets, hung from wires, that would enclose their cubicles. The unromantic appearance husband and wife would make to each other, clothed in rags, emaciated in body multiplied chances of mutual irritation each day's drab routine would present.

The practical difficulties weighed heavy on many minds. By this time the Camp had shaken down. Various inmates had contrived their own ingenious methods of making this existence tolerable, devices to secure more room by beds slung from the ceiling or in one case by a quadruple decker which exacted from the topmost occupant a steeple-jack's agility. To disturb all this, to turn the Camp upside down in a flurry of chaotic carpentry, was a prospect they shuddered at.

The most likely difficulty was in everybody's thoughts, though I was criticized as indelicate for mentioning it in an open letter which I posted on the bulletin board. This was the likelihood of pregnancy. Our Camp diet, it was true, did not conduce to erotic yearnings, but there were some people who needed no stimulus. What if the accident they pooh-poohed should happen? How could a child so conceived be properly nurtured? What special demands would be made on the Camp's dwindling food-stocks?

Despite urgent appeals for a plebiscite, the Committee refused to put the issue to a vote. They pushed ahead their plan for co-habitation, and even seized on the grade-school, converting it into what scoffers nicknamed the Rabbit Warren. But they did have to modify the total conversion of the Camp's living quarter which they had sought. Many couples remained outside the scheme. Only the middle barracks was subjected to this doubtful domesticity. The single women's barracks and the men's preserved their freedom intact; in the latter, indeed, we gained space and came to congratulate ourselves that we were rid of all the impatient husbands.

Our Japanese commandant in this crisis, a benign man, was shocked by the angry passions it engendered. He had gone so far as to permit a wedding, even before general co-habitation was mooted. It was an extraordinary ceremony, solemnized before an outdoor altar in what had once been a sunken garden. All the sentimental fussiness of weddings at home was adhered to. "I love you truly," was sung; a flower girl scattered petals, a ring-bearer toddled precariously ahead of the bride along a path carpeted with the multi-useful

304

sheets. Just as the rites were commencing, however, the Commandant came bustling in from Baguio; in one hand he brought a bouquet of scarlet flowers for the bride to carry, in the other, a bottle of wine.

Nothing so genuinely original, of course, could be allowed to taint the conventional humdrum of the marriage. While the participants faltered, shocked by the interruption, puzzled how to decline the Commandant's kindness, Nellie McKim extricated them from their dilemma. Employing the tact which pulled the Camp out of many worse plights, she explained to the baffled officer the American bride's curious predilection for white, the funeral colour, but told him that his brilliant bouquet would be exactly right for the reception. The wine, too, was inappropriate, for the bride was a missionary, and her groom, although originally a miner, had been lured to the fold. The wine did not appear at the reception. Who drank it was, for days afterward, the subject of intriguing guesses.

Thus, by Japanese encouragement, we had come the full circle from their earlier prohibition against commingling to benevolent insistence that husbands go to bed with their wives. In but one case did connubial bliss produce the predicted result. It was evoking also the predicted plea for special favours but, luckily for the couple concerned and the bulging offspring, our rescue intervened.

My participation in the General Committee's travail covered our last months of internment. To safeguard the school's interest, progressively slighted (as I felt) by the current Committee, I put up my name in August 1944 for what proved to be our final election. After eight months away from its counsels I was back once more mulling over familiar but ever harsher problems.

The school gained little by my return. Events were driving us and scarcities of food, clothing, medicine obsessing us till but one thought weighted down our meetings – how to survive. As if this were not enough to turn us grey-headed, the Japanese augmented our troubles by further encroachment on quarters already too limited.

The final crisis came when they commandeered the two-story cottage that had served so effectively for our hospital. For days we struggled with schemes to re-allot living space. Just when we had got everybody moved and settled, we received notice that the Camp was to be shifted to Manila.

For the third time, with cheerfulness undaunted but on a scale so straitened as to make earlier observances seem lavish, we had made a show of celebrating Christmas. Good will was expressed by a handful of peanuts, a lump of panocha, a full strength cup of coffee. The next evening, I was playing bridge with friends, when I received a summons, as peremptory as it was mystifying, to a hastily summoned meeting of the General Committee.

What I heard was startling. Yamato had come suddenly to ask for some shoes which he had left in our cobbler's shop to be repaired.

"I need them when I go to Manila," he explained.

"Oh, are you going to Manila?" asked the Chairman, hopefully.

"You are going too," said Yamato.

Thus the news was broken. It had been broken just as abruptly to our guard. Without troubling to clarify his actions to the Commandant, an officer had appeared and stationed his own soldiers around the Camp. Not till he had completed their disposition did he divulge the secret that we all were to be transferred "to a place near the coast" – as we heard it, though rumour defined that place as Bilibid, the abandoned prison where the Japanese had herded their military captives through months and years of abject misery.

At this meeting, fired alike by excitement and elation, the General Committee transformed itself into a new body. It became, much like what the war's first exigencies once made it, three years earlier, an emergency body almost self-organized to confront difficulties no one could measure or predict. Gone were the niceties of Woman's Suffrage or Cohabitation. Our first concern was to add to our numbers other aggressive, energetic talents, and to choose a Safety Committee that could ease our departure into the unknown.

Camp Holmes was ended.

* * * * * * * *

In post-war reminiscences Camp Holmes has been always the forgotten camp. The military camps, by reason of their suffering, their heroism, shine rightly in a garish limelight we would not presume to challenge. But we were jealous of our place among the civilian camps, and nothing galls us more than to be asked, "Were you at Santo Tomas?"

It is true that Santo Tomas and its mid-war offspring, Los Baños, numbered their inmates by thousand where we could claim only hundreds, but Santo Tomas, at least, had privileges we were never allowed; its prisoners could live as families in little private shacks built for their own use, they could have meals sent in, laundry sent out, could take week-end leave, take their pick of Red Cross supplies, monopolize opportunities for repatriation. Such privileges, of course, favoured those who could pay for them.

Not only did we avoid these sharp distinctions between rich and poor; we escaped to a large degree Santo Tomas's differences of caste. Into the Manila camp were swept the scouring of the China coast, an indiscriminate assortment, whereas we were nearly a unit and, in the end, better hardened to endure the privation of the final months.

The following tribute to our spirit is excerpted from my diary. Describing our Christmas Eve observance in 1942, it takes on unique value because it was written at the time, and not in glamourous retrospect.

"In the evening…the pageant. A Christmas tree outside the school house shone brilliantly with its many coloured lights. We sat on the hillside waiting until from behind the hospital we heard the Adeste Fideles; two by two came the choir hidden by darkness except for the coloured lanterns they carried. The serene harmony of their voices contained an indomitable note which made me proud to be a member of this camp. Nothing could discomfit the glorious assurance of the music, an augury, if there was one, that truth and freedom and decent regard for the rights of men will yet be victorious. We looked forward to the time when the voice of the bully will be heard no more in the land and God's love in mankind will assert its real strength. The singing accompanied lovely tableaux in the pine-girt bower, the Blessed Mother and St. Joseph at the manger, the coming of the shepherds with young goats bleating their interest in the scene and then subsiding to tranquil contemplation of the manger, and finally, one by one, the approach of the Three Kings. It epitomized the wording of a message I got, 'Wishing you a Merry Christmas and a Hopeful New Year." Finally the lights were put out and the moon rose…"

Our celebrations of Christmas never faltered. Seen now, a full twenty years later, they were almost idyllic. When we were dragged once more into the maelstrom of Christmas at home, into the frantic shopping, the harassing importunity of a festival so corrupted that it makes its greed only gaudier by glittering tinsel, we envied the little homemade gifts, the cards coloured by crayon, such as gave our Christmases behind barbed wire a brightness heartfelt and indelible.

But there was special excitement to Christmas in 1943; prompt to the day itself arrived the one Red Cross shipment we received. Six were sent; only one got to us. Our feud with Santo Tomas began when we found out that the Manila camp, a year before, had put our share of the first shipment into their own stores, justifying this selfishness by the excuse that it might not have reached us. Possibly they were right. After our rescue in '45 we saw Filipino looters carrying off Red Cross boxes which they had plundered from Japanese Army warehouses. Almost certainly the Japanese took our other allotments, but for the misappropriation of that first allotment we blamed not the enemy but our fellow Americans.

For the time being, however, the distribution of Red Cross boxes on Christmas Day 1943 erased all bitterness. To make sure that they came intact the Japanese had permitted our own men to meet the consignment in Manila and accompany it in the train's freight cars, and in the buses from Damortis. Only once did this enemy liberality falter. After the boxes had been received, the guard insisted on our opening them to remove from every packet of Old Gold cigarettes the offending label; "Freedom. Our heritage has always been freedom – we can not afford to relinquish it – Our armed forces will safeguard that heritage, if we, too, do our share to preserve it." Thanks to the guards' calling to our notice this inflammatory slogan, the torn wrappers were smuggled into many a pocket, and there were few persons who could not repeat its message word for word.

As to the boxes themselves, fulfilment for once outdid anticipation; the solid truth outvied rumour. Instead of the cartons weighing 15 lbs. that we had been led to expect, each of us received a case weighing 47 lbs. By the time I had carried our family's four cases up the hill from the bodega and across the parade ground to my wife's cubicle I was staggering, but from the happiest exhaustion I have ever known.

Without this food I doubt whether many of us could have survived. Some people, of course, ran through their supply at a prodigal rate, but we husbanded ours so carefully that we still had one tin of Spam to celebrate our rescue, thirteen months later. One 12 oz. tin of corned beef, for example, used to last the four of us for three meals. On that exultant Christmas morning, however, when we took stock of our treasure, the first craving we satisfied was for cheese. Cheese on crackers! – we were almost grateful to months of privation for the relish appeased by this simplest of fare.

Yet not to our physical survival alone did these Red Cross boxes contribute but to the morale that sustained this survival. So providently had their contents been chosen, so fastidiously packed, that they reminded us even better than the Old Gold slogan "that our flag was still there."

We had still nine months to wait ere we saw victory promised from the skies. It was a day we had feared as well as hoped for. Committee meetings increasingly were concerned over how the Camp might react to the appearance of American 'planes. In the war's first months the Japanese had rubbed spirits sore with posters advertising boastfully the fall of Singapore, of the Dutch Indies, of Bataan, and Corregidor. Our turn to boast they might not admit.

We kept warning our people, when the tide turned, not to infuriate what were still our guards by intemperate rejoicing.

To the Camp's credit they showed admirable control on the late September morning when the American 'planes did come. The day before, we had seen high in the blue a reconnaissance 'plane which the knowledgeable identified as American; unlike the Japanese, its motors were synchronized. Yet the arrival of Americans in force came so naturally that many of us wakened but slowly to awareness that this was the real thing.

At work in the school, I for one was so absorbed in correcting papers that the noise of bombs barely pierced my consciousness until a teacher rushed in shouting the incredible news: American 'planes were attacking. Some months before, the Tribune's military commentator had tried to explain to its Manila readers their air-raid drills as an act of grace. Americans in force, he declared, never would penetrate the Japanese defences but, on the off chance that some stray 'plane might wing through and drop a few bombs, the Imperial Army was conducting these drills, instituting them out of sheer kindness to save the populace even the slightest damage from raids so futile.

What we witnessed was not a stray 'plane; we were witnessing the impossible, an attack by squadrons that had confounded the expert and brought American power to bear, thousands of miles across the world's broadest ocean, and in defiance of bases which, at the war's outset, the enemy had seized in arrogant confidence that these conquests were permanent.

From our height we could look toward the China Sea and watch our 'planes smashing up Poro, the port of San Fernando. For the moment, however, their objective was not clear to us. Only afterwards, and from members of the Japanese staff, was their target explained. We learned, too, that they had preceded this day's action by a devastating assault on Manila. But we needed nothing more than what our own eyes had seen. Freedom, victory were in the air.

These hopes were re-enforced by further raids, by admissions from the Commandant that the Americans might put a million men into the Philippines. They had at least a hundred air-craft carriers off the Islands, he conceded, and went on to complain that he could not imagine where they had got them; before the war they had owned not more than five. When the Americans came, he told our Committee, he and his staff would take to the hills. We were not to follow – which provoked smiles from all who heard it. Nothing was farther from our desire than prolonging acquaintance with him or his underlings.

What gave this Commandant's words greater credence was the fact often demonstrated that he hated us. A man disposed to indiscreet extremes, to ungovernable rages, he soon repented his words, and tried to recall these damaging admissions. The hundred air-craft carriers, he next announced, had all been sunk. He was too late. We believed what we wished to believe, and for once were right to do so.

All of us in our secret thoughts must have recognized that freedom might exact an ordeal by fire. At no stage had the Japanese accepted international amenities. If they had been truculent during the triumphing months when the Far Eastern empires of America, Britain, Holland crumpled under attack, what would they be when victory turned to ashes and their only course was to sell their lives to the last man? I had a theory, bred from experience in China, that Orientals are harder to deal with in success, more amenable when defeat seems inescapable. It was a precarious theory. The Japanese are not Chinese. Although our civilian staff grew friendlier, evidently ready to cut their losses, no one could count on similar appeasement from a soldiery whose desperate tradition was suicide.

Daily we were confronted by our commandant's vacillating temper. He set the entire camp to scraping away sod from the hill-sides in a belated scheme to grow *camotes* – a project begun preposterously in the rainy season when a typhoon or even a thunder storm could wash away our plantings. Claiming that we spent too much time cooking, he ordered our precious hot-plates collected, and then remitted his order. Further angered about the accelerated rate at which we were losing weight, he denounced every representation from our doctors, cursed them as fools, declared they were fitter for work in the fields than for the practice of medicine. To refute their claim that this outdoor labour was pushing the Canp faster toward starvation, he began weighing people himself – and abandoned it still more abruptly on his discovery that the doctors had not exaggerated but understated the truth. Yet it was after this, after a trip to Manila from which he returned ailing with kidney stones, that he made not only his disclosures about American naval forces and the near likelihood of American landings, but ended with the astounding statement that the kidney stones were probably a punishment for his harsh words.

Back of his moodiness and despite his more amiable spells lurked memories that could not reconcile him to seeing us go scot free. He had been in the first contingent to land at Davao. Their arrival, of course, had procured liberation for the many Japanese civilians interned in what, before the war, had been a thriving Japanese colony. Unhappily, this liberation had not been effected without violence. As they fled before the invaders, the Filipino guards turned their guns on the captives whom they were releasing, an act of senseless butchery in which no American soldiers were involved but for which the United States, as the dominant power, was properly responsible. This atrocity the Commandant set his mind to repay.

These grim chances did not dampen our elation. Gladly we welcomed black-outs, growing depressed only when the lights were not dimmed. We watched Japanese convoys coming back from the mountains, their trucks burdened with white boxes containing the ashes of their dead. In other trucks we saw troops returning from the pursuit of guerrillas; they were slumped in exhaustion, sprawled half asleep. Their Filipino drivers, though wearing the uniforms of the constabulary organized by Japanese to support a puppet government, boldly held up their hands in the V-sign for Victory. However perilous the crisis ahead of us, all we asked was that events keep moving. Eagerly, impatiently, we fretted for the next decisive step. When would the Americans land?

* * * * * * * *

When would the Americans land? Our answer came in a manner almost too extraordinary to believe. As the spinners of tall tales used to begin, "It is a long story" – but in this case it is a true story, true and, in the same breath, incredible.

From the early months of internment recreation had demanded its necessary place in our life. Outdoors, men resorted to softball, making up teams, Seniors, Juniors, Missionaries, High School, whose rivalry persisted until they were too famished to play. Even more widely practised were the sedentary pastimes. Perfect for chess was the endlessness of our captivity. Time did not matter. The game's true addicts could settle down for two or three hours of a contest unbroken except for infrequent grunts of approval or dismay. But the largest following was for contract bridge.

Twice a week the mess-hall tables were reserved for tournaments that succeeded each other in unbroken sequence. The other nights were taken up by private contests. With lighting as dim as ours, contract was easier on the eyes than books even when the cards grew so dirty that we had to look twice not to confuse clubs with spades. The Japanese restricted us to one 40-watt bulb for every four persons. Since they did not supply the bulbs, it was sometimes necessary, in making up a four, to make sure also that at least one of the four owned a light globe. Fortunately, these were pre-war light bulbs; they had been made more honestly than was to be the case not alone with bulbs but with almost everything of past-war manufacture. The bulbs which we secured in 1942 lasted most of us into 1945. So irreplaceable did they become that twice, when the filaments in my light broke, I spent hours tapping it with my finger until they caught again and fused. Had we been equipped with today's workmanship, we should have groped through the war in darkness.

Our bridge, too, was pre-war. Culbertson was our patron saint. The war was not quite long enough for us to absorb all the intricacies of his well-publicized system, but we gave his gilt-covered handbook the earnestness people once gave to their Bibles. Ely Culbertson helped us survive evenings whose tedium the Japanese diverted only once with a movie – and then got

311

the reels so mixed that the hero was clasping the heroine (George Raft and Carole Lombard) before the villain had done pursuing her.

A fixed part of our calendar was three family contests wherein my wife and I engaged weekly. These filled the nights between the perpetual tournament. Each was against another married couple, but the most prized was our weekly bout with Sidney and Blanche Burnett. Sidney's system was his own – flavoured with a dash of poker, a high spirited bravado, that made this rivalry gloriously competitive. Since we had kept a cumulative score from the beginning, we fought each point as though the war's issue depended on it.

In time I came to believe that it did. They were friendly engagements, and played out in Blanche's tiny cubicle at the hospital, where she worked. Every Tuesday, the wives in turn prepared some delicacy, cakes cooked from ersatz materials, pie with papaya rinds masquerading as apples, jelly roll concocted from rice flour, coffee that at least we could boast was both hot and wet, but the game was the thing. Through the days in between, Sidney and I looked forward to Tuesdays, and came keyed to outwit the other. Victory was sweet, defeat tragic.

During much of the war our scores see-sawed, but in the summer of 1944 the Burnetts amassed a formidable lead. I would come hopeful and go back to the barracks dejected. It was then, in grim fun, that I declared the Americans would not land until we were plus. As weeks wore on with no improvement, the jest turned to conviction. In a mood more serious than mocking I tried to persuade Sidney that it was his patriotic duty to let us win. What is more, I infected others with my belief. They began to hang the war's outcome on our play, waiting eagerly when we returned to our cubicles and hailing each Tuesday's failure with a groan.

Not till late September did we creep within measuring distance of our opponents, although there had been one time in August when Frances misplayed a doubled and redoubled grand slam vulnerable which would have put us ahead. I let her know in no minced terms what that play had done to history.

At last, early in October, we concluded a desperate battle +2. Throughout the ensuing days I waited for some sign of change, some hopeful rumour. Nothing happened. Scan the skies as we might, no portent of victory intruded on what had become a depressing calm. Downcast over the failure of my own private portents, I reviewed the last session's score and was about to give it up when, with abrupt excitement, I disclosed an error in my totals. We were not +2; no one was anything. Our score was tied at zero all, 0-0. The error had developed from a penalty against our opponents; without questioning it, I had written down Sidney's figures for the set, never dreaming that he would overpenalize himself, overpenalize himself by the +2 which had put us in the lead.

This reprieve, however, gave but temporary encouragement. In the next two weeks the Burnetts once again forged into the lead. But in the third week our luck turned. Every card favoured us; we could not hold a bad hand. By curfew time we had wiped out our opponents' commanding lead, and done even better: we had emerged +1. This time there was no mistake. I checked and double-checked our figures. As I recorded our victory in my diary, I added, "May the omen prosper."

Next morning, we were lining up for roll-call when a friend sidled up to me.

"Did you hear the news?" he asked.

"No, what news?"

"The Americans have landed in Leyte."

My diary now had a second entry: "The omen of the bridge score was magnificently propitious and dramatic in its fulfillment."

I could not write more lest by some chance I betray the secret of how we had learned about Leyte, for this news was no rumour. It came by accident. Up to the first appearance of American 'planes, the Japanese had for a year or more permitted sick people, whose treatment was beyond our diminished resources, to be taken to the Baguio General Hospital. There they were kept, supposedly isolated in a ward by themselves and cared for by their own physician, their own nurse. The arrangement was far from leak-proof; Filipino physicians on the hospital staff risked their own safety to slip furtive items of news to our own doctors. By October, the Japanese had cancelled this accommodation, but late in the month Jim Halsema came down so desperately ill with a liver abscess that Oura, the Commandant, was prevailed on to permit his transfer to Baguio. That same night, the night of our victory at the bridge table, Halsema's accompanying physician gleaned the momentous news. Except for Frances's messing up that redoubled grand slam, we might have shortened the war by two months!

Bridge was one way of seeking the illusion of freedom. The friendship that accompanied these games was no illusion; it was the real thing. It tested to the quick the values of an understanding acquaintance, tested them in a situation rubbed clean of the usual social gloss. Similarly our internment proved the realities that unite a family. Few modes of life could have lacked more devastatingly the graces on which a family thrives. Privacy did not exist. For three years we were assailed, day and night, by intrusive din; we had no home, no comforts, no certain future, yet it was a common experience that never were parents and children dearer to one another, more keenly warmed by the quiet, patient heroism which privation made richly evident.

For me and many others, our imprisonment tested and proved also the genuineness of our religious hope. When some of our priests first proposed a daily Mass, I was opposed, stubbornly convinced that this was not practicable, Fortunately, I was overruled. This half hour in the dark before dawn became the best part of each day, a moment of freedom snatched from eternity.

It did not matter whether our altar was a makeshift box or, as eventually the case, a *tampipi*, a wicker basket, draped with its fair linen cloth, in a Bilibid cell-block. It did not matter whether we were worshipping in a converted chicken-house, or in a drafty matshed that shook to every foot-step, or within the concrete walls and steel bar of the Bilibid cell. It was a time when all weariness fell away, even when we were most bitterly starved, unable to sit for five minutes without twisting to the discomfort of bones that cut through the skin, we still could kneel, unsupported, on that concrete Bilibid floor and forget the discomfort.

From my place beside the schoolhouse window I used to watch every morning the hills above Camp Holmes emerging from darkness, and the Japanese sentries striding to and fro along the ridge, their slouchy figures, their guns, their bayonets, black against the dawn. Yet they could not hem me in. Stronger in my sight were the two candles flickering on either side of the crucifix. Peace and refreshment came from the mystery invoked at the altar. I could fancy no other way to begin the day as happily.

The war had brought about a gradual sifting of things we counted important. At first, there had been worry over the home we left, the possessions which had occupied that home, placed long ago with intent and loving care where they could keep us daily company. By degrees our anxieties shifted. We worried about food, about hunger, and finally, in thoughts we hesitated to divulge, we worried over the prospect of an ultimate violence which we might not survive. But at Mass even these worries were drained of fear. We learned, haltingly perhaps, with lapses from the moment's courage, yet with ever more tranquil conviction, that whatever happened could not hurt us. Even death's claims were not final.

None of this should imply, of course, that we did not cling to life, cling to it eagerly and hopefully. It meant simply that our faith was not predicated on bodily survival: we were not staking our belief on a bargain with God.

The Camp's knack for carrying on life cheerfully no matter how attenuated made a distinct impression on the Japanese appointed to our custody, particularly to the Commandant of our middle period. This man, Rokuro Tomibe, I have mentioned for the fairness and justice he showed us. He evinced no shadow of the vindictive animosity that characterized the Harvard Ph.D, Mukaibo[64], nor was he given to our final commandant,

Oura's, unpredictable outbursts, alternations of insane fury and abject conciliation such as made us suspect tertiary syphilis.

On the morning when we were crowding around the trucks that were to take us to Manila, one man accidentally bumped Oura with the canteen he had slung on the end of a stick. Instant was Oura's wrath. Snatching the canteen, he slammed it to the ground. There it stayed. The owner scorned to pick it up, leaving it in mute accusation until the commandant himself picked it up and handed it back.

Oura's impatience flared gain at Bilibid when, in making the rounds of the prison courtyard, he was obstructed by hospital sheets hung on a rope to dry. With no concern for the toil that washing these sheets had required, toil protracted by hunger and Manila's sultry heat, he slashed the rope with his sword and let them fall to the cindery ground.

Tomibe was of different calibre, patient, sympathetic, greatly concerned that we not quarrel among ourselves but live up to our own best standards. He might have remained with us to the end except for the escape, in April 1944, of two men who skipped to join the guerrillas. They had good reason to do so, for they held reserve commissions in the Army[65], but whether they were right in doing so was debatable. The penalty fell not on them but on their friends, and on the whole Camp. Its infliction was removed from Tomibe's more lenient hands and administered by the Kempei-tai.

Japanese justice took no account of individuals. Little as the Camp could do to prevent any person's escaping if he chose, since it had but a token fence, a lightly strung barrier of barbed wire, it still was guilty in Japanese eyes. The Kempei-tai's special victims were the men who had lived nearest to the fugitives in the barracks' cramped quarters. They were taken to an apartment in Baguio and tortured, tortured by methods which, I was ashamed to discover from books in the Camp library, had been employed by American soldiers, forty years earlier, on Filipinos – "Gugus," they called them – taken prisoner during the Insurrection. This fact did not sweeten the torture.

Kempei-tai procedure made it almost as dangerous to be innocent as to be guilty. Whatever happened, the victim could not afford not to confess the things, usually trivial, which the police knew that he knew. Where to draw the line called for a nicety of judgement hard to preserve when one is strung up by the thumbs, with shoulder agonizingly dislocated from having stool or chair kicked out from beneath one's feet, and then beaten between each question, or burned with cigarettes. One man said, afterwards, that he would have confessed anything no matter how absurd, confessed to murdering his mother or assassinating the Japanese Emperor. From his suspended position he could see out the window, see people in the street halted and staring up aghast at the screams they heard. Who was screaming? he wondered, till it came over him that it was his own screams they were listening to.

The man who emerged from this ordeal least scathed was physically the weakest of the prisoners thus tortured. But he was the most alert, and confounded his inquisitors by talking so much, by rattling on at so garrulous a pace that the police were baffled. They could not sift fact from frenzy.

This resort to torture Tomibe had no power to prevent – there was always a bewildering conflict of authority between the several Japanese agencies – but he left no doubt of his disapproval. Without question, his intervention did keep the secret police from pushing their brutality to a fatal issue. He got the accused men back and seems to have restrained the Kempei-tai from embarking on wholesale savagery. After four or five men had been maltreated, this harrowing inquisition was dropped.

But we lost Tomibe. He was superseded as being too friendly to his captives. For some weeks, however, he stayed on while Oura was learning the ropes. During this equivocal tenure he mystified us by what must have been references to the first Battle of the Philippine Seas. This victory he hinted at to Miss McKim by quoting in French from Cyrano de Bergerac, a quotation he smilingly declined to repeat. It sent many of us scurrying around for copies of the play. All we could find was one scene in a bound volume of the Golden book. An English translation, it gave us, alas, no clue!

So cordial was our respect for Mr. Tomibe that, when he departed, the Camp lined up to cheer him. Long after the war, a letter of his, written to one of his former prisoners, bore his own tribute to Camp Holmes.

"It was the first time," he wrote, "when I came to that camp that I became contact with American people."

"In my idea of the United States and her people, to say in a word, they had been a hedonistic people who are sometimes dogmatic and selfish, just as characters I used to see in movies of Hollywood monopolizing the world wealth in the most favoured land. It was not until I had my living with them that I noticed my idea was wrong and at the same time I learned many things. The chief items of which are as follows.

1.   Collective life, organization and its management.
2.   Education and aspiration.
3.   Fusion of religion into life.
4.   Combination of labour with machinery.
5.   Food life.
6.   Courtesy and order.
7.   Health and sanitation, etc.

316

"But the matter with which I was most impressed was your belief in your victory with which five hundred persons were united as if they had been members of a family. In truth they had a harmonious living. This was, of course, due to the strenuous efforts of the Committee which I appreciated very much but all internees' action under their directions were also worthy of applause. It is a fact that it is not in one's best days that a man's real value is displayed but in diversity. In this sense it is a matter for admiration that you had a living of perfect order and peace under such unfavourable circumstances…"

He in turn had been a prisoner of war and, we were thankful to hear, exonerated in the war crimes trials by the testimony of his American captives. The spirit he showed in meeting his own time of adversity is best described in his own words.

"Ten months have elapsed since I became POW and as a prisoner, now I have an indescribable feeling when I compare our present life with your internment life. Nowadays we are having a peace and composed life but there had been much confusion before we recovered our normal state of mind. For sometime after our surrender I was also afloat on the same waves of confusion.

"Incessant bombings, mortars' or tanks' howling, unbearably hard life in the hills, comrades' faces who died of Malaria or starvation and shouts of insult we suffered of both Philippine soldiers and civilians, all these things occurred to me successively like nightmares which drove me into almost desperate state of mind. It was at the beginning of November last year after a short time since my having been captured that our daily ration was only 0.4 pound of rice per man a day, which may have been due to the transportation and fractuation of number of men interned. Under these circumstances it was so hard for us POWs to move; we felt dizziness even to stand up that there were many troubles with food. There were some who were so radical as to raid kitchens, when I plunged myself into the mob, shouting to them with tears 'Our home country lost in the war, we lost our weapons and hoisted a white flag. But we never have cast justice and virtue we should observe. What is this starvation? What is such hardship? We must not lose nobility to endure any adversity without mental perturbation…' When I said as far as this point I felt keenly our defeat and at the same time I regained the way to live on…"

Men like Rokuro Tomibe ameliorate the wasteful hatred of war. They give hope that man may yet find strength in an understanding truer to the real genius of humanity than the distorted differences which from caveman days have bequeathed the impulse to hate and to kill all persons of strange tongue and alien skin. Most assuredly, our acquaintance with Tomibe helped promote that renewed affection for Japan which came quite swiftly and naturally after the war even to those like ourselves who had suffered the corroding bitterness of that conflict. Tomibe's home in Kyoto became an object of pilgrimage to many from our Camp, and all who visited him came away with hearts grateful for his hospitality and warmed by heightened respect for a true gentleman. They rejoiced that in Japan's regained prosperity he too was flourishing[66].

* * * * * * * *

Tomibe was not the only Japanese patriotically dedicated to his country's cause yet determined to deal fairly with his enemy prisoners. These examples of good treatment I am taking pains to stress because the opposite, the savagery of the Bataan Death March, the callous cruelty of O'Donnell and Cabanatuan, of the hell-ships whose stifling holds our men were crammed or a voyage to Japan that for many ended in death by bomb or torpedo or by a crazed struggle to escape suffocation, these have been fixed in public memory.

Perhaps some of what the military prisoners suffered can be explained by the Japanese attitude toward surrender. Until late in the war, the Japanese military mind made no allowance for the soldier who laid down his arms. He was beyond the pale, an outcaste, a man without a country. That we should think differently they could not imagine. If a soldier could not die fighting, by their code, he must kill himself. Never must he submit.

From civilians observance of this code was not expected. If they were subjected to atrocities, as seems to have happened in Borneo and the Dutch Indies and Malaya, their ill-treatment probably should be blamed on the capricious tyranny of the Japanese officers put over them. In every war, prison camps breed atrocities. They did so between our own Americans of North and South, men of like race, like speech, like habits, in the War Between the States. War puts over their fellows men unfit for this authority, hateful, sadistic, inflamed by their power to inflict pain. Of such men Japan supplied her share, but in Camp Holmes, while we had some of this type, we had other who resisted the prying suspicions of the Kempei-tai to uphold our security from injustice. Theirs was no easy task. So divided was Japanese authority, so many were the cliques intriguing against each other and ready to denounce any fair-minded officer as "soft," that the latter was hard pressed to withstand inter-service jealousies, let alone seeking to feed prisoners in a hostile country with money which the American advance was reducing to worthless paper.

In the war's ebbing months our only persistent enemy was Oura. Our contact with his subordinates grew strangely friendly. The composition of our guard had changed; the old line regulars of the Imperial Army had been called to the battle lines, their place taken by reservists. Our dealing, however, were not with guards any longer but with a staff that seemed more civilian than military. One such was Masaki, whose father was a general described by Gunther as "dangerous." Masaki minced no words about our treatment calling it stupid. In the first World War his father had commanded an internment camp for the Germans seized at Tsingtao. The younger Masaki took pride in showing us a photograph of the Christmas dinner with which the Japanese had feasted their prisoner. Enviously we looked at the lucky Germans gorging themselves on turkey. We had blundered into the wrong war.

Masaki tried to atone for our privations. He brought letters from friends at Los Baños. He cheered us by news of the American landing at Lingayen. He seemed disappointed by our setback at the Battle of the Bulge.

Still more practical was the help given us by the supply sergeant Sugano. Completely won over by his respect for Miss McKim, he made bold to disobey Oura's orders – this after our transfer to Manila – and smuggled in rations far in excess of the starvation diet which the Commandant had enjoined. That he was risking trouble was patent from his request that the Committee not publicize the amount of food we were receiving, supplies that brought us for the first time the concentrated nourishment of soy beans. Almost gleeful was his comment when making his final delivery: this, he said, should last us.

These men appeared eager to see the war end, even if it cost them defeat. Others we came to admire by an astonishing reversal of the dislike, the better resentment, we first harboured against them. Such a man was Major Sakashita, final commander of the guard. To have a major, where once we had had corporals or sergeants, controlling the troops marked real improvement in our status. Sakashita was all soldier, brusque, punctilious, efficient. Though he took no step to curry favour, he proved exceptional in that what he promised he performed. If he had guaranteed us certain rights, he was prompt to punish any underling foolhardy enough to violate these rights.

The most intriguing character, however, was the interpreter, Yamato. For months we loathed him. Strutting up and down at roll-call with the perkiness of a cock-sparrow, Yamato was the butt of much muttered obscenities. His English was as pompously absurd as his parade ground strut.

Even before his arrival, the bulletin board often entertained us.

"As your life is not a detective novel," one notice read, "of course, you must not intend to communicate with outsiders without being examined, don't have interest in trying your chance. If you continue doing such unlawful acts, we have to become more strict, which you would not prefer and it is just the same on our side."

Yamato's style was more individual. After promising that our interrupted subscriptions to the Manila Tribune would be resumed except when the news was "bad" – he did not say "bad" for whom – he notified us in June 1944 that no further issues would be forthcoming; he did not wish us "concerned about social occurrences outside." He wanted to make us, he wrote further, "an exemplary camp." His thoughtfulness was wasted. Rocketing prices were evidence enough of occurrences which he might have labelled "anti-social!"

Quite plainly the occurrences were continuing.

"Time changed the circumstances," he advised us, two months later. "We must realize the cold fact of emergency," and went on to a stern warning. "Bear in mind, please, that we must not for ever stand still in the status quo ante….To revise the loose manner of consumptive living you must realize the real purport of the Camp Store…"

With the little the Camp Store then had to offer, it was growing impossible for us to realize that it had any purport, but we solemnly accepted his peroration,

"These all we say not for ourselves but for your food's sake in this pressing time of emergency."

We responded by a plausible show of skinning our hillsides of grass, aware though we were that the camotes we planted never would be harvested.

Yamato was fond of what he called "clarifying statements" which, far from clarifying, actually muddied our relations with Oura and with Major Sakashita. As official interpreter he insisted on doing what Miss McKim could have done a hundred times better. Reasons of "face" would not let him admit this. But occasionally he could cite chapter and verse for interpretations which the ambivalence of the English language hid from our understanding.

Such was the case in a colloquy with our chairman when the latter asked permission to go up the hill to "check" the water supply.

"You mean there is too much water?" he asked.

"No, the water is very low; I want permission to check the pipe line."

Out came Yamato's dictionary. Moistening his fingers, he thumbed the pages till with a triumphant smile he pointed to the disputed word.

"But check," he indicated. "That means to stop. You wish to stop the water."

"No, we want to see if there are any leaks."

"Ah-h!" Light broke. Exultantly Yamato sucked in his breath. "Ah-h, you wish to <u>examine</u> the pipe."

"Yes," sighed the chairman, "we want to examine the pipe."

More inhalations, and then,

"Ah-h, I must ask the Commandant. I fear he will not give permission because the ro-caw condition is very bad."

"But what does roll-call have to do with the pipe-line?"

"Ah, the ro-caw condition is no good. There are many guerrillas. Perhaps it is very dangerous."

Now the chairman, too, saw light.

"Oh, you mean the local conditions!"

"Yes, the ro-caw conditions – I will ask the Commandant."

A Hallowe'en party taught me to see much more than the ludicrous in Yamato. This party, given for the children, he attended as censor. It was hardly a party to brag about, but the children and some adults made as brave a show as possible, decking themselves with what odds and ends of finery they still had left. Refreshments were meagre. For prizes the youngsters were given cigarettes, a premium the Master of Ceremonies advised them not to scorn, since by October these had become the Camp's most stable currency.

What intrigued Mr. Yamato most was the kimonos worn by several girls, my own daughter among them. Warmly he spoke of an American magnanimity generous enough to costume their children in enemy dress. I withheld comment, accepting the compliment rather than explain that the girls were wearing kimonos because these were the easiest to improvise.

His remark, however, had started us both off in so cordial a vein that we talked until time for the party to disband. For the first time, I perceived Yamato's fine dignity as a man. He was from Kyoto, a city I loved. Familiar scenes came to our lips the Kamogawa rippling brightly over the long streamers of cotton cloth stretched beneath its swift, transparent current so that the green, red, blue, orange dyes of their gay patterns might set, the cedar floors of the Chion-in, the nightingale floors, creaking birdlike music under the pilgrim feet which through centuries had polished their boards glossy black, the crown of temples on the city's surrounding hills, shining crimson in the sunlight, vanishing in misty rain.

"I found much that was very appealing in this talk," I wrote in my diary, " a sense of cordial good will toward Mr. Yamato himself, who impressed me as a very lonely soul, grieving (though he did not mention it) for a son killed in action and anxious for the well-being of his family in Kyoto. Acquaintance dispels anger; I felt sorely impatient at this divisive tragedy of war which brings only cruelty, destruction and hatred in its train and mars so much beauty, beauty of man's building, beauty in the human spirit. It was ghastly to think of no better solution to this conflict than the laying of waste of so fair and lovely a country as Japan, but even worse that laying waste of understanding between peoples now enemies which, if properly developed, could have made the whole world a place fair to live in. Mr. Yamato and I parted in a mood of genuine friendliness; I was much touched by his farewell words to Frances, "I thank you for your husband.'"

Not long afterward, Mr. Yamato appeared at the office, his eye blackened, his face bruised. The Commandant, whose devious authority he had tried always to uphold, had repaid this loyalty by knocking him down.

For a brief moment Yamato forgot his official decorum. He measured his job of interpreter by a new scale.

"When I go back to Japan after the war," he announced, "I will tell them about this militarism."

But for him there was to be no "after the war."

* * * * * * * *

The night after Christmas 1944, we learned, as abruptly as our guardians, that Camp Holmes was ended. It had been a tranquil Christmas, warm and sunny. For days the Kitchen gang had skimped to give us a double portion of rice for breakfast, with sugar, coffee, a banana, and for the rice the unwonted luxury of syrup. Many of us even had milk on our rice. This had been given by Andrew Chicay, a Filipino friend, who added to his three years' record of generous kindness not only this milk but a whole cow. Although the guard appropriated one shoulder, there was meat enough to feast us one last time with hamburgers; this, with a further festival helping of rice and candied camotes, and with "submarined" coffee, made dinner – as I wrote – both "ample and appetizing." To quote my diary further, "It was the first day in weeks that I have not been hungry. . .Late in the evening, with (friends) we enjoyed coffee on the parade ground, getting pleasure from the Christmas trees and the moon and relaxing to the contentment of well-filled bellies…"

Next night all was chaos, the Camp turned to bedlam. Lights were left shining until midnight; after they were turned out, darkness still did not extinguish the hubbub, as men tore to pieces the quarters to which, during three long years, they had devoted tireless ingenuity, eking out meagre materials to make them habitable.

I, for one, could not watch this happy vandalism without qualms. Almost reluctantly I roused to the fact that I could not shelter myself longer within the slowly acquired amenities of our little cubicle. It represented a degree of progress wordlessly gratifying when I contrasted it with the elbow-to-elbow promiscuity into which we had been dumped, thirty-three months before – the aching discomfort of those first weeks, without bed or table, chair or light. Within its modicum of privacy, my ears shut to adjacent babble. I had contrived to focus my mind on blessed hours of study, on preparing classes I looked forward to, day after day. I take naturally to ruts. Even the recognition that this existence must be shattered before we again could be free could not ease the pangs of seeing it ripped apart.

Just how we were to be freed we dared not guess. After three years' stagnancy, merely to be moving inspired hopefulness. I cannot recall that any of us was perturbed by the possibility of such worse moves as the removal to Japan that snuffed out in hell-ships the lives of many military prisoners. Our Japanese staff themselves backed up our optimism and seemed to relish our prospect of release. Yamato, in first breaking the news, said that we were being concentrated near the coast by request of the American government; our repatriation might come in a few days. Others admitted that MacArthur had landed, quite unexpectedly, on Mindoro, an ideal springboard for leaping the Verde Island Passage and staging a short, quick advance on Manila. What became ever more certain was that we were destined first for Bilibid. In the ponderous concrete hospital, erected long ago by the Americans as an annex to the old Spanish prison, we were to be quartered, so we heard, until ships could take us home.

Bilibid was no name to conjure with. We had gleaned echoes of what American prisoners had suffered there, but all this, our informants assured us, belonged to the past: Major Watterous, in pre-war days an eye-specialist known to many of us, had cleaned out the place, made it habitable. His reputation for getting things done left no room for further doubt.

Everything which the Japanese divulged was true – to a point. What they knew, they told us. Negotiations indeed were in progress for turning over Manila, and our transfer was part of the arrangement, all to be consummated in early January. To this the Japanese high command had agreed. Having lost too many men already in last ditch combat, they did not wish their Philippine-based forces trapped in defending an outworn capital. But in their system interservice rivalry went to cut-throat lengths. The Army might propose; their Marines disposed. Let the Army clear out, they taunted; they would stay, stay to die and in the revered Nippon tradition make certain that their foes died with them. None of this did we or our Japanese staff anticipate.

For the transfer to Manila we were divided into two groups. My family and I were in the first, picked to depart on the morning of the 28th, less than thirty-six hours from our initial warning. For the three hundred of us fourteen small trucks were provided. Since each truck had to carry five or six guards, heavily accoutered with guns and grenades that jabbed us at inconvenient angles we had no room for more than a suit-case apiece. The day before, the Camp's butcher detail had slaughtered what was left of our livestock, and our cooks had worked around the clock preparing meat, chicken, rice to allow each of us a packet of cold food. All bedding, except blankets, we had been ordered to discard; Japanese buyers thronged the Camp, but many of us had kept pads or mattresses for one last night's sleep, deeming this more valuable than the cup or two of coffee which was the most their sale would purchase. One camp-cot I did squeeze into our truck. The rest of our belongings we left behind, packed in standpipes which the Japanese assured us would follow in a day or two – a promise none of us put much faith in.

Tightly jammed though we were, with only suit-cases or blanket-rolls to sit on, we departed in gala spirits. Baguio, its streets seedy and overgrown, quickened our interest; we gaped at the concrete pill-boxes guarding every turn of the spectacular zigzag descent to the plains. In the morning sunshine, which spread before our eyes the golden promise of a world so long shut off from our narrowed vision, we felt already free. Worriesome moments came only when our convoy, instead of pursing the Manila road, turned off to Rosario, a seaport on the Lingayen Gulf. The diversion was ominous. Were we to be shipped, after all, to Japan?

If such was the Japanese purpose, American submarines had vetoed it by sinking already the ships that might have taken us. More likely, our side-trip was what the American Army labelled "snafu." Before we could grow too perturbed over being stalled in a town wholly absorbed by measures to resist invasion, our convoy turned around and rejoined the Manila road.

All day we stemmed the current of an army on the move, an army in strategic retreat. Just as they had commandeered Rosario's houses, Japanese soldiers had overflowed the country-side. Their guns bristled from every farm-house; their cannon were hidden under haystacks. In the narrow road, bumpy with pot-holes, our trucks were swept continually by the leafy camouflage that protruded from oncoming vehicles. We were making jolty headway against an itinerant forest, a river of greenery stemming our progress mile after mile, a mechanized Birnam Wood that dwindled Macbeth's baneful portent to a straggle of shrubs.

Yet it was not all mechanized. Many field pieces were being dragged by horses, still more by Japanese soldiers. Even the carretela, the Philippine cart of all trades, depended on man's strength as often as on horse's. Its passengers and freight were jammed in bowers of waving bamboo. Some soldiers were walking Christmas trees; from head to foot they were hung with nets so thickly interthrust with bamboo branches that the man barely could be seen within his verdant tent.

At noon our little convoy paused from bucking this endless tide. In the drowsy provincial town of Binalonan we halted. Our selves and baggage were strung along the edge of a weed-ragged plaza, across which stood the Spanish church typical of these towns, its squat walls adobe, its roof rust-streaked iron. But the church porch, we noted, was piled to the ceiling with boxes of ammunition.

During our Binalonan stay I came near being thrust into premature freedom. Dressed in what seemed the most convenient costume for this journey, a dirty white cassock and an equally soiled sun-helmet, I was wandering down the line to talk to friends from other trucks when some guards began haranguing me to be gone. Not till we had rounded up an English-speaking member of the staff was their anger explained. They had mistaken me for a Spanish padre and accused me of mingling unlawfully with their prisoners.

By the time we resumed our journey we were sick of Binalonan. It had been pleasant at first to rest on the parched grass and to eat our portions of chicken and cold rice. But two hours in the noon sun was enough. When we learned, however, that instead of the fourteen trucks, barely sufficient to bring us from Camp Holmes, we now were to have but nine, we were sicker yet.

This reduction necessitated leaving most of our baggage by the roadside. Yamato's announcement that it would be brought the next day and that for anything lost we should be compensated by the Imperial government evoked jeering laughter. Those ultimate dregs of our possessions were valuable only for their immediate usefulness. For that they were priceless, but their intrinsic value, in terms of post-war compensation, was small change not even worth totalling.

Greatly depressed, we had just squeezed into our new conveyance when we were turned out again. Major Sakashita had second thoughts. A few metres down the road he commandeered a shed; here he had us transfer our whole dispersed straggle of baggage, and even put his soldiers to work helping us, a job they did with surprising good will. So effectively did he secure the stuff that, against all expectations, it did catch up with us, two days later, and so saved the Imperial Government from calculating compensation – which, if it followed the generous alacrity of our own Government, might perhaps have been doled out to us in devalued currency by the year 1990.

No ride can I recall to match the excruciating discomfort of the hours that ensued. So tightly were we wedged into our diminutive truck that we could not move so much as a cramped foot without getting our neighbours

325

to make squirming adjustment. To untwist an arm required a plebiscite. We did stop once or twice for bodily relief, which was more than had been allowed during the morning trip, when men suffering from dysentery had been compelled to relieve themselves by squatting over the tail-gate of the plunging truck. Long since, we had discarded all niceties; the roadside was our latrine. Embarrassment over such matters was a trifle compared with the protracted torture of the ride itself.

Hour upon hour we jolted forward over a road quite obviously unrepaired since before the war. Our spirits sank too low for us to joke about our misery. No longer jeering, we bounced across pot-holes as our drivers, reckless enough to have been recruited from Tokyo taxis, scraped the oncoming traffic and, once, knocked down a carretela, horse and all, down an embankment. We did not have room even to extricate the packets of rice and chicken we had saved for supper.

The few airplanes we saw brought, of course, their own anxiety. Fortunately, none were American[67]. They could not have ignored a target so inviting as was offered by these crowded roads. If darkness lessened our hazard from the sky, it made the hazards of the road loom up monstrous and precipitate, for our convoy, like the traffic bearing down on us, was proceeding without lights. Only our lead-car would flash on lights briefly to indicate our approach. The moon we had counted on soon disappeared behind clouds, and the clouds chilled us with spurts of drizzling rain.

Dark and silent cowered the countryside. Its moribund state weighed still more heavily on our dampened courage when, long after midnight, we began winding through Manila's vacant streets. Behind bolted doors, tight-shut windows, the city cringed. Mile on mile, shut in by adobe walls that reverberated to our clatter, we rumbled along till time lost all meaning. We even had grown used to the aching numbness of postures we could not change.

Somewhere near two we passed through Bilibid's dismal gate. Section after section of this mediaeval prison we traversed, halting at each inner barrier until at last we stopped outside the entrance to our quarters, Bilibid's abandoned hospital. A ponderous three-storied structure, this was America's only addition to the old Spanish penitentiary. It had been erected early in the century when concrete construction called for walls five feet thick. Whether the top story had been bombed, or partially dismantled before the war, we could not determine. In the dim light its great empty-faced windows gaped like entrances to a huge black cavern, and cavernous indeed were the vast dark halls into which we lugged our blankets.

Dark though it was, one dismaying fact was immediately evident. The renovation we had heard about was a myth. All we could find to alleviate

326

bedding down on the concrete floor was a heap of mattresses. Prudence warned us to leave these mattresses alone, but we were too tired to care. For people as thin as we were, hip-bones do not adjust even tolerably to a concrete floor. Like everybody else I dragged out a mattress, propped up a suit-case at my head to keep my mosquito net out of my face, and collapsed into a sleep bombs could not have disturbed.

* * * * * * * *

Daylight showed how foolish we had been to yield to the temptation of the mattresses. From the seams of my net we evicted more than fifty bed-bugs. They were in our blankets, lurking in Frances's camp-cot, whole colonies, round, brown disks bloated from their nights' feeding and smelling sickish sweet, like castor oil, when we squashed them.

This, the Camp's first contact with vermin, cried for action. As yet we had no quorum for a Committee meeting. Several members were not due from Camp Holmes until the next day. The best I could get from the one doctor in our contingent was a recommendation that the mattresses be thrown out. This I transformed into an order and, with the willing, effective help of another committeeman, my Roman colleague, Father Sheridan, organized active parties to persuade or cajole our fellow prisoners to get rid of their mattresses. Although a few grumbled, we pushed this disposal with such brisk momentum that people soon were hurling their mattresses out the windows. Our plan had been to burn them; this the Japanese spared us by appropriating them for their own use.

It was too late, of course, to rid ourselves of bugs, but we kept them within manageable limits. Some mornings, I would find four or five in my net, some days, none. What had worried me most was the prospect of lice, the haunting threat of typhus remembered from famine relief in China. How we escaped this plague still puzzles me, but escape it we did. Though we had scorned the mattresses, we did make use of the bunks, many of them double-deckers, scattered through the halls. They were crudely made, pieced out of whatever odds and ends of hardwood the prison's former occupants, veterans of Bataan and Corregidor,[68] could lay their hands on. In cracks and nail-holes they too harboured vermin, but in numbers we could deal with. Their boards, at least, were softer than the floor.

Our predecessors at Bilibid had left us, we soon found, infinitely more poignant mementoes of their tenancy than their crude furniture or their verminous mattresses. Up and down the grey murky walls they had scratched hundreds of names, their own, together with names and addresses of relatives and friends whom they begged some future reader to notify of their presence

327

at Bilibid, or more ominously, of their removal to Japan. We could feel too the merciless tedium of a confinement much worse than ours, for we saw the calendars some had scratched to keep track of days and months and years whose monotony threatened to obliterate all distinctions of time.

Outburst of angry bitterness and despair also were recorded, none more disturbing than one inscription which spoke out with literate eloquence: "Words cannot fully express nor can the mind conceive the trials, hardships and tortures we have endured at the hands of the Japanese. We are broken mentally, physically and spiritually by a nation of perverts (the Japs). We leave it to you incomers to wreak our vengeance." Another anonymous writer more succinctly god-damned his own Army, Navy, and Marine Corps.[69]

For many of these men these inscriptions were a last utterance. Hundreds of the died in the fatal attempt to ship them to Japan. At Bilibid, however, in the next section to ours, still remained several hundred military prisoners, men too sick to be taken to the transports. From a second floor balcony we could see them pacing their yard but, except for some furtive attempts at communication, they and we lived rigidly apart.

In our midst, however, were the graves of men whose final horizon was the tall, wire-topped wall that enclosed us. My count of these graves never was twice the same; my highest total was 165; others counted 180. Each grave had its cross, a few marked with the Star of David; in the centre stood a larger cross inscribed with the four meaningful initials, I.N.R.I. Who made these crosses I do not know; all were exactly alike and of finished workmanship. Around them clustered huge cannas, yellow and red, the cannas which brighten even hovels in Manila as they brightened Bilibid's barren, cindery courtyard, But at nights rats as big as rabbits prowled these tragic graves.

Little time, nevertheless, did we commiserate with the dead. Our own prospects offered small ground for the hopefulness that had spurred our departure for Manila. Compared with Bilibid we remembered Camp Holmes as a palace. In the vast, vacant wards each family squatted where it could. Our own first roosting place was within an entanglement of steel rods evidently dumped through an upstairs hall when war halted the demolition of this obsolete prison. Such accommodations were only temporary until the committee could assign space in an arrangement less helter-skelter. Eventually, we took up room in a ward and proceeded, like everybody else, to knock out the sheets of galvanized iron wherewith the Japanese had sealed the tall windows.

The change gave us not only light and air but an intriguing view of a side street almost beneath us, and a more distant view of Quezon Boulevard. We could see people at their doorsteps and note the absence of taxis, *carretelas*, ox-carts, all the variegated traffic that used to clog Manila's narrow streets.

Once again the Camp displayed its resourcefulness in meeting exigencies that should have daunted, above all people, the supposedly luxury–loving American. Little privacy did the promiscuous tenancy of these wards allow, nothing but the protection of a few ramshackle double-deckers, yet somehow men, women, and children managed to group themselves into cubicles, and to dress and undress without any sense of being conspicuous. Dressing and undressing, of course, were not complicated; in Manila's climate, shorts were garb enough for the men, shorts and brassiere for many of the women. Often I ruminated, after this continuous exposure to the female torso, how romantically provocative it would be to see women wearing blouse and skirt. Strip without tease becomes insufferably dull.

In our state of near-starvation it is doubtful whether the most glamourously erotic of strip-teases would have excited more than a moment's glance. During our last months at Camp Holmes we had been losing weight at a steady pace, four or five pounds a month. In Bilibid the pace was accelerated; each day we felt weaker as we wasted to gaunt, loose skinned skeletons. So sapped of energy that we halted between each step of our long journey to the outdoor latrines, and faltered for minutes debating whether it were worth the effort to tie a loosened shoe-lace.

So thin were we that to sit in any position soon became torture. Yet sit we had to, sit for the two hours at a time waiting the afternoon's dole of rice. Our tail-bones cut through what little flesh we had left. In the evenings we sometimes sat propped against a buttress of the walls, but even the pillows we took out to sit on could not relieve for long the acute, cutting discomfort of our bones.

Our rations had been reduced to rice, and for a few days even the rice failed us. We had to be grateful for a tablespoonful of mouldy corn-meal at breakfast, another spoonful at dinner. After nearly a week without vegetables the doctors gave the Camp permission to pick the leaves of talinum, an innocuous plant, little better than a weed, which Bilibid's earlier tenants had bequeathed us. Within the hour the plants were stripped bare. One evening, when we were fortunate enough to get *camotes*, Frances spilled our allotment while trying to shield her plate from pouring rain. By good luck there were seconds enough for her to obtain another portion, but she did not stop content with this. Out she went into to the darkness and scraped up from the cinders the fragments she had dropped.

If things had continued thus, few of us would have lived to be rescued. That we survived should be credited, in large part, to the Japanese supply sergeant Sugano whose stealthy enhancement of our provisions I have mentioned. He slipped in stocks of food well above the seven hundred caloric limit which Oura had enjoined. Aside from procuring rice when worm-eaten

329

corn-meal seemed all we could hope for he went on to flavouring it with soy-bean residue, the scraping of pots in which soy-beans had been cooked, and even overwhelmed us with the soy-beans themselves – diet too rich for our undertaxed stomachs.

They were part of supplies which, he told Miss McKim, should last a month, and then added, with a smile, "I think that will be long enough."

His prediction that these supplies would last long enough was timed accurately; we were cooking a mess of soy-beans on the night the Americans invaded Manila.

For weeks we had heard and even seen the war coming nearer. On the 6th of January, feast of the Epiphany, I was saying Mass within our iron-barred chapel. I had just reached the Preface to the Sanctus, "Therefore with angels and archangels and with all the company of heaven," when a thunderous rumble of exploding shells outvoiced our liturgy. Squadrons of B-24's had begun dumping their formidable cargo.

Every morning thy came over, thirty, forty, sixty, seventy of these great 'planes, maneuvering with an imperturbable dignity that reminded me of the fleets of Spanish galleons I had seen carved in colourfully painted wooden panels in old churches. Through the brown puffs of flak, of anti-aircraft gunfire, they wheeled, never faltering, never quickening their majestic pace. The Japanese sent up no 'planes to oppose them; their own 'planes, like their fields, were torn wrecks. Only once did we see their gunfire from the ground find a mark.

A single chance shot struck a Liberator. Breathless we watched as flames began to crawl and curl along its giant wings. As the fire broadened, the 'plane pulled out of line. One by one its crew took to parachutes. In horror we saw the first 'chute plummet to earth without opening, another catch fire and plunge its victim to his death. Other men were luckier and floated safely down, although a rumour spread unchecked that these men escaped only to be slaughtered when they landed.

This one casualty, out of the hundreds of American 'planes we watched make their deadly assaults unscathed, sobered us all. Some in our camp had forgotten that the game was "for keeps." Sentimental inmates soon had shaped a legend to complete this tragedy. It happened, next day, that two squadrons were wheeling one above the other in what these spectators declared was a cross – from which the more imaginative saw a wreath dropped. Two months later, on our way home, we met men of the 5th Airborne who had flown with these squadrons. Highly amused were they at anyone's fancying that they had time to drop wreaths over each fallen 'plane. The truth was that one squadron had arrived ahead of schedule and was maneuvering frantically to avoid collision with the other. So much for a pretty story!

Still more spectacular were the light 'planes. These we could see at closer quarters as they dived upon their targets. Recklessly they swooped, spouting flames from a forward cannon and so nearly overtaking the bombs they dropped that their wings fluttered from the concussion. Behind the house-tops we would lose them, and wait fearfully until up they soared, graceful and deadly.

Manila by now was seething with oil-fires, with huge molten bubbles rolling skyward cradled in sulphurous smoke. Night and day, far and near, explosions shocked our ear-drums, much of this destruction evidently done by the Japanese themselves. Not till dusk did they put any 'planes into the air, but one night early in January they slashed the sky with searchlight beams, the only drill of its kind we saw, and done for what purpose we could not determine. This display they did not repeat; by dawn they had dismantled the searchlights and removed them. Across the street from Bilibid one of these lights had been concealed inside a dwelling. No sooner had the Japanese removed it than looters poured in and stripped the place bare, carrying off every stick of lumber they could get their hands on.

Despite these signs of enemy withdrawal our mood shuttled between hope and fear. Masaki had given us word that MacArthur had come ashore from the Gulf of Lingayen, the same coast where the Japanese had landed in force three years before. To this news Yamato later added his characteristic bit: the Americans were advancing slowly because – as he put it – they were "protecting their behind." Cheered as we were by this information, in some minds still lurked dismal conjectures that Manila might be by-passed, that the Luzon landings might be only a side issue, a detention of Japanese forces while MacArthur's chief offensive pushed on to China.

Over these malign possibilities I tortured myself unreasonably. My pessimism was not shared by most of my colleagues on the Committee. They seemed to me almost fatuously optimistic over the certainty of our release, and they devoted one meeting to a rash of plans, plans for making contact with the Swedish Consul, for issuing passes, and deciding who should, and should not, go out, all flagrantly assuming that the turnover would be smooth and peaceful.

To this assumption I objected: Manila was an Oriental city, and my experience of Oriental cities led me to believe that the turnover was more likely to be violent. I urged that we prepare for fire, even prepare for rampaging soldiery. When the Committee's minutes were posted, several people took me to task for needlessly frightening the Camp. In the upshot, my predictions came nearer the facts. We soon forgot about calling the Swedish Consul.

Yet January had its spells of strange calm. Each morning, first collecting a can of hot water from the Kitchen, we could make soluble coffee and drink it slowly in the pre-dawn coolness of the roof while we saw daylight gathering slowly and all too tranquilly behind the eastern mountains. They were hours pleasantly meditative, strangely peaceful.

On two nights, also, I took my turn at the gate, where our "bull-squad" was keeping watch lest any nocturnal crisis catch us by surprise. These midnight hours at the gate were so quiet that it was hard to believe we were surrounded by the homes, the living, breathing inhabitants, of a great city. From a far distance I could hear Japanese voices, and faint noises as if men were loading a truck. Even this chattering sounded unreal, the drowsy hubbub of a dream. There were no detonations to shatter the trance. The stillness depressed me; the war seemed to have passed on, and forgotten us.

During these weeks our Japanese staff had grown lackadaisical. Much of the time they left us to conduct our own roll-call. Having lost their own list in the removal from Camp Holmes, they were dependent on ours. On one night only did they feel compelled to call their own roll: something, a rat, perhaps, had tripped the wire on the wall top and set off an alarm.

Since Bilibid was without lights, our keepers had first to borrow from one of their prisoners the only electric torch still equipped with batteries that functioned. Before they could get this torch, they had to rouse the committee's chairman and, through his help, locate the man who had the flashlight. This took much groping through sepulchral darkness till, accompanying the chairman, the guards could pause before each ward while he read the names of its supposed occupants. Ludicrously the formula was followed. Out of the blackness voices would respond, but no attempt was made, or could be made, to ascertain who was answering. All these futile proceedings accomplished were to expose the poverty of an army no longer able to supply its soldiers with equipment as rudimentary as a flashlight, and the breakdown of its knowledgeable control over our movements.

Yet we were still prisoners, impatient of any pause in the workings of our release, any decline into routine, however slipshod. The daytime bombings continued. Never did we conceive the slightest fear that the bombs might drop on us. But the now familiar sight of American 'planes, of the white star circled on their wings, no longer satisfied us. We could not be rescued from the air. What we longed to hear was the reverberation of American guns.

They came at last, distant booming to the southwest, the unmistakable tongues of heavy artillery. For an hour or two they would resound, prompting excited guesses as to the American strategy. Oddly, we did not look for relief from Lingayen, even though we knew that landings had been made there. We were set in stubborn conviction that these were feints to pull the Japanese forces north. Our hopes still were turned to Mindoro and the Verde Island Passage. When the guards called the gunfire a guerrilla attack – "bandit" was the word they used – we shrugged off their explanation. But they were right. The gunfire came no nearer; it swung off to the east and appeared to dwindle. Our hopes fell.

Yet at this low moment things began to move. Before we really were aware of it, lulled dismally by more quiet nights, the war at last was snatching us up in a momentum we had been disappointed too many times to credit. Gunfire accelerated its tempo till it was audible from all directions, even in daytime. The Japanese, who often amazed us by the care they took to do things almost comical in their inappropriateness, had brought in, of all things, a piano to make noisier halls which I already had described as the "sounding board of pandemonium." That any artillery could out-boom this tumult showed how near the fighting had approached.

Demolition too had quickened, tearing the air ragged, night and day, by violent detonations. What particularly primed our curiosity were the crowds we could see massed on the roof of the Great Eastern Hotel[70]. We had to imagine what they were looking at, what they were waiting for, but their excitement spurred ours. Confident we now were that we would not be by-passed. No one gave thought to the sobering perils of the ordeal so soon to engulf us. We were ready, hopeful, in a mood to which one small boy gave vent by scraping on the prison's mildewed wall the dots and dashes of "V for victory." Vainly the Formosan guards tried to wipe out this irrefutable omen.

* * * * * * * *

For me the great day dawned to nothing more drastic than a double dose of Epsom salts. I thought that I had fallen victim, at this momentous stage, to our latest epidemic of dysentery, a fear luckily not fulfilled. But it was a day of dragging myself down stairs and up stairs on profanely toilsome trips to the latrine.

Late in the afternoon events took a turn that banished further worry over dysentery. We heard a sudden roar, saw a 'plane come hurtling from the north, then another, and another, till we had counted nine, all coming down Rizal Avenue, banking just short of us, and turning as if to scan Quezon Extension. Back in our cubicle after roll-call, I noticed unwonted activity in our street, people running, looking north, then scattering, taking cover as if apprehensive of being fired at. I could hear the rattle of machine guns, and thought guerrillas must be attacking, but downstairs I heard from excited lips that American tanks in great numbers had been coming into Quezon Boulevard[71]. It seemed incredible, yet just the thing to be expected in this incredible campaign.

333

That these were American tanks the Japanese were not yet prepared to concede. On the authority of Major Ebiko, supposedly Oura's superior, although Oura had continued in unwelcome charge of our welfare, these tanks were not American but Japanese; he even hinted that they were the vanguard of fresh Nipponese forces. Since we had been ordered down to the ground floor, no one could dispute this until one of our men, taking advantage of dusk, slipped up to the roof.[72]

From this height he could look down on tanks clattering through the narrow lane below our wall. The light was too dim to reveal their insignia, but he heard one man, standing in an open turret, hail the next tank.

"Hey, Harvey," the man called "where the hell are you going? You've been down this street once before."

That voice did not come from the vanguard of fresh Japanese forces. It was the voice of freedom.

Even when people at last were convinced that the Americans had come, they kept their exhilaration under tight control. All around Bilibid the advent of the tanks had erupted into a lurid clash of gunfire. "By now," as I wrote in my diary, "hell was breaking loose: the heavily rhythmic drumming of American machine guns, 50 calibre, was drowning the lighter, ineffectual sounding 27 calibre of the Japanese, while into a welter of star shells and tracer bullets thundered the 3 inch guns[73] of the tanks, blasting houses from which sniping had broken forth."

What peril we risked from that blasting we neither knew, nor considered. Weeks later, long after our rescue, we heard how trigger-happy those tanks had been, and how they ached to bombard the blank, massive darkness of Bilibid. They had come, not with a hundred tanks, as I had estimated, but with only seven, and with eight hundred men in half-tracks. By much agile movement they sought to give this effect of a really large force, and to bluff the Japanese into retiring south of the Pasig River.

In this they succeeded. To free the great concentration camp at Santo Tomas was their first objective. They did not know that prisoners still were quartered in Bilibid. Had our guard provoked retaliation, we should have been destroyed by our own guns.

Luckily for us, our guard now consisted largely of Formosans. Although they set up a tank trap at the gate and lugged a machine gun and bottles filled with gasoline to the roof, they were in no mood to invite trouble. They did not share the Japanese zeal to die fighting for the Emperor, but wanted only a chance to surrender. Their apathy Major Ebiko must have sized up; after a visit to the roof he assured us that the guards would not shoot. He still tried to convince us that the tumult we were listening to was merely a guerrilla attack, while Oura, some time later, came through the halls laughing as if enjoying a great joke. What the Japanese really felt was expressed later by another of the staff. "The Americans," he said, "They never do what we expect."

Our chief concern was the fires breaking out in the houses near Bilibid, fires flaring with a hot violence that threatened to span the narrow lanes and ignite the mosquito nets and bedding on our upper floor. Only after a futile attempt to push the iron shutters back across the yawning gapes of the windows did we discover that two streets, not one, separated us from this conflagration.

We were too elated to worry. Gathered in groups on the lower floor, we chattered and laughed through the explosive night, broaching our last tins of food – our family was down to half a tin of corned beef – in assurance of the plenty soon to be ours.

One solitary figure did not share our elation. All night long, Yamato had stood watch outside, making sure that any of us who went to the latrines did not expose ourselves rashly. In the glare of shells lighting up the darkness his world was crashing around his shoulders. Little could he care whether we were hurt or not, yet we had been committed to his charge. It was his job to assure our safety. Throughout the night's tumult he kept his station, an example of faithfulness to duty such as most of us were too absorbed in our own excitement to note or to admire.

By daylight, things had quieted. Houses in the neighbourhood still burned. Sprawled in the middle of Quezon Boulevard lay a dead Japanese soldier. All day it was left there slowly bloating as the sun mounted. Where the tanks had gone to we did not know. The only recognition we got was from the pilot of a Piper Cub who waved as he drifted by. We did not know, of course, that American forces had entered Santo Tomas and set up headquarters. We knew nothing except that we were free – but it was freedom curtailed by a warning to remain inside Bilibid.

Our release and this warning had been given us simultaneously by Major Ebiko. The notice of release he had sent over, shortly before noon, after first calling down the guards from the roof. This document, "originally dated the 7th January," (I quote my diary) "was read in hushed silence to the crowd packed into the hall. Father Sheridan started God bless America – too high; then the Star Spangled Banner – again too high. People wept." From the balcony Ethel Herold broke out an American flag, long hidden, to which every woman in Camp had contributed at least one stitch. For this moment they had kept it ready, a moment too heavy with emotion to be accepted except simply.

Exhausted by the night's excitement I, like many, rested through the afternoon, but I wakened in time to see my first American soldiers. They

335

were crossing an intersection down the street overlooked by our window, and crouching as they dodged, with rifles and machine guns, into the houses adjacent to our compound. Quite evidently they were dislodging snipers, whose menace had worsened after the initial shock of the American attack. These G.I's – a name we had not yet heard – might have been men from Mars. They were not the Army we had known, three years before. Their jungle-green mechanic-style uniforms were different, their weapons, the steel helmets that overlapped their necks. What surprised us most, however, was their size. So accustomed had we grown to the skinny, rib-ridged torsos of our fellow inmates that these newcomers looked more than gigantic; they looked fat.

To see them was reassuring, for the tanks had disappeared. No longer under guard ourselves, we had begun to worry about trouble from Japanese stragglers or from Manila's always lawless riffraff. Yet none of us thought it odd that the American forces had made no contact with us. Too many things absorbed our interest. We had made our own contact with the military prisoners remaining in the sector next to ours. These were the men luckily too sick to be removed to Japan, some eight hundred in all. Within the six weeks since we had halted in dark uncertainty outside the gate to our ruined hospital, perhaps forty graves had been dug, two score men buried where on that black night there had been no graves at all. Later, from these same prisoners, we were to see men too sick to respond to their rescue, a boy in his early twenties fighting off food, fighting off medicine, and dying frenziedly determined not to acknowledge the freedom that had come too late.

Yet the resilient courage that still enlivened the great body of these men amazed us, for beside their treatment we had suffered no hardship at all. Right up to their release they had operated two radio receiving sets in quarters where a mouse would have been hard put to it to hide; they had kept abreast of the war's developments far more accurately than we. Quite properly they were the first Bilibid inmates to be discovered by the rescuing soldiers. It happened in the late evening while one of our Committeemen was visiting old friends among them.

Outside a wooden side-gate they heard a man saying,

"How the hell do we break in here?"

"Brother," exclaimed an inmate, "how in the hell do we break out?"

"What! Are there Americans in there?"

Spurred by an emphatic affirmative, the G.I's knocked down the barricade. Big, burly men, they confronted with awe the skeleton-thin expendables of the old Army whose grim surrender they had avenged. They were a detachment form the 37th (Ohio) Division; their officer was a Major

Wendt, from Cleveland. That was all we ever learned about Major Wendt but, like the almost legendary Harvey, his name we would not forget.

"Why, we thought you were all dead!" they cried, greatly bucked up at freeing prisoners whom the 1st Cavalry had overlooked. To have found and released any prisoners of their own was a prize they no longer expected. The 37th had travelled on foot, fighting their way from the original landing point on the Gulf of Lingayen whereas the Cavalrymen had come mechanized by a shorter route from Zambales[74]. Since men in other divisions tended to scoff at the 1st Cavalry as MacArthurs's pets – a privileged status repudiated by the 1st Cavalry in gusty language! – the elation these Ohio soldiers felt in scoring off their rivals was as jubilant as our own joy in being welcomed at last to the fold.

We had become, in official language, "Civilians Recovered from Enemy Occupied Territory" – dry paraphrase of a highly dramatic fact.

* * * * * * * *

That night, a machine gun duel, and spent slugs battering the iron screen over our window, tumbled me out of my cot and down to the floor. The Japanese, too, were not doing what we expected. Free we might be, but it was freedom curbed by a battle that was to keep us confined to Bilibid for weeks, a resistance waged to the death by sixteen thousand Japanese including their Special Landing Forces.[75]

None of this did we anticipate on the morning that followed our rescue. Victory was in our hearts. Blithely we talked to the many G.I.s. from the 37th who came crowding into our prison, eager for a first glimpse of American women and children. None of our women, at that moment, could have qualified as pin-ups, but to troops whose recent sight of womanhood had been restricted to New Guinea's fuzzy-wuzzies, a white face, however lean, looked glamourous.

The G.I.s had kept up on their vitamins! During those early encounters we were puzzled as to why so many of them persisted in walking upstairs to look out the second floor windows. We had forgotten that these windows overlooked the women's outdoor showers. But even this explanation seemed to us silly. Who would go to such trouble to stare at a scrawny nudity less inviting than when at least partially concealed by the tattered, faded remnants of Camp garb?

Correspondents were as prompt visitors as the G.I.s. They had much to tell. A Nisei, they said, had been planted in the Japanese Headquarters; dangerously privy to their secrets, he had kept MacArthur informed about Japanese plans. From him, they declared, had come word that all men and boys in the prison camps were to be taken out on Tuesday, the 6th. This was the warning which had galvanized the American forces to undertake their swift sortie against Manila. If their information was correct, MacArthur had put this crisis up to his troops and inspired the race that saved us.

As the day progressed, we were hustled back into the brutal realities of war. Japanese mortar shells were lobbed into the narrow stretch of open ground between our building and its buttressed walls. Shell-bursts at such close quarters almost blinded as they deafened us, yet they hit nobody outside nor did they penetrate our hospital's gaping windows. An explosion withindoors would have been disastrous, for they scattered an incendiary substance so cool to the touch that one boy had picked up a piece and brought it inside where it heated swiftly to combustible temperature and burned his hands.

Our bombardment, however, was brief. Santo Tomas was a more serious target, justifiably so, since the American Army had made it a division headquarters. Before the Japanese were done with that huge camp, nearly a hundred people had been killed by their roving cannon. Throughout their ordeal, prolonged for several days, we used to watch shells making gaps in the University tower, and grew so inured to these attacks that we would go on washing, at an outside sink, the cans that served us for dishes while, a bare hundred feet above our heads, the shells rumbled by like a subway express.

Only on that first day was our camp deliberately bombarded, though stray shells often came our way at night. By a second sense we began to distinguish between Japanese guns firing at us and American guns firing over us. Many a night I would waken when, from a new angle, the enemy started shooting their captured 4.2's, guns taken at Bataan, whereas I would sleep through an American cannonade and exclaim, next morning, how quiet the night had been!

No noise, no tumult, indeed could compete with that first day's frightening tempo. Although our initial exposure to Japanese artillery did not persist, there was the ping of sniper's bullets, there were the ear-stunning explosions as, one by one, key buildings, detonated from some central point, erupted against the sulphurous-smoky sky. Fires from this demolition swelled to such gigantic size that they towered over us, an advancing wall of flame, of oily, billowing smoke, two miles wide, two hundred feet high.

By nightfall the Army decided that Bilibid was untenable. Momentarily they expected its building to be torn apart by hidden explosives. On an instant's notice we got word that we were to be moved to a safer place outside Manila. We were to take only what we could carry; except for women and children trucks were not available. The men must expect to walk for perhaps two miles before they could be picked up.

What we could carry posed a sore problem. In our weakened condition suitcases were too heavy. We were assured, however, that our removal would be only for the night; Bilibid would be guarded, and whatever we left behind would be safe. So we narrowed our selection to blankets and mosquito nets. Only last minute prudence prodded me into slipping inside my blankets the three volumes of my war diary before I joined the straggling procession out the rear gate and down a lane garishly illuminated by the fire.

But the Army did better than they had promised. No sooner had we reached a nearby thoroughfare than we were halted and told to await trucks that were coming for us. On each side of the street Filipinos thronged in huge numbers watching both the movement of American troops and the awful backdrop of flames against which their crowded, flimsy houses stood out, black and doomed. So vast was this livid holocaust that despite its ominous roar, despite the sharp crackling of the fire and the stunning concussion of each new explosion, noises heard above the crowd's surging talk, we still could not tell whether it actually threatened this area. Certainly, the people's note was more gaiety than fear.

We were the heroes of the hour. While we waited, men brought us chairs, plied us with *basi* and brandy. Eagerly they queried out our experiences in prison and told harrowing tales of their subjugation to an enemy they could not speak of without hate. As we climbed into our trucks, everybody joined in crying, "Good bye. Come back soon."

Scarcely were we loaded in what was commodious luxury compared with the discomfort of our endless ride from Camp Holmes than we were startled by a new noise, a vibrant murmur that began far down the street and with irresistible power swelled to a double fortissimo of tumultuous acclamation. Suddenly, a jeep came hustling along to marshal our procession; from a staff held upright it displayed an enormous American flag, the Stars and Stripes, springtime bright in their colours, which the crowd greeted in immense unison, singing, weeping, shouting. For one glorious moment history shone, brilliantly focussed before our eyes.

* * * * * * * *

Our destination was Ang Tibay, an abandoned shoe factory on Manila's outskirts. We were billeted on upper gangways, a half floor from which we looked down on the main floor and on the pitiable spectacle of prisoners who had not come through the war as fortunately as we. These were the sick, the precariously sick, of the military prisoners confined next to us at Bilibid. Among them was the boy we watched fighting off the doctors as they tried to minister to him, falling from paroxysm into paroxysm till in gentler, sobbing spells his face and body relaxed in death. Here were others – "psychos" – who had lost all awareness, who looked out on the stimulating activity around them with blank, uncomprehending eyes.

Our attention was demanded more actively by G.I.s – an ever-changing group, they squatted on the floor to talk to us. They were our first intimate introduction to the new Army. A remarkable introduction it was, to men whose quality almost suffocated our hearts with pride that we could call ourselves their countrymen. They were shock troops, and had fought their way up the bitter pathways of the Solomons and New Guinea. This friendship with the Army which began that night suffered no letdown in the weeks of continued acquaintance soon to follow.

Long after that garish night, when we had arrived in San Francisco and were revelling in hot water and soap, and sheets on our beds, we discovered our ten year old daughter weeping out her heart in the unwonted luxuries of the bath room.

"What on earth is the matter with you? her mother asked.

Between sobs, Ann stammered, "I am – l - - lonely for my soldiers."

We understood.

That these men were brave goes without saying. What amazed us was their gentleness, their considerateness for us that night when we took refuge at Ang Tibay. For days and nights they had been fighting their way to Manila; some, when we met them, had had no sleep for thirty-six hours, yet their one thought seemed set on making us comfortable. Their intelligence, too, astonished us. For them there was none of the old "theirs not to reason why, theirs but to do and die" spirit supposedly necessary to making a good soldier. They knew the wherefore of their arduous campaign, the strategy, the tactics, and took pride in explaining these intricacies to us, volunteering them with a fine satisfaction over what their outfits had achieved.

Undoubtedly they grumbled, they complained; later, during the hand-to-hand struggle for Manila, they used to scoff at their leadership and claim that this battle was being waged solely to save MacArthur's pent-house atop the Manila Hotel. Good soldiers, at heart they were civilians who, to fight well, had needed first to convince themselves that the war made sense. This rescue of prisoners, men, women, children, whom they themselves had freed, gave the conviction they had come to its ultimate personal clincher.

I remember only a few of the men we met that night, and chiefly that they were men of marked individuality, like the student of anthropology from Cincinnati who had been able to send home the artifacts collected during his staging in Fiji, or the young farmer from Illinois, who looked beyond violence to his peaceful fields. They preferred, however, to hear our experiences than talk about their own. Individuals they were, but individuals from a great crowd in whose outward confusion there was an ever-present note of purpose, of activity unregimented, yet drawing from every man his particular part in the large work being done.

In the open space outside the shoe factory this activity fascinated me. For some time I lingered before a radio loud speaker, which was blaring forth the news of our own rescue, news up to the minute of our removal from Bilibid to Ang Tibay. I heard a statement from Henry L. Stimson, Secretary of War, that told us more about ourselves than we yet knew. I saw General Kruger push in through the crowd; his rank betokened only by the four stars painted on his helmet; across his shoulder a carbine was slung. On the edge of the crowd strange vehicles were assembling, tanks of startling shape, bizarre names, dukws, alligators, jeeps. Yet back of it all, and ever apart from it all, flared the burning city, that stupendous wall of flame. Occasionally, I would withdraw a few feet to regard it, to remind myself of the homes, the hopes, the happiness engulfed by that monstrous fire. I could smell the crackle of burning timbers; the concussion from fresh explosions rattled my teeth.

We had little chance, little temptation, to sleep that night. Besides the excitement to keep us awake, there were the mosquitoes, vicious, biting hordes. I managed two hours' uneasy rest and then got up to take my place with G.I.s in the line waiting to wash at a pump in a field nearby. It took me an hour of moving forward step by step before I could reach this one pump, and our only available water, gushing from a well the Japanese had neglected to destroy.

Breakfast cost a wait even longer. The Army, despite the many accumulating evidences of its power, had as yet only a precarious foothold in Manila. It had outrun its supplies, outrun its transport. Its engineers were exhausting themselves, toiling round the clock to rebuild bridges. To feed eleven hundred rescued prisoners taxed its resources.

But breakfast, when it did come, was a miracle – 10 in 1 cereal, ration of eggs and bacon, hot chocolate, packets containing biscuits, fruit bars, lemonade powders. A late afternoon lunch stirred further excitement over beef and bean stew, and coffee. This food, concocted from the despised K-rations, the G.I.s sniffed at; to us it was a feast for the gods.

By afternoon, however, the strain of sleepless nights was wearing us down. The news that we were to return to Bilibid was darkened by rumours that everything we left behind had been looted. The fire had come so near the prison, so the report ran, that the military police had been withdrawn, whereat a Filipino mob, undeterred by the blistering heat, had swept through the deserted building, plundering all they could lay their hands on. This rumour we tried not to believe. Eventually, we had to accept it. Through hot, tedious hours, unable to rest, unable to relax, we waited for the promised convoy to return us to our shambles.

The return was too thrilling for comfort. Instead of going in a 'bus, our family had acceded to the insistence of a friendly soldier that we ride in his jeep, our first experience of this hardy vehicle. Starting late, we had to catch up with the convoy and, several times, nearly lost it. Much as we admired the rabbit-like agility of the little car, its knack of leaping pot-holes, we were fearful of getting lost in a section of Manila which we knew none too well, and our driver not at all. All we could think of was the target we made for snipers.

As things turned out, the whole convoy went the wrong road, and took us to Santo Tomas, giving us our first (and, I hoped, a last) glimpse of this huge camp, whose verandahed building towered like an old-fashioned seaside hotel, while its inmates swarmed through the one-time college campus, crowds in a chattering, holiday mood, evidently elated over the artillerymen set in their midst.

Bilibid was a dejected contrast, a place of solitary desolation. Our non-descript furniture had been shoved around or pushed over, the concrete floors littered with refuse, everything of value stripped bare. Only one thing worth salvaging did I find, a Book of Common Prayer. Whose it was I don't know, but it seemed left providentially for my use. Just as my library had been reduced now to one cockroach-chewed prayer-book, my other possessions had been reduced to the bedding I carried, to the bedraggled clothes I was wearing, shorts, a torn shirt, socks knit from string, tennis-shoes broken out at the toes. We reached bottom – and so had our spirits.

Frances had fallen sick with dengue, and no longer cared whether she lived or died. Geoffrey and I groped in twilight through jumbled chaos till we recovered for her a wooden bed – the camp-cots had gone – and the rest of our makeshift furniture. Like our fellow victims we reassembled as best we could the unit we had occupied before our rescue. In the night's gathering gloom Geoffrey and I secured our new issue of K-rations and sat outside on the steps to eat it. Even food, more food than the two of us could manage, lacked the magic to dispel our utter, cheerless despondency.

* * * * * * * *

Six more weeks we were to remain in Bilibid, six weeks during which an unexpected and bitterly contested battle was fought over our heads. That first night of our return, we were unwilling to face even three more days of Bilibid. In the ensuing days, however, our mood changed until, in the end, we became almost sorry to say good-bye to the old derelict prison.

It had accumulated a host of memories, particularly of new friends made among our rescuers, that we felt guilty at leaving them to confront months of campaigning still ahead while we ran out on the dangers they were to suffer, dangers for which some might never come home.

These were a curious six weeks. The Japanese marines had elected to fight to the death. Only by being blasted out of their pill-boxes in room after room of Manila's fortress-staunch public buildings were they finally overcome. In their holocaust they took thousands of Filipinos, people of other nations too, hostages put to fiery death during mad orgies of massacre. To root them out of Intramuros, the ancient walled city where they had made their utmost stand, exacted a wholesale bombing that could not distinguish between friend and enemy.

For three of the six weeks we were close to the vortex of almost continual bombardment. American howitzers, two miles behind us, were loud enough to have been across the street. In the day-time their thunder was augmented by 'planes. We watched them dropping bombs on the City Hall, on schools further south, watched buildings disrupt in a geyser of fire. Across the Pasig a Japanese flag continued to wave from the Post Office, Manila's latest and sturdiest public structure, a bastion of concrete and steel. One morning, our artillery overwhelmed it with several hundred shells. The flag, the "fried egg," went down, resistance ceased, yet before the day's end the Japanese were back again. They had returned through the sewers.

All this lapsed into routine stuff. I suggested once to a mother that after the war she would need a riveting hammer to lull her children to sleep. Heavy artillery we got use to, though we were disconcerted by reports that the enemy had stationed naval guns in the eastern hills, cannon which would roll out from caves at daybreak to shell the city at random. For some reason, to be killed by accident seemed much worse than to be killed deliberately. But our bombers saved our worry: they sealed the caves by day, our cannon pinpointed them at night.

Only when the machine guns began barking did we have trouble sleeping. They would wake me instantly. We all knew what shooting of this kind meant: the Japanese were trying to break through the defenses that pinned them to the Pasig's south bank. Every desperate tactic they resorted to: they worked their way across the sunken ships in the bay, they launched sneak attacks by boats on the river, one evening they pushed forward so vigorously in a banzai charge that American re-enforcements were rushed to repel them. The Pasig was a bare quarter of a mile distant. Had these enemy sorties succeeded, they might have overrun Bilibid.

Our rudest awakening came one morning just before dawn, when a bomb, dropped from the air, exploded a scant hundred feet from our window. The

343

concussion blew out our iron shutters, sent them crashing to the ground, yet without shifting empty food-cans from the window sill. It bent the tall prison wall. Saddest of all, it shattered to bits a whole tank crew who had been sleeping in hammocks across the street. For us, this was a nearer miss than the Japanese shell which holed a house opposite us, a house from which the G.I.s soon ejected the sniper. Who dropped our one and only bomb we never learned. One rumour declared that a Japanese 'plane had slipped in only to be shot down in the harbour. Another more accepted report told that the bomb had been dropped accidentally by one of our own 'planes.

Yet much of the night fighting we watched as though we had no part in it but like spectators enthralled by a display of fireworks. The star shells, red and blue and green, were always beautiful, and the brilliant yellow flares illuminating great areas of the murdered city as they drifted slowly down on Manila's shattered roofs. When the fighting passed and we depended only on the moon's paler rays, we missed their romantic beauty, the quiet radiance of their descent.

Gunfire, star-shells, machine gun duels were subordinate, after all, to the keen delight of renewing acquaintance with amenities of which we had long been deprived, the taste of bread and butter, of bacon, of the steaks flown us from Los Angeles. To put on underwear again was exhilarating, the olive-drab shorts and vests of Government issue, to be given magazines, no matter how old, to receive tooth paste, soap, razor blades. So keenly did we revel in these tokens of the homeland's bounty that it was almost worth while to have gone without them for three years to know the happiness discoverable in life's simplest things. The surfeit of peacetime never could match the sharpened relish which this largess of freedom brought us.

War and Peace would have made the right title for those weeks. The two went on simultaneously. One war-time habit we could not discard: we craved rice. The Philippine Civilian Aid Unit which took over our kitchen was better able to satisfy this need than the richer abundance of Army food. Rice they supplied with the stews they cooked. At the same time, however, that we were emerging from the attitude, ingrained by three years' privation, of wondering where our next meal was coming from, we suffered scarcity of water.

Blowing up the pumping stations, the Japanese had reduced Manila's water supply to a trickle. We had taken some precaution against a complete stoppage by digging shallow wells amid the graves. This water, happily, we never were quite reduced to utilizing. It was probably brackish, for we were but a few feet above tide-marks, and our imagination would have flavoured it always, no matter how drastically it was boiled, with the taint of the corpses from whose vicinity it was drained. To our relief, the trickle persisted, giving

344

us enough to wash out the cans from which we ate our food, enough to fill the buckets wherewith we rinsed out the sloping trough of our latrine.

These open latrines, from our first arrival at Bilibid, had been a sanitary hazard. While we still were prisoners, some of our men had contrived an ingenious arrangement to discourage flies. They had made a framework from the steel rods, the old structural re-enforcement culled out of the hospital walls when they were being dismantled. Over these rods, suitably bent, they had pulled, in covered wagon fashion, some green nets which the Japanese Army had discarded.

This contrivance stirred Oura's anger. It was an insult to use the Imperial Army's equipment for so degrading a purpose. Here Yamato, with rare tact, intervened, explaining to the Commandant that these were second hand nets – and the conclusion obvious: their use to screen toilets was but a second hand insult. Oura let them stay.

Compared to these bad dreams of a past so recently outlived, the thunderous hostilities of the present, though fought over a no man's land to which Bilibid was uncomfortably adjacent, were an epic, heroic in its dimensions, and ours a rare privilege of witnessing it. Within three days of our rescue we were visited by the great Captain of it all, the hero who, while still living, had created his own legend, General Douglas MacArthur.

His visit was wholly informal and friendly. Among our number were friends he had known from earlier years in Manila. My diary speaks merely of his looking "heavier than before the War," and that "to the echo of our cheering (he) inspected our chaotic quarters." I cite these details because, long afterward, his friend, General Whitney, published in Life magazine a highly charged account of that visit in which he contrasted the behaviour of Bilibid's military and civilian prisoners. The former, he said, even to the feeblest, stood at rigid attention by their cots when their General walked by whereas we civilians clawed at him in demoniacal frenzy. The scene, as he described it, could have been matched only by hysterical 'teen-aged girls mobbing the latest pelvic contortionist to prod their shrill fancy.

Where General Whitney got this account I do not know. He might have mixed our reception with the one given the General at Santo Tomas – we were welling to believe anything libellous about Santo Tomas! – but his story was not even remotely true of us.

As an eye-witness of MacArthur's visit to Bilibid, I wrote to Life contradicting their story. This letter they did not print. Instead, they wrote quashing my protest with the pompous statement that they had their own reliable sources of information. Before the correspondence was closed I received from an acquaintance of my daughter's two photographs of MacArthur in Bilibid – no crowds, no clawing, but the General chatting at entire ease with a few of our camp-mates. These pictures, though they refuted Life's story, I did not send in lest the magazine appropriate and suppress them. Their all-wise attitude, however, left me wondering how much modern history is being tailored to what the editors of a bloated weekly chose to pronounce as truth. For them to suppress not only my first hand impressions but the written support of my diary makes one ask whether a subscription list numbered in millions entitles such periodicals to manufacture history after their own image.

Even MacArthur himself was not infallible. He had not envisaged the prolonged, wearying duration of the battle for Manila. On the 26th February we were given a concert by the band of the 32nd Division. According to my diary,

"They had been waiting at Tarlac to come in for a Victory parade which MacArthur had scheduled prematurely for the 10th February and had come to play at Malacanan (Palace) tomorrow and at a parade now fixed for the 10th March. Fresh from the road they greeted us with breathtaking heartiness as the first American civilians they had seen in months and years. Grouping their chairs in front of the main steps they gave us a brief concert which moved us to the core by the precision, superb tone and perfectly modulated balance of their playing. The concrete walls of the derelict hospital were a peerless sounding board and even picturesque behind the shelter of their great global mango-trees and with the full moon slowly lifting through the dark foliage. Tremours shook me as I listened to the Star-Spangled Banner and, with their playing, even Land of the Morning had dignity, though not the majestic implications of the National Anthem played by the soldiers who had made its promise of freedom and victory a reality."

I added further:

"All these bandsmen were further encouraging tokens of what we have observed on every hand, the pleasant, gay, gentlemanly quality of American soldiers. They are boys to be proud of and we shudder to think that a single one of them should be killed by the fanatical, shifty coolies deployed against them."

This reference to the Japanese was less than fair, tainted by wartime emotions; as to our appraisal of the G.I., I did not feel at the time, nor have I felt later, that what I wrote was overdrawn.

* * * * * * * *

Slowly the Battle of Manila passed beyond our range. While we were held almost within its vortex we knew far less about its progress than people at home. Rumours of massacre were rife; their harrowing details we could never confirm. Not until three weeks after our rescue were we able to emerge from Bilibid and see for ourselves what price the retaking of the city had exacted. Except Warsaw, we were told, no city had been more fearfully destroyed.[76]

The Escolta, Manila's venerable shopping street, a narrow, crooked alley which even before the war had choked over its incongruous medley of horse-drawn and motor-driven traffic, was now impassable. The floors of its concrete and steel buildings had flopped over one another like wilted pancakes. The parallel streets, however, had been made partially viable by Army trucks, which ground down their rubble, stuffing it into potholes to make a rough and ready surface.

Along this dubious highway we walked down to the banking district. The Hongkong & Shanghai Bank, the National City Bank, and all the others had been gutted. They stank with rotting corpses. Across the pavement were strewn Japanese bank-notes, often in packets amounting to thousands of pesos, "mickey mouse money" not worth the toil of stooping to pick it up.

Replacing the broken arches of the Jones Bridge, a bailey bridge spanned the Pasig. Fort Santiago, the ultimate hell of Japanese prisons, now flew the American flag. From its dungeons some prisoners had come back to sunlight wild-eyed, raving. To the south, beyond the river, the roof of the Legislature was burning. It had been newly bombed, a good riddance, we hoped, for like many of the public buildings first erected by the American government, it was a concrete mimic of Washington's classical architecture, its unshaded windows as unsuited to the glaring tropical sun as its columns and porticoes were stupidly pretentious. The Ice Plant, which did not pretend to be anything but ugly, was still a stronghold of Japanese defenders whom our Army, rather than fight them from room to room, undermined and then blew up with an explosion that rattled our teeth and stunned our eardrums.

As we explored the now unfamiliar, indeed unrecognizable, street, we wondered how Manila's site could ever be cleared sufficiently to permit rebuilding, how the bay could ever be cleared of its upended Japanese ships. To remove the whole city to some adjacent site looked more feasible.

Even these excursions told but part of the tale. Geoffrey and I had the chance to accompany an officer from the C.I.C. while he helped two German-Jewish couples from Santo Tomas seek out what was left of their homes. This took us considerably south of the Pasig into such residential areas as Ermita, an area of wooden bungalows so completely flattened by fire that one couple could not even be sure where their vanished house had stood.

347

We came back by Dewey Boulevard, still labelled Koa, a scenic drive which I remembered fondly for many promenades along its sea-wall, promenades at the sunset hour, when a west wind dispelled the afternoon's heat and Manila's polyglot inhabitants turned out to inhale the clean sea-breeze and watch the waves flinging foamy crests from the rocks. Now what villas survived looked down on empty paths. The royal palms that we had admired as they grew year by year to a tall colonnade were mere shredded stumps, desolate wreckage like the acacias which once had roofed Ermita's sleepy back streets.

Our goal was the Episcopal Cathedral of SS. Mary and John. Though we had been warned what to expect, we could not grasp such appalling ruin. The church's two west towers had been toppled into the street, its massive concrete walls were riddled and broken, of the dome nothing remained but twisted steel girders atop which leaned a melted cross. To continue from my diary:

"Bits of stained glass glittered from the debris, the brass candle-sticks from the high altar lay amid the rubble. . . In the crumbling masonry which had buried the pavement many feet deep we had to walk warily because of the unexploded Japanese shells which lay everywhere, and walk with a particularly cautious eye on the wing-tailed mortar shells which the slightest jar might explode. Booby traps too we had to guard against. The building reeked with the stench of Japanese dead; in the nave, partly concealed by a collapsed arch, lay one corpse, the face hidden, the naked belly distended, trousered legs asprawl; another in full uniform – the dirty khaki we remembered so bitterly – had his head flung back and the skin drawn back taut from his teeth, presenting a snarl which death had made hideously permanent. He might have been a mummy, but other corpses I saw had rotted away or been eaten away till the ribs were bare and the flesh little more than dissolving piles of foul-smelling, putrescent grease outlining what had been a man's torso. Often they had not human semblance; they were just rags and rotted meat. The flies swarmed around us, gluing themselves to our legs and our arms with a horrid tenacity which our frantic flicking of handkerchiefs could not discourage. . .

"Such destruction, miles of it, was too thorough, too violently chaotic to credit. We were glad to turn away from it, but we had one last reminder of the defiled city in a truckload of Jap bodies, loaded six deep, which rumbled past us filling our noses with the appalling corruption of its smell which pervaded Ermita like a miasma and wafted from the shambles of the government buildings. For hours my nostrils were full of it."

348

I might well have said, "for days." Wherever we went in Manila there were lurking whiffs of this stench. Beneath every pile of rubble lay unburied, nameless bodies. Not until the wrecked houses were cleared would their bones be uncovered, mute victims to the insanity of a war that gained nothing for its conspirators, but left the world a sadder place to live in.

* * * * * * * *

Day by day the community we had known so long as Camp Holmes was falling apart. The Battle of Manila had ended on the morning of the 23rd February in a tumultuous barrage; from every angle and with unslackening rapidity, from six until half-past eight, shells were furled into Intramuros, after which the guns fell back into phenomenal quiet. What I had predicted came true: so accustomed had we grown to noise that this abrupt silence was uncanny. At night we could not sleep. We missed the cannonade's lulling rhythm.

No sooner had the air-fields been cleared than the Army began repatriating some first batches from our number, flying them to an unnamed destination there to await passage home, as their orders put it in oddly guarded language. It was a secret we all knew: they were being flown to Tacloban, on Leyte. Each day took away more of our members, but the officer in charge of Bilibid still wished us to retain our General Committee and had us draft new committeemen to replace those who had gone.

When we first returned from Ang Tibay to our plundered prison I and my family would have started home on ten minutes' notice; in the intervening weeks our eagerness to be on our way had waned. Such attractive friends had we made among the G.I.s that we were reluctant to bid them good-bye. Ann, in particular, had lost her ten year old heart to a military policeman. She hung around the gate, one in a bevy of adoring maidens who offered worship to its stalwart guardian.

Her adoration was more than mute. Addressing herself to a very patient young man, Bill Haskins, she hailed him in verse:

(1)   "I love those hazel eyes of yours
        That twinkle in the light,
        They twinkle like the little stars
        That twinkle in the night.

(2)   "But in the dark I see your smile,
        Your teeth are pearly white,

349

Your eyes and smile must be the style
To make the whole world bright."

To her mother she explained the circumstances of this lyric: "I thought of the first verse last night in bed and the other this morning in the toilet."

Ann's taste in soldiers took her far afield in streets scarcely yet safe enough for her and her sub-teen friends to explore. From one such expedition, undertaken without our permission, she returned trailed by a military retinue whom her blonde hair had drawn like a magnet. She was a fantastic spectacle, her face grimy and nearly snuffed out by a G.I. helmet while from her shoulder was slung a carbine.

"Mummy," she cried in exultant tones, "here are some soldiers I've brought you."

Behind her came three soldiers, two of them drunk. Her leading escort was a skyscraping sergeant, a Texan, who shambled in not too steadily. He had been guzzling the rot-gut whisky with which Filipinos, at extortionate prices, poisoned their liberators. The corrosive potion, however, had not stifled the Texan's gallantry. Promptly putting his hand on Frances's shoulder, he invited her to go out with him to dinner – an invitation he would have been puzzled to make good in a city whose one-time restaurants were cinders and its bright lights candles. The other two were Californians, one of them of Portuguese extraction, a man bursting to unload his woes, his frustration, on any sympathetic ear. Mine became that ear.

He was a pathetic figure. For thirty-seven months he had been away from home; liquor and the sight of women and children had worked on him like a catalyst, loosing a whole wartime's pent up longings for his young wife, and fear lest she forget him. On the Bilibid roof-top, away from the unceasing hubbub of our crowded quarters, I listened to his voice going round and round the same worries, the same repeated doubts.

While I was held to this fruitless talk, unable to break away, help came in the arrival of a group of First Cavalrymen with whom we had been foregathering each evening. It was help I was dubious about, having heard what he thought about the First Cavalry. Yet I failed every attempt at persuading him to seek out his buddys, who had gone off to explore Bilibid's further social attractions. Nor could I isolate him in our corner of the roof when it was cheerfully evident that my friends were expecting me at their party.

The moment he learned that they were First Cavalrymen he froze. Their offer of a drink he could not accept unless he could pay for it. Fortunately, they perceived his state well enough to ignore the insult. By great tact they dissipated his resentment and made him feel so welcome that when the Texan sergeant returned to nudge him into starting their long journey back to their engineering outfit near Stotzenburg, he was in no mood to go.

To hell with the Army, he exclaimed. He would outstay his leave, he would go A.W.O.L., he would not check in till he damn well felt like it.

The Texan opposed no argument. To each brashly voiced threat he kept insinuating, "Larry, you gotta go."

Perhaps a dozen times he had been rebuffed, with Larry waxing ever more explicit about what the Army could do, when suddenly, to our amazement, the unvarying refrain, "Larry, you gotta go," hit its mark.

"You think so?" inquired Larry, collapsing into a meekness truly dramatic. For a long moment he was quiet, then shrugged his shoulders. "O.K." he sighed – and off he went, docile as a lamb.

The First Cavalrymen who had handled Larry with such flawless empathy were friends we had made, some days before, when they had come to entertain our camp with a Special Services programme. Almost every evening thereafter they joined some of us on Bilibid roof to enjoy the luxury, magnificently appreciated on their side and ours alike, of talking with new acquaintances, people among whom we had not talked ourselves dry during three years of war.

Even before our rescue Bilibid roof evoked tranquil, poetic associations. Next to its chunky parapets Frances and I used to sit savouring our tin cupfuls of soluble coffee while we watched sunrise behind the eastern mountains, and the swift, magical dispersal of night's gloom. Now we were watching the warfare ebb behind these same mountains, and feeling almost sorry to see the excitement of hours when we had lived history fade away. Bursting shells still flared over those hills, but each night they were remoter. Manila remained a ghost city, its houses like Bilibid lit by the pale luminescence of candles until on one of those evening we were startled to realize that the cars in the streets, the multitude of military vehicles had turned on their headlights. The Army had closed its chapter on the Battle of Manila.

Besides the First Cavalry we had other visitors, chief among them our Bishop, Bishop Binsted, newly released from the camp at Los Baños where American forces in a maneuver remarkably co-ordinated had brought guerrillas, paratroopers, amphibious tanks to overwhelm the Japanese garrison at exactly the moment when they had stacked arms and were doing their morning push-ups.

Bishop Binsted was one of two thousand prisoner thus rescued. A year prior to the outbreak of war, he had been transferred from his diocese in Japan. The right man in the right place, he played a hero's part. Since he spoke Japanese fluently, he knew how to deal with the Nipponese invaders. His home they seized to accommodate members of their high command,

351

but they allowed him to occupy one wing. There, under their eyes, he busied himself supplying his countrymen in the prison camps. Others engaged in this activity were caught and beheaded, among them the Methodist pastor and his wife, but the Bishop did his work so circumspectly that he emerged from its brutal hazards unscathed.

Our liveliest society, however, was the cavalrymen. They had unearthed a cache of liquor left by some Spanish merchant. Most of this booty was requisitioned by their colonel for the regimental mess, but they managed to crack the necks of bottles enough to stimulate our evenings. What we drank was a mystery; it had been dosed so heavily with coca-cola syrup that we never knew for sure whether it was whisky, brandy, or gin, but it made us happily voluble and livened our sessions far beyond the ten o'clock curfew when all soldiers were supposed to depart. Our laughter even penetrated the concrete floors beneath, provoking complaints from sundry old ladies who, though not averse to being saved by the G.I.s, did not like being kept awake by them.

So tolerably had we settled down into this existence, curiously suspended between war and peace, that the summons to start home, though expected daily, burst upon us with shocking abruptness. Letters from home had been reaching us; gradually we were getting clothed; now we were purged of vermin in what my diary records as a "Gobi desert storm of white dust." This was the miraculous D.D.T. It did its job; bed-bugs were finished. Despite my skepticism, not even one of the flat disc-like creatures ever crawled out of the seams to confound modern science.

Next we were initiated into the Army procedure mockingly described as, "Hurry up and wait" – up at four, breakfasting at seven, boarding our 'buses at nine, idling away three or four hours amid the devastation at Nichols Field before our eight 'planes were air-borne. However tedious the wait, we had not learned, as yet, to complain; we had too much to be grateful for. Even the G.I.s we talked to were not grumbling; benefitting by the system of rotation leave recently ordained, they too were on their way home.

One man told us in brimful elation that this was the first "break" he had had since joining the Army. He spoke too soon. He was in the ninth and last 'plane, the 'plane after ours. In heading down through clouds to land at Tacloban, the pilot drove his 'plane headlong against a mountain ridge – no survivors.

Our C-47's were luckier. For most of us this was our first flight, though too routine to be spectacular except when the pilot swung across Manila Bay and over Corregidor, off which island a cruiser was planting shells into cliffside tunnels, sealing under rock slides the remnants of the Japanese garrison. Nichols Field already had demonstrated the accuracy of our bombing.

Japanese 'planes by the score, mere wreckage scorched and twisted, had been pushed off the runway. From this misshapen junk protruded wings, apple green and circled with a red sun almost set. Manila Bay was as formidably cluttered with up-ended ships, while Corregidor could have passed for deserted ruins dug up by archaeologists from the steppes of central Asia.

What we could see from the C-47's tiny windows was but fragmentary glimpses soon obscured by clouds above which our motors droned so casually that they lulled many of us to sleep. I woke once to see the base of mount Mayon tapering into grey overcast and, next, the open roadway of Tacloban teeming with carriers, destroyers, landing craft, huge transports, whole navies imparting a brief bustling importance to this lethargic provincial town.

At Tacloban we joined the Army. Women and children were taken to a hospital down the coast; the rest of us, supplied with G.I. clothes, settled in the tents of a rotation camp where we swarmed three times a day to a chow line that doubled and redoubled in serpentine folds, inching forward to have our aluminum mess-kits smacked full of hot food.

The camp was in swampy ground. So recently had its tents been pitched that there had not been time to sand the muddy paths, but we were up on board floors and enjoying brilliantly lighted quarters where we sat, the centre of interest from our tent-mates, from officers eager to hear our story. To me the fact most miraculous was that we could sit a few feet above marsh-land yet never once hear the whine of mosquitoes nor squirm from their sharp-pronged assault on our bare knees. This miracle D.D.T. had worked; in our minds, after three years sequestered from the achievements of modern medicine, it was astounding enough to rival what the Army had done on the battlefield. It promised a victory over pestilence, over the age-long course of malaria, such as portended (we believed, alas, too naively) a new world as free from disease as it was now to become secure against tyranny and hatred and war.

The Army's only link with the past was the camp-cots we slept on. No one had improved on them. But we thought for a moment that one other tradition still held when we woke to a bugle blowing reveille. Who blew that bugle, and why, we never learned. The call was not repeated. On the garish night when American tanks first invaded Manila some of our Spanish-American War veterans at Bilibid had kept hearing bugles. They even identified the calls. They were hearing ghosts.

Our rotation camp bothered little about military punctilio. I cannot remember seeing any soldier salute an officer. The camp's was a casual life in which we sat on our cots or wandered to the seashore nearby to watch a never-slackening procession of trucks rattling by, or 'plane coming in, four or five minutes apart, to roll to a stop on their wire–mesh landing field.

353

We met other civilian repatriates from the central and southern islands; they had done better than we, staying out of Japanese reach in the mountains of Negros and Mindanao. One man, escaping with his wife barely hours ahead of the enemy, had been compelled to wait while his wife gave birth to a baby. This infant, when but ten hours old, they had entrusted to a Filipina nurse. Seven months later, she met them and returned the child to its mother.

Atrocities were vouched for so grewsome that the recital turned our stomachs, but the war mentality was not restricted to the enemy. On our side too it produced quirks which we thoroughly approved, constricting our hearts to a cold impersonal anger that sanctioned what in normal times we would have labelled murder.

One G.I., an electrician, told of spending seventy-eight days with the infantry as they fought up the Leyte hills. In this fighting quarter was neither asked nor given. After one sortie the Americans found the body of a man from their outfit: his feet had been burned off, his eyeballs gouged out, his forearms and hands flayed. Not surprising was it then that the electrician, when he surprised a Japanese unarmed in a fox-hole, made no bones about shooting him, but before he could pull the trigger he was checked by his victim's exclaiming in English,

"Don't shoot, or you'll go to hell."

Going to the edge of the fox-hole, he squatted down.

"Where did you learn about hell, you bastard!" he demanded.

The man's answer shocked him. This Japanese had lived in San Francisco, his own home town. For several minutes they chatted affably about places they both knew well, a conversation they prolonged with mutual pleasure until an impatient sergeant cut them short.

"Come on," he yelled, "we gotta get out of here. What're you doing?"

"Just talking to a Jap from San Francisco," replied the G.I.

"Well, make it snappy."

Turning to the Japanese, the electrician asked, "Well, where do you want it?"

The Japanese hesitated, then put his hands behind his back, as he said,

"Between the eyes.

"Brother," the electrician assured him, "that's exactly where you're going to get it," – and he shot him.

Not one of us dissented from the complete rightness of his action.

* * * * * * * *

Three days were more than enough of Leyte; we had ten - by which time I was turning psycho. Some husbands hitch-hiked rides down the coast to

354

see their wives, but I stuck to the camp and its nondescript beach, vacillating between each day's several choices in boredom. To be clothed, fed regularly, relieved of work, responsibility, worry, was too drastic a change. My nerves needed pressure to steady them. With nothing to worry about, I had to invent worries. Even when our names were posted for departure, I lay awake most of a night imagining some hitch.

One hitch, indeed, we did suffer, but it was on an apt culmination to the dreariness of our ten days' wait at Tacloban. It was the hitch to which seasoned G.I.s were inured, the proverbial haste to arrive nowhere. Having had our impatience already tormented by twelve hours' postponement of the plans first announced, we arose after midnight, drank coffee and ate sandwiches in the Casual Mess Hall, then at two climbed into trucks for the short ride to Tacloban's improvised port. The women and children, we knew, had embarked, the day before, aboard our transport, a rakishly handsome Dutch liner, the *Klipfontein*.

Beside the pontoon she lay, dark and silent. An hour passed, two hours, three, but still nothing happened. The pontoon by now was crammed with departing passengers. Not only ex-prisoners but soldiers, all assembled before the crack of dawn. What was holding us up no one knew, though there was a multitude of guesses, all profanely worded, which narrowed down to two: The holds were not yet cleared, and the transport commander was asleep. Finally the colonel of our rotation exploded.

"Sergeant," he called out, "go and wake up that major, - and don't wake him up gently!"

The only persons who did wake up were our wives. Attired in Red Cross negligees, they appeared on deck, and tried to cheer us by tossing us oranges. But even this comfort palled as dawn lightened and the sun climbed, hotter by the minute. Our colonel did his best for us, securing K-rations for a mocked up breakfast. Still the *Klipfontein* slumbered. Not till we were staggering under noon's violence, slowly broiling on the pontoon's griddle-hot plates, did the ship put out gang-planks and take us aboard. I had just strength enough left to drag two duffel bags into the forward hold allotted to us and plop them on one of the four-decker bunks that had been cramped into its stifling confinement. My first act was to make sure I had all twelve copies of our travel orders; this was no niggling issuance in quintuplicate or sextuplicate, but a whole dozen! We shuddered to calculate how many ships were needed to carry to the South Pacific mimeographs enough to maintain this gargantuan output. They must be held ready, we were warned, to be produced on demand. Assiduously I put them at the top of my duffel bag whence, with perverse ingenuity, they worked their way to the bottom. Time and again I would dump out the bag's miscellaneous contents, fish out the straying documents, fix them once more at the top. I still have all twelve; they were never asked for. Munitions may run short, men and supplies go astray – but no war can be fought without paper.

Travel orders vexed us less, however, than the other orders given us aboard the *Klipfontein*, orders that depressed our spirits to an ebb even more dismal while we were but half recovered from our eleven hours' vigil on the pontoon. These new orders prohibited all male ex-prisoners from visiting their families amidships except between two and four each afternoon. On such visits they were restricted to the starboard deck and one of the ship's two lounges.

Who had made these regulations we never could learn. The American transport officer, according to the chaplain, his intermediary, blamed the Dutch captain – in whose eyes, trained to European caste distinctions, (it was said) we were steerage. The Dutch officers pooh-poohed this accusation; they didn't care where we went. Their sole concern was navigation. The fault, they insisted, was the transport commander's. As for the Navy gun-crew, their attitude was a plague on both their houses. For us, however, graduates of an internment camp, the rule smacked of our one-time subjection to the Japanese edict against "commingling."

Whatever its source, the regulation did not stay long in force. Three years of internment had made us expert at breaking rules. We soon invented a dozen excuses for haunting the first class precincts. One excuse was even valid: four men, glorified by huge red celluloid buttons labelled "Sentry," were on duty patrolling the decks to make sure that on child fell overboard. Though these guards were supposed to change on the hour, the buttons multiplied like rabbits. Then there was the hour when the PX was open; no one presumed to obstruct an American citizen's right to drink coca-cola. It was a husband's duty, too, to care for his wife when she was seasick – and who was to diagnose the gravity of her illness? Certainly not the Army doctors, young and unpractised in gynecology. So successful was our lawbreaking that, before we departed New Guinea, the South West Pacific's top transport officer came aboard to rescind all major limitations on our movements. We now could inhabit the first class deck and share one of the lounges.

"But everyone's been doing that any way," he was told.

"Yes, I know; but we might as well make it official."

This is jumping ahead of the story. At the pace we set from Leyte we seemed unlikely ever to reach New Guinea. We were travelling in convoy, some forty or fifty of us, landing craft, destroyer escorts, a freighter or two and, standing out, monumentally vulnerable, the 16000 ton *Klipfontein*. As usual, our destination and route, officially secret, was known unofficially to everybody – Biak, Finschhaven, and thence past Guadalcanal on the long haul to San Francisco. Just ahead of us, however, as we emerged from the

Leyte Gulf, was another convoy whose secret was better kept. Its four hundred ships filled the sea. Turning north, while we turned south, its foremost vessels were hull-down on the horizon before the aftermost had drawn away from us. Not till news came of the bloody assault on Okinawa did we know where they had gone.

Our pace, of course, was set by the slowest craft in our convoy. Only one thing could have been slower – our twice-daily crawl to meals, 0630 to breakfast, 1630 to dinner. This was by way of the "Burma road," a tortuous passage down into the bowels of the ship. "Bowels" was an apt metaphor; in our twisty, dark meandering, we could well have been threading the *Klipfontein*'s intestines. Eventually we did come up again to sunlight in the approach to a mess-hall far aft. But by now we ex-starvelings were spoiled; forgotten were rice, and carabao sinews flavoured with cockroaches. Ably seconded by the G.I.s, we were learning to gripe at what, a few weeks back, would have been nectar and ambrosia.

The first night out, each of us was given a fresh pear; we were given also an Atabrin tablet apiece, a confection so new to me that, instead of swallowing it at once, I let it dissolve on my plate. The result was a pear so bitterly coated that only by stern will-power did I gulp it down. The whole way across the Pacific I regretted that pear. Never again were pears on our menu. Oranges and apples we had in plenty, but nothing else would satisfy me but the pear I had let spoil.

Such annoyances, absurdly important at the time, were further symptoms of the tension that ensured on our release from tension. Only slowly did concentration camp relax its grip, only by small degrees could we adjust ourselves to freedom. Our grudge against the Santo Tomas camp had not abated; in the weeks between rescue and departure we had chalked up new grievances, the mishandling of our mail, shoved aside in their office where it might have gathered dust till the war's end except for the determined woman who pushed past their denials that we had any mail, and found it there, the arrogant appropriation of relief supplies, of shoes and clothing, with only left-overs for us to pick from. So acutely did these grievances rankle that, aboard the *Klipfontein*, our Camp Holmes-Bilibid group, a minority of course, held stiffly aloof from the Santo Tomas people. This was not deliberate pettiness but simply that we felt nothing in common with the other camp. Casual words we might exchange, little more.

My dominant memories, however, fix not on the trifles that bulked so ridiculously large; they dwell on mysterious twilights, morning and evening, when tightly cinched up in kapok jackets we kept vigil through the hours most liable to submarine attack. Out on deck, while night was still dark, we would come and there remain till daylight filtered through the clouds that hung perpetually over equatorial seas. One by one, the convoy's many ships would take shape, dark, silent hulls drifting into the dawn. A strange quiet hushed us all until the captain woke a new day's chatter, announcing in guttural accents, "Der schmoking lamp is lit."

Between the Philippines and New Guinea, G.Q. was no fancy precaution. Off Hollandia, in moonlight that made the *Klipfontein* a silver target, two torpedoes were let loose at us, Luckily, we now were traveling on our own, and turned up a burst of speed that shook us from mast-head to keel, speed sufficient to outrun any submarine. In convoy, our ship would have been a sitting duck.

Once clear of the islands, however, and traversing the interminable vacancy of the Pacific, we grew progressively disinclined to forsake our bunks and (in the Navy phrase) hit the deck. At Biak and Finschaven we had taken aboard close to two thousand soldiers. Through morning and evening stand-to they packed the deck in a wedge too solid for latecomers to force passage. Yet before we were half way across the Pacific the deck was so empty that those who still responded to the morning call looked lonely.

Daily we went through a solemn farce: the master sergeant, surveying us from his stance on the top deck, would ask the corporal in formal military idiom whether everyone was present. Everyone was present, the corporal assured him – from which reply the logical deduction was that several hundred G.I.s must have fallen overboard since we left New Guinea. In time, military procedure was reshaped to fit facts: as we entered colder climates, our orders were amended, and we were dispensed from going on deck. At the call of "Now hear this," all we now had to do was dress and stand by our bunks. All we did, naturally, was stay in our bunks.

Another problem to which the transport commander addressed himself more stringently bore results as comical as they were futile. On her preceding voyage the *Klipfontein* had carried to San Francisco a cargo of Australian wives. Before the commander could steady his nerves after this shattering experience he found himself again saddled with a shipload of women. True, these women had been prisoners and long absent from a beauty parlor, but for two months now they had been eating good food; no longer were they gaunt and sunken-eyed. They had begun not only to feel desirable but to desire – a heady situation when followed by the covetous eyes of two thousand soldiers.

Frances was standing, one morning, by the rail looking down on the troops sprawled across the hatches of an after well-deck.

"I wonder what they are thinking about," she remarked to a nearby sentry.

"Lady," was his fervent reply, "don't never ask!"

These sentries were a final measure adopted to keep the soldiers, if not pure in thought, at least pure in deed. They were stationed on the companionways and at every strategic point to prevent the G.I.s from striking up acquaintance with the women passengers. The officers were subject to even stricter regulation, not an easy matter, for they, like the women, were quartered in first class accommodations amidships. As a token barrier, a rope was stretched down the middle of the recreation deck, supposedly to keep military and civilian personnel apart. At night it was not even a token. The *Klipfontein*, of course, was travelling without lights; her decks were obscured by a darkness truly Stygian. So little heed was paid to the rope that, by a last edict, all officers were banished to their cabins at nine o'clock. Whether this proved effectual I doubt. The transport's aspirations were amply expressed by a calendar in the ship's office: the date of our expected arrival in San Francisco was ringed with a pencil, and above it in frantic capitals were inscribed three eloquent words, "Girls! Girls!! Girls!!!"

* * * * * * * * *

Our course home was more roundabout than the routes taken by most of our fellow prisoners. It was, in fact, a tour of places which the war had dragged out of the mists of geography to make forever famous. If we had been given our choice, we would have chosen the direct route; we had seen too much of what it meant to become famous by war.

Yet there was excitement in approaching a place like Biak in the company of the same troops who, a few months earlier, had blown its coral beaches to grey dust. It was fascinating to proceed in throbbing haste along the New Guinea coast, to see its volcanoes rising in naked, sharply tapered cones out of the sea, to look up at mountains heaped into gigantic ridges where the jungle poured skyward through fissured valleys to disappear, mysterious and unexplored, in the clouds veiling its summit, twelve thousand feet above sea-level.

Suddenly, with no warning except a blinking of lights, we had turned into Finschhafen's contrived harbour, our last landfall on this vast island. On a scale to match its huge, looming bulk was the military equipment fetched here to the world's end. In its brief moment of glory Finschhafen had burgeoned into an unceasingly bustling port, stocked with all the implements of modern warfare. Yet but a few hundred yards across the bay wood-smoke drifted from thatched roofs. Fuzzy-wuzzies paddled canoes out from a village where life adhered to age-old savage ways. Barely a mile back hovered the jungle, waiting to smother every sign of this activity and reduce its jeeps, its tanks, its 'planes to rusting wreckage. Naked children would play in these desolate relics and improvise legends of Finschhafen's greatness.

Such thoughts sifted through my mind as I watched this incongruous juxtaposition of frantic hustle and primitive somnolence. For the moment, however, the present was too impressively with us to make credible how swiftly its signs would pass.

The soldiers we were taking aboard crowded our holds. They cherished no regrets at seeing the last of New Guinea. Some were "psychos," mental cases broken by combat. One youngster fought every attempt to lead him up the gang-plank. He had to be shipped home by 'plane. Those who were brought aboard had their foreheads daubed with gentian violet to distinguish them from their saner comrades. One man I remember from watching him on deck, where he would stand by the hour, rigid, unmoving, empty-eyed. If anything of interest penetrated his dimmed mind, he did not turn merely his head but his whole body. He was being taught to feed himself, a process that took half a morning, half an afternoon. The day when he stooped to pick up a magazine, like a baby reaching for a trinket, to glance at it however vacantly, was a landmark in the doctors' hopes that some day he might recover. He had flown fifty-two missions; just before the fifty-third, he was found sitting by his bunk, his mind gone.

These men bespoke the cost of victory. Of that inestimable price we were mindful as we steered through rain-squalls past New Britain and into the Coral Sea. Guadalcanal's sullen coast, kept safe now by American destroyers, woke reminder of how anxiously we had tried to glean news of the fearful warfare, of how we cherished the oddly candid admission of a Japanese admiral, published in a Tokyo newspaper, that if they lost Guadalcanal they lost the war. By the time we passed its blurred shores, they were receding in history, their glory and their tragedy a short-lived flare-up from which they were sliding back into the unstoried remoteness that had made the Solomon Islands a synonym for the end of the earth.

That "end of the earth" feeling haunted us as we passed other islands scarcely less famous. The steep mountains of the Santa Cruz group where huge trees outlined the slopes like bristles on a hog's back, the Ellice Islands, just the tops of palms above a watery horizon, these dwelt in primeval stillness. To imagine them dragged out of their legendary isolation, compelled to take part in western civilization's more efficient homicide, seemed not only an unfair intrusion but too fantastic to believe. Who could have imagined that they would affect the destiny of Washington or Chicago or New York?

Washington, however, reached out to us in mid-Pacific, dismaying us with word that Franklin Roosevelt was dead. So out of touch with American politics had we been – Yamato had labelled Camp Holmes's straw ballot for

360

Roosevelt "an imaginary election" – that no one aboard the *Klipfontein*, not even the soldiers, seemed to know who was President in his place. Some of us guessed McNutt! When at last we learned that our new chief was Truman, there was great conjecture as to who Truman might be. I for one thought gloomily of Lincoln's death in the hour of victory, and of all the trouble that followed his tragic removal from a job which he alone could manage – but President Truman's plainspoken voice reassured us.

Our thought, nevertheless, still lingered with the dead President. The ship prepared to honour him. A voice over the loud-speakers asked for a volunteer to blow taps. Of the two thousand soldiers on board not one responded. If buglers there were, they hid their light under a bushel. They had learned too thoroughly the Army rule "never to stick your neck out!" In ceremonies faultily labelled "In Memorium," American and Dutch officers united to pay a tribute certainly sincere but culminating far from majestically in the Star Spangled Banner amplified, scratches and all, from a record player.

Grief for the late President did not persist. Just as he had passed, so the war was passing from our consciousness. We were out of it, hard put at times to believe that we had ever been in it. Reports of the assault on Okinawa, of civilians rescued from Baguio, came through the scenes already as remote as the rumble of distant thunder. In an impersonal way we were sorry for the men still fighting, still battling to gain points of vantage for what might be the costliest action of all, the attack on Japan's mystically invulnerable shores. Ours was the sympathy one gives on hearing that a not too intimate acquaintance has contracted cancer. The shores we looked to were east, not west.

We were in our own hemisphere now, and pushing steadily north, away from the equator, a fact attested by each day's acuter chill. No longer did I wake exuding rivulets of sweat, nor climb up on deck in the small hours to seek gasping relief from the hold's tightly screened stagnation. The woolen shirt and trouser, the heavy lined jacket, issued at Tacloban, had welcome use.

Clothes, like food, were still luxuries we did not take for granted. When, the day before San Francisco, an order went out that all things to be discarded should be piled on a forward hatch-cover, ready to be dumped overboard at dusk, we were shocked to see what was thrown away, new boots, rain-coats, overcoats, jackets, shirts, articles we would have clung to long after they were threadbare. So sharply had internment taught us their value that we gladly would have helped ourselves from the heaped-up hatch-cover, but Army rules did not permit this, just as Army book-keeping was not equal to salvaging left-over stores, stores in most cases brand new which could have gladdened a horde of dispossessed people. Over the side they went; the G.I.s did not want the bother of carrying them ashore. To us this extravagance was more shocking than many larger, more tragic experiences. No country, however rich, had the right to dispose so wastefully of its abundance. It was, unhappily, too appropriate a symbol of the ruthless havoc with which America, long before the war, had been slashing and destroying the most opulent heritage into which ay nation had ever been privileged to enter. War merely aggravated this trait, hurling into the Pacific shiny new boots, the heavy woolen overcoats, we quondam prisoners coveted.

There were other preparations for San Francisco, a whole series of instructions, of injunctions calculated not only to effect a smooth landing but, it was hoped, a decorous return to a country populated with females. There was to be no whistling, no cat-calls. Who devised this code of etiquette I do not know, but I cannot conceive of any man fool enough to believe it would be obeyed. I had seen transports arriving from France after the First World War, heard the ebullient outcry as doughboys hailed every skirted passenger aboard the Hoboken ferries. The new breed of soldier, twenty-five years later, had a different nickname, but they were not likely to stand in reverent attention at the spectacle of American womanhood. The first glimpse of silk-stockinged legs would rouse the predictable reaction; from men starved of sex it would ring with the lusty overtones of rape – and it did.

Our thoughts as we cut smoothly through the dark sea toward America surged with expectation of the Golden Gate, theme of so many pessimistic jingles – "Golden Gate in Forty-Eight," and the like. Long before dawn we groped our way for the last time along the Burma Road and, in a shiveringly cold wind, across the after deck to a skimpy breakfast. The meal was rushed through, and we were piled topside with our duffel bags so that not one minute need be lost in cleaning out holds and evacuating the ship. As the night thinned, we could see the darker California coast and, at last, the tall towers of our hearts' cherished destination, the Golden Gate Bridge. A huge cheer from hundreds of throats greeted the sight. Exactly midway between the two towers rose the sun.

It was the dawn of a new day, but for me it brought back another morning, a morning when I was young and had risen early to see this same sun brighten with its first beams the tapering slopes of Fuji. Between those two sunrises stretched a lifetime.

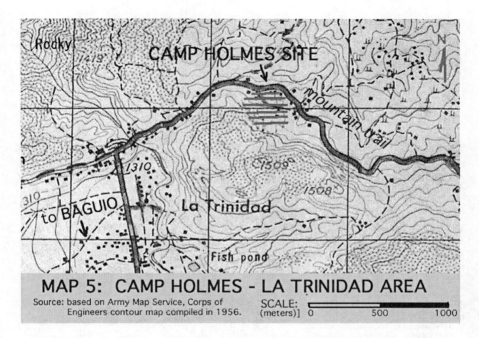

MAP 5: CAMP HOLMES - LA TRINIDAD AREA

Source: based on Army Map Service, Corps of
Engineers contour map compiled in 1956.

SCALE:
(meters)] 0   500   1000

CAMP HOLMES SITE *(above) shown below arrow. Area is approximate. Wood crews worked hills to the South. Based on a 1956 Army Map Service contour map. Elevations in meters, contour lines every 20m.*

POST-WAR PHOTO OF CAMP HOLMES SITE *(below) showing foundations of main barracks. Camp Holmes was destroyed Jan. 7 1945 less than two weeks after its inmates were sent to Manila (courtesy of Ralph Longway whose mother, Inez, took this photo in 1947)*

363

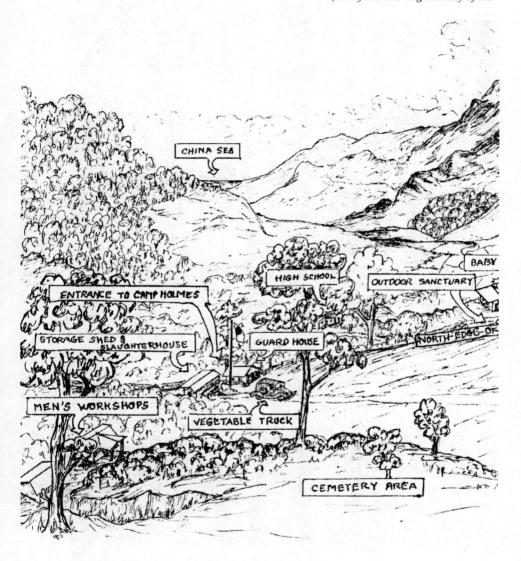

Fern Harringtons's **PANORAMIC VIEW**
(use of this drawing courtesy of the

This half of Fern Harrington's drawing shows places mentioned in the text including: the High School (later relinquished), the Work Shops where the "Ball & Chain" for diplomas were made, the Guard House where inmates could listen (for a while) to broadcasts by "Tokyo Rose".

364

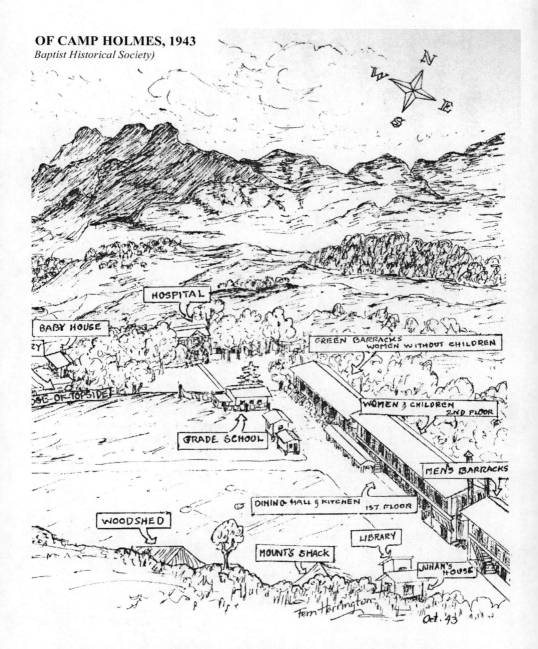

This half of Fern Harrington's drawing shows other places mentioned in the text including: the Men's Barracks where VHG and Geoffrey lived; the Women's Barracks where Frances and Ann lived, behind which was the community cook stove; the dining hall where VHG had his first job as waiter, also site of weekly entertainment and of the production of Our Town; the hospital where General Committee meetings were held, as well as the long run bridge contest between the Burnetts and the Gowens that determined the timing of MacArthur's return (p. 312-p.313).

SCHOOL

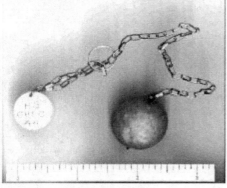

THE GRADE SCHOOL *(above), a converted chicken house that was moved from near the pigpen to a more central location. Later a similar building, not much bigger, became the High School (Courtesy of Robert Foley whose father, Rupert took this photo at great risk with a camera smuggled into Camp)*

"We had been promised an academy; we were given a shack... .It was an overgrown matshed, roofed with second hand iron full of nail-holes that had to be plugged with tar..." (p.292)

BALL AND CHAIN FOR DIPLOMA *This Ball and Chain made by Fabian Ream for daughter Nora, class of 1944. The ball is from fossilized limestone, the chain from the back of a comb, and the plaque from a 10 cent piece. Her two classmates also received a "ball & chain." (Photo and text courtesy of Ralph Kuttner)*

"I could not forget how Camp Holmes pupils conserved paper by writing their letters so small – three lines where we would write one – that today I need a magnifying glass to read my few surviving samples of their work." (p.289)

EXCERPT FROM STUDENT JOURNAL *(actual size)*

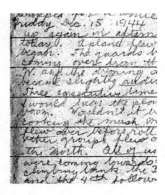

BILIBID PRISON

GRAVES OF AMERICAN SOLDIERS
(right) that lined the north and east walls of Bilibid Prison. Edge of the guard house can be seen on the right.

"In our midst . . .were the graves of men whose final horizon was the tall, wire-topped wall that enclosed us. (p.328)

VIEW OF BILIBID, 1949 *(below) This shot shows, beyond the central cell block tower, the northern, civilian quarter of Bilibid formerly used for the Camp Holmes internees, rebuilt as a hospital. (From a postcard from Fr.Sheridan to Elmer Herold courtesy of Betsy Herold Heimke)*

MAP OF CIVILIAN QUARTER OF BILIBID *(below) This plan view comes from a journal kept by Geoffrey for the last two and a half months of internment. Written in pencil its lines and text were redrawn to make them legible.*

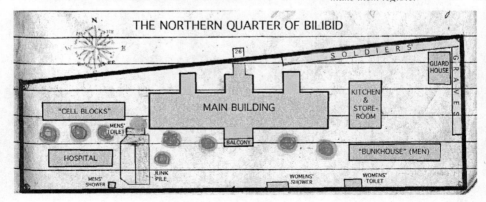

THE NORTHERN QUARTER OF BILIBID

N

26

SOLDIERS'

GUARD HOUSE

GRAVES

"CELL BLOCKS"

MENS' TOILET

MAIN BUILDING

KITCHEN & STORE-ROOM

HOSPITAL

BALCONY

"BUNKHOUSE" (MEN)

MENS' SHOWER

JUNK PILE

WOMENS' SHOWER

WOMENS' TOILET

BATTLE OF MANILA

MANILA IN FLAMES *(above). When this photo was taken, 7 Feb, 1945 the front line, as can be seen in Map 6, was north of the Pasig River, only a km. away from Bilibid Prison (oval structure in foreground). Its inmates had just returned after evacuation from a fire that reached Azcarraga St. immediately to the south of the prison compound.*

MORTAR BATTERY IN BACK-YARD *(left). The towers and walls of Bilibid Prison can be seen behind.*

AFTER THE BATTLE

LEGISLATIVE BLDG BEFORE *(right)* **AND AFTER** *(below right)* **THE BATTLE OF MANILA.**. *Both pictures from Robert Ross Smith "Triumph in the Philippines" Dep't of the Army, 1963, pp 304-305.*

"To the South, beyond the river, the roof of the legislature was burning. It had been newly bombed, a good riddance, we hoped, for like so many of the public buildings first erected by the American government it was a concrete mimic of Washington's classical architecture, its unshaded windows as unsuited to the glaring tropical sun as its columns and porticoes were stupidly pretentious. (p.347)

JAPANESE PRISONERS LEAVING BILIBID PRISON *(left, taken late March, 1945) They were on work detail to clean up debris from destruction "that was on the scale of Warsaw. . . and smaller only than the battles of Berlin. . . and Stalingrad." Quote from Connaugton, Pimlott and Anderson "The Battle for Manila, p.15.*

GOING HOME SOON

MAIL LINE *(above). The American Red Cross collected some 600 letters for Bilibid civilian internees delivered shortly after they had been liberated. Prison walls can be seen in background.*

ORDERS HOME *(below) Official orders were required for civilian internees to be repatriated A total of 47 names were listed. Gowen family names are at lower left. No one had enough possessions to use the 50 lbs. that was authorized!*

C O N F I D E N T I A L

HEADQUARTERS
UNITED STATES ARMY SERVICES OF SUPPLY
OFFICE OF THE COMMANDING GENERAL   -AGSXP 24 -

15 March 1945
SUBJECT: Orders.   APO 707

TO   : Personnel concerned.

        Pursuant to auth contained in letter, Hq, USAFFE, dated 4 Mar 45,
file FEGARP 704, subject: "Civilians Recovered from Enemy occupied Territory"
and Radio CG USASOS 4448, the following named civilians (US Citizens), liberated
from enemy held territories in SWPA WP to a port in the US by first available
water T. Pers will report to Comdr of Port on arrival for further instructions.
Air T by mil acft. auth to APO 72, where water T to the US will be provided.
50 lbs personal baggage auth while traveling by air. TCNT.   TDN.

        DORTHY GARWICK   CARROLL HINDERLIE
          VINCENT H GOWEN   MARY W HINDERLIE
        FRANCES GOWEN   MAREN HINDERLIE
        GEOFFREY GOWEN   ROY M HIX
        ANN GOWEN   INA RAE HIX

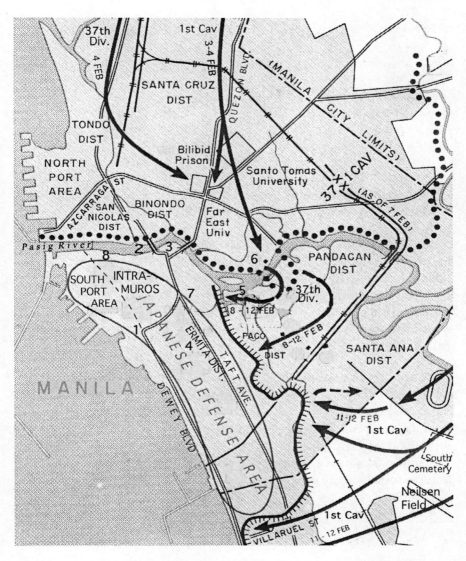

MAP 6 -- THE BATTLE OF MANILA

→ U.S. AXIS OF ADVANCE, DATES INDICATED
●●●●●●●● U.S. FRONT LINE, EVENING, 7 FEB
▯▯▯▯▯▯▯▯ U.S. FRONT LINE, EVENING, 12 FEB

SOURCE: based on Robert
Ross Smith *"Triumph in
the Philippines"* Dep't of
the Army (1961), Map VI

1 MANILA HOTEL
2 JONES BRIDGE
3 GENERAL POST OFFICE
4 EPISCOPAL CATHEDRAL
5 PROVISOR ISLAND
6 MALACAÑANG PALACE
7 LEGISLATIVE BLDG
8 FORT SANTIAGO

SCALE MILES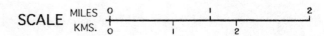
KMS.

Epilogue

AFTER THE WAR Father Gowen and his family moved to the old family home on Bainbridge Island across Puget Sound from Seattle.

For several years he taught at Lakeside School in Seattle. When an Episcopal church was built on the island he left Lakeside and became the full time rector of Saint Barnabas where he served until he retired in 1961. In the following years he continued to assist at Saint Barnabas on occasion. He performed weddings and baptisms and funerals. He tutored students, held a weekly literature class, and continued to row his boat in the waters around Bainbridge.

During this time he kept up an active correspondence with friends and former students from his days in the Orient. Many made the trek to Bainbridge Island to visit and recount old days. In 1977 (long after these memoirs were penned) he attended the first major reunion of Camp Holmes survivors in San Francisco. There, after 34 years, he met again Mr. Rokuro Tomibe commandant of Camp Holmes in 1943, the honored guest and featured speaker of the reunion.

Father Gowen remained active until the last few months of his life when cancer began to take its toll. He died in 1984 at the age of 91. Twenty three years later, at the closing ceremonies of the 2007 Camp Holmes Internees Reunion, attendees listened to a performance of, and then joined in singing the Camp Holmes School Song that he had written 63 years earlier. The song was performed and videotaped for the occasion by the chorus of the Lynden Christian High School of Lynden, Washington, the school of four of his great-grandchildren.

Appendix A:
Reflections on Chinese Literature and Drama

IN NANCHANG I first learned to speak Chinese. I won't say I mastered it. That is a different matter. Foreigners who really mastered Chinese were a rare breed. I am skeptical whenever I read of Europeans acquiring an Oriental language so completely in a year or two that, when suitably disguised, they could pass as natives. In China I met a few who, after years of residence, might have managed this – but they still could not claim to have mastered Chinese; it demands too many diverse skills. Fluent they might be without knowing the characters or, if they could read characters, this was not guarantee that they could write them. Mastery then I certainly could not claim, but a growing adeptness in both speaking and reading quickened my desire to be at home in Chinese culture.

Although this desire I fulfilled only to a fractional degree, the pursuit was exhilarating. It introduced me to the Chinese novel and the Chinese drama.

The two are intertwined. Most Chinese dramas in my day drew either on the great epic novels like the Three Kingdoms or novels like the Dream of the Red Chamber which move through the domestic relationships and intrigues of a Chinese family, always of course a family in the classical mould. The Chinese theatre also borrowed many episodes from collections of short stories.

One of these collections, Chin Ku Ch'i Kuan, I had read earlier, quite startled by the explicit detail of its love passages. Lured by a remark in Gile's Chinese Literature, I had tried to secure a novel called the Chin P'ing Mei; this, he said, would require the nerve of a Burton to translate. When I asked for it at Chinese bookstores, the salesmen laughed in my face and denied having it. I tried a fresh tack: on the advice of an English friend then visiting me I included it in a list of several books which I asked my teacher to purchase for me. Back he came with all of them – except the Chin P'ing Mei!

My friend, fortunately, had a teacher less fastidious. He made no scruples about getting him a copy, nor a second one for me, my friend having assured him that he wanted a copy in each hand, so intensely was he enjoying its ribaldries. A satire on the corrupt practices of the late Ming court, the Chin P'ing Mei might not be reckoned shocking in an age when Henry Miller can pass the censors, but it will never be Sunday School reading. On the other hand neither is it prurient. It does not grovel in perversion but wreathes its people in the glimmering twilight of the loneliness, the tragic vacancy, to which their own wilful follies conduct them.

In several respects Chinese novels resemble English novels of the early 18th Century, especially such masterpieces as Fielding's Tom Jones or Joseph Andrews. There are marked differences, of course: the Chinese author does not indulge in Fielding's editorial comment, he does not stand aside to exclaim with inimitable irony on the vanities and follies of his characters. Nor is he limited to "boy gets girl;" with him it is "boy gets girls!"

But the plots are similar, rambling, discursive, straying from episode to episode. If the Chinese works allow more scope for poetry, they compare with the English in humour, humour rather than wit, and often raffish. In books as out of them, Chinese laughed at very elementary jokes. I was present once at an important educational meeting graced by the Governor of Kiangsi and all the top gentry, an imposing array clad in brocaded satins who quite forgot their dignity over a spectacularly vulgar song contributed to the programme by a school principal. In this ditty the catch line of each stanza ended with "ba'ba," an infant's output which Western mothers confine to his diaper. As the teacher cleverly turned the lines so that one by one from the Governor down everybody present was "ba-ba," His Excellency and the distinguished official sitting with him rocked themselves hysterical with laughter.

Such humour pervades Chinese novels and with it – a further characteristic of 18th Century England – a gaily tolerant relish for sexual exploits. "Boys will be boys," they agree and if the Chinese setting, with its abundance of concubines, female cousins, pretty slave-girls, offers them wider opportunity to be so, it is a situation of which Tom Jones, tumbling farmers' daughters in the bushes, would have availed himself with gusto.

Oddly enough, a Chinese author, writing masterful English, has given us original works that display all the finest marks of the Chinese novel. In Lin Yu-t'ang's Moment in Peking, as in his later books, we see how admirably this type of fiction can be expressed in English. Both English and Chinese are loosely textured languages; in both, grammar has almost disappeared, and for the same reason, the centuries during which the basic tongue was spoken but not written. In England this happened after the Norman Conquest, when Norman French, the court tongue, joined Latin, the language of scholars, to oust Anglo-Saxon as a literary medium. In China the literary language, Wen Li, and the spoken language Kuan Hua or Mandarin, existed separately, side by side. But the novels which scholars did not appraise as literature, were forerunners of a movement that eventually, in the 1920s, raised the vernacular – under the name of Pai Hua or Clear Talk – to respectable acceptance for books, plays, and newspapers alike. Thus resulted a style so akin to English narrative style that Lin Yu-t'ang, writing like a native in what was not his native language, has given us novels exactly in the vein of Chinese domestic fiction.

I have stressed "domestic," because the heroic novels were on a different scale, even if the style, diffuse and episodical, was similar. I have read but one, the San Kuo, or Three Kingdoms, the greatest of them all, a book so well known that its scenes, used in numberless decorative panels, are painted without explanatory characters. The San Kuo should be ranked as perhaps the world's most richly variegated epic. Heroic courage and fidelity, pathos, humour, romance, brilliant inventiveness in the strategy that plans its wars and the tactics directing its battles, all these parade magnificently through nine hundred close-printed pages.

Its time is the break-up of the Han dynasty, 220 A.D., but its narrative of the civil wars that ensured, the shifting of alliances that waged their quarrels across the length and breadth of China, described just as aptly the China which I knew, the China of the *Tuchüns*, the War-Lords.

The *Tuchüns*, however, had no one in their ranks fit to rank with the San Kuo's three heroes, Liu Pei, king of west China, and his two friends, Chang Fei, and Kwan Kung (deified later as God of War), nor with the genius, Chu Ko-liang, who used the resources of the spirit world as well as the natural in directing Liu's campaigns. Liu, Chang and Kwan were the three "brothers of the Peach Orchard," having taken there an oath of eternal fidelity from which they never wavered. Chu Ko-liang's association with the three was stamped by the same unswerving loyalty.

How much of the book is history, how much fiction, is for sinologues to argue. Such distinctions did not worry me, so absorbed was I in the unfailing interest of the story. This interest took its breath-taking hold from the men and women who people the novel. In every word, every deed, they are alive, while the scintillating changes of scene and mood through which they move reveal them as both human and heroic. The unknown author transfers to us his own sometimes mocking affection for a doughty warrior like Chang Fei who, surprised by an enemy army when his own forces were absent, could think of no better defense than to bellow at them. His voice is prodigious.

The enemy are checked. We see them hesitate, falter, look at one another with a startled query in their faces. These are the slow beginnings of the panic which they struggled to check – until Chang bellows again. No longer do they hesitate. Tumbling over each other's heels they break into flight.

Chu Ko-liang in a similar plight did not have Chang Fei's redoubtable voice to help him. He too had been surprised, this time within a walled city which he had no soldiers with him to defend. Not for one moment did he show alarm. Ordering all the city gates to be thrown open, he mounted a t'ing tzu, the high rooftop platform where Chinese restaurants serve their guests in hot weather. Here he had a feast brought to him, course by course. In plain sight of his foe he sat, calmly eating and drinking, but such was his reputation for military cleverness that the enemy, suspecting a trap, dared not attack.

Supreme in Chinese history as a strategist, Chu Ko-liang could have matched wits with Ulysses. His moves were the moves of the chess board. His most daring feat was carried out to the discomfiture of an ally, Sun Ch'uan, whose loyalty he rightly suspected. Although they were mutually engaged in a campaign, Sun Ch'uan was so embittered by jealousy of his more brilliant comrade that he sought excuses to be rid of him. On this occasion he asked Chu Ko-liang (or K'ung Ming, as he was often called) what weapons they should employ against the enemy.

"Bows and arrows," said the latter.

"But we are short of arrow heads; how many must we have?"

Kung Ming did not waver in his reply, "One hundred thousand."

"Ai ya! That's impossible!"

"I can get them for you."

"We must have them quickly," Sun Ch'uan protested. "How soon can you get them?"

"I'll have them here in three days," said K'ung Ming.

"Can you guarantee that?"

"Of course."

Sun Ch'uan pressed home his advantage.

"Will you stake your life on it?"

To these fantastic terms K'ung Ming agreed.

Sun Ch'uan, now certain that he had his rival at his mercy, made doubly sure by ordering all his arrow-makers to work slowly. But K'ung Ming did not even trouble to approach them. So far as Sun's spies could ascertain, not once did he depart from his tent but remained inside, feasting and drinking wine. On the third morning he went to Sun Ch'uan.

"It is time to get the arrows," he announced. "I want twenty boats made ready; each must have a drum, and each must have its deck covered with straw."

Much mystified, Sun Ch'uan had the boats prepared and, with K'ung Ming directing them, set out up the Yangtze in a dense fog. Carefully they groped their way until they were opposite the enemy encampment, whereat K'ung Ming ordered the drums to be beaten loud and strong.

The enemy forces, soldiers of T'sao T'sao, China's arch-rebel, could not see their foe, but they could hear them. In a frantic attempt to repel the attack which they thought imminent they began shooting arrows wildly in the direction indicated by the drums, arrows which piled up on the strawed decks of sun Ch'uan's boats. At last, calculating that each boat had taken in not fewer than five thousand K'ung Ming said, "It is time to take our arrows back to camp."

"But how did you know the third morning would be foggy?" asked his discomfited ally.

"After living on the Yangtze all my life," K'ung Ming replied, "I would be pretty stupid not to foretell the weather three days in advance."

He was better at such guesses than I. Fourteen years on the Yangtze still left me puzzled as to the probabilities of its weather even one day ahead!

In many ways K'ung Ming is the hero of the San Kuo. Outliving his friends, the three sworn brothers of the Peach Orchard, he embarked on campaigns, particularly against Burma, in which he used weapons unmatched until the British employed tanks in World War I. One formidable opponent he captured and released time and again until this adversary at last conceded that K'ung Ming was the better man.

His death was in the epic tradition. Observing his star one night, he was startled to see it wavering. On hurrying to the astrologers he learned that only one measure could save him: for a week he must keep a candle alight in his tent.

This entire week K'ung Ming devoted to nursing the fateful candle. Never once would he leave it but hovered over it day and night until gradually the star regained its vigour. Seven nights had gone by and six days; only hours remained to make his future assured. But almost at the moment when K'ung Ming was expecting to terminate his long vigil a friend, unaware of what was happening, came to consult K'ung Ming – and left the tent flap open. Before K'ung Ming could rush to shelter the flame, the draught had blown it out. All the world wondered at the great star that fell. With it fell Chu Ko -Liang.

Other tragic episodes in the San Kuo are recorded in pages equally poignant. So intimate are the ties binding Liu Pei and his two great adjutants of the Peach Orchard Oath that when death breaks up their tight-knit brotherhood it shocks the reader like the death of a close friend. We can feel the extremes of Chang Fei's sorrow at beholding the apparition of Kuan Yu, who came to tell of his murder by T'sao T'sao. These ghostly appearances outweigh in the chilling grief they provoke even their great counterparts from Hamlet and from Greek tragedy.

But no incident can excel the devotion shown by Sun fu-jen, Liu Pei's wife, when told a false report of her husband's death. Quite unwillingly she had been detained by Sun Ch'uan, her brother, who had kept his sister from rejoining her husband in west China. As fickle and undependable in his association with Liu Pei as he had been with Chu-Ko Liang, he did not wish to see her involved in what he looked forward to as Liu's certain downfall. But he overplayed his hand. Sun fu-jen's response was suicide. Into the Yangtze she leaped, and so ardent was her desire to be united with her husband that her body floated upstream against the current.

Across the river from Wuhu, where for five years I lived, her body was pulled ashore and buried. Her simple grave was still there, sheltered by the temple built over it. The current still ran so strong that we had to make an extended detour to prevent our sampan's being carried down stream. With the Yangtze swirling past us in yellow turbulence, this legend of the dead woman stemming the river's irresistible strength became a tribute as heroic as it was tender to a wife's loyalty – and to a husband whose charm must have been remarkable to outweigh what we would regard as the handicaps of his personal appearance – for the record describes him as seven feet five inches tall, with eyes that could see behind his back, ears reaching to his shoulders, and hands hanging to his knees!

* * * * * * * *

To follow Chinese drama a knowledge of the San Kuo was essential and indeed a like familiarity with other novels, both heroic and domestic. My hankering for the Chinese theatre began at Nanchang where the billings adhered to tradition in offering not just a single play but a series of dramatic excerpts from different cycles, to be continued week by week like the Perils of Pauline in our first movies. They did not end, it is true, with the heroine tied to the tracks and an express train hurtling toward her at sixty miles an hour, nor with this much abused damsel prone before a buzz-saw inching nearer and nearer to her throat. But if we can imagine our theatre drawing its material week by week from successive books of the Iliad and the Odyssey as well as the Decameron, we can picture the dramatic use made of San Kuo and the other great books of Chinese fictional literature. One evening's performance rotated through a widespread programme, epic themes, heroic themes, mixed with farce, comedy, opera, and bawdy satires on the pranks of Buddhist and Taoist monks. Presented in their several courses these plays dished up – as Shakespeare did in one play or in such a historical series as Henry IV and V – something palatable to every man's taste.

The show began about seven and ended nearer one than midnight. The theatre made as few concessions to comfort as the Chinese restaurant. It was a barn. Groundlings sat in the pit, the elite in a narrow balcony which overhung three sides of the auditorium. The seats were wooden benches but in the balcony there were tables as well, a convenience for setting down the tea-pot and tea-cups which are an inseparable part of all Chinese social activity. Although the Chinese had not learned to mix popcorn with drama, they enjoyed peanuts and melon seeds, substitutes equally noisy, if any noise could outdo the strident click of the stone drums in the orchestra. These drums were unbreakable; my ears were not.

The stage was bare. The illusion of scenery had to be created by the actors' skill. In this they were aided by many conventions; when once these were mastered by the spectator, scenery and props could be forgotten. Some props there were, of course, but these too followed conventions which had to be understood before the action was intelligible. Most of them were attended to by stagehands, almost as active in the play as the actors themselves although by common agreement between cast and audience they never seemed part of it. Warily a stage-hand would drop a flat leather cushion behind an actor so soften the impact when he was supposed to fall. He would cover the face of a dead man with a cloth, generally red, to indicate his demise; even if the actor remained on his feet, the moment his face was covered, he was dead. I saw school boys, once, performing Julius Caesar, indicate the great man's ghost by chalking his face and stuffing paper in his eyes and nose. But for stage-hands and actors alike the most versatile of props were paper flags.

Two flags thrust either side of the actor indicated that he was riding in a sedan chair. Flags sprouting from between a general's shoulder blades indicated the number of armies he commanded. Heroes from the historical novels were indeed a magnificent spectacle, their official robes brilliantly embroidered in the traditional style (dragons, clouds, rocks, foaming waves), their eyes pointed upwards at the outer corners in an asterisk of black paint, their faces half hid by flowing white beards, a sign of venerable prestige as well as virility since not till he was forty did a Chinese presume to flaunt a mustache, and even at that age often could not manage more than a few sparse hairs to lend him this dignity.

Props and costumes the actors supplemented by gestures again strictly enjoined by custom. These were a gesture to indicate that the actor was riding horseback, another that he was crossing a bridge. If I had not had at my elbow a Chinese friend thoroughly versed in the elaborate pantomime of these dramas I would have come away hopelessly mystified as to what I had been witnessing.

For the amateur theatre-goer there was the further drawback of the language. Many of the plays, perhaps most of them, used the literary speech instead of the vernacular; only by study of the plays, or of the books from which they were drawn, could they be understood. The farces were more easily intelligible; even I could join in the guffaws which greeted their bawdy innuendoes, but for a detailed awareness of what was being said, I depended on my friend's running commentary.

In one respect I was fortunate: most of the romances were taken from the Chin Ku Ch'i Kuan, The New and Old Wonders, a book of short stories which I had read. They included the story of the boy who substituted for his sister as bride at a wedding. His family, hearing that the bridegroom was gravely ill, demurred to sending his sister to be married by proxy lest she be condemned to premature widowhood. Her brother therefore went dressed as a girl, only needing to conceal with a plaster the fact that he had had both ears, instead of only one, punctured for ear-rings. Despite the bridegroom's inability to attend, the ceremonies were held, the contract signed.

No one had detected the imposture and all would have passed off properly if the groom's sister had not felt sorry for the lonely bride and offered to keep her company on her wedding night. In a further ebullience of spirits she even suggested to the supposed bride that they pretend to be the newly married couple. It did not take long for these endearments to become so intimate that – as one needed no great Chinese scholarship to guess – nature took its course. The old nurse, who had listened in dismay to the bed creaking, was the first to guess a secret that soon was no secret at all. In a manner typically Chinese, however, the story's ultimate problem was how to untangle a whole skein of betrothals so that the errant couple might wed. Both the boy who had masqueraded as his sister and the bridegroom's sister, the girl who led him into mischief, had to be rid of future spouses to whom they were plighted. In a country where engagement is as binding as marriage this required a social finesse such as only a Chinese matchmaker could manage. But all ended happily, with the families thus involved linked by two weddings instead of one.

As drama, another tale from the Chin Ku Ch'i Kuan rose to more remarkable heights. Its plot was one dear to the writers of Greek and Latin comedies and, by derivation, to Shakespeare – the separation in infancy of [identical] twins. The play showed the brother, a handsome young man, searching for his sister from whom the exigencies of a famine had parted him while they were still babies. In such crises girls were sold into slavery; it was not surprising that his inquiries led to a brothel. His sister, he learned, was a sing-song girl, and absent on her nightly round of feasts. Without revealing his errand he awaited her return, stubbornly resisting the enticements of the other girls. But when his sister returned and he had followed her to her bedroom, he was balked of making himself known by the grotesque mishap that she was too drunk to comprehend. Time was wasting; in desperation, he resorted to an expedient one could look for only on the Chinese stage: he made her sick, even pulling off his silk jacket so that she could vomit into its folds.

What could have been ludicrous was performed with a tense delicacy that made me want to weep while I laughed, and the recognition of brother and sister soared to heights of lyric beauty, beauty golden-toned in the graceful blending of the two voices, the gloriously dramatic fulfilment of music cascading its blithe notes like a peal of silver bells. It stirred me then to tears and has enthralled me ever since, leaving memories bright as enamel which time cannot tarnish.

This, of course, was grand opera; Chinese drama depended as much on the sung word as on the spoken. But the Nanchang theatre was in the forefront of a changing tradition: instead of assigning women's parts to female impersonators, it gave them to women. As with England's Restoration drama, the introduction of actresses added a piquancy not entirely theatrical, and the girls who played these parts played also on the special allurements of their sex. But China's most lavishly worshipped actresses were still men. Of these the greatest was Mei Lang-fang.

This remarkable performer who, a number of years later, was to win applause even in New York, I saw in Peking. When he was acting the stir around the theatre was like the commotion around New York's Metropolitan Opera House when Caruso was billed to sing. Instead of cars, however, there were carriages, glassed-in broughams arriving by the score. The theatre, more Western in design than Chinese, outdid in comfort and splendour Nanchang's ramshackle playhouse; the audience, refreshing itself with bottled lemonade instead of melon seeds and tea, also seemed more Western in attitude than Chinese. It sounded odd to hear a Chinese gentleman reprove a Chinese woman in front of him not in Mandarin but with a curt command in English, "Sit down!"

Although they followed the traditional cycle, the plays obviously were regarded as curtain-raisers; at times they barely made headway against the chatter of an audience assembled for but one purpose, to see and hear Mei Lang-fang. Not until eleven was he booked to appear.

His entrance hushed the chatter; tense silence gripped every spectator. Before a backdrop of white satin, brilliantly embroidered with a huge peacock.

381

He began what to all intents and purposes was a protracted solo, a solo lasting for an hour and sung throughout in falsetto. He was impersonating Lin Yai-yo, one of the several heroines of the Hung Lou Meng. A synopsis of its plot I can best quote from the quaint English of the programme.

"Adopting from the famous Chinese novel 'Dreams from the Red Chamber," the play is well written and carefully transformed into music. These passages from the chapter 'Ta Yu Buries the Flowers' are the most beautiful and tasteful of all. The story runs:

"While Pao Yu, the young gentleman is reading 'The Western Paradise,' a famous romance, among the rocks in the garden, Ta Yu, his sweetheart, happens to come and reads it also. On seeing her so attached to the romance he teases her with jokes from the very book; she scolds him with charming and bewitching air, and at last, he asks for pardon. Then she gathers the falling flowers from the ground. She pities the flowers because she thinks that she herself will be tortured and marked by the Time just as it is done to the flowers. She believes that the youth is just like the spring and will vanish without the least hope of delaying. Then she buries the flowers weeping and singing with pity,

'Being scoffed as a fool I bury the flowers,
Yet I wonder in other days who will bury me?'

Was the concluding question of her sorrowfulness."?

Something of the magnitude of Mei Lang-fang's genius can be gauged by remembering that he wrote the words and mustc to his plays in addition to acting them. The perfect correlation of these talents shone through his performance, a performance whose marvellously subtle modulations of tone I have heard rivalled only by Sarah Bernhardt in La Phedre. But Mei Lang-fang was a man impersonating a young girl, and doing so in a falsetto with a tenderness, a gentle delicacy in the use of his voice, a clear, lyric intonation on the highest notes, that made us breathe and weep with the moody heroine. We forgot that this was acting; we were sharing with a girl in her 'teens, youth's first tragic puzzlement over a life that sweeps away health and love and happiness like chessmen from a game concluded too soon. The burial of the flowers and Tai Yu's lament were the play's only action yet for an hour, almost unaided, Mei Lang-fang swept our emotions across the whole magical range of his singing then lulled them into an unbreathing trance, his voice supported by an orchestra which, in moments of surpassing loveliness, quieted to the tranquil harmonies of flute and harp.

Acting at this level enforces its universal, its timeless contacts. It brings up from the heart men's hopes, their cravings and fears, and clarifies them by ennobling expression. How deeply Mei Lang-fang had seen into the souls of the heroines he personified I learned, a year or so later, when one of my pupils, a girl sensitively poetic in her daydreams yet courageous enough to stand against the communist agitators who strove to disrupt her school, ended a composition with questions worded almost in Tai Yu's phrasing,

"Why do the flowers fade? Why do the blossoms fall? Why do men die?"

Appendix B:
Two Heroes of the American
Occupation of the Philippines.

THIS HAPHAZARD CHRONICLE would be one-sided if it gave credit only to the Mission for bringing a primitive people safely into a world more dangerous than the pinched world they had known. Americans pretty generally have overlooked what used to be called the days of the Empire. They have ignored or forgotten heroes of their own nationality whose names should be revered so long as we are proud of being American.

With the Igorots American officers succeeded where the Spanish had failed. They won his allegiance, and won it not by military conquest but by fair and friendly dealing, won it so solidly that when a plebiscite was taken to register the will of the Filipinos as regards Independence, the Igorots of our district voted 8-1 to remain under the American flag. Like the Moros of the South they did not get their wish, and perhaps, in the long run, it was better so, but the vote was a tribute to the American officials (as well as the missionaries) who gained this unique trust.

Many illustrious men had toiled to this end, but I will mention only two, last of the line, because I arrived in time to witness what they were doing. These two were Leonard Wood, Governor General in the middle '20's, and John Chrysostom Early, last American Governor of Mountain Province.

But for the tragic tendency of politicians to shy off from strong men, Leonard Wood might have been elected President in 1920. The politicians preferred Warren Gamaliel Harding, a man they were confident, and alas rightly, that they could control. Yet Harding, the small town politician, deserves credit for appointing the Philippines' greatest Governor General to replace the worst. He dispatched Wood to succeed Francis Burton Harrison, with whom the Island had been saddled for eight ruinous years by the visionary idealist, Woodrow Wilson. This paradox is easier to lament than to explain.

For Leonard Wood to accept Harding's summons and return to the Philippines was not only a hug sacrifice, it was a death warrant. It required him, in the first place, to decline the chancellorship of the University of Pennsylvania, an offer exceptionally congenial to a man who, soldier though he was, devoted his prime concern to the arts of peace. More gravely, it put him beyond reach of surgical attention which he could neglect only at mortal risk.

Early in his career, while Governor General of Cuba, he had suffered a head injury from a falling chandelier, an injury that caused recurring tumours and necessitated periodic operations. Only in Boston, at the skilled hand of Dr. Harvey Cushing, was this surgical treatment available. But so demanding were the problems which Leonard Wood dealt with as Governor General that he postponed this treatment too long. When at last, in 1927, he was prevailed on to return to America, he went home to die.

His predecessor had not dared go home. He had settled in Scotland where he stayed until the Commonwealth was inaugurated in 1935. Apparently to collect on earlier favours he then returned to Manila, took Philippine citizenship, secured a political appointment, and very soon afterward disappeared from public notice.

The fruits of Burton Harrison's eight years in office did not disappear so handily. From 1913 to 1921 his single policy had been to undermine all that Americans before him had laboured, self-effacingly, to achieve. He had wiped out a dedicated civil service, turned administration over to Filipino politicos, sat idly by while they put the Government into business – and milked its profits. Whether he was carrying out Woodrow Wilson' order or pampering his own sloth is a question best buried along with the Manila gossip which debated it avidly for years. What remained was the corruption, the political mess, Leonard Wood was sent to purge. Even a man as brave, as duty-directed, as the new Governor General could have been excused if he had chosen to decline his appointment. But the General was not the man to dodge a tough assignment. As he said to one of his staff, a man too ready to quit, "You need to practise resignation less and perspiration more."

When Manuel Quezon, the dominant politico, had announced, "Better a country run like hell by the Filipinos than like heaven by the Americans," he described just how he and his fellow partisans had been running their country. But it had not been run by the Filipino people; it had been run by a clique as careless of the people and their welfare as a South American junta. Wood's fault in their eyes was his concern for all the people of the Philippines, for the tao, the peasant, as well as the cacique, the vested landowner. The tao, mired in debt from cradle to grave, was the pure-blooded Filipino; his rulers

– and creditors – were of mixed ancestry, their veins flowed with Spanish blood and Chinese.

The plight of the tao Leonard Wood set himself with indignant compassion to remedy. He was determined that they should have an honest government, a policy which necessitated pulling it out of the business enterprises, the bank, the sugar centrals, long mismanaged by politicians to their private enrichment. Instantly resentful of this assault on their perquisites, the officials tried to boycott his administration and bring it to a standstill. They failed. Even if he had to operate the machinery of government single-handed, the Governor General would not be bluffed; he kept the wheels turning. Grimly he confronted the current catch-cry of Independence.

Agitation for Independence had served the politicos well. It saved them from ever having to redeem their election promises. Whether they actually wished for Independence is debatable, certainly not if it led to canceling their exemption from paying American tariffs, or to the economic collapse sure to follow. They had no passion for a country too poor to pay them their inflated salaries. To demand Independence, however, seemed safe; nobody at that time could believe that the United States would grant the demand. Not only did this agitation relieve them from any need to offer a specific programme; it was an issue which they could utilize ad infinitum and ad nauseam, playing high-pitched tunes on the heart-strings of the rabble.

General Wood was no politician. He could not brook sham issues when real issues cried to be dealt with. On a visit to a provincial town he was confronted at a banquet by the usual oratory. He cut it short.

"Gentlemen," he said, "when I was coming up the stairs to this banquet hall, I heard sounds of moaning under the stairs. I went to investigate, and discovered an insane woman chained to a post. These are the things to which we had better give our attention before we talk about Independence."

His talk fell flat. I wish that he had been aboard the interisland steamship in which I once traveled from Mindanao to Manila. On a lower deck we had the spectacle of an insane man chained between two stanchions, where for six days he was left to wallow in his own filth. The Governor General had the authority to do something about it; our only response had to be the craven one of staying out of earshot so that we could not hear the man's piteous cries.

Leonard Wood's response was always the practical one which brushed aside theory. He was a man big enough to find time for little things. Such was his action when Mrs. Wood, returning from an afternoon's drive in Baguio, told of seeing an Igorot boy afflicted with a harelip, and how she had made the mother promise to bring her child next day to the clinic to have the deformity corrected.

The mother's promise did not suffice for the General. Off he went in person to the hut where the boy lived and brought him in his own car to the clinic. In person he made sure that the operation was performed. On his scale the Governor General never was important enough to weigh his own time against a child's happiness.

When he came back to the Philippines, one of the men he persuaded to return with him was Jack Early. Against opposition from the Philippine Legislature he made him Governor of the Mountain Province. Governor Early was as reluctant to return as his friend and superior. While flush with youth he had enrolled in the erstwhile Civil Service only to see it butchered by Burton Harrison. Seeing no future to a Philippine career he had gone to Spokane and, by the early 20's, was profitably engaged in business. To give up his developing prospects was a sacrifice almost foolhardy but, as he once told me, when he measured his own sacrifice against the General's, he could not refuse.

The hardship was aggravated by measures which the Legislature had taken to make his position in the Mountain Province unacceptable to Americans. This they had manoeuvred by cutting his salary till it was less than enough to subsist on. Only by securing him a secondary appointment as Superintendent of Schools (which he was well qualified to fill) did General Wood guarantee him a living wage.

Governor Early was a big man, big both in body and spirit. In college he had been one of Washington State's football heroes. His physical endurance outwore every limit. Undaunted by trails that slid down into the tropics and up once more into the chilling winds of the temperate zone, trails baked by the oven heat reflected from cogon grass till every step became head-splitting torture, trails that skirted dizzying chasms in a zigzag so precarious that I have seen Americans crawl on hands and knees along their crumbly edge, he continued to inspect every inaccessible corner of his immense province. Since he was too considerate to weigh down the mountain ponies with his big-boned frame, he obtained, after unraveling much red tape, an Army mule to carry him on his travels.

On one of these inspection tours, he was caught by a typhoon on Pulog, the Philippines' second highest mountain, ten thousand feet above the sea. The darkness was impenetrable, the rain an unceasing deluge propelled by gale winds that tugged at his feet like the malevolent back eddies of the Ilocos coast. His Igorot retainers lay down under what shelter they could improvise, but Governor Early looped a roped around a pine tree, striving to keet warm, ever aware that hidden in the night's screaming chaos lurked a precipice awaiting the single false step that could hurl him to his death.

But death used simpler means to claim its victims. When grey dawn filtered through the fog, Governor Early discovered that he alone had survived. All his companions were dead, dead from exposure. They had perished with the same fatalistic acceptance as a man lying down exhausted in Arctic snow.

Many such exploits the Governor's oversight of the Mountain Province forced on him. Other adventures he sought, as when he descended on a rope's end to sound what was reputed to be a bottomless pit in the honeycombed limestone at Sagada. He found no bottom. The stones he dropped into this shrub-hidden cavern sent back no sound.

Not surprisingly his physical courage built him into a legend, but this played only one, and that a less considerable, part in Governor Early's matchless ascendancy over Igorot hearts. Bodily strength supported a character of rare gentleness and compassion; intuitively he understood primitive people and won their trust.

In this he was frequently at odds with the Constabulary and with their legalistic efforts to conform the Mountain peoples to legislative enactment, to bend their shoulders to lowland-manufactured law they neither agreed to nor comprehended. Whenever he had disorders to resolve, Governor Early told me, he would try to keep out the Constabulary; many of his settlements, he admitted were by Philippine statute illegal but by tribal justice right.

So thoroughly did he pursue this policy that, when an American constabulary man refused to marry an Igorot girl after getting her pregnant, the Governor threatened to let the old men deal with him by village custom. The American knew what that would bring – judgement with a head-axe! Quickly he accepted marriage.

Cancer ended Governor Early's career in the Mountain Province; it never downed him. Through three agonizing years he fought his disease every step. When no longer able to travel mountain trails, he took up Henry Stimson's offer to work at Malacañang, the Governor General's palace, as advisor on the "Non-Christian Tribes." He even accompanied Stimson on a visit to the southern islands, where the Moros accorded him the same unequivocal trust as the Igorots. None of his duties would he spare himself. In his office he kept a couch; here he would lie down for a spell, if the pain became intolerable, then back to his desk he returned.

He had tried every medical expedient then available. His last recourse was a newly devised operation which proposed to burn off the cancerous tissue with a white-hot iron. The plans went awry. The instruments for this drastic surgery were late in coming from the States and, to make matters worse, the only surgeon skilled in their use fell sick with a fever the night before the operation. On the spur of the moment a substitute had to be drilled in this unfamiliar technique. It was not surprising that the operation dragged long behind schedule, so long that the local anaesthetic wore off.

Governor Early described to a friend of mine some part of what he suffered during that operation. In the room, while he was telling the grim story, there happened to be present, from another of the Non-Christian Tribes, a young man whom Governor Early had persuaded Stimson to appoint to the Legislature for a constituency still too unversed in political experience to elect its own representatives.

"John C. Early," this young man exclaimed in forthright English, "you certainly have the guts!"

"Have I!" was the Governor's dry comment. "They're pretty well cooked by now."

Right up to his death Jack Early waged his battle to remain active. New Year's day 1932, he sat beside Governor General Stimson at Baguio to explain each of the festive dances with which the Igorots celebrated the holiday. This was all he was to see of 1932. That night he died.

When I told my Igorot principal the sad news, he made but one comment; "He was our father."

It was the right epitaph for a great and good man. Out of the rivalry for possession of his body the Bontocs won the right to bury him high on a cliff overlooking the twisted canyon of the Chico River. His own country may have forgotten John Chrysostum Early; savage memories are longer. In the turgid development of world politics what Governor Early contended for was as sure of defeat as his battle for health. Yet "the Empire" was a noble dream, and there were many Americans, unrecorded in our history books, who shared that dream, men whose understanding won a sure place in the hearts of a primitive, neglected people and gained the perfect commendation, "He was our father."

Notes

1   Lancelot Edward Gowen, 18 months younger. Lance became Professor of Architecture at the University of Washington, a position he held at his death in 1957 at age 63.

2   The *Persia,* only 4,356 tons, was built in 1881, purchased by Pacific Mail lines in 1905, sold to Toyo Kisen Kaisha of Yokohama in 1915 and scrapped in 1926. By contrast the *Empress of Russia,* his favorite of the "Empresses," was built in 1912 and continued in service until 1945 when it was destroyed by fire. See "The Ship's List" at www.theshipslist.com and related internet sites.

3   The Russian Volunteer Fleet was created by Tsar Alexander III as a "patriotic squadron", funded privately, to destroy British mercantile ships if war occurred between Russian and Britain over Afghanistan. As of 1902 there were thirteen ships in the fleet, all built in Britain. They made service runs between Nagasaki, Vladivostok, and Odessa, wintering in ice-free Nagasaki until after the Soviets took control. See "Oura Articles" prepared by Nagasaki Foreign Settlement Research Group at http://www.nfs.nias.ac.jp/index.html

4   The Chinese name for the Yellow River.

5   Trade between China and Britain as of early 19th century was imbalanced: tea was exported from China but no British products were exported to China in return with the result that accounts had to be settled by the export of silver. To stem the drain on the treasury the British began exporting opium to China from India. This caused conflict with the Imperial Government which had forbidden the import and use of opium and led, eventually, to the "Opium wars" between China and Britain. With superior military strength the British enforced the terms of the Treaty of Tientsin of 1860 that maintained the trade in opium and provided the basis for the treaty port system and "gun boat diplomacy" that persisted until 1927. See Encyclopedia Brittanica Online under "Western Colonialism, The Opium Wars.

6   Now known as Yantai, it is the kargest fishing seaport in Shandong province to the north of Shanghai.

7   Now known as Zhong Guo.

8   Also referred to as the Ch'ing or Qing dynasty.

9   In his original manuscript VHG adds the following description:

"This tomb had slipped into obscurity, overshadowed by the more imposing memorials to the later Ming Empowers, who had moved to Peking, the northern Capital, and taken for sepulture a huge empty landscape close to the Mongolian border. Hidden within this folded valley, guarded by stone beasts, stone warriors and statesmen, Hung Wu had not lost entirely his mystical ascendancy over the few knowledgeable scholars who sought solace from present ignominy in regret for past glory.

"They still spoke of the predictions miraculously fulfilled by his appearance. The details were vague. According to legend, seekers for a new son of Heaven were guided to recognize in this shepherd, asleep on the hillside, the destined signs in his postures as he slept. First, he was lying on his back, arms out-stretched, staff above his head, thus forming the character T'ien, or heaven, or Son. The purple he was to wear revealed itself in the wine-dark colour of his back, burned this deep hue by naked exposure to the sun.

"Hung Wu survived not only nostalgic memories of the past but in hopes for the future. He had been served by a chief minister, Liu P'o-wen, so stalwart in defending the Empire from Mongol foes that he had been permitted to build his official residence, his *kung kuan*, not facing south like all Chinese houses, but north, in vigilant watchfulness against further northern invaders.

"Liu P'o-wen still was met with on Purple Mountain. In the late hours of the night shepherds would be hailed by a mysterious stranger, who asked what hour it was, and when the Ming (a character made of <u>sun</u> and <u>moon</u>) or Bright Day would dawn.

"The shepherd's reply was always the same: "Tsao ti han, tsao ti han - it is very early, very early!" - whereat the ghostly figure would go off weeping into the darkness."

10 In 1913 China had the world's largest population, around 400 million, but whether it had the highest birthrate is questionable. Today, China's fertility rate, as reported by the World Bank, is about 2 births per female, comparable to the US and to East Asia and the Pacific. It is well below Sub-Saharan Africa (5), and South Asia (3).

11 See footnote 5

12   This term, "tong bao" in Chinese, has been used in the last half of the 20th century by the Beijing government to refer to "compatriots" living on Taiwan, Hong Kong and Macao.

13   Now known as Beijing.

14   The "Eighteen Provinces" of the Manchu (Qing) rule were considered by Westerners of the time as "China proper". They did not include peripheral territories of the empire – Manchuria, Mongolia, Sinkiang (now Xinjiang), and Tibet. Taiwan was included until 1895 when it was ceded to Japan. The concept of "China Proper" has changed over time and with the persons or entities using the term.

15   Now known as Shenyang, Mukden in Manchuria to the North East was at least 700 kms. distant by rail.

16   This passage refers to the poem by Bret Harte, first published in 1870 titled "Plain Language from Truthful James or The Heathen Chinee", a humorous account of a poker game between the narrator (Truthful James), Bill Nye (a California miner) and Ah Sin (the "Heathen Chinee") that was an important source of the stereotypical view of immigrant Chinese in the US.

17   Chihli was the name of the province in northeastern China now called Hebei. Its capital, Shijiazhuang, is located about 270 kms. south southwest of Beijing.

18   The T'ai P'ing (Heavenly Peace) movement sought to overthrow the Manchu (Qing) dynasty. Led by Hung Hsiu-ch'uan who saw himself as a messianic Christian leader, the brother of Jesus, the T'ai P'ings moved through Kuangsi and Hunan provinces, capturing city after city, eventually overwhelming Nanking in 1853. In the process buildings and monuments were systematically destroyed and inhabitants slaughtered. The movement ended in 1864 when Nanking was recaptured, with British help, and Hung committed suicide.

19   Now known as Jiu Jiang

20   The Grand Canal runs 1795 kms. from Hangzhou, about 100 mi. SW of Shanghai, to Beijing. Ancient in its origin, its present form took shape in the early 7th century. Only the southernmost section, the Jiangnan Canal that connects to the Yangtze river at Jining (about 60 km. east of Nanking) is navigable today.

21   In present day guidebooks known as "Jiuhua Shan", this mountain is located in south-east Anhui province, about 115 kms. SSW of Wuhu.

22   The term used for a Chinese official's office and residence.

23 Born in 1866 in Russia, Bakst worked as painter, costume- and scene-designer. Among other things he worked as a scene painter for Diaghelev with the Ballets Russes commencing around 1908. He lived until 1924.

24 Neither Anking nor Nanchang were treaty ports like Wuhu, Nanking, or Shanghai.

25 The first dragon flag of the Manchu (Qing) dynasty, used from 1872 to 1890 showed a blue, four-footed, five-twoed dragon on a triangular yellow field exhaling a small red sun in the upper left-hand corner. It was replaced in 1890 by a rectangular flag of similar design.

26 The horizontal stripes of this flag, from top to bottom were: red for the Han Chinese, yellow for the Manchus, blue for the Mongols, white for the Moslems (the Huis and Uighurs) and at the bottom, black for the Tibetans. This flag continued in use until 1928 when it was replaced as the symbol of the Republic of China by the familiar red flag with blue rectangle in the upper left corner with a white sun centered in it. It continues today as the flag of The Republic of China on Taiwan.

27 The Washington Naval Treaty, signed at Washington D,C. in February 1922 by the U.S.A, U.K., Japan, France and Italy that limited naval armaments.

28 Wuchang is one of three cities collectively referred to as Wuhan located at the confluence of the Han and Yangtze rivers, almost six hundred kilometers upstream from Wuhu, that has figured prominently in modern Chinese history. Wuchang, the administrative, cultural, and educational center of Hubei province was besieged for nearly six weeks commencing Sept. 1, 1926 until it fell to the advancing communist armies of Chiang Kai Shek. The other two cities of Wuhan include Hankow, the commercial center and former treaty port, and Yuchang, formerly a residential center but now mostly industrial.

29 The port city for Wuhan, over 1000 kms upstream from Shanghai.

30 Chinkiang, now known as Zhenjiang, lies almost 300 kms upstream from Shanghai, almost two-thirds the distance to Wuhu. At the time it was also a treaty port.

31 Kiukiang, now known as Jiujiang, is located in the very northernmost tip of Jianxi province, almost due north of Nanchang, about 250 kms. upstream from Wuhu and about half way from Wuhu to Hankow. It was also a treaty port.

32 Now Wuxi

33   Bishop Gouverneur Frank Mosher, second bishop of the Missionary District of the Philippines, a post he held until January, 1940.

34   A brief profile of Leonard Wood appears in Appendix B

35   Renamed the "E.J. Halsema Memorial Highway" after World War II after E.J. Halsema, who as the engineer in charge was responsible for its construction. Subsequently appointed Mayor of Baguio he and his family were interned with other foreigners in Baguio at the outbreak of World War II. He was killed March 15, 1945, when American bombs hit the Baguio hospital where he was a patient. See Halsema, p.321.

36   The reference here is to Mary Angeline, who had come with him from China in June 1927. Eventually they went on to Manila for treatment for the injuries she had received from a horse riding accident.

37   Sadly the church did not outlast American military's World War II efforts. Bombed in 1945 as part of the U.S campaign it was later rebuilt but with a different design.

38   Deaconess Ann Hargreaves who came to Besao in 1912.

39   Mary Angeline died August 7, 1928 in Manila. Her body was returned to Besao for burial.

40   The term used for the wild tribes inhabiting the mountain forests.

41   Army Map Service contour maps of Luzon, issued in 1956, label this mountain "Sipitan", but in Besao, at least, it was known as Sisipitan.

42   The reference here is to the over five hundred American teachers sent by the U.S. government to the Philippines in 1901 to establish a public school system. They arrived aboard the transport ship USS Thomas and were henceforth known – as well as those following on other ships – as the Thomasites. Though the reference to "schoolmarms" suggests that the teachers were all women, in fact according to an entry in Wikipedia, over two-thirds were men.

43   In January, 1956, Father Gowen joined son Geoffrey, then a pilot with the U.S. 7th Fleet that was visiting the Philippines at the time, and returned to the mountains. To his complete and tearful surprise as he arrived in Besao he was greeted by a huge crowd of former students who burst into the St. James School song as he deborded. The next few days, filled with dinners and celebrations, allowed him to witness the changes that had taken place.

44   The reference here is correct about the star but wrong about its distance. As many amateur astronomers know, Arcturus is relatively close, about 38 light years away.

45   The architect of this church, John van Wie Bergamini, who also supervised its construction, was later interned with his family at Camp Holmes.

46   Bishop Norman S. Binstead, formerly Bishop of Tohuco in Japan, who had succeeded Bishop Mosher when the latter retired in October, 1940.

47   Camp John Hay was one of the first Philippines targets of the Japanese; the bombing, around 9 a.m., Philippines time, December 8th followed the Pearl Harbor bombing by about six and a half hours. Bartsch, p. 56.

48   Cavite was bombed on December 9th around 1 p.m. by Japanese "Betty" and "Nell" bombers stationed on Formosa. Bartsch, p.122

49   Fort Stotsenburg was the U.S. cavalry post, established in 1902. Clark Field was constructed later adjoining it to the East. Clark Field pilots were billeted at Fort Stotsenburg.

50   Bartsch's more recent assessment places responsibility for this debacle somewhat differently: ". . .Iba radar had provided warning to Iba and Clark fields way in advance, but in a confused situation of conflicting reports coming from other sources in the Philippines, the 24th [Pursuit Group]'s commander made erroneous judgments that would cost the destruction of virtually a whole squadron of pursuit and most of the B-17s at Clark." Bartsch, p.429.

51   Don Mansell reports that an eye-witness of the landing, Woody Bartges, counted 110 vessels. (personal communication with Geoffrey Gowen)

52   Bartsch account makes clear that also critical was the use of P-40 pursuit planes which, though underpowered, had been shown by General Claire Chennault in China to be capable of successfully intercepting Japanese bombers under certain conditions: adequate warning to allow planes to achieve sufficient altitude; more experienced pilots; more time to become familiar with the P-40; and time to ensure that planes and weapons were in working order.

53   According to Jim Halsema this was Lt. Col James P. Horan. Camp Holmes internees referred to him irreverently as "the colonel who ran."

54   Nakamura was in immediate charge of the internees at Camp Holmes (and before that when they were at Camp John Hay) until shortly after the Anglican missionaries at Bontoc were moved to Camp Holmes.

55   This characterization of Spanish-American war veterans needs qualification. Though it fits some in this group, there were others who did their share of work.

56   Thanks to research by Curtis Tong who shared his findings at the February 2007 Camp Holmes reunion in St. Augustine, Florida, we have learned that Mukaibo did not have a Harvard Ph.D. He earned the equivalent of a Master's degree from Boston University School of Theology in 1932 and returned in 1936 to get a Ph.D.

57   This refers only to the entry of the Bontoc group into Camp Holmes in June, 1942. Later after the escape of Herb Swick and Richey Green there was intensive questioning by the Kempei-tei of internees thought in some way to be connected to the escapees.

58   This was Frank Mount. According to Jim Halsema he was not from Tennessee though probably from a state nearby where such skills were equally valued.

59   In her memoirs, "Keepsake", Betty Halsema Foley tells the following story about coping with the shortage of paper: "One morning when Derek Whitmarsh arrived without having done his homework, using lack of paper as his excuse, Ann Wilson reminded him that he had overlooked a good source. This was in early 1944, shortly after the arrival of our first and only Red Cross supplies. She said "Derek, your mother smokes and she got Red Cross cigarettes. Why didn't you use the back of a cigarette package?" He answered,, "We use those for T.P. (*toilet paper*). Ann answered. "Of course, but you must use it for your arithmetic homework first." See "Keepsake" p. 208.

60   The grade school was only moved from near the pigpen. Its final location, as can be seen on the Panoramic View of Camp Holmes (p.365) was near the stops leading down to the hospital.

61   David Bergamini, son of John van Wie Bergamini, architect of St. Benedict's church, Besao.

62   Don Mansell, one of the three graduates of the class of '44 at which this song was first sung, recalls VHG saying that the tune was from a German drinking song.

63   Many in Camp Holmes would not agree with this statement. Carl Eschbach, who took over as head of the General Committee was beloved and respected by many in Camp Holmes.

64   Mukaibo did not have a Harvard Ph.D. See footnote 56 above.

65   Only Herb Swick had a commission; Green did not.

66   In 1977, after these memoirs had been written, Mr. Tomibe was invited to a Camp Holmes reunion in San Francisco which VHG attended. Mr. Tomibe flew there at his own expense, bringing with

hm bronze medals, one for each attendee, that he had had cast for the occasion.

67   How fortunate this circumstance was learned later from American soldiers: strafing by American planes might indeed have occurred but for a temporary shortage of aviation gasoline on the days that Camp Holmes internees were moved. See e-mail from Betsy Herold Heimke cited in Mansell, p.231, footnote 8.

68   The most recent predecessors were likely veterans from Cabanatuan, en route to Japan. The last shipment of some 1600 POWs from there, after a two-month stay in Bilibid left on December 13th, scarcely two-weeks before Camp Holmes internees' arrival. See Sides, pp. 202-215 for the harrowing tale of their experience after leaving Bilibid.

69   The exact words, recorded in code in son Geoffrey's diary were as follows: "This is what the barber says: 'Goddamn the American army, navy, marines. Fuck 'em all. Who wants a haircut.'"

70   The reference to the Great Eastern Hotel is puzzling. Don Mansell suggests it might be to the Marco Polo hotel.

71   These were tanks of the 44th Tank Battalion, attached to the 1st Cavalry Division. See Smith, p.251.

72   The definitive account of the first sighting of American soldiers and tanks, according to Jim Halsema (discussion at his home, Dec. 7th, 2004) comes from Betty Halsema Foley's memoirs. With several others she was standing by an open, second floor window late in the afternoon on February 3rd. Trying to keep son, Michael amused, she recalls: ". . looking across rooftops to a wide avenue a few blocks away. . . I saw men and tanks. Not small tanks camouflaged with netting and bits of foliage, as we had seen used by soldiers atop Japanese tanks, but very real monsters with soldiers wearing German helmets riding ourside them. I felt I was seeing an action movie." See Foley, pp. 235-236.

73   Jim Halsema points out that 4.2" guns were being used on American tanks.

74   This is not correct. Zambales province lies west of the route through the central plains taken by the 37th Division and even further from the 1st cavalry whose route was generally to the east of the 37th Division. See Smith, Map III, The Sixth Army's Advance and Map V, The Approach to Manila. Veterans of the 37th Division claim that they might have been able to reach Manila before the 1st Cavalry but were held up by order of General MacArthur. Telephone discussion

with Gene Pope, veteran of the 148th Battalion that liberated Bilibid Prison.

75 As is well known now, this battle was not what was intended by Yamashita, the general in overall command but the result of a somewhat ambiguous command structure that allowed a determined subordinate, Admiral Iwabuchi, to fight to hold on to Manila despite Yamashita's orders to the contrary. See Smith, pp. 240-248.

76 A recent assessment puts the destruction of Manila on a par with Warsaw, and exceeded only by the destruction of Stalingrad and Berlin. See Connaughton, Pimlot and Anderson, p.15

Bibliography

Listed here are the books directly referenced in the Notes, Maps and Illustrations.

Bartsch, William H., *Doomed at the Start,* Texas A & M University Press, College Station, Texas, 1992

Connaughton, Richard et al, *The Battle for Manila,* Presidio Press, Novato, California, 2002

Clubb, O. Edmund, *20th Century China,* Columbia University Press (Third Edition), New York, 1978

Foley, Betty Halsema, *Keepsake,* Paper & Ink, Inc., Scottsdale, Arizona, 2001

Halsema, James J., *E.J. Halsema: Colonial Engineer*, New Day Publishers, Quezon City, The Philippines, 1991

Mansell, Donald E., *Under the Shadow of the Rising Sun,* Pacific Press Publishing Association, Nampa, Idaho, 2003

Miles, Fern Harrington, *Captive Community,* Mossy Creek Press, San Angelo, Texas, 1987

Sides, Hampton, *Ghost Soldiers,* Random House, New York, 2002

Robert Ross Smith, *Triumph in the Philippines*, Office of Military History, Department of the Army, 1963, Washington, D.C.

ISBN 142510520-3